CURRICULUM CONTENT FOR STUDENTS WITH MODERATE AND SEVERE DISABILITIES IN INCLUSIVE SETTINGS

Diane Lea Ryndak
University of Florida

Sandra Alper
University of Northern Iowa

Allyn and Bacon
Boston • London • Toronto • Sydney • Tokyo • Singapore

To Bertha, my mother, and Seth, my son, for your love.
To Michael Pagels, for your support and encouragement that makes anything possible.

Editor-in-Chief, Education: Nancy Forsyth
Series Editor: Ray Short
Editorial Assistant: Christine Shaw
Marketing Manager: Kathleen Hunter
Production Editor: Catherine Hetmansky
Editorial-Production Service: Ruttle Shaw & Wetherill, Inc.
Cover Administrator: Suzanne Harbison
Composition Buyer: Linda Cox
Manufacturing Buyer: Megan Cochran

Copyright © 1996 by Allyn & Bacon
A Simon & Schuster Company
Needham Heights, Mass. 02194

Library of Congress Cataloging-in-Publication Data

Ryndak, Diane Lea
    Curriculum content for students with moderate and severe
disabilities in inclusive settings / Diane Lea Ryndak, Sandra Alper.
        p.   cm.
    Includes bibliographical references and index.
    ISBN 0-205-14667-8 (casebound)
    1. Handicapped children—Education—United States—Curricula.
    2. Mainstreaming in education—United States.   I. Alper, Sandra K.
    II. Title.
    LC4031.R96   1996
    371.9'046—dc20   95-6135
                                                             CIP

Printed in the United States of America

10 9 8 7 6 5 4 3 2   99 98 97

CONTENTS

PART II   *The Curriculum Content Identification Process and Its Use with Education Teams in Inclusive Settings*

PART III   *Applying the Curriculum Content Identification Process to Curriculum Areas*

APPENDICES

CONTRIBUTORS

Sandra Alper, Ph.D.
Professor and Chair
Department of Special Education
Schindler Education Center
University of Northern Iowa
Cedar Falls, Iowa 50614-0601

Roberta Anderson, Ph.D.
Assistant Professor
Department of Special Education
221 Rackham Building
Eastern Michigan University
Ypsilanti, Michigan 48197

Jennifer R. Butterworth, Ph.D.
Director, L.R.E. for Life Project
University of Tennessee
Knoxville, Tennessee 37996

Grace Cross
Graduate Student
Special Education Department
310 Townsend Hall
University of Missouri–Columbia
Columbia, Missouri

James Charles Green, Ph.D.
Consultant
Missouri Department of Mental Health
Columbia, Missouri

Marilyn Jean Jones
Doctoral Student
Special Education Department
310 Townsend Hall
University of Missouri–Columbia
Columbia, Missouri

Robert McMullen
Parent/Teacher Trainer
Special School District
    of St. Louis County
St. Louis, Missouri

Victoria McMullen
Doctoral Student
Special Education Department
University of Missouri
Columbia, Missouri

Sheri L. Menscher
Curriculum Specialist
Special School District
    of St. Louis County
St. Louis, Missouri

Patricia J. Miller
Parent/Teacher Trainer
Special School District
    of St. Louis County
St. Louis, Missouri

Diane Lea Ryndak, Ph.D.
Assistant Professor
Department of Special Education
G315 Norman Hall
University of Florida
Gainesville, Florida 32611-2503

Lech Wisniewski, Ph.D.
Assistant Professor
Department of Special Education
221 Rackham Building
Eastern Michigan University
Ypsilanti, Michigan 48197

Sarah D. Weidler, Ph.D.
Associate Professor
Dept. of Elementary Education and Reading
321C Bacon Hall
State University College at Buffalo
1300 Elmwood Avenue
Buffalo, New York 14222

PREFACE

I know that most men, including those at ease with problems of the greatest complexity, can seldom accept even the simplest and most obvious truth if it be such as would oblige them to admit the falsity of conclusions which they have delighted in explaining to their colleagues, which they have proudly taught to others, and which they have woven, thread by thread, into the fabric of their lives.

—*LEO TOLSTOY*

Change is never easy, especially when it involves a large number of individuals and an established system; yet change is necessary when innovative practices demonstrate greater effectiveness than past services. For years the education system has provided special education and related services to students with disabilities and systematically developed a dual service delivery system comprising different settings, different curricula, different services, and different service providers between students with disabilities and nondisabled students. The creation of that dual system had its basis in conclusions that now are suspect due to the outcomes from an innovative practice—inclusion.

Our experiences with the inclusion of students with moderate or severe disabilities in the general education settings they would attend if they were not disabled have caused us to rethink how, when, where, and by whom educational services are provided. The speed and breadth of the growth the students demonstrated, the increase in their alertness and time-on-task, their demonstration of unexpected cognitive and functional abilities, and the establishment of nurturing relationships with nondisabled classmates, have been eye opening and thought provoking for us, as well as many other professionals in general education, special education, and related services. Responses to these findings have included both personal and systemic changes, because the inclusion of students with moderate or severe disabilities in general education calls for collaboration among all service providers. As these changes continue, we are approaching the development of one educational service delivery system that serves all students.

This book has two purposes. First, it provides a process with which education teams can identify curriculum content for students with moderate or severe disabilities in inclusive settings, defined for this book as the general education settings each student would attend if he or she did not have disabilities. Because of the nature of inclusive settings and the long-term goal for students to transition into inclusive adult settings, this curriculum content identification process gives equal emphasis to functional and general education content, allowing each education team to decide if one or both emphases are appropriate for an individual student during a given academic year. Second, this book provides information on curriculum content areas traditionally included in both special education and general education curricula and examples of how the process can be used in each of those areas.

The book is organized into four parts. Part I provides introductory information on the inclusion of students with moderate or severe disabilities in general education settings, and how inclusion relates to other trends both in general education and in the philosophical approaches to services for students with moderate or severe disabilities (Chapters 1 and 2). Part II describes the curriculum content identification process (Chapter 3) and the role of family members, friends, and other education team members both when identifying curriculum content for a student (Chapters 4 and 5) and in implementing instructional activities in relation to that content (Chapter 6 and 7). Part III discusses content traditionally included across curriculum areas and the application of the curriculum content identification process in relation to those areas. For instance, Chapter 8 discusses the importance of opportunities for students with moderate or severe disabilities to interact with nondisabled peers of the same chronological age and how education teams can use the process to maximize opportunities to interact and facilitate interaction. Chapters 9, 10, and 11 discuss, respectively, (1) the ecological domains that special education programs traditionally address to meet the functional needs of students with moderate or severe disabilities, (2) the areas in traditional special education curriculum that have parallels in the general education curriculum, and (3) the areas in traditional special education curriculum that do not have parallels in the general education curriculum. In addition to describing the content of each area, these chapters provide examples of how education teams can use the process to identify the content from each area that is most meaningful for the instruction of a specific student with moderate or severe disabilities that academic year. Part IV provides information on topics that are relevant to the identification of appropriate curriculum content for students with moderate or severe disabilities and on the provision of effective instruction on that content in inclusive settings. Chapter 12 discusses how an education team can address excess behaviors in inclusive settings. Chapters 13 and 14 address the needs of students with physical and medical needs in inclusive settings. Finally, Chapter 15 discusses the transition process across ages and settings for students with moderate or severe disabilities. The appendices include profiles of six students, describing (1) their performance before inclusion in general education settings, (2) information gathered through the use of the process, (3) their annual goals and educational program after completion of the process, and (4) their performance after inclusion. For one student this information is expanded into a more complete case study (Appendix B).

When a task of this magnitude is undertaken, a number of people are drawn into the experience and thus share in the task completion. Knowing that we cannot possibly name each of these people, we would particularly like to acknowledge certain people and groups of people. First, we would like to thank specific colleagues who challenged us, allowing us to expand our thoughts about inclusion, about viable functional and general education curriculum content, about adaptations for inclusive settings, and about a viable process to allow for maximized instruction in inclusive settings: Mary Beth Doyle, Susan Mason, David Pomerantz, Beverly Rainforth, and Maureen Smith. Second, we would like to acknowledge the irreplaceable efforts of parents and other education team members who shared their insights about the process and gave feedback on components: Karen Bald, Barb Cain, Coleen Carroll, Nancy Militello, Anne Scherff, Robert Schooley, Lynne Sommerstein, and Jennifer Weaver. Third, we would like to express our appreciation to the students with moderate or severe disabilities who were patient as their educational teams went through trial and error procedures, attempting to maximize the effectiveness of their educational services in inclusive settings, and whose successful pioneering efforts in inclusive settings would not be denied: Jonathan, Mark, Matthew, Michelle, and Todd. Fourth, we recognize that we could not have completed this book without the efforts of numerous individuals who willingly gathered information for and proofread chapters, figures, and appendices, especially the graduate students in the Moderate and Severe Concentration at the State University College at Buffalo. Fifth, we wish to publicly recognize the patient and diligent efforts of the people at Allyn & Bacon whose expertise helped bring this book to fruition, especially Ray Short. Finally, we particularly wish to thank the people who, through their collegial support and encouragement, gave us the impetus to undertake this book and, therefore, are most responsible for its existence: Patrick Schloss and Barbara Sirvis.

INTRODUCTION

Recently an advocate for persons with disabilities lamented that the authors of PL 94-142 (Education of the Handicapped Act [EHA] of 1975) had been weak in mandating education in the "least restrictive environment" rather than mandating that all children receive educational services in general education settings. While we might wish that EHA had been stronger or clearer, we must recall the state of special education in 1975. At that time Congress had found that more than half of the 8 million children with disabilities in the United States received inadequate or inappropriate educational services, and another 1 million were excluded from public education altogether. To rectify this intolerable situation EHA mandated that priority be given first to developing programs for children with disabilities who were not receiving any educational services and second, to improving programs for children with the most severe disabilities who were receiving inadequate educational services.

At the time we were excited about the possibilities this legislation presented, particularly the new opportunities for children with moderate or severe disabilities. There were debates in our literature about whether *all* children were, in fact, educable. The debates, however, centered on children with moderate disabilities, unwittingly limiting the meaning of the word *all* by excluding children with severe disabilities. New technologies of applied behavior analysis and systematic instruction were emerging, allowing us to demonstrate that not only children with moderate disabilities, but also children with *severe* disabilities, were capable of learning. Curricula based on standard developmental sequences were developed, resulting in watered-down versions of age-inappropriate content. A new organization, the American Association for the Education of the Severely and Profoundly Handicapped (now The Association for Persons with Severe Handicaps) formed to advance our professional knowledge and share this knowledge nationally. There was an information explosion that fueled a virtual social movement. What a great time to be in the field!

In 1975 our victories for students with moderate or severe disabilities seemed major, as we procured adapted wheelchairs for people who had spent years in bed;

hired a *certified* special educator for a class that aides, foster grandparents, or other volunteers had served, established a class, regardless of the location, where there had been *no* services. No, in 1975 we were not concerned with inclusion; we were dealing with issues that were much more basic. Even in 1985, most advocacy efforts focused on modifying educational services to better prepare students for adult life in integrated environments by providing services in public school buildings; providing opportunities to interact with nondisabled peers during lunch, recess, and special subject areas; arranging for *special friends;* and providing community-based instruction during school hours.

It was around that time, however, that parents began asking why their child with moderate or severe disabilities could not attend the same schools as their other nondisabled children; why services did not follow children to their home schools; why their children could not, and should not, be educated in general education classes. Such questions opened new debates in our professional organizations and agencies, advocacy organizations, professional literature, and popular literature. These debates continue today. They reflect beliefs about preparing students to participate in an inclusive society, concerns about effective education for all students, and concerns about escalating costs of special education during a period of economic recession. One camp believes that inclusion is a philosophical and theoretical battle that sacrifices children; another fears that it is a cost-cutting measure that would eliminate special education and related services from educational programs; and still another believes it is a civil right issue that is an integral component of school reform. Now, some twenty years after the two landmark cases (i.e., *Pennsylvania Association for Retarded Citizens v. Pennsylvania*, 1971, *Mills v. Board of Education of Washington, D.C.*, 1972) that became the foundation for EHA by establishing the right of *every* student to a free appropriate public education in the least restrictive environment, the courts have entered the debate about the conceptual and logistical meaning of the term *least restrictive environment.*

The EHA, reauthorized as the Individuals with Disabilities Education Act (IDEA) of 1990, requires states to assure that:

> . . . *to the maximum extent appropriate, children with disabilities, including children in public or private institutions or other care facilities, are educated with children who are not disabled, and that separate classes, separate schooling, or other removal of children with disabilities from the regular education environment occurs only when the nature or severity of the disability is such that education in regular classes with the use of supplementary aids and services cannot be achieved satisfactorily. . . . (20 U.S. Code sec. 1412[5])*

Recently, the courts have started interpreting this least restrictive environment mandate as favoring education of all children with disabilities, including those with moderate or severe disabilities, in general education settings with the use of supplementary aids and services. In three recent cases (*Board of Education of Sacramento City Unified School District v. Holland*, 1992; *Rafael Oberti v. Board of Education of Clementon, New Jersey*, 1992; and *Statum v. Birmingham Public Schools Board of Ed-*

ucation, 1993) U.S. District Courts concluded that a continuum of placements is required, but the general education setting *must* be considered first; more restrictive placements are acceptable *only when it has been demonstrated* that the child does *not benefit* when placed in general education settings *with supplementary aids and supports.*

In addition to litigation we have increasing numbers of educational programs in which children with all types and levels of disabilities, and of all ages, are included successfully in general education settings with appropriate aids or supports. Thus, we know it can be done, and the courts tell us it must be done. The remaining questions are: *Will* it be done; *when* will it be done; and will it be done *well?*"

In our philosophical victory, however, we cannot sacrifice what we worked so hard to discover over the last two decades: how to provide intentional and intensive effective instruction for students with moderate or severe disabilities on meaningful curriculum content that will positively effect a student's life both now and in the future. How we define these concepts has changed considerably since 1975; but, we rejected ineffective instruction on watered-down curriculum then, and we must be vigilante to do the same now. Instruction on functional and general education content in general education settings *does not mean* watered-down curriculum content; it *does not mean* ineffective instruction. Instead, it means intentional and intensive effective instruction in different settings (i.e., general education settings) and the blending of functional content and components of general education content that are most relevant for a particular student with moderate or severe disabilities.

There is sufficient knowledge about effective educational services for students with moderate or severe disabilities in general education settings to guide education teams involved in this endeavor. As special education services become more decentralized, our challenge is to disseminate that knowledge, move beyond philosophy and generality, and detail strategies for day-to-day instruction. This book helps meet that challenge by providing information that is both fundamental and essential about curriculum content and curriculum modification.

While we were not concerned with inclusion in 1975, we have evolved and we are now concerned. While inclusion undoubtedly holds many new challenges and may take us down a meandering path on the road to intentional and intensive effective instruction in general education settings, the only possibility is to go forward and grow with it. What a great time to be immersed in this field!

Beverly Rainforth, Ph.D.
State University of New York at Binghamton

1

THE RELATIONSHIP BETWEEN FULL INCLUSION AND OTHER TRENDS IN EDUCATION

SANDRA ALPER

Objectives

After completing this chapter the student will be able to:

1. Define full inclusion.
2. Identify some of the issues and controversies surrounding full inclusion.
3. List the benefits of full inclusion for students with disabilities.
4. Identify advantages of full inclusion for students without disabilities.
5. Discuss similarities and differences between full inclusion and normalization.
6. Describe the relationship between full inclusion and deinstitutionalization.
7. Discuss how full inclusion is related to the concept of least restrictive environment.
8. Articulate the similarities between mainstreaming and full inclusion.
9. Discuss some of the obstacles to successful mainstreaming of students with mild disabilities that are important considerations for advocates of full inclusion.
10. Discuss why many educators have called for reform in education.
11. Describe how the demands for reform in education are related to full inclusion.

Key Terms

Full inclusion   Normalization
Age-appropriate skills   Mainstreaming
Functional skills   Least restrictive environment (LRE)
Integration   Free and appropriate education (FAPE)
Deinstitutionalization   Educational reform

Public Law (PL) 94–142, the Education of All Handicapped Children Act of 1975, won the right to a free and appropriate public education for all students, including those with the most severe disabilities. Today, a growing number of parents and educators are arguing that "appropriate" education for students with severe disabilities means receiving services within the same general educational settings as students without disabilities. Programs for students with severe disabilities have been referred to as "the last bastion of segregation" within the American educational system (McDonnell & Hardman, 1989). Although there has been an increase in the number of these students who receive services in the same schools and classrooms as their brothers and sisters and neighbors, the majority are still educated in separate settings and, in some cases, separate school systems (Danielson & Bellamy, 1989).

Students who are typically labeled as experiencing severe disabilities have moderate-to-severe levels of mental retardation in addition to one or more other disabling conditions (e.g., communication deficits, physical aggression, self-abusive behaviors, self-stimulating responses, seizure disorders, visual impairments, hearing impairments, medical disabilities). The American Association on Mental Retardation (AAMR) (Luckasson et al., 1992) defines mental retardation in the following way:

> *Mental retardation refers to substantial limitations in present functioning. It is characterized by significantly subaverage intellectual functioning, existing concurrently with related limitations in two or more of the following applicable adaptive skill areas: communication, self-care, home living, social skills, community use, self-direction, health and safety, functional academics, leisure, and work. Mental retardation manifests before age 18.*

The AAMR Ad Hoc Committee on Terminology and Classification further characterized mental retardation by the degree of appropriate support services needed by the individual. Thus, while individuals with severe mental retardation may need an array of support services throughout life, persons with mild mental retardation may require support services on an intermittent basis (Luckasson et al., 1992).

Students with moderate to severe disabilities encounter a number of specific learning difficulties. They learn at a significantly slower rate than other students. They have difficulty maintaining the skills they have learned, and in generalizing skills learned in one situation to other situations. It is hard for them to combine skills that were initially learned individually. These students pose difficult challenges to educators. Full inclusion of these students in regular classrooms is a complex process with far-reaching implications for all educators. Descriptions of two students follow.

Bryan is a fourteen-year-old boy who has been diagnosed with moderate mental retardation. He has Down syndrome. Bryan lives with his mother, father, and an older sister. He attends his neighborhood junior high school where he takes general education classes in language arts, math, science, social studies, home economics, and physical education. Bryan's general and special education teachers work as a team to develop functional skill objectives in each of his classes. His primary needs focus on learning functional academic, vocational, and domestic skills that will enable him to live and work in the community. Bryan belongs to a Boy Scout troop and enjoys attending sports activities at his school.

Maryanne is a ten-year-old girl who has been diagnosed with severe mental retardation. Her disabilities are believed to have resulted from a lack of oxygen and other complications during labor and delivery. Maryanne's mother was fifteen years old at the time, and the child was placed in foster care while still an infant. She lives in a group home with two other youngsters. Maryanne is friendly and enjoys being in class with other students. She does, however, cry and throw tantrums when frustrated. Maryanne is verbal, but her speech is difficult for others to understand. She has very poor motor coordination. Maryanne attends a general fifth-grade classroom. She changes classes for art, music, and physical education. A personal aide has been assigned to her throughout the day and works closely with the general-education elementary teachers in developing Maryanne's educational program.

Full Inclusion Defined

Full inclusion is the term most commonly applied to the practice of educating students with moderate to severe disabilities alongside their chronological age peers without disabilities in general classrooms within their home neighborhood schools (Brown et al., 1983, 1989a, 1989b; Gartner & Lipsky, 1987; Giangreco & Putnam, 1991; Lipsky & Gartner, 1992; Stainback & Stainback, 1989; Wheeler, 1991). Full inclusion includes physical integration, social integration, and access to normalized educational, recreational, and social activities that occur in school.

In addition to philosophical support for full inclusion based on ideals of humane treatment, democracy, and equal opportunity for all persons, a legal base supports of this concept. The doctrine of "separate but equal" public education programs was struck down in *Brown v. the Board of Education* in 1954. Section 504 of the Rehabilitation Act of 1973 prevents discrimination in programs that receive federal financial assistance on the basis of membership in a particular class. This means that students cannot be denied access to public education programs solely on the basis of a disability. Public Law 94–142, the Education of All Handicapped Children Act of 1975, mandated that students with disabilities be placed in the least restrictive environment (LRE), or the educational environment most like that of age peers without disabilities. This federal law further mandated that students with disabilities not be removed from the general education setting unless it is documented that they would not benefit from instruction in these settings with appropriate supports and resources.

Full inclusion has significant implications for virtually every facet of public education. Our attitudes and values about the educability of *all* children, curricula, the roles of professionals from a variety of disciplines, transportation, administrative arrangements, and the very nature of teacher training programs in higher education are all affected by inclusion. There are implications for *all* students in the public schools, as well as for their parents, teachers, related service providers, and administrators. There are also implications for the community at large as more and more students with severe disabilities are provided the opportunity to grow up, go to school, work, and live in the community.

Because of its many facets and far-reaching implications, full inclusion is best conceptualized as a set of practices or processes. Bates, Renzaglia, and Wehman (1981) and Williams, Fox, Thousand, and Fox (1990) have identified several education practices that support full inclusion. These include:

1. age-appropriate placement in general educational settings
2. age-appropriate and functional curriculum and materials
3. instruction in natural training settings outside the school
4. systematic data-based instruction
5. social integration
6. integrated therapy
7. transition planning
8. home–school partnerships
9. systematic follow-up evaluations

Many of these practices have been empirically and socially validated as "best practices," or indicators of program quality (cf., Snell, 1987; Williams et al., 1990). We describe in the remaining chapters of this book many of these practices as they are used with students with severe disabilities in inclusive settings.

While there is a growing base of philosophical, legal, and empirical support for full inclusion (Alper & Ryndak, 1992), some educators disagree, passionately at times, on how full inclusion should be implemented. One topic of debate concerns whether all students with severe disabilities should be served in inclusive settings, or if placement decisions should be made on a case-by-case basis (cf., Leiberman, 1992; Lipsky & Gartner, 1992; Stainback & Stainback, 1984; 1992; Vergason & Anderegg, 1992). Another question relates to the degree of inclusion—that is, should students with severe disabilities be served in general education classrooms for the entire school day or for only part of the day (Schloss, 1992). Embedded in these controversies is the issue of choice. If a full continuum of services as mandated by PL 94–142 is provided, then parents retain the opportunity to choose either a more or less restricted education for their children with disabilities.

In the remainder of this chapter, we review the advantages of full inclusion for students with and without disabilities. Then we discuss the relationship between full inclusion and other trends in education. This relationship is important because it can help us to understand the historical context in which full inclusion evolved. It can also help us to understand and be more sensitive to the many issues and arguments that surround full inclusion today.

Advantages of Full Inclusion

Benefits for Students with Disabilities

Alper and Ryndak (1992) reviewed literature pertaining to full inclusion. They noted a number of advantages of inclusion for students with disabilities. First, spending the school day alongside classmates who do not have disabilities provides many opportunities for social interactions that would not be available in segregated settings (Sasso, Simpson, & Novak, 1985). These opportunities allow students with disabilities to improve their communication and social skills. In addition, friendships between students with and without disabilities may result. A second advantage of full inclusion is that students with disabilities have appropriate models of behavior. They can observe and imitate socially acceptable behaviors of students who do not experience disabilities (Brown et al., 1983, 1989a). The third benefit of inclusion is that teachers often develop higher standards of performance for students with disabilities (Brown et al., 1989a; Snell, 1987). Both general and special educators in inclusive settings expect appropriate conduct from all students. In addition, students with disabilities are taught age-appropriate functional components of academic content, which may never be part of the curriculum in segregated settings (e.g., science, social studies, interactions with persons without disabilities.) Finally, attending inclusive schools should increase the probability that students with disabilities will continue to participate in a variety of integrated settings throughout their lives. Acquiring functional academic, social, vocational, and recreational skills should help to prepare students with disabilities to live and work in the community after they leave school.

Benefits for Students without Disabilities

Students without disabilities have a variety of opportunities for interacting with their age peers who experience disabilities in inclusive school settings. First, they may serve as peer tutors during instructional activities (Gurry, 1984; Stainback, Stainback, & Hatcher, 1983; Slavin, as cited by Fiske, 1990). Second, they may play together during recess. Third, they may play the role of a special "buddy" during lunch, on the bus, or on the playground.

Critics have voiced concerns that full inclusion will in some way "short change" students without disabilities in terms of instructional time and teacher attention. If properly implemented with appropriate resources, however, full inclusion can result in several benefits for students without disabilities (Alper & Ryndak, 1992). First, these students can learn a great deal about tolerance, individual difference, and human exceptionality. Second, they learn that students with disabilities have many positive characteristics and abilities. Third, students without disabilities have the chance to learn about many of the human service professions such as special education, speech therapy, physical therapy, recreation therapy, and vocational rehabilitation. For some, exposure to these areas may lead to career choices. Finally, full inclusion offers the opportunity for students without disabilities to learn to communicate and deal effectively with a wide range of individuals. This should better prepare these students to fully participate in a pluralistic society when they are adults.

Relationship between Full Inclusion and Other Trends in Education

Normalization

The philosophical basis for full inclusion has its roots in the principle of normalization. This movement originated in Scandinavia in the late 1950s. Bank Mikkelson was, at that time, director of services for persons with mental retardation in Denmark. He is usually given credit for first articulating the *principle of normalization,* or allowing persons with mental retardation to experience normal lifestyles.

Bengt Nirje, executive director of the Swedish Association for Retarded Children, stated: "The normalization principle means making available to the mentally retarded patterns and conditions of everyday life which are as close as possible to the norms and patterns of mainstream society" (Kugel & Wolfensberger, 1969, p. 181). Nirje reported the minutes of a meeting held by fifty young adults with mental retardation in Malmo, Sweden, in 1970. This group talked about their lives and issued a strong statement demanding normalized residential, vocational, and recreational opportunities in the community (cited in Wolfensberger, 1983).

The normalization philosophy quickly spread throughout western Europe, Canada, and the United States. Advocates of this philosophy argued for better (i.e., more normal and community-based) residential, educational, vocational, and leisure opportunities for persons with mental retardation. Wolf Wolfensberger (1972) was the primary proponent of normalization in the United States and Canada. He expanded the concept in his definition of the principle of normalization as "the utilization of means that are as culturally normative as possible in order to bring about in potentially deviant clients' behaviors that are as culturally normative as possible" (p. 87).

Deinstitutionalization

A corollary of the principle of normalization was the movement toward deinstitutionalization in the United States. Some of its chief proponents were parents and mental retardation professionals who knew firsthand of the inhumane conditions inside institutions. Dr. Burton Blatt, a renowned special educator and tireless advocate for the human and legal rights of persons with mental retardation, and Fred Kaplan, a photographer, published *Christmas in Purgatory* in 1966. This photographic essay of conditions inside institutions was later published in *Look* magazine. The startling photographs of life inside institutions horrified the American public.

Blatt and Kaplan observed and photographed children and adults tied to chairs, locked in isolation rooms and cages, wandering aimlessly with little or no supervision or meaningful activity in large and sterile "dayrooms," and sleeping in rooms full of wall-to-wall cribs or beds. Many of Blatt and Kaplan's photos reflected frightening similarity to conditions in the concentration camps of Nazi Germany. Burton Blatt (1969) lamented:

> *There is a shame in America. Countless human beings are suffering needlessly. They are the unfortunate victims of society's irresponsibility. Still others are in anguish, for they know or suspect the truth. Wittingly, or unwittingly, they have been forced to institutionalize their loved ones into a life of degradation and horror. (p. 176)*

During the next few years repeated and shocking accounts of abuse and neglect in institutions for the mentally retarded all across America were made public. Journalists and human-service professionals uncovered and reported cruel and inhumane conditions in Willowbrook in New York, Beatrice State Hospital in Nebraska, Pennhurst in Pennsylvania, Belchertown in Massachusetts, Partlow State School in Alabama, and others (Biklen & Knoll, 1987). Parents and other advocates banded together to file class-action lawsuits designed to end the wretched conditions in institutions. More and more demands were made on state agencies to develop and fund residential familylike group homes and educational, vocational, and recreational opportunities in the community for persons with mental retardation. Federal support and financial assistance became available in the 1960s primarily as a result of the Kennedy family's firsthand experience with mental retardation and their political influence.

Relationship of Full Inclusion to Normalization and Deinstitutionalization

Many similarities exist between full inclusion and the principle of normalization and its corollary deinstitutionalization. They may be grouped into three basic categories: (1) similarities in philosophy, (2) similarities in implementation, and (3) similarities in outcome.

Similarities in Philosophy

Embedded in both the principle of normalization and full inclusion is the idea that people with and without disabilities hold the same values. Factors that contribute to the quality of life (e.g., friendships, choice, freedom, normal rhythms of the day, week, and year) are the same for all people.

Burton Blatt (1987) eloquently articulated the values inherent in normalization and deinstitutionalization (and full inclusion). He pointed out that the controversy surrounding these trends have been argued in two ways. Some authors (e.g., Vergasson & Anderegg, 1992) defended separate programs for people with and without disabilities. The basis of this position is that some persons, because of the severity of their disability, require separate programs to achieve their maximum level of functioning. (Indeed, this is the primary argument in favor of separate school settings for children with severe disabilities.) The counterpoint (Blatt, 1987) is that people are entitled to live free in natural settings, irrespective of what environment enhances their academic skills. Blatt (1987) wrote, "Abraham Lincoln did not emancipate the slaves in order to promote their school capability or vocational viability. The slaves were freed because people deserve to live free...." (p. 238).

Those opposed to full inclusion argued that it is just another educational fad with no empirical base. Blatt (1987) contended that issues surrounding full inclusion of persons with disabilities in schools, places of work, and residences in the community are not empirical questions but rather questions about our values. Normal settings are good by definition. They do not have to be justified by empirical studies. Do we hold the same values for all people, or is there one set of values for "us" and another for "them"?

Similarities in Implementation

Similarities in applying the principle of normalization and full inclusion in school programs are clearly evident in the Program Analysis of Service Systems (PASS 3) instrument, authored by Wolfensberger and Glenn (1975). PASS was developed to quantitatively evaluate the degree to which any human service program (e.g., special education programs, group homes, nursing homes, sheltered workshops) had implemented the principle of normalization. While PASS can be used to evaluate a program, it can also serve as a teaching guide for those trying to implement normalization.

The PASS instrument shares several similarities with more recent guidelines regarding quality indicators of educational services for students with severe disabilities (cf., Williams et al., 1990). These shared elements include:

1. Physical integration.
2. Social integration.
3. Emphasis on age-appropriate activities that result in acquisition of new, useful skills as opposed to activities that merely fill up the day. Physical integration is not enough. The support services required by students with disabilities must be available in the general educational settings.
4. Facilities that are the same in location and appearance as those for students without disabilities.
5. Normal length and rhythm of the school day for students with and without disabilities. The school day is the same length for everyone. Everyone eats lunch during the same block of time.

6. References to students and programs that are respectful and dignified. For example, students with behavior disorders who are approximately ten years old are referred to as "fourth graders" rather than as "BD kids."
7. Staff who have been trained in meeting the needs of the students. Staff from a multitude of disciplines work together in collaborative teams in the same schools and classrooms (Rainforth, York & MacDonald, 1992).

Similarities in Outcome

The principle of normalization and the practice of full inclusion are both directed at achieving the same outcome. The goal is that persons with moderate to severe disabilities will be able to grow up and live, work, and recreate in normal settings in the community. Brown and his colleagues (1989a; 1989b) argued that "segregation begets segregation." These advocates of full inclusion pointed out that segregated and separate school settings do not offer students with disabilities the opportunities to learn the skills necessary to function in the community as adults. Segregated school programs do not have the same expectations, functional activities, opportunities to practice skills learned in natural settings, or normal role models as general educational settings. Brown et al. (1987) reported that students with moderate-to-severe disabilities in Madison, Wisconsin, who were included in general educational settings were more likely to work and live in integrated settings in the community as adults than were their counterparts who had been educated in separate settings.

Least Restrictive Environment

The Education for All Handicapped Children Act of 1975 guarantees that all students with disabilities have the right to a free and appropriate education in the least restrictive environment (LRE). PL 94–142 (1975) requires that "to the maximum extent appropriate, disabled children, including children in public or private institutions or other care facilities, are educated with children who are not disabled, and that special classes, separate schooling, or other removal of disabled children from regular education environments occur only when the nature or severity of the disabilities is such that education in regular classes with the use of supplementary aids and services cannot be achieved satisfactorily" (Sec. 612.5).

The intent of the LRE clause of PL 94-142 is that students with disabilities be educated alongside their chronological age peers who do not have disabilities. Further, special educational services should be provided in the schools the students would normally attend if they did not have disabilities (Gartner & Lipsky, 1987; Sailor et al., 1989).

Tucker (1989) observed that school systems attempting to comply with the LRE regulations of PL 94-142 have sometimes interpreted the concept too narrowly:

> *Virtually everyone would agree that the word* environment *means more than location. Yet when paired with the term* least restrictive *in the application of services for students who are disabled, the term has remained almost exclusively a*

term of literal placement without reference to conditions or circumstances that exist in that location. (p. 456)

Tucker suggested an alternative interpretation of the LRE concept based on the individual needs of the student. Within this perspective the key question is, what are the most normal conditions under which a student's needs can be met? It is important to note that the term *conditions* refers to the supports and supplemental aids needed and not to a specific setting. For example, a child with a hearing impairment may need a hearing aid or an oral interpreter, rather than a separate classroom.

Tucker's program-oriented concept of LRE is consistent with full inclusion in at least three dimensions (Tucker, 1989). First, both LRE and full inclusion are directed at maintaining the student in the general educational setting:

> *Is there any type of student need (i.e., a need defined by a given disability) that cannot be provided in the regular classroom, given all of the necessary support that might be required? I have asked that question many times, and the answer has always been a qualified no. (p. 457).*

Second, both concepts emphasize educating students with disabilities alongside their chronological age peers who do not have disabilities. Third, both LRE and full inclusion assume that supplementary support personnel and services can be delivered within general educational settings (Alper & Ryndak, 1992; Rainforth et al., 1992; Tucker, 1989).

Mainstreaming

Mainstreaming refers to providing individualized special education services to students with disabilities while they remain in general educational settings for the majority of the school day. The mainstreaming movement gained momentum shortly after the passage of PL 94–142 in 1975. Initially, the emphasis was on maintaining students with mild disabilities in general education classrooms.

Kaufman, Agard, Gottlieb, and Kubic (1975) described three basic components of mainstreaming. These were integration, educational planning, and clarification of responsibilities.

Integration

Kaufman et al. (1975) described three types of integration. *Temporal* integration is the mere physical placement of a child with disabilities in a general classroom. *Instructional* integration refers to opportunities for students with disabilities to participate in the full range of instructional activities as students without disabilities, even though they may not be expected to master the same academic skills. *Social* integration means that students with disabilities are provided opportunities to interact socially and participate in extracurricular activities with students without disabilities. Kaufman et al. argued that all three types of integration needed to occur if mainstreaming were to be successfully implemented.

Educational Planning

Kaufman et al. (1975) pointed out that an individualized educational plan should be carefully developed for each student with a disability placed in the mainstream. This plan was to be developed by a team of general and special educators working in concert with the parents and the student. Again, the idea was emphasized that mere physical placement of the student with disabilities in the general classroom did not constitute mainstreaming.

Clarification of Responsibilities

Kaufman et al. (1975) argued that the responsibilities of all professionals who participated in the education of a particular student with disabilities needed to be clearly specified in writing. This meant that open and direct communication and collaboration between parents and special and general educators was imperative. No individual had sole responsibility for the education of a student with disabilities placed in a mainstreamed classroom.

Birch (1974) reviewed successful mainstreaming programs across the United States. He recommended the following guidelines for implementing mainstreaming:

1. The concerns of parents, special and general educators, administrators, and students about expectations for behavior in the classroom, instructional materials and methods appropriate for students with disabilities, classroom organization, and the adequacy of support services available should be dealt with before mainstreaming is implemented.
2. Efforts must be made to shape and reinforce positive teacher attitudes. Attitudes associated with successful mainstreaming include the belief that all students can be educated, flexibility, acceptance of the idea that not all students have to master the same content, and willingness to communicate and collaborate with other professionals and parents.
3. Inservice education is critical.
4. Removing students with disabilities from the mainstream should be a last resort.
5. Parents need to be informed and empowered participants in mainstreaming efforts.

Birch's comments are as germane to our discussion of full inclusion today as they were to mainstreaming in 1974.

Similarities between Mainstreaming and Full Inclusion

Although mainstreaming was focused on students with mild disabilities and full inclusion is directed at students with moderate-to-severe disabilities, it should be apparent from the preceding discussion that the two concepts have several similarities. First, both concepts are philosophically grounded in the struggle for the extension of civil rights. Proponents of mainstreaming and those of full inclusion have argued that isolation, exclusion, and separation on the basis of disability are as injurious as they are on the basis of race or sex (cf., Herlihy & Herlihy, 1980; McDonell & Hardman, 1989). Second, mainstreaming and full inclusion are both directed at placement of students with disabilities in general educational settings alongside their friends, neighbors, and sisters and brothers without disabilities. Third, both mainstreaming and full inclusion share elements of implementation.

The lessons of history are important to learn, even in a field as young as special education. Many mainstreaming efforts were doomed from the outset because they involved moving students with disabilities into general classrooms without the necessary support services. Administrators, teachers, parents, and students without disabilities were neither prepared nor equipped to meet the needs of these students. Many became bitter opponents of mainstreaming as a result of faulty implementation. Whether advocates of full inclusion will be able to avoid the same mistakes remains to be seen.

Integration

As we have noted, integration consists of both physical and social integration of students with and without disabilities. Social integration is a critical component in efforts to normalize and mainstream educational environments for learners with disabilities. Cullinan, Sabornie, and Crossland (1992) noted that while students with mild disabilities have been physically integrated into general educational settings for some time now, their social integration in these settings has often been unsuccessful. These authors defined social integration as membership in a group in which a child is: "(a) socially accepted by peers, (b) has at least one reciprocal friendship, and (c) is an active and equal participant in activities performed by the peer group" (p. 340).

A common concern in implementing integration involves grouping. The formation of homogeneous ability groups of students without disabilities for instruction in academic areas such as reading and math has been debated by educators (Fiske, 1990; Slavin, 1987; Stallings, 1985; Swank, Taylor, Brady, Cooley, & Frieberg, 1989). Increasing emphasis is being placed on strategies that promote social integration by advocates of full inclusion. Several innovative options for grouping students who have diverse learning and behavioral characteristics have been developed.

The use of flexible grouping has been suggested as an alternative to homogeneous ability groups. Flexible groups are fluid and dynamic. They may be formed and reformed depending on the goal to be accomplished (Harp, 1989; Unsworth, 1984).

Slavin (1987) and Stevens, Madden, Slavin, and Farnish (1987) described the use of cooperative learning groups. Students in cooperative learning groups work as a team to accomplish some common group goal. These authors cited evidence demonstrating higher achievement by students in cooperative groups than those in traditional ability groups. An example of a cooperative learning-group project follows:[1]

In a fifth-grade elementary classroom groups or "pods" of four to five children who varied in ability were formed into wagon trains. Each group was given a description of the family members they portrayed in the wagon trains. Wagon-train families then worked together on a number of academic assignments related to the general theme of western expansion. Each wagon-train family earned points or "miles" for accuracy and turning in the assignments on time.

Another option for grouping students who vary widely in ability is peer tutoring (Brown et al., 1983; Good & Brophy, 1984; Gurry, 1984; Stainback & Stainback, 1989). Peer tutors who do not have disabilities can teach students with disabilities a wide array of functional academic and social interaction skills. Hofius (1990) pointed out that siblings are an often overlooked resource for tutoring.

Strully and Strully (1989) are respected authors who also happen to be parents of a child with severe disabilities. They advocate the development of strategies that foster social integration. In particular, they emphasize the importance of the formation of friendships between students with and without disabilities. The author described the use of special "buddy" systems that can sometimes blossom into genuine friendships between students with and without disabilities. A student without a disability can serve as a helpful "buddy" to a student with disabilities in a variety of school and nonschool settings.

Reform in Education

The question of how to restructure schools to achieve excellence is an ongoing concern in the field of education (Brookover et al., 1978; Edmonds & Frederiksen, 1979; Robinson, 1985). School reform is a major concern today because of a number of problems facing the schools and the larger society. These problems include large numbers of students with and without disabilities who drop out or fail, high unemployment rates of persons with disabilities, the increasing need of U.S. employers for a skilled labor force to compete on a world market, violence and drugs in the schools, and high rates of pregnancies among youngsters who are ill-equipped to be parents.

Lipsky and Gartner (1992) identified three distinct phases of school reform. The first phase emphasized external factors such as higher standards for graduation, new curricula, more stringent teacher certification criteria, and continued education by teachers in service as a requirement for maintaining employment. The second phase of school reform focused on the roles played by adults in education. Parental choice, teacher empowerment, and local school-based management were all highlighted. The authors charged that neither of these attempts at school reform paid much attention to the needs of students with disabilities. Citing dismal statistics on drop-out rates and levels of unemployment after graduation from special education, Lipsky and Gartner called for a third wave of reform—one that focuses on the needs of the student.

Lipsky and Gartner (1992) argued that meaningful and significant educational reform is best measured by increases in student learning. Successful school outcomes, according to these authors, are more accurately reflected by what students learn rather than by what teachers teach. They called for educational changes focused on (1) respect for all students, (2) actively engaging students in the learning process, (3) teaching students the functional skills they will need for successful post-school outcomes, (4) providing all students with the supports and instructional strategies needed for learning, and (5) making parents and the community partners in education.

The reforms called for by Lipsky and Gartner are in concert with full inclusion. Their recommendations would support the education of all learners in the general education setting. These changes place accountability on adults for the learning outcomes of students, including those with moderate and severe disabilities. They imply that all students are assumed to be capable of learning. If a student is not learning, the problem is presumed to be due to an ineffective education program, rather than to some psychological or behavioral impairment within the student who requires separate services. If fully implemented, the changes advocated by Lipsky and Gartner would mean an end to the dual system, or separate education, of students with and without disabilities.

Summary

In this chapter we have described full inclusion as a set of practices associated with successful learning outcomes for students with disabilities. The similarities and differences between full inclusion and other trends in education were reviewed. Full inclusion has roots in a rich tradition of philosophical, legal, and empirical support. Educators, parents, and advocates working to implement full inclusion have historical antecedents that offer direction. The lessons learned from our previous efforts in normalization, LRE, and mainstreaming, all precursors of full inclusion, are well worth reviewing. They contain suggestions that can facilitate full inclusion, while helping us avoid repeating mistakes of the past.

References

Alper, S., & Ryndak, D. L. (1992). Educating students with severe handicaps in regular classroom settings. *The Elementary School Journal, 92,* 373–387.

Bates, P., Renzaglia, A., & Wehman, P. (1981). Characteristics of an appropriate education for severely and profoundly handicapped students. *Education and Training in Mental Retardation, 16,* 142–149.

Biklen, D., & Knoll, J., (1987). The community imperative revisited. In R. F. Antonak & J. A. Mulick (Eds.), *Transitions in mental retardation,* Vol. 3 (pp. 1–27). Norwood, N.J.: Ablex.

Birch, J. (1974). *Mainstreaming: Educable mentally retarded children in the regular classes.* Minneapolis: Leadership Training Institute/Special Education, University of Minnesota, pp. 2–3.

Blatt, B. (1969). Recommendations for institutional reform. In R. Kugel & W. Wolfensberger (eds.), *Changing patterns in residential services for the mentally retarded* (pp. 175–177). Washington, DC: President's Committee on Mental Retardation.

Blatt, B. (1987). The community imperative and human values. In R. Antonak & J. A. Mulick (Eds.), *Transitions in mental retardation: The community imperative revisited* (pp. 237–246). Norwood, NJ: Ablex.

Blatt, B., & Kaplan, F. (1966). *Christmas in purgatory.* Boston: Allyn & Bacon.

Brookover, W. B., Schweitzer, J., Schneider, J., Beady, C., Flood, P., & Wisenbakeer, J. (1978). Elementary school social climate and school achievement. *American Educational Research Journal, 15*(2), 301–318.

Brown, L., Ford, A., Nisbet, J., Sweet, M., Donnellan, A., & Gruenewald, L. (1983). Opportunities available when severely handicapped students attend chronological age appropriate regular schools. *Journal of the Association for the Severe Handicapped, 8*(1), 16–24.

Brown, L., Long, E., Udvari-Solner, A., Davis, L., VanDeventer, P., Ahlgren, C., Johnson, F., Gruenewald, L., & Jorgensen, J. (1989a). The home school: Why students with severe intellectual disabilities must attend the schools of their brothers, sisters, friends, and neighbors. *Journal of the Association for Persons with Severe Handicaps, 14*(1), 1–7.

Brown, L., Long, E., Udvari-Solner, A., Davis, L., VanDeventer, P., Ahlgren, C., Johnson, F., Gruenewald, L., & Jorgensen, J. (1989b). Should students with severe intellectual disabilities be based in regular or in special education classrooms in home schools? *Journal of the Association for Persons with Severe Handicaps, 14*(1), 8–12.

Brown, L., Rogan, P., Shiraga, B., Albright, K., Hessler, K., Bryson, F., Van Deventer, C., & Loomir, A. (1987). *A vocational follow-up evaluation of the 1984–1986 Madison Metropolitan School District graduates with severe intellectual disabilities.* Madison: University of Wisconsin and Madison Metropolitan School District.

Cullinan, D., Sabornie, E. J., & Crossland, C. L. (1992). Social mainstreaming of mildly handicapped students. *The Elementary School Journal, 92,* 339–351.

Danielson, L. C., & Bellamy, G. T. (1989). State variation in placement of children with handicaps in segregated environments. *Exceptional Children, 55,* 448–455.

Edmonds, R. R., & Frederiksen, J. R. (1979). *Search for effective schools: The identification and analysis of city schools that are instructionally effective for poor children.* (ERIC Document Reproduction Service No. ED 179 396)

Fiske, E. B. (1990, January 3). More and more educators agree that grouping students by ability is misguided. *New York Times,* p. 19.

Gartner, A., & Lipsky, D. K. (1987). Beyond special education: Toward a quality system for all students. *Harvard Educational Review, 57*(4) 367–395.

Giangreco, M. F., & Putnam, J., (1991). Supporting the education of students with severe disabilities in regular education environments. In L. H. Meyer, C. Pech, & L. Brown (Eds.), *Critical issues in the lives of persons with severe disabilities* (pp. 245–270). Baltimore: Paul H. Brookes.

Good, T., & Brophy, J. (1984). *Looking in classrooms* (3rd ed.). New York: Harper & Row.

Gurry, S. (1984). Peer tutoring and the severe special needs students: A model high school program. Washington, DC: U.S. Department of Education, National Institute of Education. (ERIC Document Reproduction Service No. ED 245 463)

Harp, B. (1989). What do we put in the place of ability grouping? *Reading Teacher, 42*(7), 534–535.

Herlihy, J. G., & Herlihy, M. T. (1980). Why mainstreaming? In J. G. Herlihy & M. T. Herlihy (Eds.), *Mainstreaming in the social studies* (pp. 2–7). Washington DC: National Council for the Social Studies.

Hofius, D. (1990). *Training children to promote social interactions with their mentally retarded siblings.* Unpublished manuscript, University of Missouri, Department of Special Education, Columbia.

Kaufman, M., Agard J., Gottlieb, J., & Kubic, M. (1975). Mainstreaming: Toward an explication of the construct. *Focus on Exceptional Children, 7,* 1–12.

Kugel, R. B., & Wolfensberger, W. (1969). *Changing patterns in residential services for the mentally retarded.* Washington, D.C.: President's Committee on Mental Retardation.

Leiberman, L. M. (1992). *Preserving special education . . . For those who need it.* In W. Stainback & S. Stainback (Eds.), Controversial issues confronting special education (p. 13–25). Boston: Allyn & Bacon.

Lipsky, D. K., & Gartner, A. (1992). Achieving fall inclusion: Placing the student at the center of educational reform. In W. Stainback & S. Stainback (Eds.), *Controversial issues confronting special education* (p. 3–12). Boston: Allyn & Bacon.

Luckasson, R., Coulter, D., Polloway, E., Reiss, S., Schalock, R., Snell, M., Spitalnik, D., & Stark, J., (1992). *Mental retardation. Definition, classification, and system of supports* (9th ed.). Washington, DC: American Association on Mental Retardation.

McDonnell, A. P., & Hardman, M. L. (1989). The desegregation of America's special schools: Strategies for change. *The Journal of the Association for Persons with Severe Handicaps, 14,* 68–74.

Rainforth, B., York, J., & MacDonald, C., (1992). *Collaborative teams for students with severe disabilities.* Baltimore: Paul H. Brookes.

Robinson, G. (1985). *Effective schools: A summary of research.* Arlington, VA: Educational Research Service.

Sailor, W., Anderson, J. L., Halvorsen, A. T., Doering, K., Filler, J., & Goetz, L. (1989). *The comprehensive school.* Baltimore: Paul H. Brookes.

Sasso, G. M., Simpson, R. L., & Novak, C. G. (1985). Procedures for facilitating integration of autistic children in public school settings. *Analysis and Intervention in Developmental Disabilities, 5,* 233–246.

Schloss, P. J. (1992). Mainstreaming revisited. *The Elementary School Journal, 92,* 233–244.

Slavin, R. E. (1987). *Cooperative learning: Student team. What research says to the teacher* (2nd ed.). Washington, DC: National Education Association.

Snell, M. E. (Ed.). (1987). *Systematic instruction of persons with severe handicaps* (3rd ed.). Columbus: Charles E. Merrill.

Stainback, S., & Stainback, W. (Eds.). (1992). *Curriculum considerations in inclusive classrooms: Facilitating learning for all students.* Baltimore: Paul H. Brookes Publishing Co.

Stainback, W., & Stainback, S. (1984). A rationale for the merger of special and regular education. *Exceptional Children, 51*(2), 102–111.

Stainback, W., & Stainback, S. (1989). Practical organization strategies. In S. Stainback, W. Stainback, & M. Forest (Eds.), *Educating all students in the mainstream of regular education* (pp. 71–87). Baltimore: Paul H. Brookes.

Stainback, W., Stainback, S., & Hatcher, C. (1983). Non-handicapped peer involvement in the education of severely handicapped students. *Journal of the Association for the Severely Handicapped, 8*(1), 39–42.

Stallings, J. A. (1985). *A study of basic reading skills taught in secondary schools* (Report of Phase I findings). Menlo Park, CA: Stanford Research Institute.

Stevens, R. J., Madden, N. A., Slavin, R. E., & Farnish, A. M. (1987). Cooperative integrated reading and composition: Two field experiments. *Reading Research Quarterly, 22,* 433–454.

Strully, J., & Strully, C. (1989). Friendships as an educational goal. In S. Stainback, W. Stainback, & M. Forest (Eds.), *Educating all students in the mainstream of regular education* (pp. 59–68). Baltimore: Paul H. Brookes.

Swank, P. R., Taylor, R., Brady, M., Cooley, R., & Freiberg, J. (1989). Outcomes of grouping students in mainstreamed middle school classrooms. *National Association of Secondary School Principals Bulletin, 73,* 62–66.

Tucker, J. A. (1989). Less required energy: A response to Danielson and Bellamy. *Exceptional Children, 55,* 456–458.

Unsworth, J. (1984). Meeting individual needs through flexible within-class grouping of pupils. *Reading Teacher, 38,* 298–304.

Vergason, G. A., & Anderegg, M. L. (1992). Preserving the least restrictive environment. In W. Stainback & S. Stainback (Eds.), *Controversial issues confronting special education* (p. 45–54). Boston: Allyn and Bacon.

Wheeler, J. J. (1991). *Educating students with severe disabilities in general education settings: A resource manual.* Pierre, SD: South Dakota State Department of Education, Office of Special Education.

Williams, W., Fox, T., Thousand, J., & Fox, W. (1990). Level of acceptance and implementation of best practices in the education of students with severe handicaps in Vermont. *Education and Training in Mental Retardation, 25*(2), 120–131.

Wolfensberger, W. (1983). Social role valorization: A proposed new term for the principle of normalization. *Mental Retardation, 21,* 234–239.

Wolfensberger, W., & Glenn, L. (1975). *PASS 3: Program analysis of service systems.* Toronto: National Institute on Mental Retardation.

Endnotes

1. The example of the wagon train project was implemented by Mrs. Joyce Stanley in her fifth-grade classroom in Columbia, Missouri.

2

AN ECOLOGICAL APPROACH TO IDENTIFYING CURRICULUM CONTENT FOR INCLUSIVE SETTINGS

SANDRA ALPER

Objectives

After completing this chapter the reader will be able to:

1. Describe those to whom the term *moderate to severe disabilities* applies.
2. Describe the major learning characteristics most commonly observed in students who have disabilities.
3. Describe the developmental, preacademic-skills and functional academic-skills approaches to curriculum development.
4. Discuss the major features of the ecological approach to curriculum development for learners with severe disabilities.
5. Identify curriculum domains based on natural settings.
6. Conduct task analyses of skills required in natural training settings.
7. Develop an ecological inventory.

Key Terms

Community-referenced curriculum
Curriculum
Developmentally young
Discrepancy analysis
Domain
Ecological inventory

Preacademic
Prevocational
Readiness
Skill synthesis
Social consensus
Social validation

Environment   Subdomain
Generalization   Subenvironment
Learning rate   Subjective validation
Medical model   Task analysis
Mental age

Students who have moderate to severe disabilities are a diverse, challenging, and rewarding group of individuals with whom to work. They have so many unique individual qualities that to group them all together under one diagnostic label can be misleading. Generally speaking, the term *moderate to severe disabilities* applies to children, adolescents, and adults who have been labeled trainable mentally retarded, severely and profoundly handicapped, autistic, deaf, and blind, or severely emotionally disturbed. As noted in Chapter 1, these individuals usually have moderate to severe levels of intellectual impairments in addition to one or more other types of disabilities. They represent approximately 1 percent of the general population. If any generality can be made about these individuals, it is that the only characteristic they have in common is their need for support and services from others (Sailor & Guess, 1983; Falvey, 1989).

Learning Characteristics of Students with Moderate to Severe Disabilities

Students who have been labeled with moderate to severe disabilities demonstrate a number of unique learning characteristics. First, they tend to learn at a significantly slower rate than do their age peers who do not have disabilities. Zeaman and House (1963) first demonstrated that students with moderate levels of mental retardation tend to respond to new problems in a trial and error fashion. They take longer than their peers without disabilities to focus on the relevant stimulus dimensions of a task and find the solution. Because of this difficulty, they may learn less material (Gaylord-Ross & Holvoet, 1985).

Second, students with severe disabilities experience difficulty in maintaining the skills and knowledge they have acquired (Horner, Dunlap, & Koegel, 1988). They require frequent opportunities to practice new academic and functional skills. Curriculum must focus on skills that they need to use frequently in school, at home, and in the community.

Third, students with severe disabilities often have great difficulty in generalizing skills learned in one setting to a different situation (Haring, 1988; Stokes & Baer, 1977). A student who learns to use money to make a small purchase in the school cafeteria, for example, cannot be expected to perform the same skills in the grocery store or at McDonald's. These settings often vary along a number of dimensions, including which persons are present, cues, materials, and consequences. Difficulties in generalization experienced by students with moderate to severe disabilities makes training in natural settings, or the settings in which the skills taught are actually performed in daily life, imperative.

Finally, students with moderate to severe disabilities find it extremely hard to combine skills that have been taught separately. For example, ordering a meal in a restaurant requires reading, math, social, and communication skills. Educators cannot teach these skills separately and in different contexts and then hope that the student will be able to synthesize them when confronted with a functional task. Thus, teaching functional skills in the natural contexts in which they are performed is necessary.

After reviewing the learning characteristics of students with moderate to severe disabilities, Alper and Ryndak (1992) concluded that despite their difficulties, there is little empirical support for educating these students in segregated settings or in artificial or simulated situations. Rather, they learn more efficiently if taught within the contexts in which they will have to function when not in school, that is, in the same settings frequented by persons without disabilities.

It should be obvious from the previous discussion that students with moderate to severe disabilities present a number of challenges for educators. The discussion now turns to identifying curriculum content for these students in inclusive settings. First, we define curriculum. Then, several traditional approaches to developing curriculum are reviewed. Finally, the ecological approach for identification of curriculum content is presented, along with several examples.

Curriculum

The term *curriculum* often brings to mind a purchased package of materials, objectives, and activities that guides the teacher's instruction. Rainforth, York, and Macdonald (1992) suggested that this view is too narrow, however, because it neglects the students, parents, and other providers of services to students with moderate to severe disabilities. They favored Eisner's (1979) perspective from which curriculum is viewed as a theoretical model reflecting beliefs about an appropriate scope and sequence of education.

The approach used throughout this text views curriculum as consisting of several distinct phases (cf., Snell, 1987). These phases each require instructional decisions by the educational team members. The phases, or instructional decisions, involved in curriculum development are:

1. What outcomes are desired for the student?

    Outcomes appropriate for the individual student are determined by consideration of the settings in which it is desirable for a student to function after schooling. These outcomes are basically similar to those typically achieved by students without disabilities (e.g., to live and work in the community, to participate in social and recreational activities with friends, to be able to make choices about one's own life).

2. What skills must the student learn in order to achieve those outcomes?

    To work in the community the student needs to learn the vocational and related skills necessary to get and keep a specific job. To maintain friendships, the student needs to learn certain social and communication skills.

3. How should those skills be taught and by whom?

Based on the empirical literature on best teaching practices (Falvey, 1989; Snell, 1987), what specific instructional strategies are needed for this student to learn?

4. Where should instruction take place?

What training settings located in school and in the community are appropriate? The student's learning difficulties and the desired outcomes are both considered here.

5. How should the curriculum be evaluated?

What skills can the student perform independently in nonschool environments? Have the outcomes been reached?

Traditional Approaches to Curriculum Development

Psychologists and educators first became aware of the learning capabilities of persons with moderate to severe disabilities in the 1960s. At that time, much of the early experimental work on operant conditioning and applied behavior analysis was conducted with participants who resided in institutions (see Mercer & Snell, 1977, for an excellent review). Before that time, persons with moderate to severe disabilities who were institutionalized were cared for but were thought to have very little ability to learn new skills.

Three traditional approaches to developing curriculum content for persons with moderate to severe disabilities in educational programs are: (1) the developmental model, (2) the preacademic skills or readiness approach, and (3) the functional academic skills approach.

Developmental Model

The developmental model of curriculum was based on theories of normal child development (Gesell & Amatruda, 1947). Normal children tend to acquire gross-motor, fine-motor, perceptual, cognitive, social, and communication skills in a fairly predictable sequence (e.g., most children babble before they use words and roll over and crawl before they learn to walk). Using this model, normal developmental sequences of skills were taught to students with disabilities (e.g., Bricker & Bricker, 1974).

The developmental model of curriculum was also based, at least in part, on early conceptions of students with moderate to severe disabilities as eternal children. Indeed, one of the first textbooks that addressed the education of this population was entitled *Training the Developmentally Young* (Stephens, 1971).

The developmental model is essentially a norm-referenced approach based on the normal development of young children who do not have disabilities. Specific skills and the order in which to teach them are specified for the teacher. It was originally assumed that teaching these same sequences of behaviors to students with disabilities could help them to overcome many of their delayed developmental disabilities.

The developmental approach to curriculum development, while appropriate for many young children, has a number of disadvantages for students with moderate to severe disabilities. First, strict adherence to a normal pattern of skill development can preclude an individual being taught more functional skills. Rainforth, York, and Macdonald (1992) noted that some educators and therapists have spent years trying to teach the next skills in the normal developmental sequence. As a result, more useful and functional skills have not been taught because they are presumed to be too developmentally advanced.

A second disadvantage of applying the developmental model to curriculum development for students with moderate to severe disabilities is that it encourages the use of activities and materials appropriate for infants and young children but inappropriate for adolescents and adults (Wilcox & Bellamy, 1982). This model, with its emphasis on the skills developed by normal young children, can limit the opportunity to learn more age-appropriate and functional skills required by adolescents and adults, such as vocational and community access skills. The lack of these skills can lead to perceptions of incompetence and lowered expectations for these individuals by others (Bates, Morrow, Pancsofar, & Sedlak, 1984).

Third, curricula based on normal sequences of development do not provide for teaching functional response alternatives. A number of authors have shown how tasks can be modified so that students with moderate to severe disabilities can participate (Brown et al., 1979; Falvey, 1989; Snell, 1987; Wilcox & Bellamy, 1982). For example, a student who cannot count change, read, or write can still be taught to push the cart in the supermarket, locate desired items to be purchased, and pay for them using only one-dollar bills. Rainforth, York, and Macdonald (1992) pointed out that curriculum based on normal sequences of development do not reference the functions and contexts that confront the student in daily life in the community, at home, and at school.

Basic Academic Skills Approach

Closely related to the developmental model approach to curriculum development is the basic academic skills approach. Wilcox and Bellamy (1982) described this model in detail. The basic skills approach, according to these authors, assumes that normal behavior and development are based on a group of core skills. These core skills are those typically taught to children without disabilities in the early elementary years (e.g., reading, arithmetic, written communication). Objectives such as using money, telling time, reading, and writing a story are analyzed into their component academic skills.

Wilcox and Bellamy (1982) pointed out a number of disadvantages in applying this approach to developing curriculum for students with severe disabilities. First, the curriculum is primarily concentrated on the traditional academic "three Rs." Nonacademic skills that students with disabilities need to master, such as making a bed, cooking, ordering food in a restaurant, and appropriate social skills, may be neglected. Second, the academic skills are often taught in isolation. Reading, arithmetic, and writing are often taught in separate time periods of the school day with separate materials and tasks. Yet, shopping for groceries requires that the student be able to perform several different skills within the same task. In addition, there is no guarantee that the student with moderate to severe disabilities will be able to generalize skills learned in isolation to the functional context in which they are actually performed in daily life. Third, the basic academic skills taught may be different from those needed by the student with disabilities to perform a functional task in a natural context. This is particularly the case in situations in which there is more than one way to perform the functional objective. For example, students learning to use money may learn to count by ones, fives, tens, and so on. Making a purchase in a store, however, may be accomplished by a student with disabilities who has learned to count only one-dollar bills (Test, Howell, Burkhart, & Beroth, 1993).

Functional Curriculum

Many special educators have adopted a functional-skills approach to developing curriculum for students with severe disabilities. Within this approach, functional skills that are performed in daily life are task-analyzed into a sequence of observable and measurable responses. Tasks such as washing dishes, riding the bus, ordering a meal in a restaurant, and many other functional skills performed at home, at work, at school, and in other community settings are task-analyzed and taught.

The functional-skills approach has several advantages over developmental approaches for students who experience moderate to severe disabilities. First, the curriculum is based on functional and age appropriate skills needed by the student in a number of school and nonschool settings within the community. Learning to perform these skills enables the student to perform more independently in a variety of settings and often raises the expectations of others who observe the student performing in a competent manner. A second advantage of the functional-skills approach is that many of the skills taught are performed by persons who do not have disabilities. Learning to perform many of the same day-to-day tasks performed by people without disabilities increases opportunities for integration and social interaction. Third, the use of task analysis as a strategy to identify specific responses to be taught facilitates individualization. A particular task may be analyzed into any number of discreet steps, based on the unique strengths and weaknesses of the student.

Rainforth, York, and Macdonald (1992) identified one major disadvantage of the functional-skills approach. According to these authors, the functional-skills approach lacks a clear organizational framework. Because there are no universal criteria for determining what skills are functional and relevant for a particular individual, the potential exists for idiosyncratic curricular content.

The Ecological Inventory Approach to Identifying Curricular Content

The ecological approach to identifying curricular content for students with severe disabilities was developed in response to at least two situations. First, the more traditional models of curriculum posed a number of disadvantages for teachers and students, as discussed above. Second, educators and parents recognized the need for curriculum revisions when the results of several follow-up studies of special-education graduates were published (e.g., Frank, Sitlington, Cooper, & Cool, 1990; Hasazi, et al., 1985; Mithaug, Horiuchi, & Fanning, 1985; Wehman, Kregel, & Seyfarth, 1985). These follow-up data revealed that students with disabilities were not making a successful transition from school to adult life in the community. Instead, they experienced high rates of unemployment, segregation from their chronological age peers, and, in some cases, stayed at home with no meaningful activity for long periods of time.

Educators began to discuss what outcomes for students with moderate to severe disabilities were desirable after graduation and how curriculum might be designed to meet them. Wilcox and Bellamy (1982) synthesized the literature on quality of life, the value of competence and independence, the value of work, and normalization. They proposed three dimensions with which the adult lives of persons with moderate to severe disabilities might be assessed to evaluate the success of schooling. These dimensions were: (1) degree of participation in community activities and organizations, (2) degree of independence or extent of reliance upon others, and (3) productivity or the extent to which one is involved in paid and unpaid work.

Consistent with these three dimensions, Brown and his colleagues (1979) described an ecological inventory approach. Ecology refers to the interrelationships between people and the environment. The ecological approach to curriculum is unique in that it emphasizes the stimulus features of specific settings in which people are expected to function and the importance of conducting training in those settings. The term *inventory* refers to the process of systematically analyzing natural settings in the community, school, and at work to identify the skills needed for one to function independently in those settings.

Identifying Curriculum through the Ecological Inventory

Lou Brown and his colleagues (1979) at the University of Wisconsin originally described the ecological approach as centered on four areas of the curriculum, or domains: community, vocation, community access, and recreation-leisure. (See Falvey [1989] for an excellent discussion of curriculum development within each of these domains.) The domains represent basic areas of day-to-day life for all people. Recently, York and Vandercook (1991) recommended that school be considered a fifth domain because it represents such a substantial part of the daily lives of all children and youth.

The steps in identifying curricular content using the ecological inventory approach developed by Brown and his coworkers are:

1. Select the domain of choice (e.g., school).
2. Identify environments within the domain in which the student needs to learn to function (e.g., homeroom classroom, lunchroom, bathroom, playground).
3. Select subenvironments that are of priority for the student (e.g., the storytime area of the classroom, cafeteria line).
4. Identify activities within each subenvironment in which the student is to be included (e.g., listening to the teacher read a story and then discussing it with other students, standing in line in the cafeteria, selecting a place to sit down and eat lunch, washing hands after using the bathroom).
5. Task analyze the priority activities into their component skills.

Examples of ecological inventories developed for students of three different ages are shown in Figures 2.1, 2.2, and 2.3.[1]

Major Features of the Ecological Approach to Curricular Development

The ecological inventory approach to identifying curriculum content is characterized by several features. First, this approach is consistent with the learning difficulties experienced by students with moderate-to-severe disabilities. The emphasis is on teaching functional and age-appropriate skills in the settings in which they are performed. Thus, difficulties the student may have in generalizing skills learned in one setting to another setting may, to some degree, be avoided.

Domain: Domestic

Environment: Home

Subenvironment: Bedroom

Skill: Dressing in the morning

Task Analysis:

1. Put on clean underwear.
2. Put on socks.
3. Put on shirt.
4. Put on pants.
5. Fasten pants.
6. Put on shoes.
7. Tie or fasten shoes.
8. Look in mirror to check and make sure everything's done.

FIGURE 2.1   Ecological Inventory for Elementary School

Domain: Domestic

Environment: Home

Subenvironment: Kitchen

Skill: Make macaroni and cheese from box

Task Analysis:

1. Ask permission to make macaroni and cheese.
2. Gather materials: measuring cup, large sauce pan, box of macaroni-and-cheese dinner, stick margarine, milk, wooden spoon, drainer, and large bowl. (Egg timer optional).
3. Using the measuring cup, measure six cups of water into large sauce pan and place on stove.
4. Turn on correct stove burner.
5. Wait until water begins to boil.
6. Pour macaroni into pot of boiling water and stir with wooden spoon until macaroni is soft, (Could use egg timer set at seven minutes.)
7. Turn off correct burner.
8. Use hot pad to remove macaroni pot from stove and slowly pour the macaroni into the drainer.
9. Pour drained macaroni into large bowl.
10. Using the lines on the stick of margarine, measure out one-quarter cup (four lines) margarine and add to macaroni in bowl.
11. Using the measuring cup, measure out one-quarter cup milk and add to macaroni in large bowl.
12. Add contents of sauce packet to large bowl.
13. Stir with wooden spoon until all mixed.
14. Put large sauce pan, drainer, measuring cup, and spoon into dishwater.
15. Put margarine and milk back into refrigerator.

FIGURE 2.2   Ecological Inventory for Skills at the Middle School Level.

Second, the ecological inventory approach fosters local referencing. Many packaged curricula containing elaborate sets of objectives and activities have been published. Two problems are often present when using these programs. The skills required to ride the bus, use local recreation facilities, or shop vary from community to community. The skills necessary to use local transportation in Buffalo, New York, are very different from those required in Columbia, Missouri. Even in situations where the skills needed to perform a task are the same in two different geographic areas, local standards and performance expectations may vary (Wilcox & Bellamy, 1982). The ecological approach focuses on the skills needed by students to function in settings they must frequent in their own community and neighborhood.

The third major feature of the ecological inventory is that skills identified to be taught are determined to be functional and relevant through social validation (Ka-

Domain: Vocation

Environment: Community

Subenvironment: Bus

Skill: Riding bus to work

Task Analysis:

1. Go to bus stop at designated time.
2. Wait.
3. Pay driver and get transfer ticket.
4. Find seat on bus and sit down.
5. Follow route to transfer site.
6. Pull cord to get off bus at appropriate time.
7. Transfer to other bus.
8. Give driver transfer ticket.
9. Find seat and sit down.
10. Pull cord to get off at appropriate time.

FIGURE 2.3   Ecological Inventory for Skills at the High-School Level

zdin, 1982). In the process of analyzing each subenvironment, activities are identi-fied that are: (1) generally believed to be important by consumers, parents, teachers, and others and (2) performed frequently by chronological age peers with-out disabilities in the same setting.

The process of social validation of skills leads to a fourth major advantage of the ecological approach. Because skills identified to be taught are performed by people without disabilities, students with disabilities are provided with many op-portunities to engage in the same activities as more competent persons. This can serve to raise the expectations of others. The competence–deviance hypothesis (Gold, 1980) holds that the more competence a person demonstrates, the more oth-ers will tolerate deviance, or differences, in that person.

Fifth, the ecological approach emphasizes access to normal settings and oppor-tunities to interact with persons without disabilities. The benefits of integration for persons with and without disabilities are significant and were reviewed in Chapter 1.

The sixth characteristic unique to the ecological inventory approach is that it encourages the educational team, including family members, to consider future normalized environments that are desirable for the individual student. As Brown and his colleagues (1979) observed, teaching students with severe disabilities to function in natural community and school environments early in life can increase the probability that they will remain in less restrictive community settings after schooling.

Finally, the ecological approach fosters early and ongoing family involvement. The process of considering desirable future outcomes for the student with disabilities (Forest & Lusthaus, 1987) encourages family members and others who participate in the educational team to view the student as a unique individual with strengths and assets, as well as challenges.

An Application of the Ecological Inventory Approach in General Education Settings: COACH

Giangreco, Cloninger, and Iverson (1993) developed an assessment and planning tool useful in identifying curriculum content for students with disabilities in general education settings. *Choosing Options and Accommodations for Children* (COACH) was developed based on the following assumptions:

1. The design of curriculum should be related to life outcomes that are valued by many people.
2. Families are consumers and partners in the design of curriculum.
3. Collaboration is essential in the design and delivery of quality education.
4. Curriculum objectives should be developed based on priorities and outcomes valued by the family rather than professionals representing different disciplines.
5. Problem-solving strategies are instrumental in the design of effective curriculum.
6. Special education is appropriately conceptualized as a service rather than a physical placement.

Curriculum development as advocated by the authors of COACH utilizes ecological inventory strategies within a family-centered approach. COACH should prove to be a valuable asset to educators from a variety of disciplines and families as they work together to design a curriculum that results in positive outcomes for students with disabilities in school and the larger community.

Summary

In this chapter we reviewed several traditional models of developing curricula for students with severe disabilities. We discussed a number of difficulties when these traditional models, particularly those based on normal sequences of development in young children without disabilities, are applied to curricula for students with severe disabilities. Finally, the ecological inventory approach was described. This approach is considered favorable with its emphasis on functional and age-appropriate skills required to function in a variety of home, school, vocational, recreational, and community settings. We have also seen how this approach fosters interaction between persons with and without disabilities.

References

Alper, S., & Ryndak, D. L. (1992). Educating students with severe handicaps in regular classroom settings. *The Elementary School Journal, 92,* 373–387.

Bates, P., Morrow, S. A., Pancsofar, E. & Sedlak, R. (1984). The effect of functional vs. nonfunctional activities on attitudes of nonhandicapped college students: What they see is what we get. *Journal of The Association for Persons with Severe Handicaps, 9*(2), 73–78.

Bricker, W., & Bricker, D. (1974). An early language strategy. In R. L. Schiefelbusch & L. Lloyd (Eds.), *Language perspectives: Acquisition, retardation, and intervention* (pp. 431–468). Baltimore: University Park Press.

Brown, L., Branston, M.B., Hamre-Nietupski, A., Pumpian, I., Certo, N., & Gruenewald, L. (1979). A strategy for developing chronological age-appropriate and functional curricular content for severely handicapped adolescents and young adults. *Journal of Special Education, 13,* 81–90.

Eisner, E. W. (1979). *The education imagination: On the design and evaluation of school programs.* New York: Macmillan Publishing Co.

Falvey, M. A. (1989). *Community based curriculum: Instructional strategies for students with severe handicaps* (2nd ed.). Baltimore: Paul H. Brookes Publishing Co.

Forest, M., & Lusthaus, E. (1987). The kaleidoscope: Challenge to the cascade. In M. Forest (Ed.), *More education/integration* (pp. 1–16). Downsview, Ontario: G. Allan Roeher Institute.

Frank, A., Sitlington, P., Cooper, L., & Cool, V. (1990). Adult adjustment of recent graduates of Iowa mental disabilities programs. *Education and Training in Mental Retardation, 25,* 62–75.

Gaylord-Ross, R. J., & Holvoet, J. F. (1985). *Strategies for educating students with severe handicaps.* Boston: Little, Brown.

Gesell, A., & Amatruda, C. S. (1947). *Developmental diagnosis.* New York: Harper & Row.

Giangreco, M. F., Cloninger, C. J., & Iverson, V. S., (1993). *Choosing options and accommodations for children.* Baltimore: Paul H. Brookes.

Gold, M. W. (1980). *Try another way training manual.* Champaign, IL: Research Press.

Haring, N. G. (Ed.). (1988). *Generalization for students with severe handicaps: Strategies and solutions.* Seattle: University of Washington Press.

Hasazi, S., Gordon, L., Roe, C., Finck, K., Hull, M., & Salembier, G. (1985). A statewide follow-up on post high school employment and residential status of students labeled "mentally retarded." *Education and Training of the Mentally Retarded, 20,* 222–234.

Horner, R. H., Dunlap, G., & Koegel, R. L. (1988). *Generalization and maintenance: Life style changes in applied settings.* Baltimore: Paul H. Brookes.

Kazdin, A. E. (1982). *Single-case research designs: Methods for clinical and applied settings.* New York: Oxford University Press.

Mercer, C. D. & Snell, M. E. (1977). *Learning theory research in mental retardation: Implication for teaching.* Columbus, OH: Charles E. Merrill Publishing Co.

Mithaug, D. E., Horiuchi, C., & Fanning, P. N. (1985). A report on the Colorado statewide follow-up survey of special education students. *Exceptional Children, 51* (5), 397–404.

Rainforth, B., York J., & Macdonald, C. (1992). *Collaborative teams for students with severe disabilities.* Baltimore: Paul H. Brookes Publishing Co.

Sailor, W., & Guess, D. (1983). *Severely handicapped students: An instructional design.* Boston: Houghton Mifflin.

Snell, M. (Ed.) (1987). *Systematic of persons with severe handicaps* (3rd edition). Columbus, OH: Charles E. Merrill.

Stephens, B. (Ed.). (1971). *Training the developmentally young.* New York: John Day Co.

Stokes, T. F., & Baer, D. B. (1977). An implicit technology of generalization. *Journal of Applied Behavior Analysis, 10*(2), 349–367.

Test, D., Howell, A., Burkhart, K., & Beroth, T. (1993). The one-more-than technique as a strategy for counting money for individuals with moderate mental retardation. *Education and Training in Mental Retardation, 28,* 232–241.

Wehman, P., Kregel, J., & Seyfarth, J. (1985). Transition from school to work for individuals with severe handicaps: A follow-up study. *Journal of the Association for Persons with Severe Handicaps, 10*(3), 132–136.

Wilcox, B., & Bellamy, G. T. (1982). *Designing of high school programs for severely handicapped students.* Baltimore: Paul H. Brookes Publishing Co.

York, J., & Vandercook, T. (1991). Designing an integrated education for learners with severe disabilities through the IEP process. *Teaching Exceptional Children, 23*(2), 22–28. Zeaman, D., & House, B. J. (1963). The role of attention in retarded discrimination learning. In N. R. Ellis (Ed.), *Handbook of mental deficiency,* pp. 159–223. New York: McGraw-Hill.

Zeaman, D., & House, B. J. (1963). The role of attention in retarded discrimination learning. In N. R. Ellis (Ed.), *Handbook of mental deficiency,* pp. 159–223. New York: McGraw-Hill.

Endnote

1. The authors would like to acknowledge the contributions of Nicole Werner and Michelle Meenahan, who developed the ecological inventories included in this chapter.

3

THE CURRICULUM CONTENT IDENTIFICATION PROCESS: RATIONALE AND OVERVIEW

DIANE LEA RYNDAK

Objectives

After completing this chapter the reader will be able to:

1. Provide a rationale for a process of identifying curriculum content that blends functional needs and general education curriculum needs.
2. List and discuss steps for identifying a student's priority functional needs.
3. List and discuss steps for identifying a student's priority general education curriculum needs.
4. Describe how to negotiate annual goals and why negotiation is appropriate.
5. Develop meaningful annual goals for inclusive settings.
6. Discuss the various locations in which instruction may occur and a process of identifying locations for each goal.

Key Terms

Blending
Community inventory
Family inventory
Discrepancy analysis
Inventory of general
    education curriculum
Inventory of general
    education settings

Negotiation
Peer inventory
Priority needs
Related services
Student performance

Rationale for a Blending Process

Because the material on which a student receives instruction determines the potential benefits from educational services in the form of skills acquired for use upon leaving school, an education team has the responsibility to consider carefully all possible curriculum content when identifying annual goals for a student. The team should select content that maximizes the student's acquisition of meaningful activities and skills in both current and future environments (Brown et al., 1979a, 1979b; Mount & Zwernik, 1988; Salisbury & Vincent, 1990). The education team should pay particular attention to the development of natural support networks that will benefit the student throughout life (Perske, 1988). (For an in-depth discussion of natural support networks see Chapter 4.) This is a massive responsibility, and an education team cannot view the identification of curriculum content for a student as just one of many tasks that comprise their job. Rather, it is only the first of many steps that will determine the nature and extent of that person's participation in life, both as a student and as an adult.

Identifying curriculum content for a student involves a number of steps requiring decisions that are based on judgements. Because curriculum content, by definition, will vary from student to student, the team judges the relevance and importance of every activity and skill for each student. Each team member naturally bases judgements on past experiences and personal values. While it is unlikely that multiple teams would identify the same set of curriculum content for one student, teams that hold the same values and share similar experiences tend to identify content that, when viewed in its entirety, leads to similar short- and long-term benefits for a student. The process a team uses to identify curriculum content reflects their values. Effective teams gather the best information possible in relation to the immediate and final outcomes desired for a student. These teams then formulate their *best guesses* about the activities and skills that will be most meaningful for that student in both current and future environments and provide instruction on those activities and skills during the ensuing school year.

Curriculum content for a student in inclusive settings could and should emphasize a blending of that student's functional needs and the curriculum content presented in the general education settings. By blending these needs the education team enhances the student's (1) independence in both the inclusive settings and adult life and (2) participation in general education activities with peers. The team also allows for teaching both general education content and functional content during general education and functional activities in the classroom, the school, and the community. In this way, both general education and functional content are reinforced during instruction in various settings and activities across the day.

Blending needs necessitates a process for identifying curriculum content that would be most appropriate for a specific student to learn at that time—a process that incorporates both functional activities (including building friendships and natural support networks) and general education curriculum content. This type of process allows education teams to fulfill the intent of inclusion in general education settings and maximize the benefits of inclusion. To accomplish this, the team first must gather information about the student's participation in activities at home, at school, and in the community. Education teams use the ecological approach of identifying curriculum content described in Chapter 2 to gather information about the student's functioning within environments and across domains.

Although this content is critical for students with moderate or severe disabilities, it is insufficient when used alone to determine curriculum content for a student in inclusive settings. When an education team considers only functional curriculum content for a student, it makes three assumptions. First, it is assumed that the student cannot learn and benefit from any of the curriculum content being presented to the general education class. A number of students with moderate or severe disabilities have, in fact, demonstrated across settings knowledge they acquired along with their general education classmates (Flowers & Houck, 1991, 1992; Oubre, 1991; Schooley & Ryndak, 1991; Sommerstein, Schooley, & Ryndak, 1992; Weaver & Ryndak, 1992). While the amount of demonstrated knowledge varies by student, students evidently are acquiring information that similar students in self-contained classes are not acquiring. Unless an education team also focuses on general education curriculum content and deliberately identifies the most relevant components of that content for the student with moderate or severe disabilities, they are leaving to chance the components on which that student actually will receive instruction. If instruction is to occur in general education settings, is it not the responsibility of the education team to carefully select for the student the most meaningful components of the curriculum content taught in those settings and focus instruction on those components?

Second, it is assumed that, by definition, partial participation in general education class activities will lead to the acquisition of relevant social skills, academic knowledge, and functional activities. While partial participation in general education activities provides opportunities for interacting with classmates, the instruction provided during those activities will determine the degree to which these opportunities lead to skill acquisition. Instruction may take the form of antecedents (e.g., cues, directions, models) or consequences (e.g., feedback on performance, reinforcement, error correction). In addition, the instructor may be a peer or adult. As such, instruction can flow quite naturally within the parameters of any activity. The absence of planned instruction, however, leaves to chance the amount of learning that actually occurs for a student, especially the amount of learning on predetermined components of the curriculum. If partial participation is to occur, is it not the responsibility of the education team to carefully select the part(s) of the general education activity for which the student with moderate or severe disabilities will have responsibility and to provide instruction for that student to increase the probability of success and the extent of participation?

Third, it is assumed that because a student with moderate or severe disabilities is in a general education class, both the general education teacher and the student's classmates will understand and accept that the student is indeed a part of that class, as are the nondisabled students. While there are limited data supporting the belief that students with disabilities who attend a general education class on a part-time basis are not truly considered part of that class (Schnorr, 1990), there is beginning to be evidence that full-time placement alone does not constitute belongingness (Sommerstein et al., 1992; Weaver & Ryndak, 1992). Unless completely involved in the identification of relevant curriculum content, including components of the general education curriculum, general education teachers perceive that they merely are providing an environment in which the special education teacher (and possibly related services personnel) can provide their "special" instruction to their "special" student (Idol, 1993; Orelove & Sobsey, 1991; Vandercook & York, 1990; Vandercook, York, & Forest, 1989). This perception negates the intent and benefits of inclusion. This negative perception can be avoided by: (1) including the general education teacher in all planning and curriculum content identification procedures; (2) systematically considering, with the general education teacher, whether each component of the general education curriculum content is relevant for the student; and (3) carefully selecting, with the general education teacher, any relevant component of the general education curriculum for possible inclusion in the student's curriculum content. If a student with moderate or severe disabilities truly is part of a general education class, and the purpose of that class is to present information to all students and develop their skills, is it not the responsibility of the education team to include the student in every aspect of that class?

To avoid making these assumptions, the education team must consider fully both the general education setting and curriculum content when identifying content on which instruction will be provided for a student, regardless of the type and extent of the student's handicap. For each area in which information is gathered, the education team first lists all possible curriculum content that is relevant for the student and then prioritizes the content *only for that area.* The education team then reviews the prioritized lists of content for all of the areas and uses that information to develop annual goals for the student's individualized education program (IEP), which will define the emphasis of instruction for that student during the next year.

This curriculum content identification process emphasizes (1) the role of the family and other education team members in identifying curriculum content for a student, (2) the blending of functional and general education curriculum content during instruction, and (3) the provision of instruction on both functional and general education content in general education settings, the school building, and the community. An education team uses this process as they are determining the curriculum content to be emphasized for a student during instruction. Figure 3.1 depicts the steps in this process. Because the IEP legally dictates (by the Individuals with Disabilities Education Act [IDEA]) the content that instruction *must* address, the team should complete this process before the development of the student's IEP or individualized family service plan (IFSP).

Gathering Information to Identify Priority Functional Needs

As described in Chapter 2, Brown and his colleagues (1979a,b) provided a pedagogical framework for obtaining information that is useful in identifying activities and skills that are functional for a student. The curriculum content identification process described in this chapter begins by extending the use of inventories across

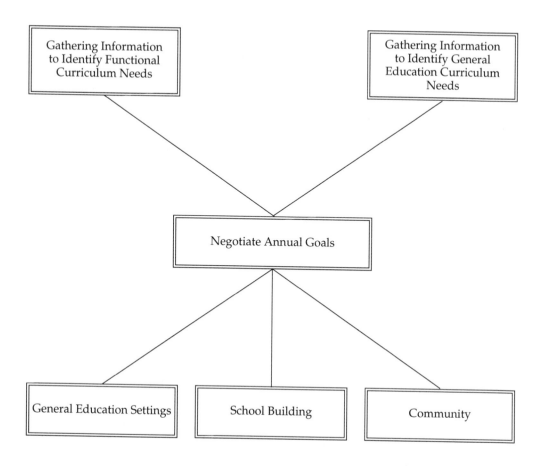

FIGURE 3.1   Curriculum Content Identification Process Flowchart

people and settings that play a major role in that student's life. The education team uses the information obtained from these inventories to prioritize the student's functional needs for instruction in the coming school year. Inventories included in the process are family, peer, and community inventories.

In addition to using information from inventories to identify priority functional needs for a student, this section describes effective use of information from related services assessments, records, and other prior information available when determining priority functional needs. The education team reviews these with consideration for (1) how the values they reflect correlate with the values inherent in inclusive services and (2) how the student's described needs relate to the full participation in activities at home, at school, and in the community. Finally, the process emphasizes the student's preferences in functional curriculum content to be addressed in instruction the next school year. Figure 3.2 summarizes the steps completed in the process to gather information to identify a student's functional needs. The steps in the process are in a specific order both in Figure 3.2 and in the follow-

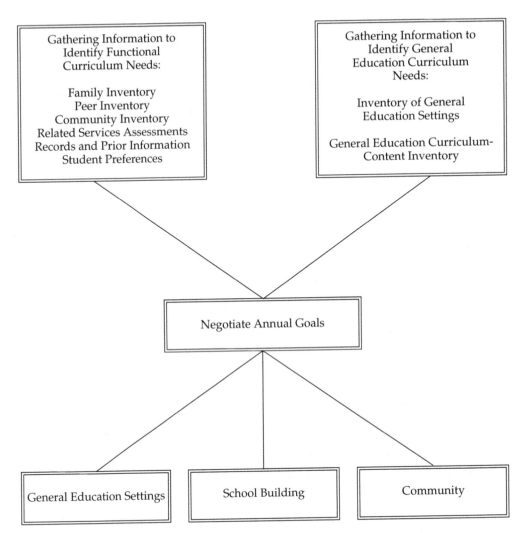

FIGURE 3.2 Steps Completed to Gather Information to Identify Functional Needs

ing sections, but the team can complete most of these steps in any order. The family inventory should be completed first, however, because it provides valuable insight into both the student's performance in natural situations and the family's educational priorities. This information may affect how the other steps are completed.

Family Inventory

A family inventory (Giangreco, Cloninger, & Iverson, 1993; Ryndak, Doyle, & Osborne, 1989; Turnbull et al., 1985; Winton & Bailey, 1988) is a tool education teams use to acquire information from a student's family members that will assist in identifying the activities and skills that, when learned, would most effectively allow (1) the student to more fully participate with their family, neighbors, and friends in activities within the home and community, and (2) the family to complete daily or weekly tasks more easily. While some education teams send home a survey-type instrument for the family to complete and return, the most effective method of completing a family inventory is to interview the family in their home, using a survey-type instrument both to guide the interview and for recording responses. While this format ensures that the areas included on the instrument are addressed fully, it also allows the education team to expand the questions in areas of specific relevance for the student. In addition, the interview process itself generates more information than a written instrument alone. It allows participants to clarify comments, expand information from general ideas to specific examples, enhance knowledge and understanding of a student's life, and bring into focus the family's hopes and dreams for the student.

Cohen, Agosta, Cohen, and Warren (1989) summarize some disturbing variations in family structures in the United States, including: (1) the lack of legal ties between adults living together in a household, (2) no male head of household, (3) a teenage female head of household, (4) a sharp drop in household income due to divorce or separation, (5) mothers working outside the house, and (6) restructured families that include stepparents and stepchildren. In addition, the increase in households that are ethnically diverse raises culture-related issues. The interviewer considers carefully each of these variables during the completion of a family inventory. The completion of this inventory in the family's home can provide helpful insights about the student's role in the family's life, as well as the family system itself and potential needs for family support services (Cohen et al., 1989).

Although information from a family inventory can be endless and the process is at times overwhelming, the team can control the information by focusing on the purpose of the family inventory. Specifically, the family inventory should assist the education team in identifying activities and skills for inclusion in instruction during the ensuing school year. Activities and skills identified through the family inventory most effectively should allow (1) the student to participate more fully with their family, neighbors, and friends in activities within the home and community, or (2) the family to complete daily or weekly tasks more easily. To accomplish this, there may be several areas and domains in the family inventory.

Personal Profile

This area contains information relevant to the student across domains and environments. In addition to demographic data, information gathered includes (1) the manner in which the student makes choices and interacts with others, (2) items, people, and activities that the student likes and dislikes, (3) physical and other management needs demonstrated by the student throughout the day, (4) health and medical concerns, and (5) issues related to ethnic diversity that effect the student's participation in inclusive settings.

Home Life

Information is gathered about activities in which the student participates every day of the week at home, specifically including the morning routine, afternoon events, evening activities, and bedtime routine. All activities of daily living and activities in which the family participates regularly occur during these time periods. For each time period information is gathered on (1) the responsibilities completed by the student, (2) the extent of the student's participation, (3) the needs demonstrated by the student, and (4) the frequency and type of interactions in which the student engages. The team carefully considers how the student's participation in family life is influenced by ethnic diversity. Two questions consistently are asked: what could their child learn to do more independently that would help make daily life easier for the family, and for what home life activity does their child demonstrate a preference for learning?

Community Activities

There is a wealth of information that the family can provide on a student's participation in community activities, including opportunities to participate, extent of independence during participation, interactions with family members and/or friends during participation, and desire to participate. The team collects such information in regard to the student's use of (1) recreation facilities, (2) leisure options, (3) restaurants, (4) shopping facilities, and (5) chore-related community environments (e.g., banks, laundromats). In addition, the education team gathers information about how the student accesses these environments, and about options available for travel to, from, and within the environments.

Work

Regardless of the student's age, the education team gathers information on work history, including work at home, at school, and in the community. The student's likes and dislikes in relation to jobs, working environments, job hours, and proximity of coworkers are recorded in as much detail as possible. The education team notes job-related skills (e.g., staying on task, completing work independently, interactions with authority figures) and demonstrations of the student's work ethic. Even if of primary-school age, the family can supply information on the student's job-related skills and work ethic based on performance on tasks at home and in school. As the student ages, he or she gives more detailed information on work preferences and the feasibility of specific jobs available in the home community. The feasibility of specific jobs, and the degree to which emphasis is placed on employment, may vary across families of diverse ethnic backgrounds.

General Education Curriculum

In addition to gathering information from the family about a student's participation in life at home and in the community, the family inventory assists in focusing on the benefits from inclusion in general education settings that the family desires and foresees for the student. While initially families generally focus on the social benefits derived from interacting with nondisabled peers of the same age, there are other benefits that inclusive settings offer for students with moderate or severe disabilities. Discussing the academic subjects, units, and desired outcomes from participating in the general education curriculum for nondisabled students assists family members in envisioning the student's participation in classroom activities. In considering a student's participation, identification of specific components of the general education curriculum that would be beneficial for the student is possible. These components may include: (1) rudimentary knowledge related to content of specific units, (2) detailed knowledge related to content of one or more specific units, (3) general work skills or personal values demonstrated through partial participation in units, and (4) generalized use of functional activities within all classroom activities. The family's views of which components of the general education curriculum are the most relevant for a student both in that school year and in the future assist an education team in identifying relevant curriculum content for that student.

Future Hopes and Dreams

Because the purpose of education is to prepare a student to function as independently as possible in both current *and* future environments, education teams must form a legitimate vision of the future environments in which the student most likely will participate. This vision must coincide and keep pace with the family's vision. For this reason, family inventories include a section that asks the family to describe their hopes and dreams for a student's future, specifically in relation to where they foresee the student living, working, being at leisure, and accessing community resources. These hopes and dreams will vary with the family's history, values, ethnic background, and socioeconomic status. The hopes and dreams are projected for three and five years into the future, as well as for after completion of the education program.

Functional Needs Priorities

At the end of an interview for the family inventory, education team members ask the family to prioritize what they perceive the student needs to learn for participation in activities both at home and in the community. While there may be a number of activities for possible inclusion in the student's curriculum content, the education team must determine the order of importance for these activities. Of consideration when prioritizing activities is the degree to which the activity generalizes across inclusive settings. Throughout this discussion, education team members share their perceptions of the relative importance of each functional activity and the relation of each activity to the student's current and future environments. Following this discussion, however, the emphasis should be on the family's perceptions.

General Education Priorities

In addition to prioritizing the student's functional needs, the family also prioritizes components of the general education curriculum identified as possible curriculum content for the student. Family members should consider which components of the general education curriculum the student will use most frequently across settings. By selecting those activities, the team can address the student's difficulties with generalization. Again, while the education team discusses the relative importance of components of the general education curriculum with the family, the focus should be on the family's priorities.

Priority Needs Inventory

Given the two lists of priorities in functional and general education curriculum content, the family then combines the two lists, resulting in one list of the family's perceptions of priority curriculum content for the student. In developing this list, the family may choose all or some of the items from either list. In addition, they may identify needs that arise across settings. The final list of the family's priorities, therefore, may incorporate only functional activities, only components of general education curriculum content, or a combination of functional and general education curriculum content, as well as activities that occur across settings.

Peer Inventory

The importance of establishing relationships and natural support networks for students with moderate or severe disabilities demands that education teams consider curriculum content that allows each student to interact in a meaningful and effective manner with peers at school, in their community, and in their own ethnic group. To identify that curriculum content, education team members must first determine the topics about which the student's peers interact and the ways in which they interact. To accomplish this in a manner that eliminates the adults' perceptions of what is relevant to the student's peers, education teams conduct a peer inventory that includes peers both at school and in their community.

A student's peers may divulge a wealth of information covering a myriad of areas. Some of these are:

1. preferred school events and weekend activities;
2. favorite leisure activities, locations, and companions;
3. current age-appropriate trends in colloquialisms, music, and styles; and
4. how and where to "hang out" with friends.

Because being able to converse on a topic is not enough to be accepted as part of a group, the information from a peer inventory should direct the education team toward the peer group's preferred appearances, activities, and interaction styles (Chin-Perez et al., 1986; Haring, 1991; Haring & Breen, 1989). With this information the education team can complete a discrepancy analysis (Gaylord-Ross & Browder, 1991; Hoier & Cone, 1987) between the student's appearance, participation in activities, and interaction style and that of the student's peers. This discrepancy analysis determines the activities and skills the student must acquire to increase the probability of interacting successfully with peers at school and in the community.

There are a number of formats used to conduct peer inventories at various ages. For example, at the primary level education teams have used whole language exercises, show-and-tell sessions, and art projects to obtain relevant information from students. The teams have used similar exercises at the elementary level along with surveys that require simple written or drawn responses. More sophisticated exercises are appropriate for use in middle and high schools, including more complex written surveys, video projects, essays for newspapers or school magazines, photograph essays, or computer-generated reports. Gathering information about current or potential coworkers must be quick and completed in a manner that is unobtrusive in the work setting. While time consuming, direct observation of interactions between peers also has been effective to supplement information from a peer inventory. The formats used are irrelevant. The key is that the education team obtains information from the student's peers about the skills and knowledge that are critical for that student to acquire to increase the probability of successful and effective interaction with peers.

Upon completion of a peer inventory and possible direct observation, an education team lists the curriculum content that potentially would assist the student in participating with peers more effectively, especially across settings and peer groups. The team prioritizes the items on this list without regard to priorities from other inventories.

Community Inventory

While the family inventory provides some information on environments and activities available in the student's home community, education teams expand on this information by going directly to that community and conducting an inventory. The purpose of a community inventory is to identify both (1) the resources available in a student's community for living, working, and playing and (2) the resources the student's peers frequently use, especially resources to which the student does not already have access through family activities (Brown et al., 1983). A community inventory describes the resources available within a specific range of the student's home. Figure 3.3 includes a worksheet used by some education teams to gather information for a community inventory. This information helps the education team identify activities and skills that would assist the student to participate more fully with peers in the home community. The distance from the student's home for which a community inventory is completed will vary depending upon the nature of the community (i.e., urban versus rural) and the number of options appropriate and necessary for a student. For example, when attempting to identify work options within a rural home community for a student with multiple disabilities, it may be necessary to extend the range for which the community inventory is completed by several miles before finding enough feasible options to allow the student and education team choices. The range of a community inventory for the same student in an inner city, however, may not need to exceed a few blocks.

Upon completing a community inventory, the education team compares the resources available in the student's home community with the preferred activities of

Student: _____   Address: _____   Date of Inventory: _____

Domain: _____   Description of Inventory Range: _____

Resource	Location	Activities	Cost(s)	Clientele	Dress Code and Average Dress	Hours	Travel To and From	Accessibility

FIGURE 3.3   Community Inventory Worksheet

the student, the student's peers, and the student's family. In addition, a discrepancy analysis may determine how the student's performance in any community location differs from the performance of same-age peers. Through these comparisons the education team identifies the community resources that would be most beneficial for the student to learn to access, thereby increasing opportunities to participate more fully with peers and family members in the community. From these resources, the education team develops a list of community resources that would be most beneficial to include in instruction for the student in the ensuing school year.

Related Services Assessments

Public Law 94–142 (the Education of All Handicapped Children Act [EHA] of 1975, reauthorized as the Individuals with Disabilities Education Act [IDEA]) defines related services as:

> . . . *transportation and such developmental, corrective, and other supportive services (including speech pathology and audiology, psychological services, physical and occupational therapy, recreation, and medical and counseling services, except that such medical services shall be for diagnostic purposes only) as may be required to assist a handicapped child to benefit from special education, and includes the early identification and assessment of handicapping conditions in children (20 U.S. C.$1401[17]).*

According to Rainforth, York, and Macdonald (1992):

> *The phrase* as may be required to assist a handicapped child to benefit from special education *suggests that the related services of physical and occupational therapy and speech/language pathology must both relate directly to the child's educational program and be provided in such a way that the child receives a greater benefit from the educational program than if related services were not provided. . . . both educational relevance and student benefit are addressed when therapists integrate their knowledge and skills into instruction provided in the context of routine daily activities that comprise the student's educational program, whether at school, in the community, or at home. (p. 26)*

In conjunction with this interpretation, assessments on a student's needs in a related service area (e.g., occupational therapy, physical therapy, speech/language pathology) focus on the student's performance across naturally occurring environments, and the consequent need for a related service to improve the student's performance. For a student who receives educational services in inclusive settings, those environments include: (1) the general education classroom, (2) other school and community settings in which the student's class participates in activities (e.g., lunchroom, library, hallway, art room, bus, locations of field trips, playground), and (3) other school, home, and community environments identified as priority environments for instruction of either functional or general education curriculum content for that student during that school year. Giangreco et al. (1993) stated that:

> related services should be provided to enable students to pursue family-centered, discipline-free IEP goals as the focus of their educational programs, other relevant learning outcomes that provide for a well-rounded school experience, and general supports . . .(p. 9).

Without reference to how a student demonstrates a specific need within a specific environment and how the related service will directly impact on the student's performance within that environment, an identified need becomes tangential to the student's potential educational program. IDEA, therefore, does not consider it a related service need.

If a related service assessment identifies a need for service that will improve the student's performance in specific environments, the education team discusses those needs, the activities, and environments in which those needs were identified, how the related service will improve the student's performance in those activities and environments, and the relative importance of each of those activities for the student. To assist in identifying potential functional curriculum content for inclusion in the student's education program, the education team prioritizes the activities for which the related service will improve the student's performance, emphasizing those activities that occur across settings.

Records and Prior Information

Valuable information can be gleaned from a student's records and other information from prior education services (e.g., discussions with prior education team members, written products). Depending on the type of prior education services provided and the values demonstrated by those education teams, however, the information may provide varying degrees of insight into either relevant curriculum content or effective instructional strategies for the student. For instance, if there is a change in a student's placement from a self-contained class or building to a general education class, the information available from prior education teams most likely will not describe the behaviors and skills one would expect from the student in the general education class. Because the environments are dramatically different (i.e., different stimuli, expectations, and consequences), the student conceivably will view the general education class as a "new" setting and will determine the appropriate behaviors to be exhibited there by observing the behaviors of others. In addition, if the prior education team's values are not consistent with those of the education team in the inclusive setting, the probability that the teams would identify similar curriculum content for the student's education program is extremely low.

For these reasons, education teams attempt to determine the values demonstrated by prior education teams by reviewing the types of services provided and the curriculum content believed to have been most critical for the student during those services. The more consistent these are with inclusive services and the values espoused by the current education team, the more informative records and other information will be. Education teams from inclusive settings review records and other information with constant attention for insight into the student's probable performance, learning style, and learning rate in the general education classroom and other naturally occurring environments in the school, home, and community. This will be the most valuable information from records when determining relevant curriculum content for the ensuing school year. From this information the education team will determine possible curriculum content and prioritize that content for possible inclusion in the student's IEP for the next school year.

Student Preferences

Any education team would be remiss if they did not identify and strongly consider a student's preferences when determining curriculum content. One of the focuses of education, after all, is to teach a student to make decisions (Helmstetter & Guess, 1987; Kennedy & Haring, 1993) based on knowledge of the options and to deal with the consequences of that decision. Initially, instruction on choice making uses information from reinforcement assessments, thus verifying that the student learns how to make choices by having at least one option that is a personal high preference (Green, Raid, Canape, & Gardner, 1988, 1991; Wolery, Ault, & Doyle, 1992).

When identifying a student's preferences for curriculum content to be included in instruction, therefore, it is the education team's responsibility to provide enough information to allow the student to make an informed choice between viable options (Nietupski & Hamre-Nietupski, 1987). While options for general education curriculum content during the primary and elementary years may be limited, as they are for all students, the number of options increases as a student progresses into middle school and high school. The number of options increases at the primary and elementary levels, however, when considering instruction in the community. The number of community-based options greatly increases, again, as the student enters middle school and high school, with time in the community and the number of activities completed in the community increasing.

As with the information gathered from the other sources listed previously, the education team prioritizes the curriculum content preferred by the student. Again, the education team should consider which of the preferences will be helpful for the student across settings and peer groups. The team will review and compare the content on this prioritized list with the content of the prioritized lists from the other sources of information as they make final decisions on curriculum content for the school year.

Gathering Information to Identify Priority General Education Needs

Thus far the education team has gathered information related only to identifying functional curriculum content that will assist a student to participate more fully in activities with peers and family members at home, in school, and in the community. In addition to this information, education teams need similar information related to identifying general education curriculum content that is relevant for the student (see Figure 3.2).

Inventory of the General Education Setting

Numerous variables about the general education setting are relevant when identifying curriculum content for a student with moderate or severe disabilities. While a list of those variables could be endless, depending upon the specific needs of students with multiple disabilities, some variables are important for all students (see Figure 3.4). With this information education teams can perform a discrepancy analysis between the demands of the locations and the skills currently demonstrated by the student, identifying any necessary (1) changes in physical layout (e.g., amount of space between desks), (2) adaptations or additions to materials (e.g., adapted utensils or writing and drawing implements, addition of switches to electrically operated equipment), (3) skills the student must acquire (e.g., new class rules, use of a locker), and (4) modifications in instructional style (e.g., interspersing of questions on similar content for the student during class review sessions). This information will allow the education team to determine the skills and activities which are expected of all students and, therefore, would be most beneficial for the student to acquire to participate more fully in each of the general education settings. They should note if specific skills and activities have generalized use for the student across settings. The team then can prioritize the skills and activities for later use in determining the student's actual curriculum content for the next school year.

---

1. Location of various rooms (e.g., classroom, lunchroom, gym) to each other and the possible paths between those rooms
2. Areas within each room that are used for instruction (e.g., student desks, teacher desk, reading area, carpet section, small group table) and the possible paths between those areas
3. Differences in distance and ease of mobility along each path between rooms and areas within rooms
4. Location of accessible restrooms to each room
5. Location and accessibility of equipment, instructional supplies, and functional materials within each room
6. Location and method of accessing student storage areas (e.g., cloak room, locker, cubby hole) per room
7. Types of materials used during large-group, small-group, and independent instructional activities per class period
8. Class rules across instructors and rooms
9. Instructional style of each instructor

FIGURE 3.4 General Education Setting Information

General Education Curriculum Inventory

In order to identify components of the general education curriculum that are most relevant for a student, the education team reviews the instructional units and specific outcomes targeted per unit for the general education class. While school districts have an established scope and sequence to their overall curriculum which is readily available, there are minor nuances to that curriculum that are specific to every teacher in a district. For example, one school district's first-grade curriculum in language arts includes a rudimentary understanding of authors and how writing styles are demonstrated in each author's books. To address this curricular area, one first-grade teacher incorporates an "author study" emphasis across three to four weeks of instruction, interweaving the content of various books by one author during reading, language experience, art, and even some math classes. Another first-grade teacher holds "author study" class sessions, comparing authors and their books in specifically structured activities.

To identify skills and activities that are most relevant for a student with moderate or severe disabilities, therefore, the education team conducts an inventory of the specific general education curriculum to be addressed in the student's class. The team completes this by reviewing each unit completed by the general education teacher and by reviewing the outcomes that the teacher both expects and desires for the entire class. From this list of outcomes, the education team can identify the components that would be most effective in increasing the degree to which the student participates in activities in school, at home, and in the community, both that year and in the future. Figure 3.5 includes a worksheet used by some education teams during the general education curriculum content inventory. The team then prioritizes these components for future use in determining the final curriculum content for the student's next school year.

When Jason's education team needed to identify priorities from the general education curriculum (see Appendix A), they selected the special education teacher, speech therapist, and first-grade teacher as the most appropriate team members to conduct the general education curriculum inventory because of his needs and their pivotal roles in meeting those needs. These team members met and reviewed all the curriculum content that the nondisabled first graders should achieve by the end of the academic year. In addition, the first-grade teacher discussed the academic and personal growth objectives that she would like her students to achieve by the end of the year, beyond those officially covered in the general education curriculum. Because all three team members had at least rudimentary information about Jason, they already knew the kindergarten content he was acquiring and could envision the content that potentially would be within his ability to acquire. In addition, they were able to relate to his family life and peer interactions and envision the first-grade curriculum content that he could use most readily in those settings.

When the general education class receives instruction from more than one teacher (e.g., teachers of special subject areas, such as art or physical education; teachers of compartmentalized programs, such as language arts, science, and math), each teacher participates in completing a general education curriculum in-

Student:	Teacher:
Date:	Grade:
Subject:	
Unit:	

Expected Outcomes	Components Relevant for the Student	Settings and Activities for Application			
		General Education	School	Home	Community
Desired Outcomes					

FIGURE 3.5   General Education Curriculum Content Worksheet

ventory. The teachers determine for each class period the outcomes and the curriculum components that would be most beneficial for the student, especially across inclusive settings and peer groups. Again, the education team then prioritizes the selected components for future use in determining the student's final curriculum content for the next school year. For Jason, the special education teacher and speech therapist also met with the music teacher, librarian, and physical education instructor to complete general education curriculum content inventories.

Negotiating Annual Goals

Thus far in the process an education team has gathered information from a variety of sources and identified priority instructional needs for a student in relation to both functional and general education curriculum content. With information on prioritized needs for each inventory completed, the education team then reviews all of these lists of priorities and negotiates to identify the most relevant and critical activities and skills to emphasize for the student's instruction during the next school year.

Negotiation

Negotiation is the process of arranging for or bringing about the settlement of a matter through conference, discussion, and compromise with others (*Webster's Ninth Collegiate Dictionary*, 1991). In relation to an education team identifying the prioritized curriculum needs for a student, negotiation must incorporate true collaboration among team members. Hargreaves (cited in Ainscow, 1991) describes the need for

> ... *true collaborative cultures that are "deep, personal and enduring. They are not," he argues, "mounted just for specific projects or events. They are not strings of one-shot deals. Cultures of collaboration rather are, constitutive of, absolutely central to, teachers' daily work." (pp. 221–222)*

Rainforth, York, and Macdonald (1992) state that "to function as a collaborative team, positive interdependence must be structured through mutually agreed upon goals, contribution to goal attainment, and celebration of goal accomplishment" (p. 206). If an education team has established a collaborative relationship built on positive interdependence, then the process of negotiating the content of annual goals will reflect mutual respect for both the individual members of the team and the instructional content with which each member has expertise. Such mutual respect leads to an understanding of how acquisition of instructional content within one area affects acquisition of content in other areas.

For example, while fully ambulatory, Jason (see Appendix A) has low muscle tone and weak trunk muscles, resulting in physical fatigue he demonstrates by slumping over his desk during the afternoon session of his first-grade class. He currently is learning to write the letters of the alphabet along with his classmates. His education team understands the relationship between his muscle tone, physical fatigue, inability to sit with erect posture, and writing letters correctly after midday. His annual goals, therefore, reflect this relationship and incorporate the development of physical strength and endurance, as well as the demonstration of these during class activities that demand writing. The education team feels that the demonstration of improvement in strength and endurance without correlation to the activities during which he is exhibiting difficulty would be insufficient to meet Jason's educational needs.

The negotiation process used to identify annual goals may vary across education teams, but the intent of the processes is the same. Education teams objectively review the priority curriculum content items identified during information gathering activities, understand the relevance of each item to the student's current and future life, openly and nondefensively discuss the rationale for their thoughts on each item, and reach a consensus on the items believed to be most important for inclusion on the student's IEP and for emphasis in instruction during the next school year. To accomplish this, each team member is ready to agree that a curriculum item they initially believed to be critical for the student actually is *less* critical for this year than other items. If this is not the case, the team member(s) must be able to convince other team members about the critical nature of the item through logical arguments related to the student's participation in life. The focus of discussions on a curriculum item is its relative importance to the student's participation in activities in both current and future environments, the potential generalized use of it, and the degree to which it is critical for that student during instruction in the next school year.

The education team's goal is to use the multiple lists of priorities from each domain and subject area and develop one final list of priority needs *across* them (see Figure 3.6). This final list of priorities will describe the emphasized content of instruction for the student during the next school year. Upon reviewing the prioritized needs for each of the domains and areas, the education team may find it possible to complete two activities that will simplify their negotiation process. First, one item may appear on more than one priority list, allowing the education team to consolidate the items on those lists and eliminate duplications. An example occurs in Mark's student profile (see Appendix A) when *increasing interactions* and *communication skills* are included as priorities on the family, community, peer, and general education inventories. His team used these priorities to develop annual goals #1 and #2 for Mark. Second, two or more items may be related or demonstrated during the same activity, and the education team may choose to combine these items. A similar example occurs in Jason's student profile (see Appendix A) when *improve verbal language* is included as a priority in the family inventory and *speak in complete sentences* is a priority in the general education curriculum inventory. Because these two priorities are similar, a combination of the two resulted in annual goal #2 for Jason.

Once they complete these simplifying steps, the education team then reviews the remaining items to (1) determine which items are most important to include in instruction for the student during the next school year and (2) eliminate the remaining items from consideration for the next year, but hold them for consideration for the following year. The education team then lists the items selected as important for the next school year in order of priority. The team may use various methods to determine order of priority. For example, if agreement cannot be

Priority Needs: Family Inventory	Priority Needs: Peer Inventory	Priority Needs: Community Inventory	Priority Needs: Related Services Assessments

Priority Needs: Records and Prior Information	Priority Needs: Student Preferences	Priority Needs: General Education Settings	Priority Needs: General Education Curriculum

Family's Priorities	Other Team Member's Priorities	Student's Preferences

Final Priorities	
1)	6)
2)	7)
3)	8)
4)	9)
5)	10)

FIGURE 3.6   Schema for Negotiating Final List of Priorities

reached among all the team members, they may list items based on the number of team members that agree on its importance. If there is complete lack of agreement, the family may select one or more priorities, then the remaining team members may select the next priority, and so on. Whatever process is used, the task is to rank those items considered most relevant and critical to include in instruction for the student, giving equal consideration to family, student, and school personnel opinions. In addition, the team must give equal consideration to items that reflect both functional and general education curriculum content.

The final list of priorities for any student may reflect either (1) a combination of both functional and general education curriculum content (see student profiles for Jason in Appendix A and Maureen in Appendix B), (2) all general education curriculum content (see student profile for Dave in Appendix A), or (3) all functional curriculum content (see student profile for Tony in Appendix A). The intent of this process is for the education team as a whole to consider *all* relevant curriculum content for each student and to identify the most relevant and critical content for inclusion in the next year's instruction for each student.

Blending of Priority Needs within Annual Goals

With the final list of priority items for a student, the education team then develops a feasible number of annual goals that incorporate those items. The number of annual goals developed varies per school district, education team, and student but should be determined based upon the (1) degree to which items are critical for the student, (2) degree to which instruction can occur on multiple annual goals at one time, and (3) feasibility of providing instruction on all the content across the school year. Annual goals may, however, reflect more than one item. For instance, aside from reflecting only one curricular need (i.e., one functional or general education curricular need) an annual goal may reflect functional and general education curriculum needs, more than one functional curriculum need, or more than one general education curriculum need. The key to blending items within one goal is determining the extent to which the functional activities and skills included in the items are used within the same instructional activity, as well as across activities and settings. For example, Dave's annual goal #1 addresses both the priority for improving social interaction skills across activities and participating in more activities across settings (see student profile in Appendix A).

The form in which annual goals appear on IEPs also varies across school districts, as does the content recommended in the literature (Sontag, Smith, & Certo, 1977; Snell, 1993; York & Vandercook, 1991). In the guidelines for implementing IDEA, however, the *Federal Register* indicates that an annual goal should reflect

> ... *what a handicapped child can reasonably be expected to accomplish within a twelve month period in the child's special education program. There should be a direct relationship between the annual goals and the present levels of educational performance.* (p. 5470)

To incorporate these guidelines into annual goals, as well as delineate clearly the intent of an annual goal and provide a specific method of measuring the degree to which a student progresses toward meeting that intent, education teams frequently develop annual goals that include the activity during which the content will be used. In addition, annual goals may include both the student's current and projected performance levels. Figure 3.7 includes two simple fill-in-the-blank worksheets education teams have used to incorporate the components into an easy-to-read format. Examples of annual goals that education teams developed using this worksheet and that incorporate these components are in the student profiles in Appendix A.

Identifying Locations for Instruction

In addition to identifying curriculum content for an annual goal, education teams determine the locations in which the student will receive instruction on, and demonstrate acquisition of, that content. While not necessarily included within the annual goal, locations for instruction and demonstration of acquisition are important to this process for a number of reasons. First, if an education team wants a student to learn activities and skills that are functional for that student, then instruction will occur in the setting(s) in which the activities and skills are needed. The team, therefore, should select locations for instruction with attention to where the student naturally will need to complete each activity and use each skill. Second, if an education team wants a student to complete an activity or use a skill in more than one setting, then instruction will occur in more than one setting. The number of settings selected for instruction will be determined by the number of (1) current and future settings in which the student needs to complete each activity or use each skill and (2) settings required for the student to generalize, as determined by the student's past acquisition and generalization rates. Third, if an education team wants a student to learn an activity or skill as quickly as possible, then the number of instructional trials should be as great as possible. Whenever an event occurs,

---

Fill in the blanks for #1:

  a)   *Student's name*
  b) will   *increase/decrease/maintain*
  c)   *domain/area/type of skills*
  d) during   *activity or activities*
  e) from   *current level of performance*
  f) to   *projected level of performance*
  g) within one year.

or for #2:

  Student's name   will   *increase/decrease/maintain*
  domain/area/type of skills   during   *activity or activities*   from
  current level of performance   to   *projected level of performance*   within
  one year.

FIGURE 3.7   Annual Goal Development Worksheet

therefore, during which an activity or skill included in the student's annual goals may be incorporated, instruction on that activity or skill should occur. For all of these reasons, education teams identify the functional and general education activities during which a student will receive instruction on the identified curriculum content.

In selecting locations for instruction, education teams consider how instruction on both functional and general education curriculum content may occur either during functional or general education activities (see Figure 3.8). That is, instruction on both functional and general education curriculum content can be incorporated into general education activities in the classroom, school building, or on field trips in the community. Likewise, instruction on both functional and general education curriculum content can be incorporated into functional activities in the classroom, school building, home, or community. For example, Alice's annual goal to increase behaviors that demonstrate self-control can occur during instruction on both general and functional curriculum content in the classroom, the school building, her home, and the community (see her student profile in Appendix A). When both functional and general education curriculum content are blended during one instructional activity, the education team (1) maximizes the use of instructional time, (2) maximizes the probability of use of skills in settings in which those skills are needed, and (3) allows other time periods to be used for instruction on additional content. The more that instruction can address multiple content areas, the more efficiently instructional time is used.

Summary

An education team has the responsibility to consider all possible curriculum content for each student, so as to maximize students' acquisition of activities and skills most meaningful for them in both current and future environments. In addition, the team pays particular attention to the development of students' natural support networks and the existence of ethnic diversity in each student's family. Determining the curriculum content that will comprise the education program for a student with moderate or severe disabilities entails the use of judgement when making a number of decisions, and the process used to make those decisions reflects the values held by the education team.

Education teams involved in inclusive services use a process that allows for blending functional and general education curriculum needs in annual goals and instruction. This blending necessitates a process for identifying priority needs for a student that gives equal consideration to both types of curriculum content, but selects only the most relevant content for instruction for the student during the next school year. The curriculum content identification process presented in this chapter emphasizes (1) the role of the student, family, and other team members, (2) the blending of functional and general education curriculum content on the IEP, and (3) the provision of instruction on both functional and general education curriculum content during both general education and functional activities.

Student: _____   Date: _____

Annual Goal	General Education Settings			Functional Activity Settings			
	Classroom	School Building	Field Trips	Classroom	School Building	Field Trips	Home	Community

FIGURE 3-8   Settings for Instruction Per Annual Goal

The process is based on an extension of the ecological approach for identifying functional curriculum content using (1) a family inventory, (2) a peer inventory, (3) a community inventory, (4) in vivo related services assessments, (5) records and prior information, (6) student preferences, (7) an inventory of general education settings, and (8) a general education curriculum inventory. In completing each component of the process, the education team also completes a priority needs inventory for that component, to be used during the negotiation of annual goals and objectives for instruction during the next school year.

Negotiation during IEP development is a process for bringing about agreement on the content on which a student will receive instruction during the next school year. True negotiation requires that a team functions in a collaborative manner across the year, in all aspects of their interactions. Each annual goal may reflect either one functional or general education curriculum need, more than one functional curriculum need, more than one general education curriculum need, or any combination of functional and general education curriculum needs. Blending needs within one goal is dependent upon the possibility of the needs being demonstrated during the same activity.

Finally, the education team identifies the location(s) in which instruction will occur on the content of each annual goal and in which the student will demonstrate acquisition of the content. The team should select locations with consideration for the occurrence of functional activities, generalized use of the skills and activities, and maximization of instructional time. The blending of instruction for functional and general education curriculum needs during the same instructional activities maximizes the impact of instruction.

References

Ainscow, L. (Ed.). (1991). *Effective education for all*. London: David Fulton Publishers.

Brown, L., Branston-McLean, M. B., Baumgart, D., Vincent, L., Falvey, M., & Schroeder, J. (1979a). Using the characteristics of current and future least restrictive environments in the development of curricular content for severely handicapped students. *AAESPH Review, 4*(4), 407–424.

Brown, L., Branston, M. B., Hamre-Nietupski, S., Pumpian, I., Certo, N., & Gruenewald, L. (1979b). A strategy for developing chronological age appropriate and functional curricular content for severely handicapped adolescents and young adults. *Journal of Special Education, 13*(1), 81–90.

Brown, L., Nisbet, J., Ford, A., Sweet, M., Shiraga, B., York, J., & Loomis, R. (1983). The critical need for nonschool instruction in educational programs for severely handicapped students. *Journal of The Association for the Severely Handicapped, 8*(3), 71–77.

Chin-Perez, G., Hartman, D., Park, H. S., Sacks, S., Wershing, A., & Gaylord-Ross, R. (1986). Maximizing social contact for secondary students with severe handicaps. *The Journal of The Association for Persons with Severe Handicaps, 11*(2), 118–124.

Cohen, S., Agosta, J., Cohen, J., & Warren, R. (1989). Supporting families of children with severe disabilities. *The Journal of The Association for Persons with Severe Handicaps, 14*(2), 155–162.

Flowers, R., & Houck, D. (1991). *The Buffalo School District inclusion program*. Presentation at the Buffalo School District Annual Conference, Buffalo, NY.

Flowers, R., & Houck, D. (1992). *The Buffalo School District inclusion program.* Presentation at the Inclusion Conference of Western New York Schools Are For Everyone (SAFE), Buffalo, NY.

Gaylord-Ross, R., & Browder, D. (1991). Functional assessment: Dynamic and domain properties. In L. H. Meyer, C. A. Peck, & L. Brown (Eds.), *Critical issues in the lives of people with severe disabilities* (pp. 45–66). Baltimore: Paul H. Brookes.

Giangreco, M. F., Cloninger, C. J., & Iverson, V. S. (1993). *Choosing options and accommodations for children: A guide to planning inclusive education.* Baltimore: Paul H. Brookes.

Green, C. W., Reid, D. H., Canipe, V. S., & Gardner, S. M. (1991). A comprehensive evaluation of reinforcer identification processes for persons with profound multiple handicaps. *Journal of Applied Behavior Analysis, 24,* 537–552.

Green, C. W., Reid, D. H., White, L. K., Halford, R. C., Brittain, D. P., & Gardner, S. M. (1988). Identifying reinforcers for persons with profound handicaps: Staff option vs. systematic assessment of preferences. *Journal of Applied Behavior Analysis, 21,* 31–44.

Haring, T. G. (1991). Social relationships. In L. H. Meyer, C. A. Peck, & L. Brown (Eds.), *Critical issues in the lives of people with severe disabilities* (pp. 195–217). Baltimore: Paul H. Brookes.

Haring, T. G., & Breen, C. (1989). Units of analysis of social interaction outcomes in supported employment. *The Journal of The Association for Persons with Severe Handicaps, 14*(4), 255–262.

Helmstetter, E., & Guess, D. (1987). Application of the individualized curriculum sequencing model to learners with severe sensory impairments. In L. Goetz, D. Guess, & K. Stremel-Campbell (Eds.), *Innovative program design for individuals with dual sensory impairments* (pp. 255–282). Baltimore: Paul H. Brookes.

Hoier, T., & Cone, J. D. (1987). Target selection of social skills for children. *Behavior Modification, 11,* 137–163.

Idol, L. (1993). *Special educator's consultation handbook.* Austin: Pro-Ed, Inc.

Individuals with Disabilities Education Act of 1990, 20 U.S. C. 1401 (a)(17).

Kennedy, C. H., & Haring, T. G. (1993). Teaching choice making during social interactions to students with profound multiple disabilities. *Journal of Applied Behavior Analysis, 26,* 63–76.

Mount, B., & Zwernik, K. (1988). *It's never too early, it's never too late: A booklet about personal futures planning.* St. Paul, MN: St. Paul: Metropolitan Council.

Nietupski, J. A., & Hamre-Nietupski, S. M. (1987). An ecological approach to curriculum development. In L. Goetz, D. Guess, & K. Stremel-Campbell (Eds.), *Innovative program design for individuals with dual sensory impairments* (pp. 225–253). Baltimore: Paul H. Brookes.

Orelove, F. P., & Sobsey, D. (1991). *Educating children with multiple disabilities: A transdisciplinary approach* (2nd ed.). Baltimore: Paul H. Brookes.

Oubre, J. (1991). *Effects of including students with moderate and severe disabilities in general education classes.* Presentation at the State University College at Buffalo, Buffalo, NY.

Perske, R. (1988). *Circle of friends.* Nashville, TN: Abingdon Press.

Rainforth, B., York, J., & Macdonald, C. (1992). *Collaborative teams for students with severe disabilities.* Baltimore, MD: Paul H. Brookes.

Ryndak, D. L., Doyle, M. B., & Osborne, D. (1989). *Inventory of family activities and annual goal preferences.* Buffalo, NY: Severe Handicaps Technical Assistance Project, State University College at Buffalo, Exceptional Education Department.

Salisbury, C., & Vincent, L. J.(1990). "Criterion of the next environment" and "best practices": Mainstreaming and integration 10 years later. *Topics in Early Childhood Special Education, 10*(2), 78–89.

Schnorr, R. (1990). "Peter? He comes and goes...": First graders' perspectives on a part-time mainstream student. *The Journal of The Association for Persons with Severe Handicaps, 15*(4), 231–240.

Schooley, R. & Ryndak, D. (1991). *Integrating students with multiple disabilities in regular classes.* Presentation at the Annual Regional Conference of the Genessee County Special Education Training and Resource Center, Genessee, NY.

Snell, M. (1993). *Instruction of students with severe disabilities* (4th ed.). New York: Charles F. Merrill.

Sommerstein, L., Schooley, R., & Ryndak, D. (1992). *Including students with moderate or severe disabilities in general education settings.* Presentation at the Annual Regional Conference of the Genessee County Special Education Training and Resource Center, Genessee, NY.

Sontag, E., Smith, J., & Certo, N. (1977). *Educational programming for the severely and profoundly handicapped.* Reston, VA: Council for Exceptional Children.

Turnbull, A. P., Brotherson, M. J., Bronicki, G. J., Benson, H. A., Houghton, J., Roeder-Gordon, C., & Summers, J. A. (1985). *How to plan for my child's adult future: A three part process to future planning.* Lawrence, KS: Future Planning Project, University Affiliated Facility, Bureau of Child Research.

Vandercook, T., & York, J.(1990). A team approach to program development and support. In W. Stainback, & S. Stainback (Eds.), *Support networks for inclusive schooling: Interdependent integrated education* (pp. 95–122). Baltimore: Paul H. Brookes Publishing Co.

Vandercook, T., York, J., & Forest, M. (1989). The McGill action planning system (MAPS): A strategy for building the vision. *Journal of The Association for Persons with Severe Handicaps, 14*(3), 205–215.

Weaver, J. & Ryndak, D. (1992). *Identifying curriculum content for students with severe disabilities in regular classes.* Presentation at the Inclusion Conference of Western New York Schools Are For Everyone (SAFE), Buffalo, NY.

Webster's ninth collegiate dictionary (1991). Springfield, MA: Merriam-Webster.

Winton, P. J., & Bailey, D. B. (1988). The family focused interview: A collaborative mechanism for family assessment and goal setting. *Journal of the Division for Early Childhood, 12*(3), 195–207.

Wolery, M., Ault, M. J., & Doyle, P. M. (1992). *Teaching students with moderate to severe disabilities: Use of response prompting strategies.* White Plain, NY: Longman.

York, J., & Vandercook, T. (1991). Designing an integrated education for learners with severe disabilities. *Teaching Exceptional Children, 23*(2), 22–28

4

NATURAL SUPPORT NETWORKS: COLLABORATING WITH FAMILY AND FRIENDS FOR MEANINGFUL EDUCATION PROGRAMS IN INCLUSIVE SETTINGS

DIANE LEA RYNDAK

Objectives

After completing this chapter the reader will be able to:

1. Define a natural support network and describe his/her own network.
2. Describe how and why the members of a student's natural support network should participate in the student's education program.
3. List and describe variables that effect the degree to which family members and friends participate in a student's education program.
4. Describe the role of family members and friends in the identification of curriculum content for a student's education program the next school year.
5. Describe the role of family members and friends during the implementation of instruction throughout the school year.
6. List and describe strategies for education teams to facilitate the expansion of a student's natural support network.

Key Terms

Natural support network	MAPS
Support	Circle of friends

The intent of providing education services in inclusive settings is to facilitate the student's independent and partial participation in naturally occurring activities at home, at school, at work, and in the community (Brown, Shiraga, York, Zanella, & Rogan, 1984; Brown, Nietupski, & Hamre-Nietupski, 1976). The nature and intent of providing such services create a situation that not only is conducive to, but also dependent upon, extensive collaboration with family members and friends in the development and implementation of a student's education program. Collaboration with family members and friends is critical because they are most knowledgeable not only about the student, but also about the settings that comprise the student's life space (Brown et al., 1984; Giangreco, Cloninger, & Iverson, 1993) and the activities that occur in those settings. Through collaboration with these individuals, school personnel (1) identify the environments, activities, and skills most meaningful for a student's participation in everyday life and (2) facilitate the broadening of a student's natural support network. This increases the probability that the student's network will be substantial enough to support the student both during and after the educational career.

Natural Support Networks

A natural support network is the set of individuals with whom a person has ongoing interactions in everyday life, reflecting various levels of friendship, caring, support, and assistance for both parties across a variety of activities. Members of a natural support network share a mutual respect and interdependence, each receiving intrinsic benefits from interactions (Forest & Lusthaus, 1989). Across people natural support networks vary in at least three ways, including: (1) the number of individuals that comprise the networks, (2) the type of relationships established with individuals in the networks, and (3) the extent to which the networks are essential for maximal independence and participation in activities throughout life. For example, the manner in which a preschool student relies on a natural support network, as well as the types of support required from the network, is different from those of a premed college student, a junior-high student in the inner city, or a high-school student in a rural area. Each, however, has identified a set of individuals with whom he or she has developed a mutually supportive relationship built on friendship, caring, support, and assistance.

While the list of all possible members of a natural support network is endless, the number of actual members in a network is limited (see Figure 4.1). Sporadic interactions with numerous potential members, however, do not constitute the basis on which membership in that person's network is established. Rather, membership in a natural support network develops over time, through ongoing, purposeful, mutually beneficial interactions. Such interactions may provide any number of benefits for either or both parties. For example, the number of opportunities to socially interact, or the frequency with which companionship is available during routine or special events, may increase for either person. A natural support network member may become a partner for leisure activities or may provide various types

Parents	Classmates
Siblings	Coworkers
Relatives	Fellow Employees
Neighbors	Employer
Family Friends/Extended Family	Business Owners
Fellow Participants in Community or Leisure Activities	Business Employees
	Community Workers
Members of Education Team	

FIGURE 4.1   Possible Members of a Natural Support Network

of assistance (e.g., physical, logistical, or emotional) that allow a person to participate in both routine and special activities. Additionally, members of a natural support network may provide various types of support. York, Giangreco, Vandercook, and Macdonald (1992) refer to four types of support that team members provide for each other.

1. Resource support—the provision of tangible material, financial resources, informational resources, or human resources to team members.
2. Moral support—person-to-person interactions that validate the worth of people as individuals and as knowledgeable colleagues.
3. Technical support—offers of concrete strategies, methods, approaches, or ideas.
4. Evaluation support—assistance both in collecting information to monitor and adjust support and in determining the effect of support. (pp. 104–105)

While York et al. (1992) discuss support in relation to team responsibilities and the needs of team members, the same types of support occur in relation to responsibilities of a natural support network and the needs of its members.

Members of the natural support network for a student with disabilities provide that student opportunities for interaction, companionship during leisure, assistance during activities, and support in a variety of ways. For this reason, collaboration between school personnel and network members is critical when (1) identifying both functional and general education curriculum content that is most relevant for inclusion in instruction, (2) implementing instruction, and (3) evaluating the effect of that instruction.

Identifying the Natural Support Network for a Student

Snow and Forest (1987) describe a process used by peers to identify people who play certain roles in their own lives and in the life of a classmate with disabilities. This "circle of friends" process has each student draw four concentric circles around a symbol that represents themselves and list within each circle, respectively, the people with whom they have (1) intimate relationships (e.g., family members, best friends), (2) close friendships, (3) acquaintanceships, and (4) paid relationships (e.g., teachers, therapists, doctors). Each student then completes the same steps for their classmate with disabilities and contrasts the degree to which the two sets of four circles are filled (see Figure 4.2). This visual representation allows students to understand the need for peers with disabilities to develop additional, nonpaid, meaningful relationships and encourages them to become part of their classmate's "circle of friends". As stated by Forest and Lusthaus (1989), the intent of this process is to assist in the development of "a network that allows for the genuine involvement of children in a friendship, caring, and support role with their peers" (p. 47).

There is a similar process for identifying members of a student's natural support network. Instead of drawing concentric circles, however, the student draws four circles in the north, south, east, and west positions with all four overlapping

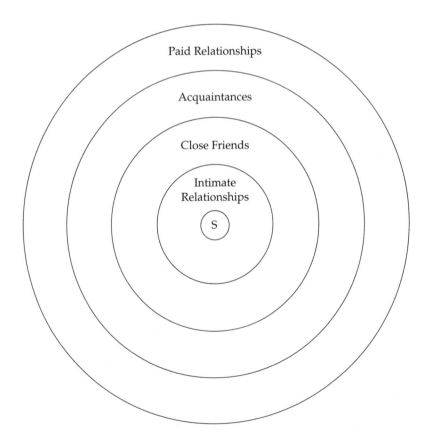

FIGURE 4.2   Circle of Friends

in the middle (see Figure 4.3). One large circle surrounds these four circles. This large circle represents all "social interaction." The four overlapping circles represent other types of benefits experienced by members of a natural support network (i.e., companionship, partners for activities, assistance, and support). Note that at the very center of this figure all five circles overlap.

When using this process to identify members of a student's natural support network, a name is placed in the circle(s) that represents the type of benefit the *student* experiences through interactions with the person named. The only people listed, however, are those with whom the student has ongoing, purposeful, mutually beneficial interactions, resulting in various levels of friendship, caring, support, and assistance. When a name appears in more than one of the four central circles, and those circles are adjacent, that name moves to where the circles overlap. If a name is in more than two of those circles, that name moves to where all three or four circles overlap. The closer the name appears to the center of the figure, the

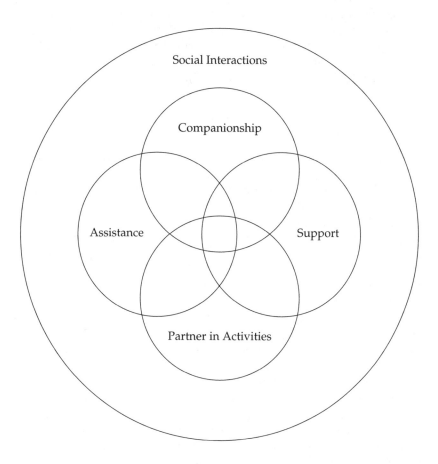

FIGURE 4.3 Identifying Members of a Natural Support Network

more types of benefit the student experiences through interactions with the person named. Finally, every person listed in one of the four central circles automatically appears in the large circle that represents social interaction, which automatically occurs when any of the four benefits occurs.

When peers complete this process for their own natural support network and that of a classmate with disabilities, the visual images project any discrepancy between the two networks. Follow-up discussions assist peers in realizing the degree to which classmates with disabilities must rely on others for support and assistance. If members of a natural support network are not available, their classmates must rely on people who are paid to support and assist them. To minimize the need for paid support and assistance, natural support networks for each classmate with disabilities must be extensive, and the education team should facilitate the membership of peers throughout the school years. As members join a student's natural support network, they should feel encouraged to participate in the student's education program.

Unfortunately, little is known about how to define an individual's social life and how to measure the extent to which it effects an individual's life (Malette et al., 1992). The importance of natural support networks in both social life and education program planning, however, increasingly is being recognized (Kennedy, Horner, & Newton, 1990; Malette et al., 1992).

Cultural Diversity and Other Factors Affecting Participation of Network Members

Both the Education for Handicapped Children Act (EHA) of 1975 (PL 94-142) and its reauthorization as the Individuals with Disabilities Education Act (IDEA) of 1990 (PL 101-476) mandate the inclusion of parents in the development of a student's Individualized Education Program (IEP). To comply with this mandate, school districts have established procedures for inviting parents to participate in major discussions of their child's IEP. Kroth (1978), MacMillan and Turnbull (1983), and some districts also encourage ongoing parental participation in the student's education program. In the majority of situations, however, encouragement has been only in the form of lip service (Lipsky, 1989).

If a student is to receive services that reflect the intent of inclusion and experience the full benefits of inclusion, school personnel must be proactive in facilitating the involvement not only of parents (Shea & Bauer, 1991) but also of other members of the student's natural support network. There is, however, a history of limited participation by parents in the development and implementation of education programs. Salisbury (1992) identifies three factors that influence the degree to which parents have been involved in education programs, and Rueda and Martinez (1992) identify three main barriers to the participation of Latino families (see Figure 4.4). Ruiz (1989) provides strategies for developing an optimal learning environment for a language-minority student. With increased focus on participation of both parents and additional network members in education programs, school personnel may want to consider these variables in relation to interaction with all network members. In addition, school personnel may want to (1) expand beyond the

A. Communication

1. Communication is not in the primary languages of parents and other network members.
2. Professionals use jargon with which parents and other network members are not familiar.
3. Parents or other network members have intellectual or physical limitations.
4. Professionals limit communication with parents and other network members to administrative tasks.
5. Professionals and/or network members have verbal and/or nonverbal interpersonal communication skills that are ineffective.

B. Perception, Attitudes, and Values

1. Professionals demonstrate an insensitivity to differences among networks (i.e., family characteristics, cultural differences, class differences).
2. Parents and other network members are viewed as adversaries rather than partners.
3. Parents and other network members are viewed as less observant, perceptive, or intelligent than professionals.
4. Priorities and expectations of parents and other network members do not match those of professionals.
5. Professionals experience profession-related constraints (e.g., time constraints, role constraints).

C. Logistical Difficulties

1. Professionals and network members have difficulty finding mutually agreed upon times for meetings.
2. Structure of meetings minimize importance of participation of parents and other network members.

FIGURE 4.4   Factors Affecting Participation of Parents and Other Network Members in Education Programs

(Adapted from Salisbury [1992]. Parents as team members: Inclusive teams, collaborative outcomes. In B. Rainforth, J. York, & C. Macdonald [Eds.], *Collaborative teams for students with severe disabilities: Integrating therapy and educational services* [pp. 43–66]. Baltimore: Paul H. Brookes Publishing Co.; and Rueda & Martinez [1992]. Fiesta educativa: One community's approach to parent training in developmental disabilities for Latino families. *The Journal of The Association for Persons with Severe Handicaps, 17*[2], 95–103.)

parents the number of members of a student's natural support network involved in the education program, (2) modify the manner of encouraging parents and other network members to participate actively, and (3) increase the extent to which information provided by parents and other network members influences the student's program.

Involvement of Family and Other Network Members in Identifying Curriculum Content

When identifying relevant curriculum content for inclusion in a student's education program, family and other network members can provide invaluable information and assistance during numerous procedures. The following sections describe three of these procedures and ways in which family and other network members proactively affect the outcome of those procedures.

Gathering Information

Because the purpose of education is to prepare students to be maximally independent and participate fully in naturally occurring activities, school personnel must focus procedures related to identifying what to teach each student on determining the activities that naturally occur in each of their lives (Shea & Bauer, 1991). Only through this information can an education team identify the most meaningful content for each student. To accomplish this, school personnel put aside their predetermined curricula, whether based in developmental theory or activities of daily living, and systematically study the variables that are important in each student's life (see Chapter 3 for details on the procedures used to study variables).

Because natural support networks and participation with others in real life settings are vital in the lives of individuals with disabilities, members of a student's natural support network are the most valid source of information about settings and activities that are relevant for that student (Hamre-Nietupski, Nietupski, & Strathe, 1992). Vandercook, York, and Forest (1989) describe the McGill Action Planning System (MAPS) as one strategy for obtaining information from natural support network members. MAPS consists of a meeting at which seven questions are answered.

1. What is the student's history?
2. What is your dream for the student?
3. What is your nightmare?
4. Who is the student?
5. What are the student's strengths, gifts, and abilities?
6. What are the student's needs?
7. What would the student's ideal day at school look like, and what is necessary to make it happen?

Through their responses, natural support network members provide a wealth of information both about the student with disabilities and about the student's relationships with others.

While all support network members are valuable sources of information, the logistics of obtaining equal participation by all members of a student's network are untenable. It is possible, therefore, for parents and a few other members to represent all the members of a student's support network and to participate actively in procedures that will identify the curriculum content to be included on the student's IEP for the next year. Parents and other participating network members, therefore, obtain information that is relevant to these procedures from other members of the student's network. School personnel, parents, and other participating network members then complete together a family inventory, peer inventory, community inventory, general education settings inventory, and inventory of general education curriculum content (see Chapter 3 for a discussion of these inventories).

Each parent and other network member may participate in all or some of these procedures, depending upon their intimate involvement in and knowledge of each procedure. For instance, school friends of an elementary student may participate only in the peer inventory and general education settings inventory, while intimate friends of a high-school student also may participate in the community and general education curriculum content inventories. The intent is to obtain participation from the individuals who are most involved in a student's life, and use that information to determine the most meaningful content for instruction for that student based on the student's daily life.

Negotiating Annual Goals

The second procedure in which family and other network members provide essential information and assistance is negotiation of content for annual goals (see Chapter 3 for details on negotiating annual goals). During negotiation procedures any education team member may become myopic, focusing on the acquisition of either isolated skills or of skills within their area of expertise, instead of the need for and use of skills within activities that are meaningful for a student in daily life. Because family and other network members are involved most intimately in the student's daily life, their assistance in refocusing the purpose of the meeting and in reaffirming the purpose of the education program being developed is essential.

There are at least three ways in which family and other network members complete these tasks. First, they insure that discussions center on activities that occur in settings frequented by the student and that those are the basis on which functional and general education content are selected for inclusion in annual goals. When discussions digress from this focus, family and other network members step in to redirect the discussion. Second, family and other network members have the knowledge base to determine the extent to which the student will use suggested functional and general education content in daily life (Hamre-Nietupski et al., 1992). If they cannot link suggested content to specific activities in the student's naturally occurring settings (i.e., general education settings, school building, home, work, or community settings), family and other network members question the content. When school personnel are unable to convince everyone of the immediate link, the education team does not include that content in the annual goals. When a link is established, family and other network members also assist in determining the relative importance of the content in comparison with other content. Third, family and other network members have the knowledge to determine when and how two or more suggested components of functional and/or general education content blend together for the student's use in daily life. This knowledge assists in minimizing the number of annual goals that need to be monitored, while maximizing the relevance of the content selected for instructional emphasis. It also assists in linking content that occurs naturally in daily settings.

Identifying Settings for Instruction

The third procedure during which family and other network members provide essential information and assistance is the identification of settings in which instruction will occur (see Chapter 3 for details on identifying settings for instruction). When discussing where instruction will occur on the content of a specific annual goal, the attention of school personnel may be limited to settings with which they immediately are familiar (i.e., general education settings, school building settings) or settings which frequently are incorporated into packaged curricula (e.g., kitchen, grocery store, restaurant, rest room). Because family and other network members have first hand knowledge of the settings frequented by the student and the additional settings to which the student has access beyond the school and traditional community settings, their collaboration in identifying instructional settings is crucial.

There are two ways in which family and other network members assist in the identification of settings for instruction. First, after agreeing on the content of an annual goal, family and other network members assist by determining all of the settings and activities in which the student can make use of the content in daily life, whether the annual goal incorporates functional or general education content. Second, during discussions of a particular setting and activity, family and other network members determine whether the student (1) likes or has the option to participate in the activity in that setting and (2) has the resources required to participate in the activity in that setting. Through this process family and other network members verify that all instructional settings are meaningful and viable for the student.

Beyond Identifying Curriculum Content

Once the education team has established the curriculum content for inclusion in the IEP, collaboration with family and other network members does not end. Family and other network members are in unique positions to continue to assist school personnel with instruction, and school personnel are in unique positions to assist family and other network members with maintaining and expanding the network itself.

Family and Other Network Members Supporting Instruction

After the initiation of instruction, family and other network members continue to interact with the student in naturally occurring settings throughout daily life. Because the content of instruction is specific for its need and use in natural settings, and because the student accesses some of those natural settings outside of the school day, family and other network members frequently are in the position to reinforce learning that is occurring at school by using instructional procedures in those natural settings (Neel & Billingsley, 1989). While formal instruction that strictly follows procedures used in school may not be feasible or desirable to family and other network members (Idol, 1993), informal instruction at home or in the community may be possible. Informal instruction may consist of loosely following instructional procedures only at times and in situations in which the instruction will not be intrusive to the ongoing events. Parents frequently conduct informal instruction, and they utilize spontaneous situations as conduits for incidental learning.

This type of collaboration should be encouraged by other education team members, however, only after discussions with family and other network members who carefully consider the complex nature of the situations in which they interact with the student (Gaylord-Ross & Browder, 1991). For example, if one parent has five children to prepare for school in the morning and to interact with after school, expectations for that parent to focus on spontaneous situations for incidental learning may not be realistic. This same parent, however, may desire to focus on spontaneous situations for incidental learning after dinner when additional adult support is available. The decision to encourage such collaboration, therefore, is made on an individual basis.

Besides assisting with instruction during naturally occurring events, family and other network members also have the opportunity to observe the student's performance and participation during activities. This observation allows them to assist in (1) evaluating the degree to which the student's instruction has been effective (Gaylord-Ross & Browder, 1991), (2) identifying additional curriculum content areas that would be beneficial for the student, and (3) determining alternate instructional strategies.

Maintaining and Extending Natural Support Networks

Malette et al. (1992) state that "neither the service delivery system nor the community as a whole has a clear understanding of what defines a 'social life', much less how to measure the extent to which it occurs" (p. 190). Newton and Horner (1993) have begun to identify strategies for developing social relationships, which are required for a social life to exist. What is clear is that natural support networks cannot develop unless potential members have opportunities to interact and develop relationships (Biklen, 1989; Stainback, Stainback, & Slavin, 1989; Strully & Strully, 1989). Schnorr (1990) described how children as young as first graders already had developed a sense of which students "belonged" in their class and which were "visitors" based on the students' full- or part-time participation in class activities. This argues convincingly for full-time participation of students with disabilities in activities with their nondisabled peers (Brown et al., 1991) if natural support networks are to develop.

In addition, many adults with disabilities do not have an extensive natural support network. They have social contacts with numerous people but few relationships that last past twelve months (Kennedy, Horner, & Newton, 1989). Even through social contacts created by secondary transition programs (Chadsey-Rusch, 1990) and employment in competitive jobs (Shafer, Rice, Metzler, & Haring, 1989), adults with disabilities seldom develop relationships that expand their natural support network.

Through their daily contact with a variety of students, school personnel are in a position to greatly influence how and when students interact with each other. Students' interactions during school hours will determine the degree and manner in which they choose to interact with each other outside of school (McDonnell, Wilcox, & Hardman, 1991). For example, if two students frequently interact socially during school hours, the chances are high that they also will interact socially outside of school when provided opportunities. Through such ongoing interactions, membership in a natural support network can develop. School personnel, therefore, can influence membership in the natural support network for specific students by providing opportunities for that student to interact with classmates (Haring, 1991; Stainback & Stainback, 1990). While interactions may center around general education, functional, or social activities, students can learn how to support and interact effectively with each other during any type of activity. The task for school personnel is to facilitate membership in natural support networks by providing opportunities for students to interact during various types of activities.

There are a number of strategies in school (Eichinger, 1990; Staub & Hunt, 1993) and in living options programs (Newton & Horner, 1993) that provide opportunities for students to interact. As described above, the "circle of friends" activity (Snow & Forest, 1987) can assist students of all ages to understand their classmates' needs for additional friends in their support network. This understanding alone, however, is insufficient to establish those needed friendships; opportunities to interact also are required. In many classrooms, teachers are using cooperative learning strategies across academic areas to maximize opportunities for interaction between students.

Cooperative learning strategies allow students to work in small groups, sharing responsibility for acquisition of new knowledge and for demonstration of that knowledge by each member of their group (Borich, 1992; Putnam, Rynders, Johnson, & Johnson, 1989; Schulz, Carpenter, & Turnbull, 1991). Henley, Ramsey, & Algozzine (1993) specifically define cooperative learning as "a method of structuring small groups of nondisabled and disabled students so that all the individuals achieve a learning goal through mutual planning and decision making" (p. 194). Strategies include: (1) cooperative goal structuring (Johnson & Johnson, 1986), (2) jigsaw (Aronson, 1978; Slavin, 1978), (3) teams-games-tournaments (DeVries & Slavin, 1978), (4) small-group teaching (Sharon & Sharon, 1976), (5) student teams and achievement divisions (Gearheart, Weishahn, & Gearheart, 1992), (6) rap sessions (Gearheart et al., 1992), (7) team-assisted individualization (Goodman, 1990), and (8) buddy systems (Gearheart et al., 1992).

As a member of a cooperative learning group, a student with disabilities supports other group members in completing the activities necessary for acquisition and demonstration of knowledge. Likewise, the other group members provide support for the student with disabilities, ensuring the acquisition of knowledge identified for emphasis in the adapted instruction. Cooperative learning activities have been effective in enhancing interactions between students with disabilities and their nondisabled classmates (Gearheart et al., 1992; Johnson & Johnson, 1981, 1986; Johnson, Johnson, Warring, & Maruyama, 1986; Putnam et al., 1989).

At some high schools, personnel have assisted students in developing student clubs whose members facilitate the inclusion of students who are in danger of being isolated during social events. Targeted students include not only those with disabilities who receive services in inclusive settings, but also students who (1) are new to the school, (2) have English as a second language, or (3) are differentiated from the general population for other reasons. A few students may attend club activities before those activities held for the entire student body. For instance, the club may hold a pizza party/pep rally for a limited number of students before a football game. When the football game is about to begin, the students attending the club event may go as a group to the game and sit together in an assigned area. Back-to-back scheduling of events allows targeted students to become part of a smaller group of students who focus on facilitating their inclusion with peers and then move with that group to the larger event.

Summary

A natural support network is a set of individuals with whom a person has ongoing interactions that reflect various levels of friendship, caring, support, and assistance for both parties. Support networks vary in the number of members, types of relationships members share, and degree to which members rely on each other for companionship, partners during activities, assistance, and support. Providing education services in inclusive settings is conducive to, and dependent upon, collaboration with members of a student's natural support network both during development and implementation of the education program. School personnel depend on members' intimate knowledge of, and interest in, both the student and the settings in which that student interacts in daily life.

The use of proactive measures allows school personnel to facilitate the active participation of family and other members of a student's support network. Proactive measures help overcome barriers to their participation, such as: (1) language and communication problems, (2) differences in perceptions, attitudes, and values, and (3) logistical difficulties. Particular care must be taken to accommodate for any cultural diversity that exists among members.

Once involved, family and other members of a student's support network can provide valuable information and assistance in the identification of meaningful curriculum content for the student during procedures for gathering information, negotiating annual goals, and identifying settings for instruction. During each of these procedures family and other network members assist school personnel in maintaining the focus of discussions on the need for and use of skills within activities that are meaningful for the student. They assist by (1) insuring that discussions focus on activities and settings frequented by the student, (2) insuring that functional and general education content selected link directly to activities and settings frequented by the student, (3) sharing information that allows two or more suggested components of functional and general education content to be linked in activities and settings, and, therefore, in annual goals, (4) determining all of the settings and activities in which the student can make use of selected content, and (5) determining whether the student actually has access to, and either likes or needs to participate in, an activity in a particular setting.

Once school personnel and natural support network members have identified curriculum content, they continue to assist each other during implementation of the education program they developed collaboratively. When feasible, family and other network members may decide to support instruction by (1) reinforcing instruction through informal instruction during spontaneous events, (2) providing feedback on the effectiveness of instruction by observing the student's performance in daily life, (3) identifying additional curriculum areas for inclusion in the student's educational program, and (4) determining alternate instructional strategies.

Finally, developing an extended natural support network for a student with disabilities is critical for long-term success in inclusive adult settings. School personnel can influence the degree of maintenance and expansion of a student's natural support network by facilitating interactions with peers at school and school events.

References

Aronson, E. (1978). *The jigsaw classroom.* Beverly Hills, CA: Sage.

Biklen, D. (1989). Making difference ordinary. In S. Stainback, W. Stainback, & M. Forest (Eds.), *Educating all students in the mainstream of regular education* (pp. 235–248). Baltimore: Paul H. Brookes.

Borich, G. D. (1992). *Effective teaching methods.* New York: Charles E. Merrill.

Brown, L., Nietupski, J., & Hamre-Nietupski, S. (1976). Criterion of ultimate functioning. In M. A. Thomas (Ed.), *Hey, don't forget about me!* (pp. 2–15). Reston, VA: Council for Exceptional Children.

Brown, L., Schwarz, P., Udvari-Solner, A., Kampschroer, E. F., Johnson, F., Jorgensen, J., & Gruenewald, L. (1991). How much time should students with severe intellectual disabilities spend in regular classrooms and elsewhere? *The Journal of The Association for Persons with Severe Handicaps, 16*(1), 39–47.

Brown, L., Shiraga, B., York, J., Zanella, K., & Rogan, P. (1984). *A life space analysis strategy for students with severe handicaps.* Madison, WI: University of Wisconsin and Madison Metropolitan School District.

Chadsey-Rusch, J. (1990). Social interactions of secondary-aged students with severe handicaps: Implications for facilitating the transition from school to work. *The Journal of The Association for Persons with Severe Handicaps, 15*(2), 69–78.

DeVries, D. L., & Slavin, R. E. (1978). Team games tournament: A research review. *Journal of Research and Development in Education, 12,* 28–38.

Eichinger, J. (1990). Goal structure effects on social interaction. *Exceptional Children. 56*(5), 408–416.

Forest, M., & Lusthaus, E. (1989). Promoting educational equality for all students: Circles and MAPS. In S. Stainback, W. Stainback, & M. Forest (Eds.), *Educating all students in the mainstream of regular education* (pp. 43–57). Baltimore: Paul H. Brookes.

Gaylord-Ross, R., & Browder, D. (1991). Functional assessment: Dynamic and domain properties. In L. H. Meyer, C. A. Peck, & L. Brown (Eds.), *Critical issues in the lives of people with severe disabilities* (pp. 45–66). Baltimore: Paul H. Brookes.

Gearheart, B. R., Weishahn, M. W., & Gearheart, C. J. (1992). *The exceptional student in the regular classroom* (5th ed.). New York: Macmillan.

Giangreco, M. F., Cloninger, C., & Iverson, V. (1993). *Choosing options and accommodations for children: A guide to planning inclusive education.* Baltimore: Paul H. Brookes.

Goodman, L. (1990). *Time and learning in the special education classroom.* Albany, NY: State University of New York Press.

Hamre-Nietupski, S., Nietupski, J., & Strathe, M. (1992). Functional life skills, academic skills, and friendship/social relationship development: What do parents of students with moderate/severe/profound disabilities value? *The Journal of The Association for Persons with Severe Handicaps, 17*(1), 53–58.

Haring, T. G. (1991). Social relationships. In L. H. Meyer, C. A. Peck, & L. Brown (Eds.), *Critical issues in the lives of persons with severe disabilities* (pp. 195–217). Baltimore: Paul H. Brookes.

Henley, M., Ramsey, R. S., & Algozzine, R. (1993). *Characteristics of and strategies for teaching students with mild disabilities.* Boston: Allyn & Bacon.

Idol, L. (1993). *Special educator's consultation handbook.* Austin: Pro-Ed. Inc.

Individuals with Disabilities Education Act (IDEA) of 1990, 20 U.S. C. 1401(a) (17).

Johnson, D. W., & Johnson, R. T. (1986). Mainstreaming and cooperative learning strategies. *Exceptional Children, 52,* 553–561.

Johnson, D. W., Johnson, R. T., Warring, D., & Maruyama, G. (1986). Different cooperative learning procedures and cross-handicap relationships. *Exceptional Children, 52,* 247–252.

Johnson, R. T., & Johnson, D. W. (1981). Building friendships between handicapped and nonhandicapped students: Effects of cooperative and individualistic instruction. *American Education Research Journal, 18*(4), 415–423.

Kennedy, C. H., Horner, R. H., & Newton, S. J. (1989). Social contacts of adults with severe disabilities living in the community: A descriptive analysis of relationship patterns. *The Journal of The Association for Persons with Severe Handicaps, 14*(3), 190–196.

Kennedy, C. H., Horner, R. H., & Newton, S. J. (1990). The social networks and activity patterns of adults with severe disabilities: A correlational analysis. *The Journal of The Association for Persons with Severe Handicaps, 15*(2), 86–90.

Kroth, R. (1978). Parents as powerful and necessary allies. *Teaching Exceptional Children, 10*(3), 88–90.

Lipsky, D. K. (1989). The roles of parents. In D. K. Lipsky, & A. Gartner (Eds.), *Beyond separate education: Quality education for all* (pp. 159–179). Baltimore: Paul H. Brookes.

MacMillan, D. L., & Turnbull, A. P. (1983). Parent involvement with special education: Respecting individual preferences. *Education and Training of the Mentally Retarded, 18*(1), 4–9.

Malette, P., Mirenda, P., Kandborg, T., Jones, P., Bunz, T., & Rogow, S. (1992). Application of a lifestyle development process for persons with severe intellectual disabilities: A case study report. *The Journal of The Association for Persons with Severe Handicaps, 17*(3), 179–191.

McDonnell, J., Wilcox, B., & Hardman, M. L. (1991). *Secondary programs for students with developmental disabilities.* Boston: Allyn & Bacon.

Neel, R. S., & Billingsley, F. F. (1989). *IMPACT: A functional curriculum handbook for students with moderate to severe disabilities.* Baltimore: Paul H. Brookes.

Newton, J. S., & Horner, R. H. (1993). Using a social guide to improve social relationships of people with severe disabilities. *The Journal of The Association for Persons with Severe Handicaps, 18*(1), 36–45.

Putnam, J. W., Rynders, J. E., Johnson, R. T., & Johnson, D. W. (1989). Collaborative skill instruction for promoting interactions between mentally handicapped and nonhandicapped children. *Exceptional Children, 55*(6), 550–557.

Rainforth, B., York, J., & Macdonald, C. (1992). *Collaborative teams for students with severe disabilities: Integrating therapy and educational services.* Baltimore: Paul H. Brookes.

Rueda, R., & Martinez, I. (1992). Fiesta educativa: One community's approach to parent training in developmental disabilities for Latino families. *The Journal of The Association for Persons with Severe Handicaps, 17*(2), 95–103.

Ruiz, N. (1989). An optimal learning environment for Rosemary. *Exceptional Children, 56*(2), 130–144.

Salisbury, C. (1992). Parents as team members: Inclusive teams, collaborative outcomes. In B. Rainforth, J. York, & C. Macdonald (Eds.), *Collaborative teams for students with severe disabilities: Integrating therapy and educational services* (pp. 43–66). Baltimore: Paul H. Brookes.

Schnorr, R. (1990). "Peter? He comes and goes . . .": First graders' perspectives on a part-time mainstream student. *The Journal of The Association for Persons with Severe Handicaps, 15*(4), 231–240.

Schulz, J. B., Carpenter, C. D., & Turnbull, A. P. (1991). *Mainstreaming exceptional students: A guide for classroom teachers.* Boston: Allyn & Bacon.

Shafer, M. S., Rice, M. L., Metzler, H. M. D., & Haring, M. (1989). A survey of nondisabled employee's attitudes toward supported employees with mental retardation. *The Journal of The Association for Persons with Severe Handicaps, 14*(2), 137–146.

Sharon, S., & Sharon, Y. (1976). *Small-group teaching.* Englewood Cliffs, NJ: Educational Technology.

Shea, T. M., & Bauer, A. M. (1991). *Parents and teachers of children with exceptionalities: A handbook for collaboration* (Second Ed.). Boston: Allyn & Bacon.

Slavin, R. E. (1978). Student teams and comparison among equals: Effects on academic performance and student attitudes. *Journal of Educational Psychology, 70,* 532–538.

Snow, J., & Forest, M. (1987). Circles. In M. Forest (Ed.), *More education integration* (pp. 169–176). Downsview, Ontario: G. Allen Roeher Institute.

Stainback, W., & Stainback, S. (1990). Facilitating peer supports and friendships. In W. Stainback, & S. Stainback (Eds.), *Support networks for inclusive schooling: Interdependent integrated education* (pp. 51–63). Baltimore: Paul H. Brookes.

Stainback, S., Stainback, W., & Slavin, R. (1989). Classroom organization for diversity among students. In S. Stainback, W. Stainback, & M. Forest (Eds.), *Educating all students in the mainstream of regular education* (pp. 131–142). Baltimore: Paul H. Brookes.

Staub, D., & Hunt, P. (1993). The effects of social interaction training on high school peer tutors of schoolmates with severe disabilities. *Exceptional Children, 60*(1), 41–57.

Strully, J., & Strully, C. (1989). Friendship as an educational goal. In S. Stainback, W. Stainback, & M. Forest (Eds.), *Educating all students in the mainstream of regular education* (pp. 59–68). Baltimore: Paul H. Brookes.

Vandercook, T., York, J., & Forest, M. (1989). The McGill Action Planning System (MAPS): A strategy for building the vision. *Journal of The Association for Persons with Severe Handicaps, 14*(3), 205–215.

York, J., Giangreco, M., Vandercook, T., & Macdonald, C. (1992). Integrating support personnel in the inclusive classroom. In S. Stainback, & W. Stainback (Eds.), *Curriculum considerations in inclusive classrooms: Facilitating learning for all students* (pp. 101–116). Baltimore: Paul H. Brookes

5

EDUCATION TEAMS AND COLLABORATIVE TEAMWORK IN INCLUSIVE SETTINGS

DIANE LEA RYNDAK

Objectives

After completing this chapter the reader will be able to:

1. Define education team.
2. List potential members of an education team and their respective areas of expertise.
3. Define collaboration.
4. Define collaborative team.
5. Describe how a collaborative education team differs from a multidisciplinary, transdisciplinary, and interdisciplinary team.
6. Describe steps completed when developing a collaborative education team.
7. Describe ways in which a collaborative education team could divide their roles and responsibilities, ensuring that all responsibilities are covered by the team.
8. Provide examples that demonstrate collaborative education teams at work.

Key Terms

Collaboration	Multidisciplinary Team
Collaborative team	Related services
Collaborative teamwork	Role release
Education team	Roles and responsibilities
Interdisciplinary team	Transdisciplinary team

Effective education services cannot be provided in inclusive settings in isolation from the activities that naturally occur in general education classes. In addition, one person cannot provide such services; rather, effective education services in inclusive settings develop through interaction and collaboration between numerous professionals, paraprofessionals, and members of a student's natural support network. When collaboration does not occur, a student's education services are fragmented, with instruction leading to the student's various objectives disassociated from either instruction on other objectives or instruction occurring in the general education class. Minimizing fragmentation, while maximizing effective instruction to meet identified annual goals, is the responsibility of each member of a student's education team.

Education Teams

The concept of an education team has evolved from that of a set of professionals from different disciplines "established in order to provide the best overall education and habilitation programs for a particular child" (Gaylord-Ross & Holvoet, 1985, p. 289) to a much broader concept. Thousand and Villa (1990) define a "teaching team" as

> ... *an organizational and instructional arrangement of two or more members of the school and greater community who distribute among themselves planning, instructional, and evaluation responsibilities for the same students on a regular basis for an extended period of time (pp. 152–153).*

This broader conceptualization emphasizes the role that every team member plays in maximizing the benefits of educational activities for every student, regardless of whether that student is eligible for special education or related services. It emphasizes the necessity of team members sharing (1) their expertise with each other, so that all students can benefit as a team member provides instruction, (2) the responsibility for developing educational activities that facilitate learning by all students, (3) the provision of instruction across instructional content areas, and (4) accountability for each student's acquisition of knowledge and skills across content areas, activities, and settings. This conceptualization of an education team eliminates the perception of any team member planning, implementing, or evaluating the effectiveness of their services in isolation from the services of other team members and highlights the importance of each team member applying expertise directly to students' needs. This conceptualization of the education team also is consistent with the definition of related services and its interpretation by Rainforth, York, and Macdonald (1992) described in Chapter 3. That is, it is consistent with their belief that the educational relevance and student benefit of related services (e.g., occupational therapy, physical therapy, speech therapy) are heightened when team members integrate their expertise into instructional activities that oc-

TABLE 5.1   Possible Team Members and Areas of Expertise

Possible Team Member	Areas of Expertise
Student with identified needs	Self-abilities, performance needs, life activities, desires, dreams, expectations
Student's natural support network (e.g., family members, peers)	Perceptions of student's abilities, performance needs, life activities, interactions with significant others, desires, dreams, expectations
Special education teachers	Methods of identifying functional needs, adaptations, curriculum content specific to special education, instructional strategies, analysis of situations, environments, and behaviors
General education teachers	Large group instructional strategies, curriculum content specific to grade level, interaction styles and content of same age peers
Special subject area educators (e.g., art teacher, wood shop teacher)	Large group instructional strategies, curriculum content and strategies specific to subject, interaction styles and content of same age peers

Content area specialists
   Reading specialist
   Math specialist
	Small group instructional strategies, curriculum content and strategies specific to content area

Education-related specialist
   Communication specialist
   Hearing specialist
   Vision specialist
   Occupational therapist
   Physical therapist
	Discipline specific expertise, strategies for developing skills in area of expertise, especially in relation to use during activities in inclusive settings

Guidance counselor	Class options per grade level, extracurricular options per building
Employment specialist	Vocational opportunities in student's community, instructional strategies for job sites, work-related skills
Instructional assistants	Awareness of student's performance across inclusive settings and subjects
Student teacher	Current instructional practices and research, link to university/college

Continued

TABLE   5.1   *Continued*

Possible Team Member	Areas of Expertise
Health professionals	Health-related effects of behavior, strategies for coping with medical needs in inclusive settings, periodic and emergency procedures
Volunteers	Fresh perceptions of student and relevance of program to real life
School or district administrator	Legal issues, policies and procedures, mechanisms for meeting building- and district-related concerns, funding mechanisms for specific materials, adaptations, or services, link to inservice training options

cur in the context of routine daily activities at school, at home, and in the community (see Chapter 3).

This emphasis on application of expertise to students' needs in natural contexts insures that students will be more successful at learning and applying new knowledge, thus participating more fully in school, family activities, and community life. Rainforth et al. (1992) argue that when education teams do not collaborate, they abdicate responsibility for the synthesis, application, and generalization of fragmented program components and shift that responsibility "onto the very people who require their assistance to meet daily challenges: students with severe disabilities and their families" (p. 10).

The size and composition of education teams vary, as they are dependent upon the identified needs of the students for whom that team has responsibility. For example, an education team that serves a student with multiple disabilities may include many individuals who have expertise across numerous areas because of the diversity and complexity of that student's needs. Table 5.1 includes a list of possible team members and a brief description of their traditional areas of expertise. An education team may consist of fewer members, however, when that team serves only students who do not require special education or related services or students who require only minimal special education or related service support. In these cases the education teams do not require expertise from as many fields to serve their students.

There are four main responsibilities of each education team member. First, when planning services members are responsible for insuring that each student's needs are considered in a discipline-free manner, while lending the benefit of their specific expertise to that consideration. For example, during the discussion of the needs of a student with multiple disabilities, each team member has the responsibility to verify that potential instructional content will increase that student's independent functioning or partial participation in daily events at school, home, or in the community. When considering instructional content, physical therapists consider their expertise in physical development and their knowledge of that student's development in conjunction with the intent of the instructional content, in relation to the student's participation at school, home, and in the community. In addition, the physical therapist raises questions that relate to the expertise of other team members, thus insuring that the team has considered the expertise of each team member and its relation to the instructional content under consideration. In this manner, the team members share the responsibility for the team staying focused on the student's educational needs in a discipline-free manner.

Second, when implementing and evaluating the effectiveness of instruction, each team member is responsible for sharing their specific expertise with other team members and acquiring relevant information and skills from other team members. This not only maximizes the effectiveness of instructional time each team member spends with students but also results in fewer "gaps, overlaps, and contradictions" (Giangreco, Cloninger, & Iverson, 1993) in educational services for any one student.

Third, each education team member shares the responsibility for the team functioning in a professional manner with open communication. To fulfill this responsibility each team member reviews as objectively as possible both their own behavior and the behavior of other team members, to determine whether the content and delivery manner of the interaction are both professional and open, inviting collegial dialogue across relevant topics. If a team member determines that his or her own behavior does not facilitate open collegial communication, it is that member's responsibility to modify that behavior, deal with any conflicts with other team members, and reach either a consensus or a compromise with other team members in relation to topics on which they vary. It is also his or her responsibility to assist other team members in accomplishing the same by providing objective, constructive, and meaningful feedback.

Fourth, each team member has the responsibility to provide support for fellow team members in a number of ways. For example, team members can support each other in relation to (1) obtaining and using resources (e.g., people, materials, funds, literature), (2) providing moral support (e.g., listening, reinforcing, encouraging, providing feedback), and (3) using technical knowledge (e.g., developing adaptations, identifying alternate strategies, developing instructional programs) (York, Giangreco, Vandercook, & Macdonald, 1992). Through mutual support, team members develop both more collegial and collaborative relationships and facilitate more effective instruction for all students in inclusive settings.

Addressing Cultural Diversity among Team Members

Upon reviewing the responsibilities of education team members, it is evident that members must be aware of the cultural differences that exist among members of their team. Sue and Sue (1990) describe variables relevant to communication that differ across cultures and that affect group interaction: (1) proxemics, or personal space (e.g., the physical distance between people communicating, arrangement of furniture for seating), (2) kinesics, or body movement (e.g., posture, facial expression, eye contact), (3) time orientation, and (4) paralanguage, or verbal and nonverbal vocal cues beyond words (e.g., loudness, hesitations, inflections, speed). If a team comprises members from cultural backgrounds that interpret proxemics, kinesics, time, or paralanguage use differently, and members are either oblivious to these differences or choose to ignore them, difficulties will prevail in developing collegial and collaborative relationships that facilitate effective instruction for students in inclusive settings. Effective communication will occur only when the team members identify and accommodate their own cultural differences within team interactions.

A Collaborative Team and Teamwork

There are a number of ways in which a group of individuals can function, each having their own theoretical perspective that dictates how members will interact with each other, as well as with students and family members. The following sections describe four types of teams, their theoretical perspectives, and the resultant manners of interaction.

Multidisciplinary Team

The Individuals with Disabilities Education Act (IDEA) of 1990 (PL 101-476) mandates that a set of school professionals, parents, and, whenever possible, the student with disabilities, constitute a multidisciplinary team for the purpose of implementing the evaluation, placement procedures, and development of individualized-education-program (IEP) for students with disabilities. Pfeiffer (1980) surmises that the intent of this mandate was to use a group process to provide safeguards against possible errors due to flaws in the judgements of individuals and to insure the greatest adherence to the due process procedures outlined in the legislation. While well intentioned, the manner in which this mandate has been implemented has not met this probable intent. In a summary of the literature, Friend and Cook (1992) identified nine problem areas that adversely affect how teams have functioned:

1. Use of unsystematic approaches to collecting and analyzing diagnostic information.
2. Minimal parent or regular educator participation.
3. Use of a loosely construed decision-making and planning process.
4. Lack of interdisciplinary collaboration and trust.
5. Territoriality.
6. Ambiguous role definition and accountability.
7. Lack of experience and training for professionals to work together.

8. Lack of preparation in effective collaboration and team participation skills.
9. Mandatory, rather than voluntary and interested, participation. (pp. 26–27)

These difficulties have led to teams of individuals from multiple disciplines that focus their interactions around the specific expertise of each member in isolation of the other members, rather than on the collective expertise of a collaborative unit (Amlund & Kardash, 1994). The personnel preparation programs for some professionals on the team emphasize a medical orientation, in which a student is viewed as a "patient" who is "sick" or "flawed" in some way, and the role of the team member is to "cure" or "fix" the student so he or she can return to the regular environment (Hanft, 1993). This medical orientation is inconsistent with the educational orientation of special and general education teachers and results in discrepant theoretical approaches to educational program development and implementation (Hanft, 1993). In most cases, educational programs that multidisciplinary teams develop can be characterized in three ways: (1) they reflect the premise that repeated isolated work on specific skills in disciplines will lead to the student's incorporation of the skills as needed during activities in natural settings, (2) they provide isolated services, or "treatment", by team members within their own areas of expertise and on separate components of a student's performance, and (3) they provide fragmented instruction focusing on isolated aspects of a student's development (e.g., fine motor, gross motor, communication, cognition).

Finally, in theory the multidisciplinary team concept views the parent as an equal partner in the development and implementation of educational services. In practice, however, because the focus of interactions is on each professional informing the remainder of the team about information from their specific discipline in relation to the student, this negates the possibility of collaboration and minimizes the parent's participation in the team process (Amlund & Kardash, 1994).

Interdisciplinary Team

Like a multidisciplinary team, an interdisciplinary team comprises individuals from multiple disciplines who focus their expertise on the educational services for a student. The manner in which an interdisciplinary team functions, however, is different. The members of an interdisciplinary team share their expertise in relation to a student and work together to develop one cohesive program for that student (Rainforth et al., 1992). To accomplish this, team members not only share their perceptions of services within their area of expertise that would benefit the student but also work with other team members to (1) understand other needs of the student, (2) understand how the student's needs across areas of expertise interrelate, and (3) develop one set of jointly planned goals and objectives for that student.

Transdisciplinary Team

Like multidisciplinary and interdisciplinary teams, a transdisciplinary team comprises individuals from multiple disciplines that focus their interactions around the specific expertise of each member, including school professionals, parents, and, whenever possible, the student with disabilities. A transdisciplinary team, however, has one added dimension—members share across disciplines information and skills from their area of expertise that relate specifically to a student, resulting in team members incorporating into their services for that student information and skills from other disciplines and sharing the responsibility for services from other disciplines (Amlund & Kardash, 1994; Rainforth et al., 1992). This practice is referred to as "role release" (Lyon & Lyon, 1980; Rainforth et al., 1992). There are four types of information shared across disciplines through role release: (1) general information on concepts and approaches related to the area of expertise, (2) specific information on practices and methods relevant to the student, (3) specific performance competencies appropriate for the student, and (4) specific interventions and methods for use with the student. In essence, various team members provide instruction across multiple areas of needs for a student to better serve that student. This allows for each team member to participate in all services on an ongoing basis and to share with other team members responsibility for the effectiveness of those services and for student growth.

In most cases educational programs developed by a transdisciplinary team reflect the premise that multiple needs of a student are interdependent and the student does not use skills in one area of development in isolation from skills in other areas of development. The team, however, focuses little attention on the settings and activities in which instruction occurs. Because of this, many educational programs developed by transdisciplinary teams do not provide instruction in naturally occurring settings, including general education classes, and in functional activities across the school and in the community.

Collaborative Team

Like a transdisciplinary team, a collaborative team comprises individuals from multiple disciplines, including school professionals, parents, and, whenever possible, the student with disabilities. The team shares across disciplines information and skills from their area of expertise that relate specifically to a student, resulting in team members incorporating into their services for that student information and skills from other disciplines and sharing the responsibility for services from other disciplines. Collaborative teams, however, are dramatically different from other teams in a number of ways. To understand these differences, let's look at components of the term *collaborative team*.

There are many definitions of collaboration and teamwork currently in the literature, each with definitive components. For the purposes of this book, *collaboration* is defined as *a STYLE of problem solving by a group of equal individuals who voluntarily (1) contribute their own knowledge and skills and (2) participate in shared decision making to accomplish one or more common and mutually agreed upon goals* (Friend & Cook, 1992; Rainforth et al., 1992; Thousand & Villa, 1989). According to *Webster's Ninth New Collegiate Dictionary* (1991), *teamwork* is *"work done by several associates with each doing a part but all subordinating personal prominence to the efficiency of the whole."* When combining these concepts, a *collaborative team* could be considered *a group of equal individuals who voluntarily work together in a spirit of willingness and mutual reward to problem solve and accomplish one or more common and mutually agreed upon goals by contributing their own knowledge and skills and participating in shared decision making, while focusing on the efficiency of the whole team.* When applied to education, the common and mutually agreed upon goal is *to provide the most effective education services for a set of students, allowing each student to maximize their participation and contribution to life at school, at home, and in the community* (Rainforth et al., 1992; Thousand & Villa, 1989).

There are a number of components in this definition of a collaborative team and its educational goal that differentiate this team from the transdisciplinary team and that are critical to understanding how and why a collaborative team functions. First, the team's purpose for existing is linked clearly to, and defined by, the needs of each student that it serves, rather than by the training and expectations of the individual team members. Because of this, all team members put aside preconceived ideas of the services they will provide for a given student and how they will deliver those services. The education team will determine those variables in response to the student's specific needs to function and participate more fully in general education classes, in the school, at home, and in the community.

Second, collaborative team members accept the concept that the team as a whole will either accomplish, or fail to accomplish, their goal. With this acceptance it is clear that collaborative team members share (1) the responsibility for success and failure in meeting a student's needs at school, at home, and in the community, (2) mutual rewards with success and the ensuing satisfaction, and (3) mutual repercussions for failure and the ensuing sense of inadequacy or insufficiency. In many ways this concept and its effects on team members are consistent with those fostered with students in cooperative learning groups (Thousand & Villa, 1989).

A third distinctive component of a collaborative team is that the concept of role release takes on additional meanings. While members of transdisciplinary teams share their knowledge and skills with each other so that instruction provided by one team member incorporates content across disciplines, collaborative teams take this concept farther and actually brainstorm on (1) the necessary instruction and services for each discipline to meet a student's needs at school, at home, and in the community and (2) how to blend instruction across disciplines to meet a student's needs within naturally occurring activities in those settings. This expansion of the concept of role release demands that each team member understands the student as a whole, and how the student's skills and knowledge from one discipline interrelate with skills and knowledge in other disciplines. For example, a student included in a first-grade class may have difficulty using expressive communication skills (e.g., use of augmentative communication system, speaking in two to three word phrases), gross motor skills (e.g., sitting on the floor while sitting upright to attend), and fine motor skills (e.g., pencil grasp, letter formation) during language arts. Rather than focusing only on the student's needs that relate to their own discipline, collaborative team members see the student in the context in which all these skills are necessary in conjunction, allowing them (1) to grasp more fully how, why, and where the student needs to use specific skills and (2) to understand better and use the knowledge and skills shared with them by other team members.

A fourth distinctive component of a collaborative team is that services across disciplines occur in natural locations. That is, assessment procedures, direct services, and consultation services occur in the locations in which a student naturally needs to use the knowledge and skills being addressed, including general education settings, the school, the student's home, and the community. Services for which the student is pulled out of, or isolated from, those naturally occurring locations are limited to two types of services: (1) services that infringe on the student's right to privacy (e.g., range of motion activities that cannot blend in to naturally occurring activities) and (2) services that cannot be blended into naturally occurring activities (e.g., exercises that strengthen abdominal muscles that cannot be blended into every physical education activity or into positions and mobility across the day).

This focus on natural locations and naturally occurring activities dictates a fifth distinctive component of a collaborative team—the schedule of services allows each team member access to the student and naturally occurring activities in natural locations across the entire day. Rainforth et al. (1992) describe a block scheduling system that facilitates individual team members distributing the time they have committed to students within one class so that each team member can observe all of the students across the day within one or two weeks. This insures that each team member can address knowledgeably any difficulty a student has encountered in relation to applying knowledge and skills from various disciplines across natural activities and locations, including the school, community, and home.

Finally, a collaborative team differs from other types of teams in the emphasis placed on the equal partnership of each team member, especially general education teachers and parents (Rainforth et al., 1992). This emphasis reflects the belief that the expertise of each team member is only relevant to a student when considered in relation to the student's functioning and participation in real life. The general education teacher has the most consistent access to the student in inclusive settings and, therefore, is most aware of the activities and locations in which the student is involved across the day, week, and school year. The parents have the most consistent access to the student after school hours both at home and in the community. Because of these unique positions, other team members are dependent on the general education teacher and parents to provide information about and insight into those real life activities and locations. Without this information, team members lose their focus and change their purpose, ultimately resorting to functioning as a multidisciplinary or transdisciplinary team.

Benefits of Collaborative Teamwork

There are four ways of viewing the benefits of collaborative teamwork. First, collaborative teamwork can be beneficial to students with disabilities. As various team members provide instruction on goals across activities in natural contexts, the student automatically has an increased number of instructional trials throughout the day. Not only will the increased number of trials lead to faster acquisition of knowledge and skills in relation to the number of days necessary to meet criterion, but the distributed nature of those trials also will increase the efficiency of those trials, resulting in the need for fewer trials. In addition, the provision of instruction during activities in natural contexts will increase the degree to which the student actually uses skills in the activities for which they are required, rather than demonstrating the acquisition of new knowledge and skills only during artificial instructional activities. Because the activities are naturally occurring in the student's school, home, and community life, the student will maintain the skills acquired because of continued opportunities to use those skills in activities. Finally, because of the number of team members providing instruction in a large number of activities and natural contexts, the student is more likely to have generalized use of the skills learned across people, settings, and activities.

Second, because of these benefits, the student's family will benefit from collaborative teamwork in two ways. They will have (1) more information on instructional strategies and methods they can use to help their family member acquire knowledge and skills more quickly and (2) a family member who is more able to participate in family and community activities because of increased skills applied in real-life situations.

Third, collaborative teamwork can be beneficial to the nondisabled classmates of the included student. For instance, as team members provide direct services in inclusive settings, the nondisabled classmates benefit from the additional direct contact time provided by the extra personnel in the room (Ferguson, Meyer, Jeanchild, Juniper, & Zingo, 1992). In addition, the nondisabled classmates derive benefits from the indirect consultation and collaboration that occur between their general education teacher and other team members. New instructional strategies and feedback on the effectiveness of current instructional strategies are only two of the many areas in which collegial dialogue could lead to benefits for all students.

Fourth, collaborative teamwork can be beneficial to education team members through technical, moral, and problem-solving support. Benefits through technical support include: (1) direct assistance in the classroom for problems related to students other than the included student (Armbruster & Howe, 1985, Ferguson et al., 1992; Idol, 1993), (2) more effective use of expertise across disciplines for all students (Bauwens, Hourcade, & Friend, 1989), (3) assistance in identifying strategies for use by family members at home (Idol, 1993), and (4) increased flexibility for grouping and scheduling (Olsen, 1968). Collaborative team members receive moral support through (1) feedback from other team members that provides reassurance of their own performance and objectivity, (2) recognition of reasons for self-worth and self-satisfaction (Johnson & Johnson, 1987a; Murphy, 1981, Shea & Bauer, 1991), (3) follow-through of instruction on school goals at home (Shea & Bauer, 1991), and (4) relationships built on trust, communication, and conflict resolution (Johnson & Johnson, 1987b). Collaborative teams receive support in problem solving when identifying meaningful content, obtaining materials and other resources, defining specific learning or behavior problems, identifying options for intervention or instruction, implementing instruction, and evaluating the effectiveness of instruction. Thousand and Villa (1990) summarize the research literature related to benefits derived by education team members in four areas: (1) survival or power, (2) freedom, (3) sense of belonging, and (4) fun.

Developing a Collaborative Team

A collaborative team is not formed over night. Given the nature of a collaborative team, team members require time to develop the necessary trusting and supportive relationships. There are some tasks, however, to be undertaken in order for a team to be formed and for that team to develop into a collaborative unit.

Identifying Members

When an education team is forming, the school identifies individuals to participate based on their relationship to a particular student, that student's educational needs, and the individual's area of expertise. For example, when a student who has mental retardation, physical disabilities, and communication deficits is included in fifth grade, there are some individuals who will be members of the education team because of their immediate relationship to the student (e.g., the student, parents, fifth-grade general education teacher, building principal). While these individuals clearly have expertise to add to the team, there are also no alternative individuals to them for meaningful participation. They are, in fact, irreplaceable.

In addition to these irreplaceable individuals, the school identifies other members based on the student's educational needs across disciplines. Affecting the educational needs of the student mentioned above are (1) the physical development that probably requires the expertise of a physical therapist and occupational therapist, (2) the communication deficit that probably requires the expertise of a speech language pathologist or communication specialist, and (3) the mental retardation that probably requires the expertise of a special educator. Assuming this is the case, one member from each of those disciplines will join the team. Unless the district which serves the student is small, there are probably optional individuals from these disciplines who could become team members, either as employees of the district or as consultants from private agencies. Expertise from other disciplines also may be necessary for the team (e.g., behavior management, medical knowledge), depending on the student's educational needs. As those needs become clear or change, members of the team will change to reflect the disciplines from which expertise is needed by the student.

Philosophical Premises

Once the school identifies individual team members, the team must agree upon some basic philosophical premises if they are to become a collaborative team. Before agreeing on philosophical premises, however, team members require some fundamental information about the other team members. For instance, team members need to know (1) the specific expertise and experience that each member brings to the team, especially in relation to the educational needs of the student, (2) each member's philosophy in relation to the purpose of educational services,

(3) each member's perception of their role within that purpose, especially in relation to the provision of direct and consultant services, and (4) each member's perception of the roles of other team members within that purpose. Once the team has discussed these topics, team members can begin to determine the areas on which they agree and disagree. For the areas on which they disagree, the discussion might include (1) how the team will function given their discrepant viewpoints on the fundamental reason for the existence of an education team and/or the roles individuals play to fulfill that purpose and (2) what the team will do to resolve any discrepancies.

Another philosophical premise for discussion among team members is the type of team on which they would like to participate. Some members may not have had experience on a collaborative team; therefore, discussing the relative benefits and limitations of collaborative, multidisciplinary, transdisciplinary, and interdisciplinary teams, in relation to the fundamental purpose for the team's existence, may lead to a more mutual understanding of what a collaborative team actually is and a broader desire to function as a collaborative team.

Once team members reach a consensus that they want to function in a collaborative manner, they then can begin to develop a shared mission statement. Rainforth et al. (1992) recommend that educational collaborative teams for students with severe disabilities should have at least two purposes, including support of students so they can achieve integrated life outcomes through attainment of the objectives identified in their IEPs and support for one another. Collaborative teams that serve students in inclusive settings will clarify these components further to maintain focus on (1) the performance of *all* students, across settings (i.e., general education settings, school building, community), (2) the performance of students with moderate or severe disabilities in real-life activities within naturally occurring settings, (3) the function of team members in direct and consultative roles, and (4) the development and use of effective collaboration and communication skills.

Handling the Logistics

For a team to function in a collaborative manner, the entire team must decide on a few logistical issues. For instance, no team can collaborate unless there are specific times allowed for collaboration to occur and procedures established for effective communication during and between those scheduled times. Allocated time should encompass both time for team members to provide direct and indirect services for students and time to meet with other team members to collaborate. While some education teams have been able to build weekly or biweekly meetings into their schedules, many teams are unable to do so and have devised alternative methods for sharing expertise and information on their student observations. Some teams have opted for the special education teacher meeting with team members, preferably in small groups, but individually when necessary. The special education teacher then becomes the coordinator of information, using various methods of sharing information with the other team members. Whatever system the team develops for collaborating, each team member must feel comfortable that the team is truly collaborative and not changing to a transdisciplinary team because of scheduling difficulties.

Many school districts find it necessary to address other issues when scheduling opportunities for team members to provide effective direct and indirect services across settings. Such issues may include the manner in which related services personnel (1) acquire students on their caseload, (2) receive assignments across students, grades, and buildings, and (3) develop schedules for short intervals per student or larger intervals per class setting. In most situations, however, the degree to which related services personnel can meet the responsibilities of a collaborative team member in inclusive settings is limited unless these issues are addressed.

In addition to scheduling issues, members of a collaborative team clearly define the tasks for which they share the responsibility and determine which member will take the lead in either meeting each responsibility or coordinating the effort of team members to meet each responsibility. Table 5.2 lists tasks for which every collaborative team will have responsibility.

TABLE 5.2   Tasks of Collaborative Teams

IEP
  Monitoring progress on IEP goals and objectives
  Coordinating instruction to ensure IEP completion
  Coordinating assessment procedures for developing next IEP
  Collaborating to develop next IEP
Communication
  Establishing form(s) of communication
  Scheduling meetings
  Preparing agendas
  Ensuring communication occurs between all members
  Communicating regularly with family members
Adaptations
  Identifying when adaptations are necessary
  Developing adaptations
  Teaching team members to use adaptations
  Ensuring appropriate use of adaptations across members
Support
  Identifying need for support
  Identifying available sources of necessary support
  Ensuring existence of support across members
Skills
  Identifying skills needed to effectively collaborate
  Determining resources necessary to develop skills
  Requesting resources to develop skills
  Scheduling and organizing training or other method to develop skills
  Insure acquisition and use of skills after training

IEP = Individualized education program.

Required Skills for Collaboration

When part of a collaborative team, members clearly need expertise in their discipline area. This expertise alone, however, does not allow members to function collaboratively, because there are skills other than discipline-specific ones necessary to work collaboratively. For instance, when providing information and skills related to a discipline to team members who have limited or no background in that discipline, an effective collaborative team member will (1) explain the need for an intervention and what comprises the intervention itself, (2) demonstrate the intervention, (3) observe others implement the intervention, (4) provide corrective and reinforcing feedback, (5) monitor implementation of the intervention over time, and (6) monitor the effectiveness of the intervention and modify it when appropriate for the student (Rainforth et al., 1992). To accomplish these, team members must be supportive and approachable, being ready to provide information and answer questions in a nondefensive and nonthreatening manner. They must communicate information clearly and in an experiential manner, constantly being alert for signs of misunderstanding or confusion. The focus of information sharing, after all, is for the team to provide the most effective education for a set of students, allowing each to maximize their participation and contribution to life at school, at home, and in the community.

Beyond skills related to developing, implementing, and monitoring discipline-specific interventions, however, team members require communication and group interaction skills to function in a manner that supports the essence of collaboration; that is, interacting voluntarily as equals focusing on the efficiency of the whole team in a spirit of willingness and mutual reward to problem solve and accomplish their mutually agreed upon goals. When collaborating, teams will encounter problems in meeting students' needs and in interacting effectively. Problem solving skills that collaborative teams require, therefore, include acting as a group to (1) operationally define the problem so that all members agree, (2) diagnose the problem to determine the probable cause(s), (3) formulate strategies to address the problem, given the probable cause(s), (4) select and implement the strategy of group choice, and (5) evaluate the effectiveness of the strategy on the problem.

Throughout their interactions, education teams make decisions about students' needs, interventions, and logistics. When acting collaboratively a team makes decisions by consensus, defined as a collective opinion, or general agreement. To reach consensus a team seeks out differences in opinion, openly discussing the underlying assumptions of each opinion. Once team members have shared this information, they must make a decision without any members changing their minds only to get a decision made and without using majority votes or similar techniques to reach a decision. Reaching a consensus requires discussion until all members understand the options and agree that one of those is more appropriate at this time, though other options may be more viable at other times.

Finally, to communicate in a manner that facilitates collaboration a team must resolve conflicts between members. Several steps can assist conflicting team members in resolving their conflict, including: (1) one of the members confronting the other to acknowledge that they are, indeed, in conflict, (2) both members jointly defining the conflict, (3) openly communicating their positions and feelings in relation to the conflict, (4) openly communicating their intentions to be cooperative with each other to resolve the conflict, (5) each member putting themselves in the place of the other team member, "taking on" their perspective, (6) coordinating their efforts to negotiate in good faith, at the same time, and (7) reaching an agreement with each other. Unless team members are able to resolve conflicts in a manner that is constructive for the team, the trusting relationships that are necessary for collaboration cannot exist or endure.

In addition to discipline-specific and communication skills, a team needs group management and leadership skills to function collaboratively (Thousand & Villa, 1989). Group management skills will assist the team to be organized and function efficiently with minimal time commitment and waste of effort. Leadership skills will assist the team to accomplish tasks while maintaining positive working relationships. Care must be taken, however, that all team members have group management and leadership skills and that no one member becomes the perceived organizer or leader of the team.

Examples of Collaborative Teams at Work

There are a number of ways in which collaborative teams work together. Three examples illustrate this point and provide some visual images of how collaborative teams can function and to what this collaboration leads.

Adapting Activities from Weekly Lesson Plans

When a general education teacher completes weekly lesson plans a week ahead of time team members have ample lead time to collaborate for the identification, development, and training related to adaptations required per lesson. One collaborative education team whose members included a general education teacher who planned over a week in advance used those lesson plans as the basis for adapting activities (Ryndak, Rainforth, & Schooley, 1993). Because of their inability to choose one mutual planning time, this team designated the special education teacher as the coordinator for information sharing. As such, the special education teacher met once a week with each team member, either singly or in small groups. During the weekly meeting with the general education teacher, that teacher shared the general education lesson plans as they were written in a weekly plan book. The two teachers discussed each of the activities planned and systematically determined how each student with a disability would participate in the activity either fully or partially and whether any of the students required an adaptation to participate. When required, they discussed the adaptation and which team member would be responsible for developing it.

For instance, when a simple curriculum or instructional strategy adaptation was necessary, the general education teacher simply made the modification while teaching. When an adaptation was necessary in the academic materials for an activity (e.g., content of worksheets, words on spelling lists, grade level of material), the special education teacher prepared those materials. When discipline-specific adaptations were required from other team members, the special education teacher took the responsibility to share the need with those members and to insure the development of the adaptation. Such adaptations included: (1) an adapted piece of equipment that allows a student with physical disabilities to participate in a specific activity (e.g., equipment to allow a kindergarten student to crawl through tunnel with peers), (2) an adapted method of participation in an ongoing type of activity (e.g., use of a typewriter as an alternative to most handwriting), or (3) a modification to an existing adaptation (e.g., altering the communicative content on a touch talker). In these situations the special education teacher met with the other team members whose expertise was relevant to the needed adaptation providing information on the general education activity planned and the ideas for adaptations considered with the general education teacher. They then would reach a consensus on the adaptation to be used and decided which team member would develop the adaptation by when. The team member responsible for the adaptation then took the lead, ensuring that an effective adaptation was ready for the student's use during the planned activity.

Using Generic Adaptations to Activities

A different situation occurs when a general education teacher does not plan far enough in advance for the team to discuss systematically the need for adaptations. One collaborative education team faced with this situation developed a strategy that utilized generic adaptations to activities (Ryndak et al., 1993). This team served a student with profound physical disabilities and apparent profound intellectual disabilities. This student's annual goals addressed needs such as answering yes-or-no questions with known answers, using a communication board with two items, and using switches to participate in specific activities. The team developed generic instructional plans for each annual goal and determined types of activities which were frequently used by the general education teacher. The team compared the generic instructional plans with these types of instruction, identifying which generic instructional plans could be implemented naturally during which types of instruction. Team members made modifications in the generic instructional plans as necessary to allow a better "fit" with various types of instruction. Team members then developed a process for deciding which generic instructional plan best "fit" the instructional activity selected at any moment by the general education teacher, and they used the relevant generic instructional plan.

For example, if the general education teacher decided to use a cooperative learning strategy during social studies, the student with multiple profound disabilities could participate in that activity by answering yes-or-no questions about the topic given a specific question format used by peers, or by using a switch *if* the activity included a power-driven apparatus (e.g., tape player, VCR). A team member would set up the apparatus and switch, while classmates initiated the activity and asked the student yes-or-no questions when appropriate.

Exchanging Roles

One collaborative education team emphasized the sharing of instruction for all students and problem solved to identify scheduling needs and instructional activities that allowed each member to participate in each subject area across the week (Bald, 1992). This allowed every team member the opportunity to either observe, teach, or collaborate about a student in the different class periods. In addition, it allowed team members to change roles and allow team members to experience the student in activities as the other team members experienced that student. For example, during a class activity when the speech therapist was scheduled to be in the classroom, she and the general education teacher switched roles, allowing (1) the general education teacher to provide instruction in the communication needs of the student with multiple disabilities while facilitating the student's participation in the general class activity and (2) the speech therapist to provide instruction for the whole class while modeling strategies that would allow the general education teacher to maximize opportunities for the student with multiple disabilities to participate. This exchange of roles met the needs of both the general education teacher and the speech therapist without a break in the general education instructional activities.

Summary

An education team comprises a student with moderate or severe disabilities and the school personnel, family members, and friends of the student who are involved in developing and implementing that student's education program. The members of an education team share the responsibility for planning, implementing, and evaluating the effectiveness of the entire education program, including both special education and related services. Across districts and buildings, education teams develop in a number of manners, resulting in either multidisciplinary, interdisciplinary, transdisciplinary, or collaborative teams. Though each approach to teaming has benefits, collaborative teaming is considered to be most effective and efficient when providing educational services for a student with moderate or severe disabilities in inclusive settings.

A collaborative education team is a group of equal individuals who voluntarily contribute their own knowledge and skills and participate in shared decision making, while focusing on the efficiency of the whole team, as they work together in a spirit of willingness and mutual reward to problem solve and accomplish one or more common and mutually agreed upon goals. Their purpose is to provide the most effective education services for a set of students, allowing each student to maximize their participation and contribution to life at school, at home, and in the community.

The development of an effective collaborative team occurs over time, with conscious effort on the part of all members toward acquiring and consistently demonstrating a variety of skills beyond those in their area of expertise. These additional skills include effective communication, role release, problem solving, consensus building, conflict resolution, group management, and group leadership.

References

Amlund, J. T., & Kardash, C. M. (1994). Group approaches to consultation and advocacy. In S. K. Alper, P. J. Schloss, & C. N. Schloss (Eds.), *Families of students with disabilities: Consultation and advocacy.* Boston: Allyn & Bacon.

Bald, K. (1992). *Providing speech therapy in inclusive settings: Collaborating with team members.* Buffalo, NY: State University College at Buffalo.

Ferguson, D. L., Meyer, G., Jeanchild, L., Jeniper, L., & Zingo, J. (1992). Figuring out what to do with the grownups: How teachers make inclusion "work" for students with disabilities. *The Journal of The Association for Persons with Severe Handicaps, 17*(4), 218–226.

Friend, M., & Cook, L. (1992). *Interactions: Collaboration skills for school professionals.* New York: Longman.

Gaylord-Ross, R., & Holvoet, J. (1985). *Strategies for educating students with severe handicaps.* Boston: Little, Brown & Company.

Giangreco, M. F., Cloninger, C. J., & Iverson, V. S. (1993). *Choosing options and accommodations for children: A guide to planning inclusive education.* Baltimore: Paul H. Brookes.

Hanft, B. (1993, March). *School based therapy: Effective consultation in the classroom.* Workshop presented in Rochester, New York.

Idol, L. (1993). *Special educator's consultation handbook* (2nd ed.). Austin: Pro-ed.

Lyon, S., & Lyon, G. (1980). Team functioning and staff development: A role release approach to providing integrated educational services for severely handicapped students. *The Journal of The Association for the Severely Handicapped, 5*(3), 250–263.

Murphy, A. T. (1981). *Special children, special parents: Personal issues with handicapped children.* Englewood Cliffs, N.J.: Prentice-Hall.

Pfeiffer, S. I. (1980). The school based interprofessional team: Recurring problems and some possible solutions. *Journal of School Psychology, 18*(4), 388–394.

Rainforth, B., York, J., & Macdonald, C. (1992). *Collaborative teams for students with severe disabilities: Integrating therapy and educational services.* Baltimore: Paul H. Brookes.

Ryndak, D. L., Rainforth, B., & Schooley, R. (1993). Planning instruction for students with severe disabilities in general education settings: Two strategies for facilitating inclusion. Buffalo, NY: State University College of Buffalo.

Shea, T. M., & Bauer, A. M. (1991). *Parents and teachers of children with exceptionalities: A handbook for collaboration* (2nd ed.). Boston: Allyn & Bacon.

Sue, D. W., & Sue, D. (1990). *Counseling the culturally different: Theory and practice.* (2nd ed.). New York, Wiley.

Thousand, J., & Villa, R. (1989). Enhancing success in heterogeneous schools. In S. Stainback, W. Stainback, & M. Forest (Eds.), *Educating all students in the mainstream of regular education* (pp. 89–103). Baltimore: Paul H. Brookes.

Thousand, J., & Villa, R. (1990). Sharing expertise and responsibilities through teaching teams. In W. Stainback & S. Stainback (Eds.), *Support networks for inclusive schooling: Interdependent integrated education* (pp. 151–166). Baltimore: Paul H. Brookes Publishing Co.

Webster's Ninth Collegiate Dictionary (1991). Springfield, MA: Merriam-Webster.

York, J., Giangreco, M. F., Vandercook, T., & Macdonald, C. (1992). Integrating support personnel in the inclusive classroom. In S. Stainback & W. Stainback (Eds.), *Curriculum considerations in inclusive classrooms: Facilitating learning for all students* (pp. 101–116). Baltimore: Paul H. Brookes.

6

ADAPTING ENVIRONMENTS, MATERIALS, AND INSTRUCTION TO FACILITATE INCLUSION

DIANE LEA RYNDAK

Objectives

After completing this chapter the reader will be able to:

1. Define adaptation, and describe how an adaptation can facilitate the participation of a student with moderate or severe disabilities in activities in general education settings.
2. Give a hierarchy of decision rules for determining appropriate adaptations for a student, and provide a rationale for its use.
3. Explain why an education team begins the consideration of adaptations with a student's needs rather than available adaptations.
4. Describe various ways an education team could divide responsibilities for determining, developing, providing instruction on the use of, monitoring the instruction of the use of, and evaluating the effectiveness of an adaptation.
5. Describe ways in which an education team can adapt general education environments to facilitate the participation of a student with moderate or severe disabilities.
6. Describe ways in which general education activities can be adapted through materials, devices, and/or equipment to facilitate the participation of a student with moderate or severe disabilities.
7. Describe ways in which instruction can be adapted during general education activities to facilitate the inclusion of a student with moderate or severe disabilities.

8. Describe ways in which an education team can identify appropriate adaptations for a student prior to general education activities beginning.
9. Describe ways in which an education team can identify appropriate adaptations for a student after a general education activiy has begun.

Key Terms

Adaptation	Friendship facilitation
Adapting environments	General education activity analysis
Adapting instruction	Generic instructional plan
Adapting materials	Peer partners
Assistive technology	Routine activity analysis
Cooperative learning	Unit plan
Decision hierarchy	Weekly plan
Ecological analysis	

Adaptations in General Education

By definition, students with moderate or severe disabilities have learning characteristics that hamper their ability to learn the same amount of information, in the same amount of time, and in the same manner, as their nondisabled peers (see Chapter 2). In addition, students with moderate or severe disabilities do not participate in all activities in the same manner as their nondisabled peers. They may participate, however, in every activity with their nondisabled peers and benefit from instruction provided during those activities when adaptations capitalize on their strengths and compensate for their weaknesses. According to *Webster's Third World Dictionary* (1994) to adapt is "to make fit or suitable by changing or adjusting," and an adaptation is "a thing resulting from adapting; a change in structure, function, or form that improves the chance of survival . . . within a given environment." York and Rainforth (1991) stated that an adaptation is "any device or material that is used to accomplish a task in everyday life" and that the purpose of using individualized adaptations in educational programs is to increase the participation of students with disabilities in activities (pp. 259–260).

When education teams focus on increasing the participation of a student with moderate or severe disabilities in both functional and general education activities that occur in inclusive settings, they systematically identify activities in which that student requires an adaptation, develop and initiate the use of the adaptation, and evaluate its effectiveness in meeting the student's need in that activity. This chapter discusses each of these tasks, and provides examples of how education teams have addressed these tasks through determining adaptations in advance of activities and determining adaptations during general education activities.

Deciding to Use an Adaptation in General Education Settings

As with augmentative communication systems (Reichle & Karlan, 1985, 1988), deciding whether to use an adaptation, and which adaptation to use, can be complex. Education teams first must agree that a problem exists in a student's ability to participate in a given general education activity (Cohen & Lynch, 1991). Second, the team ascertains that instruction in specific skills cannot quickly meet the student's need, because the student's disability prohibits the completion of the task in the same manner as the other students. This could occur for both functional activities throughout the day and general education activities across settings. After determining the need for an adaptation, education teams clarify the precise nature of the student's problem by reaching consensus on the component of the task that the student cannot complete. The team analyzes the student's strengths and weaknesses in relation to that task component. With this information team members identify an adaptation that would accentuate the student's strengths, while compensating for weaknesses, and allow the student to complete the task or participate in the activity with classmates.

When possible the team identifies an adaptation that not only meets the student's immediate need and allows participation at the moment, but that also can have a lasting role in the student's life. For instance, instead of identifying an adaptation for one math class or unit on multiple digit addition, a better use of the education team's time and the student's instructional time would be to identify an adaptation that the student *also* can use long-term. This adaptation should be usable, or adaptable for use, across time (i.e., as the student matures) and across activities and settings (i.e., general education activities, activities in the community, self-management activities at home). In addition, this adaptation should be (1) portable for use across environments, (2) appropriate for the student's age, (3) durable for frequent use or use over time, (4) least intrusive during activities and the natural flow of events, (5) within the student's financial limitations, and (6) accessible within the time and resource parameters of the education team. While all of these variables may not be relevant for the specific activity for which a student initially requires an adaptation, their consideration will prevent the development of multiple adaptations when fewer or better planned adaptations would suffice. Not only do more adaptations mean more intrusion into the flow of activities as they are retrieved, set up, used, and removed; they also mean the team members take more time in developing and maintaining each adaptation, and the student needs more instructional time to learn effective use of each adaptation.

After the team carefully conceives the adaptation, they then develop the adaptation and initiate instruction on its use during activities. Every education team handles the responsibilities involved in development and instruction differently, each focusing on the strengths of team members in terms of expertise, interest, time, and resources available. The key to a student's successful use of an adaptation does not lie in which team member fulfills which responsibility; rather, it lies with the collaborative efforts of team members in conceptualizing the most appropriate adaptation, providing consistent instruction to the student on the use of that adaptation, and consistently facilitating the student's continued use of that adaptation across all relevant activities. Collaborating to facilitate instruction on, and use of, the adaptation results in team members collectively evaluating the appropriateness and effectiveness of the adaptation in meeting the student's identified need. These evaluation efforts may result in modifying the adaptation to better meet that student's need across activities and time.

Types of Adaptations

There are many ways to adapt general education environments, materials, and instructional activities to meet the needs of a student with moderate or severe disabilities (Sailor, Gee, & Karasoff, 1993). When selecting which type of adaptation to provide for a student, the education team prefers those that allow the student to participate in the activity without the need for another person's assistance and that minimize differences between the student and classmates. This type of adaptation (1) encourages independent completion of activities, thus making the student less dependent on others, and (2) maintains the general education curriculum content, thus maximizing the complexity of the content of instruction for the student.

Some adaptations modify the environment. Environmental adaptations (Cohen & Lynch, 1991; Udvari-Solner, 1994) could be as simple as changing the location of a student (e.g., closer to the focus of an activity, minimal distractions) or changing the student's physical position (e.g., side lying, standing, seated with support from positioning equipment). To maintain the focus of instruction in inclusive general education settings, however, removing the student to another environment that is not being used by nondisabled classmates does not constitute an environmental adaptation.

The education team can make adaptations to materials, devices, or equipment which is currently used in the student's general education settings, or by adding materials, devices, or equipment to those settings (Cohen & Lynch, 1991; Nevin, 1993; Schulz, Carpenter, & Turnbull, 1991). Again, the team prefers adaptations that meet a specific need of a student and that allow the student to participate in the activity independently. They must be careful to refrain from identifying a new or innovative adaptation and identifying when or where it could be used. Rather, the impetus for selecting an adaptation is a difficulty that a specific student is experiencing in participating in an already existing activity, and the purpose is to best meet that student's need. Adaptations in materials, devices, or equipment range from simple modifications in existing curriculum worksheets (e.g., simplifying language, decreasing number of response options), to adding low-tech devices to existing materials (e.g., a grip to a pencil, a finger guide to a keyboard), and adding high-tech equipment to the learning environment (e.g., electronic communication device, automated page turner). For example, there are a number of both low- and high-tech devices available to meet the needs of students with moderate or severe disabilities, allowing their participation in general education activities. Areas in which assistive technology can meet a student's needs include:

1. Positioning (Campbell, 1993; Gearheart, Weishahn, & Gearheart, 1992; Rainforth & York, 1991)
2. Mobility (Gearheart et al., 1992; Rainforth & York, 1991)
3. Augmentative communication systems (Miller, 1993)
4. Use of computers for instruction (Ellis & Sabornie, 1988)
5. Access to devices, such as computers or communication devices (Campbell & Forsyth, 1993)
6. Control of the immediate environment (Campbell & Forsyth, 1993; Rainforth & York, 1993)
7. Hearing or listening (Gearheart et al., 1992; Schulz et al., 1991; Sobsey & Wolf-Schein, 1991)
8. Seeing or looking (Gearheart et al. 1992; Schulz et al., 1991; Sobsey & Wolf-Schein, 1991)
9. Recreation, leisure, or play (Schleien, Green, & Heyne, 1993; York & Rainforth 1991)
10. Self-care and self-management activities (Browder & Snell, 1993; Orelove & Sobsey, 1991; Snell & Farlow, 1993; York & Rainforth, 1991).

The education team also can make adaptations in the manner in which instruction is presented or in the manner in which students are expected to respond to instruction (Borich, 1992; Nevin, 1993; Schulz et al., 1991; Udvari-Solner, 1994). For instance, the size and composition of instructional groups can be modified (Cohen & Lynch, 1991; Post, 1984). In presenting instruction or directions, there may be visual materials, color coded materials, outlines, mnemonic devices, or shortened directions (Borich, 1992; Post, 1984). Each of these adaptations draws little attention to a student with moderate or severe disabilities. Their use may be appropriate whether the curriculum content for that student is the same as, or different from, nondisabled classmates. While a peer or an adult can provide personal assistance (Udvari-Solner, 1994; Villa & Thousand, 1993), such support is more intrusive than the previously mentioned adaptations. When used, the level of intrusiveness should be kept to a minimum by removing the support whenever it is not necessary during an activity (Villa, Udis, & Thousand, 1994).

When a student with moderate or severe disabilities is able to complete some, but not all, of the work presented to classmates, other instructional adaptations are possible. Work structure can be such that all students work at their own pace, receive cues that assist them in answering questions, or have different rules for completing their tasks (Borich, 1992; Post, 1984). For instance, the number of problems to be solved may be fewer, the time for task completion may be longer, the student may ask questions, or the concepts of the task may be minimal for a student. Such adaptations may allow a student to perform a task more independently while working on the same curriculum content as nondisabled classmates , and receiving instructional emphasis on the curriculum components that are most relevant.

Finally, the education team can make adaptations to the actual curriculum content presented to a student. Changes in curriculum content can take many forms, including modification in (1) the skill sequence or task presented to nondisabled students (Cohen & Lynch, 1991; Giangreco, Cloninger, & Iverson, 1993), (2) the size of steps in the same task (Giangreco et al., 1993; Post, 1984), (3) the level of skill being taught in the same task or required to complete the task (Giangreco, et al., 1993; Post, 1984), and (4) the curriculum content area itself (Cohen & Lynch, 1991; Giangreco et al., 1993). The more that curriculum content presented to a student with moderate or severe disabilities remains the same as that presented to classmates, the more the targeted student will participate in general education activities and gain acceptance as a peer (Schnorr, 1991).

Team Member Support Related to Adaptations

When identifying, developing, and providing instruction on the use of an adaptation, team members rely on each other for various types of support (Giangreco et al., 1993; Rainforth, York, & Macdonald, 1993). Written information from team members may assist in identifying or developing an adaptation, and team members have access to different materials that may be helpful in developing an adaptation (Rainforth, et al., 1993). Team members may divide the responsibility for actually developing an adaptation (Hamre-Nietupski, McDonald, & Nietupski, 1992), depending upon the expertise and time required. For example, instead of requiring additional time to implement, many instructional adaptations require a modification in the manner in which the primary instruction is presented to the entire class. The general education teacher most easily implements this type of adaptation. Other adaptations, however, require development by the special education teacher or a related service provider.

Team members also can provide each other support in identifying, developing, and providing instruction on the use of an adaptation through human resources. This type of support occurs whenever an adult must help prepare the environment in which instruction will occur, assist a student or group of students during instruction, or clean up after instruction has occurred, thus allowing another team member time to develop an adaptation. While often overlooked, human resource support can ease a tremendous amount of pressure for any team member at critical times. Careful scheduling of this type of support will insure the team maximal benefit from human resources and maximal time to develop and provide instruction on the use of adaptations.

Perhaps most importantly, however, is the support team members provide each other not only so adaptations are developed but also so they are both effective and efficient at allowing a student to participate in general education activities. To accomplish this, team members provide support as they collaboratively strategize about different types of adaptations and how each potentially could meet the student's need (York & Vandercook, 1991). The expertise and perspective of every team member is invaluable in this process, as each sees the student and the situation differently. Throughout the strategizing and development process technical support from each team member is essential, whether the identified adaptation is related to the environment, materials, or instruction. Finally, team members provide support in evaluating the effectiveness of an adaptation in meeting the student's need, both in the initial situation for which it was required and in other situations where the adaptation may be helpful. In addition to evaluating the effectiveness of the adaptation itself, the evaluation process allows team members to monitor how consistently and correctly the team is providing instruction on its use and how appropriately the student is using the adaptation across settings.

Making Decisions about Adaptations

The use of a decision-making process in relation to identifying the most appropriate adaptation has had the support of many authors for a number of years (Baumgart et al., 1982; Cohen & Lynch, 1991; Filbin & Kronberg, undated; Giangreco et al., 1993; Hamre-Nietupski, et al., 1992; Kronberg & Filbin, 1993; Sailor et al., 1993; Thousand et al., 1986). With the recent inclusion of students with moderate or severe disabilities in general education settings, additional considerations have become relevant in these processes. There are various suggested hierarchies of considerations, however. Though specific levels of each hierarchy differ, they are consistent in four ways. First, they all demonstrate a preference for a student with moderate or severe disabilities participating in the same activity as nondisabled classmates, rather than removal from the general education activity. Second, the hierarchies demonstrate a preference for adapting the environment and instruction before adapting curriculum content. Third, the hierarchies emphasize first devising adaptations that allow a student to participate in activities independently, rather than immediately creating a situation in which the student cannot participate without the support of another person. Finally, the hierarchies demonstrate a preference for maintaining the student with nondisabled classmates before considering removal from the general education setting. Figure 6.1 summarizes suggested levels of hierarchies of considerations when identifying the most appropriate adaptation for a student with moderate or severe disabilities in inclusive settings. With each level, if the education team responds affirmatively, they either refrain from identifying an adaptation, as in the first level of the hierarchy, or they identify the problem that exists for the student and strategize on the adaptations that could meet the student's need. If the team responds to a level negatively, then they progress to the next level in the hierarchy. All team members must be cautious not to respond negatively to a certain level when a new or previously unconsidered adaptation at that level would facilitate the student's participation.

Determining Adaptations in Advance

There are a number of ways in which an education team can determine in advance the adaptations a student with moderate or severe disabilities will need to participate fully in specific general education activities. While adaptations determined in advance may need modification as more information is available about the student's needs during specific activities, they are preferable because they allow the student to participate as soon as general education activities begin.

FIGURE 6.1   Decision Making Hierarchy for Identifying Adaptations in Inclusive Educational Programs

Level	References
1. Can the student participate in the class activity just like other classmates?	Baumgart et al., 1982; Filbin & Kronberg, undated; Giangreco et al.,1993; Kronberg & Filbin, 1993; Sailor et al., 1993
-if yes, do not adapt -if no, go on to level 2	
2. Can the student participate in the same class activity if the environment is adapted?	Baumgart et al., 1982; Cohen & Lynch, 1991; Filbin & Kronberg, undated; Giangreco et al., 1993; Kronberg & Filbin, 1993; Sailor et al., 1993
-if yes, identify the student's need and strategize on adaptations for the environment -if no, go on to level 3	
3. Can the student participate in the same class activity if instruction is adapted?	Cohen & Lynch, 1991; Filbin & Kronberg, undated; Giangreco et al., 1993; Kronberg & Filbin, 1993; Sailor et al., 1993
-if yes, identify the student's need and strategize on instructional adaptations -if no, go on to level 4	
4. Can the student participate in the same class activity but with adapted materials?	Baumgart et al., 1982; Cohen & Lynch, 1991; Filbin & Kronberg, undated; Giangreco et al., 1993; Kronberg & Filbin, 1993; Sailor et al., 1993
-if yes, identify the student's need and strategize on adapted materials -if no, go on to level 5	
5. Can the student participate in the same class activity but with adapted expectations or rules?	Baumgart et al., 1982; Filbin & Kronberg, undated; Giangreco et al., 1993; Kronberg & Filbin, 1993; Sailor et al., 1993
-if yes, identify the student's need and strategize on adapted expectations or rules -if no, go on to level 6	
6. Can the student participate in the same class activity but with personal assistance?	Baumgart et al., 1982; Filbin & Kronberg, undated; Giangreco et al., 1993; Kronberg & Filbin, 1993; Hamre-Nietupski et al., 1992; Sailor et al., 1993
-if yes, identify the student's need and strategize on personal assistance; train peer or adult -if no, go on to level 7	
7. Can the student participate in the same class activity but with goals on a different level of the same content?	Filbin & Kronberg, undated; Giangreco et al., 1993; Kronberg & Filbin, 1993
-if yes, identify the student's need and strategize on adaptations to incorporate different level -if no, go on to level 8	
8. Can the student participate in the same class activity but with goals from a different curriculum content area?	Filbin & Kronberg, undated; Giangreco et al., 1993; Kronberg & Filbin, 1993; Sailor et al., 1993
-if yes, identify the student's need and strategize on adaptations to incorporate goals from a different curriculum content area -if no, go on to level 9	

FIGURE 6.1   *Continued*

Level	References
9. Can the student work in the room on a logical different activity related to IEP goals?	Giangreco et al., 1993; Hamre-Nietupski et al., 1992; Sailor et al., 1993
-if yes, identify the student's need and strategize on incorporating a different activity least intrusively -if no, go on to level 10	
10. Can the student work in the building on a logical different activity related to IEP goals?	Giangreco et al., 1993; Hamre-Nietupski et al., 1992; Sailor et al., 1993
-if yes, identify the student's need and strategize on incorporating change of location least intrusively -if no, go on to level 11	
11. Can the student work on a logical community-based activity related to IEP goals?	Giangreco et al., 1993; Hamre-Nietupski et al., 1992; Sailor et al., 1993
-identify the student's need and strategize on incorporating change of location least intrusively	

IEP = individualized education program.

Determining Adaptations Based on IEP Content

An individualized education program (IEP) offers a wealth of information about a student's strengths, weaknesses, current level of performance, and projected level of performance at the end of the year in the content identified as most important for that student. Frequently, adaptations that are essential to the student's independent participation in general education activities also appear on the IEP. For instance, an IEP may indicate the student's need to use an assistive device (e.g., calculator for math activities, computer for writing activities) or have instructional adaptations (e.g., extended time for completing assignments and tests, decreased amount of work). Each of these comments can assist an education team in having appropriate adaptations available for a student prior to related activities.

In addition, an education team systematically could review the instructional content on a student's IEP and compare this content with current performance levels. Teams can perform this task for both functional and general education curriculum content included on the IEP and for functional needs not included as goals on the IEP. For example, the matrix in Figure 6.2 lists areas of functional curriculum content frequently found on traditional IEPs for students with moderate or severe disabilities. On the left hand side of this matrix are the levels in the adaptation-decision hierarchy previously described. An education team can discuss the student's level of performance in each of the functional curriculum content areas and determine the levels and types of adaptations the student may require before general education activities begin. Though the adaptations identified in advance may require refinement or modification once more, the initial adaptations at least will

FIGURE 6.2   Determining Adaptations for Functional Curriculum Content in Advance

Decision Hierarchy Level	Functional Curriculum Content						
	Communication		Choice Making	Postural Control & Manipulation of Objects	Mobility	Eating	Hygiene/ Appearance
	Receptive	Expressive					
1. Participate as classmates							
2. Adapt environment							
3. Adapt instruction							
4. Adapt materials							
5. Adapt rules/ expectations							
6. Personal assistance							
7. Different content level							
8. Different content							
9. Different activity in room							
10. Different activity in building							
11. Different activity in community							

allow the student to participate more fully in the functional aspects of general education activities from the beginning.

Similarly, an education team can determine adaptations in advance for the general education curriculum content included on a student's IEP. The matrix in Figure 6.3 provides space for team members to list up to ten components of the IEP's general education content and systematically consider the levels and types of adaptations the student may require in general education activities by using the decision hierarchy per area. Again, the team may modify or refine these adaptations as they learn more about the student's needs during activities in general ed-

Social Interactions	Socially Appropriate Behavior	Problem Solving	Performance Quality	Performance Tempo	Activity Completion			
					Initia-tion	Prepa-ration	Core	Termi-nation

ucation settings. The initial adaptations, however, will allow the student to participate more fully in the general education activities upon entering those settings.

Determining Adaptations from Unit Plans

Education teams also can determine adaptations throughout the academic year in advance of activities when there is a change in instructional units in general education classes. Figure 6.4 is an example of an eighth-grade team's identification of

Decision Hierarchy Level	General Education Curriculum Content									
	#1.	#2.	#3.	#4.	#5.	#6.	#7.	#8.	#9.	#10.
1. Participation as classmates										
2. Adapt environment										
3. Adapt instruction										
4. Adapt materials										
5. Adapt rules/ expectations										
6. Personal assistance										
7. Different content level										
8. Different content										
9. Different activity in room										
10. Different activity in building										
11. Different activity in community										

FIGURE 6.3   Determining Adaptations for General Education Curriculum Content in Advance

Grade: _____8th_____   Subject: _____Math_____   Unit: _____Pythagorean Theorem_____

Student: _____Maureen_____   Date: _____Oct._____   Teacher: _____Brown_____

General Education Curriculum Content	General Education Content Identified for the Student	Adaptations
1. Evaluate exponents $2^3+5^2-1^9$	1. Decimals $(+, -, x, \div)$; exponents to 5^2	Calculator
2. Name square, square root of given number	2. Use chart to find square	Chart of squares
3. Name legs, hypotenuse of right triangle using proper geometric notation	3. Name legs and hypotenuse by labeling leg and hypotenuse on diagram	Diagram of example
4. Given legs of triangle, find hypotenuse using $a^2+b^2+c^2$	4. Use $a^2+b^2+c^2$ and substitute all 3 numerals into a formula—are they equal?	Calculator and chart
5. Given leg and hypotenuse, find either leg using $a^2+b^2+c^2$	5. As above	Calculator and chart
6. Word problem applications	6. Directional problems only	Calculator and chart

	Embedded Functional Content	Adaptation
Preparation for Class	Have materials ready	
	Homework ready to hand in	
During Class	Ask for assistance when needed	
	With prep time, answer questions when called on	Asked question during class in advance of requesting a response
Terminating Class	Write down homework assignment	Work organizer/notebook
	Organize materials to carry out of room	Backpack
	Exit room with the flow of classmates	Prompting from peer

FIGURE 6.4   Determining Adaptations Per General Education Unit: An Example

adaptations for Maureen, a student with moderate mental retardation (see Appendix B). The adaptations are for a math unit on the Pythagorean theorem. The first part of this example identifies the general education curriculum content for the entire class, the components of that general education content most relevant for Maureen, and the adaptations most appropriate for her. The second part of this example identifies functional curriculum content, only some of which is from her IEP, for which there is instruction embedded throughout math class. Maureen's education team determined the adaptations that would best facilitate her participation throughout the class.

Determining Adaptations from Weekly Lessons Plans

When a general education teacher develops detailed weekly lesson plans, education teams can use these plans to determine the adaptations that will facilitate participation in activities of a student with moderate or severe disabilities. By using the general education teacher's traditional lesson plans, team members can discuss every activity scheduled for the week and identify the levels and types of adaptations the student will require throughout the week. For example, in a fifteen-minute meeting per week, one education team clarifies information on a kindergarten teacher's weekly lesson plans, indicating the adaptations required for a student with severe disabilities to participate per activity (see Figure 6.5). Using a code, notations alongside each activity on the lesson plans delineate the level and type of adaptation the student requires throughout the week. In addition, the team adds notations on (1) the general education curriculum content emphasized in the student's instruction during each activity, (2) the functional curriculum content for which instruction will be embedded into each activity, and (3) the best position to facilitate the student's participation. Copies of this teacher's notated lesson plans are available to each team member before these activities occur the following week.

Determining Adaptations When Limited or No Weekly Plans Exist

When general education teachers write lesson plans that include little or no detail about instructional contexts, team members have difficulty determining in advance adaptations specifically designed to allow a student with moderate or severe disabilities to participate in each activity. One approach to this situation is to identify the instructional contexts the general education teacher frequently uses and determine ways in which the student can participate in each of those contexts. Tony's education team (see Appendix A, Student Profiles) used this approach to develop generic instructional plans (see Figure 6.6) for use in his fourth-grade class. For these generic plans the teacher developed only global units per subject area, with no specific activities delineated per day or even per week. This flexibility allowed the fourth-grade teacher to synthesize content across subject areas, but the lack of specific activities created difficulty in planning adaptations that allowed Tony, a student with severe disabilities, to participate with his classmates. To deal with this situation, the team used a generic instructional plan that identified the subject area and corresponding instructional contexts the teacher frequently used for the entire class. For example, during language arts, the class frequently engaged in independent work using spelling workbooks, group work with the teach-

Teacher: _____ *Mary P.* _____   Week of: _____ *5-28* _____   Grade: _____ *K* _____

Monday	Tuesday	Wednesday	Thursday	Friday
8:50–9:03 Quiet play; journal writing	8:50–9:03 Quiet play; journal writing	8:50–9:03 Quiet play; journal writing	8:50–9:03 Quiet play; journal writing	8:50–9:03 Quiet play; journal writing
9:03–9:10 Clean-up; attendance[4]	9:03–9:10 Clean-up; attendance[4]	9:03–9:10 Clean-up; attendance[4]	9:03–9:10 Clean-up; attendance[4]	9:03–9:10 Clean up; attendance[4]
9:10–9:45 Art seed pictures[OT]	9:10–9:30 Opening read "H"; sound box book[A,P]	9:10–9:30 Opening read "Hippo Sandwich"[A,P]	9:10–9:30 Opening Discuss hippos with zoo book[A,P]	9:10–9:30 Catch up day: finish any weekly activities
				9:30–9:50 If time, terrarium lecture
	9:30–9:50 Letter H; intro. sound; practice Hh; brainstorm H words; review A,C,G,O[F]	9:30–9:50 Letter H; practice Hh; write a few Hh; write A,C,G,O[F]	9:30–9:50 Blending writing on board; write on lined paper	
10:25–11:00 Science: pop bottle terrarium (demo & lecture); read "A Seed is a Promise"				9:50–10:20 Library
	9:55–10:35 Gym[PT]	9:55–10:35 Music	9:55–10:35 Gym[PT]	10:25–11:00 Shared reading: "Hairy Bear"
11:06–11:36 Lunch[3,P]	10:40–11:00 Hh ditto	10:40–11:00 finish AM work on Hh	10:40–11:00 finish AM work on writing	
11:40–12:00 Story or movie				11:06–11:36 Lunch[3,P]
	11:06–11:36 Lunch[3,P]	11:06–11:36 Lunch[3,P]	11:06–11:36 Lunch[3,P]	11:40–12:30 Movie; Rhythm Band; Craft
12:00–12:30 Craft: May baskets[OT]	11:40–12:00 Story or movie	11:40–12:00 Story or movie	11:40–12:00 Story or movie	12:00–12:30 Movie; Rhythm Band; Craft
	12:00–12:30 Science readiness: Color Hh ditto	12:00–12:30 Shared reading: "A House is a House for Me"	12:00–12:30 Craft: blow indian ink into shape of tree[OT]	

Underlined = constant entry from week to week.
Not underlined = entry added per week.
Number = objective on IEP.
  2. independently propel wheelchair
  3. use napkin appropriately
  4. locate locker and insert/remove backpack
  5. remove and care for eyeglasses
  6. coat on
  7. say "bye" to classmates without prompting
Supporting team member during instruction:
  A = aide
  P = peer(s)
  F = facilitating/special education teacher
  OT = occupational therapist
  PT = physical therapist

FIGURE 6.5 Determining Adaptations with Weekly General Education Lesson Plans

Student: _Tony_   Start Date: _4–1_   Review Date: _5–1_   Subject: _Language Arts_

General Education Activity	Generic Instructional Activity
1. Spelling: individual workbooks	a. Use letters from worksheets, and identify letters on flashcard b. Range of motion, then pass out papers to classmates, using wrist adaptation c. Throw out paper towels, put away other materials from groups
2. Spelling: on overhead	See 1a through 1c above
3. Journal writing	a. Ask Tony yes or no questions about activities at home or school, enter responses in his journal b. Have Tony match letters in his journal to his letter flashcards
4. Reading aloud	a. Range of motion and position, then use taped stories to read preselected segments for the class b. Ask yes or no questions related to the material read aloud in class
5.	

FIGURE 6.6   Generic Instructional Plan Based on Instructional Contexts

er orchestrating from the front of the room with the aid of an overhead projector, journal writing, and oral reading. For each possible instructional context the team determined adaptations that would enable Tony to participate with his classmates and work on his IEP objectives.

A second approach to determining adaptations in advance when a general education teacher does not develop detailed lesson plans is a generic instructional plan developed around the student's IEP goals (see Figure 6.7). The team can implement such generic plans regardless of the instructional context the general education teacher uses. All team members share this information, and the student also carries copies that are available upon request. Instruction based on these generic instructional plans is embedded into both instructional and noninstructional class activities.

Determining Adaptations in Current General Education Activities and Settings

After a student with moderate or severe disabilities enters general education activities, team members may find it necessary either to modify an adaptation that they

Student: _Tony_   Start Date: ___4–1___   Subject: _Routine Activities_   Review Date: ___5–1___

IEP Goal	Generic Instructional Activity Across General Education Activities
1. Responding correctly to yes or no questions	a. Attend to instructor, and answer yes or no questions when asked in large group; reinforce verbal approximation, while accepting physical responses (yes = smile plus look to left, no = look to right) b. Respond to peers' yes or no questions related to activities
2. Indicating the desire for "more"	a. When Tony finishes a preferred activity and time remains, ask if he wants to do "more," reinforce raising his arm for "more" b. Provide only some of the required materials for Tony; when he finishes with them, ask if he needs "more"
3. Letter and object identification	a. Ask Tony to identify letters (those used during class activities) by getting light from head light on the correct card b. Have Tony use head light to identify objects used during activities, and objects in pictures (textbooks/worksheets)
4.	

FIGURE 6.7   Generic Instructional Plan Based on IEP Content

already have developed or to develop an adaptation for a need that they did not identify in advance. The following sections describe strategies for analyzing how a student currently is participating in general education activities and determining relevant adaptations to meet the student's needs during those activities.

Analysis of Current General Education Activities

One strategy for determining a relevant adaptation that allows a student to participate more fully in a current general education activity is to analyze that activity (Downing & Eichinger, 1990; York, Doyle, & Kronberg, 1992). As demonstrated in Figure 6.8, the education team completes an analysis of the instructional strategy implemented during the activity (e.g., cooperative learning strategy, lecture format with overhead projector), the configuration of student participation in the activity (e.g., small group, independent work), and the general education materials being used during the activity. With this information an education team can determine more accurately the aspect of the activity with which the student is having difficul-

Decision Hierarchy Level	General Education Activity #1 Instructional Strategy: Student Configuration: General Education Materials:	General Education Activity #2 Instructional Strategy: Student Configuration: General Education Materials:	General Education Activity #3 Instructional Strategy: Student Configuration: General Education Materials:
1. Participation as classmates			
2. Adapt environment			
3. Adapt instruction			
4. Adapt materials			
5. Adapt rules/ expectations			
6. Personal assistance			
7. Different content level			
8. Different content			
9. Different activity in room			
10. Different activity in building			
11. Different activity in community			

FIGURE 6.8   Analysis of Current General Education Activities to Determine Adaptations

ty and develop an adaptation that focuses on the appropriate component of the activity using a decision hierarchy.

Analysis of Participation in Specific General Education Settings

A second strategy useful when determining relevant adaptations for a student with moderate or severe disabilities is an analysis of the student's participation in specific general education settings. For example, some student responsibilities are specific to a particular general education setting (e.g., obtaining and paying for lunch). If a student is having difficulty completing such an activity independently, an education team can complete an ecological analysis of that setting (Browder & Snell, 1993; Sailor et al., 1993; York & Vandercook, 1991) by observing students in the subenvironment in which the task is completed and listing the steps used by nondisabled classmates to complete the activity. As illustrated in Figure 6.9, the team then can delineate the steps on which the performance of the student with moderate or severe disabilities differs from classmates. To allow independent performance of the activity, the team identifies the least intrusive adaptations the student needs by progressing through the levels of the adaptation hierarchy.

Analysis of Participation in Routines in General Education Settings

A third strategy useful when determining relevant adaptations for a student with moderate or severe disabilities is an analysis of the student's participation in the routines that occur regularly across general education settings (Macdonald & York, 1989; York et al., 1992). Completion of some responsibilities, such as being prepared for class activities and following classroom rules is subject to analysis across general education settings (see Figure 6.10). The education team may be required to conduct an ecological analysis if a student is able to participate independently in some general education settings but is having difficulty in others.

Instructional Strategies that Facilitate Inclusion

There are several instructional strategies already in use in general education settings that facilitate the inclusion of students with moderate or severe disabilities. While including a student in the class of a general education teacher who already uses such strategies is possible, other general education teachers can be encouraged to use such strategies to increase the effectiveness of their instruction for *all* students.

Cooperative Learning Strategies

Cooperative learning strategies promote the interdependence of students in their acquisition and use of knowledge. While cooperative learning strategies require

FIGURE 6.9   Ecological Analysis of General Education Settings to Determine Adaptations

Setting: Subenvironment:		Decision Hierarchy Level				
Responsibility or Skill	Discrepancy with Peers	1. Participate as classmates	2. Adapted environment	3. Adapted instruction	4. Adapted materials	

small groups of two to six students, the mere placement of students in groups for instruction or activities does not constitute a cooperative learning situation, for such groups also can engage in competitive and independent learning activities (Davidson, 1994; Johnson & Johnson, 1994; Putnam, 1993). Johnson and Johnson (1994) stated that there are five components required for a group activity to be a cooperative learning experience: (1) clearly perceived positive interdependence, (2) considerable face-to-face interaction, (3) clearly perceived individual accountability and personal responsibility to achieve the group's goals, (4) frequent use of interpersonal and small-group skills, and (5) frequent and regular group processing of current group functioning to improve the group's future effectiveness.

Davidson (1994) describes several cooperative learning strategies that have been used in general education settings, including:

1. Student Team Learning Strategies, such as Student Teams Achievement Divisions, Teams-Games-Tournaments, Jigsaw II, Team Assisted Individualization, Cooperative Integrated Reading and Composition (Slavin, 1983, 1990).

	Decision Hierarchy Level						
	5. Adapted rules/ expectations	6. Personal assistance	7. Different content level	8. Different content	9. Different activity in room	10. Different activity in building	11. Different activity in community

2. Learning Together (Johnson & Johnson, 1987, 1989).
3. Group Investigation (Sharan & Hertz-Lazarowitz, 1980, 1982; Sharan & Sharan, 1992).
4. Structural Approach Strategies, such as Think-Pair-Share, Roundtable, Numbered Heads Together, Three-Step Interview, Jigsaw, Pairs Check (Kagan, 1992).
5. Complex Instruction (Cohen, 1986).
6. Collaborative Approach (Barnes, Britton, & Torbe, 1986; Barnes & Todd, 1977; Britton, 1970; Brubacher, Payne, & Rickett, 1990; Reid, Forrestal & Cook, 1989).
7. Simple Cooperation Model (McCabe & Rhoades, 1990; Rhoades & McCabe, 1992).

These cooperative learning strategies are effective to varying degrees across different variables; however, Putnam (1993) summarized the positive effects of cooperative learning strategies in the following manner:

FIGURE 6.10   **Analysis of Participation in Routines in General Education Settings to Determine Adaptations**

Settings For Routines: a) b) c)	Decision Hierarchy Level			
	1. Participate as classmates	2. Adapted environment	3. Adapted instruction	4. Adapted materials
1. Arrives at class on time				
2. Brings required materials to class				
3. Is in seat, with materials ready, as class begins				
4. Completes transitions between activities in response to situational cues				
5. Begins tasks with situational cues				
6. Stays on task throughout activity				
7. Terminates tasks with situational cues				
8. Puts away instructional materials after use				
9. Uses instructional materials for intended purposes				
10. Uses classroom materials and equipment safely				
11. Shares materials when appropriate				
12. Works cooperatively with one partner				
13. Works cooperatively with small group				
14. Tolerates changes in classroom routines				
15. Follows classroom rules and class directions				
16. Readily accepts correcton and uses assistance to modify performance				

1. Academic achievement was most likely to occur with an incorporation of the components of positive interdependence and individual responsibility.
2. Students' self-esteem increased with students learning to value and perceive themselves positively.

Decision Hierarchy Level						
5. Adapted rules/ expectations	6. Personal assistance	7. Different content level	8. Different content	9. Different activity in room	10. Different activity in building	11. Different activity in community

3. Students became more actively involved in the learning process.
4. Students accepted peers to a greater extent, despite their weaknesses.
5. Students, especially those with moderate or severe disabilities, developed more social skills.

General education activities which incorporate cooperative learning strategies are ideal for effective instruction of students with moderate or severe disabilities (Putnam, 1993; Thousand, Villa, & Nevin, 1994).

Small-Group Instruction

Not all small-group activities incorporate cooperative learning strategies, but other small-group instruction also can be effective for students with moderate or severe disabilities in general education settings (Post, 1984). Udvari-Solner (1994) described a small-group arrangement as one in which "students are allowed to work together to complete a project . . . or to socialize and share ideas while completing individual work" (p. 61). Support provided by peers who are working independently on their own activities is the least intrusive form of personal assistance possible in inclusive settings. While peers are available for support, their focus is on their own work, rather than on the work of their classmate. Because of this, small groups provide natural situations for students with moderate or severe disabilities to work independently when possible, and yet unobtrusively request assistance from a peer when needed.

Peer Partnering

Partnering classmates with and without disabilities is an effective instructional strategy that education teams frequently use in inclusive general education settings under numerous titles. Jenkins and Jenkins (1988) stated that peer tutors can be effective in increasing the skill acquisition of classmates when partnering includes several critical components, including:

1. Highly structured lesson formats.
2. Instructional content focused on extra practice, repetition, or clarification of concepts covered in class.
3. Daily instruction until the concept is mastered.
4. Continuous or daily programs of moderate duration.
5. Training for tutors on appropriate interpersonal behaviors.
6. Class climate of mutual respect and concern, coupled with high expectations for everyone.
7. Active supervision of tutors.
8. Supportive teachers and administrators who advocate with program participants.
9. A program manager for school-wide programs.
10. Measurement of student progress.
11. Careful selection and pairing of partners.

Study buddies play a different role for students with moderate or severe disabilities. They provide support by performing tasks that the targeted student cannot do. For instance, if a student is not able to write down information provided in class, a study buddy might provide copies of written materials (e.g., class notes, homework assignments) (Jakupcak, 1993). If a student is not physically able to complete preparation and clean up tasks for class activities or requires so much time that it interferes with the activity itself, a study buddy might complete part or all of those tasks. On the other hand, instructional buddies can assist in setting up learning situations (e.g., for social interactions) and reinforcing a student's appropriate participation (Hamre-Nietupski et al., 1992).

Through these various roles, nondisabled classmates contribute significantly to the educational experiences of students with moderate or severe disabilities. Ideally, they will become members of students' natural support networks and be involved long-term in both their educational programs and lives outside of school.

Summary

Students with moderate or severe disabilities frequently are unable to participate in functional and general education activities in the same manner as their nondisabled classmates and require adaptations to facilitate maximally independent participation. Adaptations may be made to general education environments, materials, and instruction, depending upon the component of an activity during which the student demonstrates a need for assistance that cannot be addressed adequately and quickly enough through direct instruction. Rather, the student's overriding disability requires an adaptation.

The education team selects an adaptation with consideration to its (1) usefulness over time and across activities; (2) appropriateness in relation to the student's age, financial resources, and importance of participation in the activity; and (3) degree of intrusiveness in general education settings and the community. In addition, preferred adaptations allow the student to perform the same activity as nondisabled classmates without relying on another person and without changing the curriculum content. A hierarchy of decisions assists team members in determining the least intrusive adaptation to meet a student's need.

References

Barnes, D., Britton, J., & Torbe, M. (1986). *Language, the learner and the school* (2nd ed.). Portsmouth, NH: Boynton/Cook.

Barnes, D., & Todd, F. (1977). *Communicating and learning in small groups.* London: Routledge, Kegan Paul.

Baumgart, D., Brown, L., Pumpian, I., Nisbet, J., Ford, A., Sweet, M., Messina, R., & Schroeder, J. (1982). The principle of partial participation and individualized adaptations in educational programs for students with severe handicaps. *Journal of The Association for Persons with Severe Handicaps, 7*(2), 17–27.

Borich, G. D.(1992). *Effective teaching methods* (2nd ed.). New York: Charles E. Merrill.

Britton, J. (1970). *Language and learning.* Portsmouth, NH: Boynton/Cook.

Browder, D., & Snell, M. E.(1993). Daily living and community skills. In M. E. Snell (Ed.), *Instruction of students with severe disabilities* (4th ed.) (pp. 480–525). New York: Charles E. Merrill.

Brubacher, M., Payne, R., & Rickett, K. (1990). *Perspectives on small group learning: Theory and practice.* Oakvale, Ontario: Rubicon Publishing.

Campbell, P. H. (1993). Physical management and handling procedures. In M. E. Snell (Ed.), *Instruction of students with severe disabilities* (4th ed.) (pp. 248–263). New York: Charles E. Merrill.

Campbell, P. H., & Forsyth, S. (1993). Integrated programming and movement disabilities. In M. E. Snell (Ed.), *Instruction of students with severe disabilities* (4th ed.) (pp. 264–289). New York: Charles E. Merrill.

Cohen, E. (1986). *Designing groupwork: Strategies for the heterogeneous classroom.* New York: Teachers College Press.

Cohen, S. B., & Lynch, D. K. (1991). An instructional modification process. *Teaching Exceptional Children,* summer, 12–18.

Davidson, N. (1994). Cooperative and collaborative learning: An integrative perspective. In J. S. Thousand, R. A.Villa, & A. I. Nevin (Eds.), *Creativity and collaborative learning: A practical guide to empowering students and teachers* (pp. 13–30). Baltimore: Paul H. Brookes.

Downing, J., & Eichinger, J. (1990). Instructional strategies for learners with dual sensory impairments in integrated settings. *Journal of The Association for Persons with Severe Handicaps, 15,* 98–105.

Ellis, E. S., & Sabornie, E. J. (1988). Effective instruction with microcomputers: Promises, practices, and preliminary findings. In E. L. Meyen, G. A.Vergason, & R. J. Whelan (Eds.), *Effective instructional strategies for exceptional children.* Denver: Love.

Filbin, J., & Kronberg, R. (undated). *Ideas and suggestions for curricular adaptations at the secondary level.* Denver: Colorado Department of Education.

Gearheart, B. R., Weishahn, M. W., & Gearheart, C. J. (1992). *The exceptional student in the regular classroom* (5th ed.). New York: Charles E. Merrill.

Giangreco, M. F., Cloninger, C. J., & Iverson, V. (1993). *Choosing options and accommodations for children: A planning guide for inclusive education.* Baltimore: Paul H. Brookes.

Hamre-Nietupski, S., McDonald, J., & Nietupski, J. (1992). Integrating elementary students with multiple disabilities into supported regular classes: Challenges and solutions. *Teaching Exceptional Children,* spring, 6–9.

Jakupcak, J. (1993). Innovative classroom programs for full inclusion. In J. W. Putnam (Ed.), *Cooperative learning and strategies for inclusion: Celebrating diversity in the classroom* (pp. 163–179). Baltimore: Paul H. Brookes.

Jenkins, J., & Jenkins, L. (1988). Peer tutoring in elementary and secondary programs. In E. L. Meyen, G. A. Vergason, & R. J. Whelan (Eds.), *Effective instructional strategies for exceptional children* (pp. 335–354). Denver: Love.

Johnson, D. W., & Johnson, R. (1987). *Creative conflict.* Edina, MN: Interaction Book Company.

Johnson, D. W., & Johnson, R. (1989). *Cooperation and competition: Theory and research.* Edina, MN: Interaction Book Company.

Johnson, R. T., & Johnson, D. W. (1994). An overview of cooperative learning. In J. S. Thousand, R. A. Villa, & A. I. Nevin (Eds.), *Creativity and collaborative learning: A practical guide to empowering students and teachers* (pp. 31–44). Baltimore: Paul H. Brookes.

Kagan, S. (1992). *Cooperative learning: Resources for teachers.* San Juan Capistrano, CA: Resources for Teachers.

Kronberg, R., & Filbin, J., (1993). *Ideas and suggestions for curricular adaptations at the elementary level.* Denver: Colorado Department of Education.

McCabe, M., & Rhoades, J. (1990). *The nurturing classroom.* Sacramento, CA: ITA Publications.

Macdonald, C., & York, J. (1989). Instruction in regular education classes for students with severe disabilities: Assessment, objectives, and instructional programs. In J. York, T. Vandercook, & S. Wolff (Eds.), *Strategies for full inclusion.* Minneapolis: University of Minnesota, Institute on Community Integration.

Miller, J. (1993). Augmentative and alternative communication. In M. E. Snell (Ed.), *Instruction of students with severe disabilities* (4th ed.) (pp. 319–346). New York: Charles E. Merrill.

Neufeldt, V., & Guralnik, D. B. (1994). *Webster's new world dictionary of American English* (3rd college ed.). New York: Prentice-Hall.

Nevin, A. (1993). Curricular and instructional adaptations for including students with disabilities in cooperative groups. In J. W. Putnam (Ed.), *Cooperative learning and strategies for inclusion: Celebrating diversity in the classroom* (pp. 41–56). Baltimore: Paul H. Brookes.

Orelove, F. P., & Sobsey, D. (1991). *Educating children with multiple disabilities: A transdisciplinary approach* (2nd ed.). Baltimore: Paul H. Brookes.

Post, L. M. (1984). Individualizing instruction in the middle school: Modifications and adaptations in curriculum for the mainstreamed student. *The Clearing House, 58,* 73–76.

Putnam, J. W. (1993). The process of cooperative learning. In J. W. Putnam (Ed.), *Cooperative learning and strategies for inclusion: Celebrating diversity in the classroom* (pp. 15–40). Baltimore: Paul H. Brookes.

Rainforth, B., & York, J. (1991). Handling and positioning. In F. P. Orelove & D. Sobsey, *Educating children with multiple disabilities: A transdisciplinary approach* (2nd ed.) (pp. 79–117). Baltimore: Paul H. Brookes.

Rainforth, B., York, J., & Macdonald, C. (1992). *Collaborative teams for students with severe disabilities: Integrating therapy and educational services.* Baltimore: Paul H. Brookes Publishing Co.

Reichle, J., & Karlan, G. (1985). The selection of an augmentative system in communication intervention: A critique of decision rules. *Journal of The Association for Persons with Severe Handicaps, 10,* 146–156.

Reichle, J., & Karlan, G. (1988). Selecting augmentative communication interventions: A critique of candidacy criteria and a proposed alternative. In R. Schiefelbusch & L. Lloyd (Eds.), *Language perspectives: Acquisition, retardation, and intervention* (2nd ed.) (pp. 321–339). Austin, TX: Pro-Ed.

Reid, J., Forrestal, P., & Cook, J. (1989). *Small group learning in the classroom.* Scarborough, Australia: Chalkface Press. Portsmouth, NH: Heinemann.

Rhoades, J., & McCabe, M. (1992). *Outcome-based learning: A teacher's guide to restructuring the classroom.* Sacramento, CA: ITA.

Sailor, W., Gee, K., & Karasoff, P. (1993). Full inclusion and school restructuring. In M. E. Snell (Ed.), *Instruction of students with severe disabilities* (4th ed.) (pp. 1–30). New York: Charles E. Merrill.

Schleien, S. J., Green, F. P., & Heyne, L. A. (1993). Integrated community recreation. In M. E. Snell (Ed.), *Instruction of students with severe disabilities* (4th ed.) (pp. 526–555). New York: Charles E. Merrill.

Schnorr, R. F. (1990). "Peter? He comes and goes...": First graders' perspectives on a part-time mainstream student. *Journal of The Association for Persons with Severe Handicaps, 15,* 231–240.

Schulz, J. B., Carpenter, C. D., & Turnbull, A. P. (1991). *Mainstreaming exceptional students: A guide for classroom teachers* (3rd ed.). Boston: Allyn & Bacon.

Sharan, S., & Hertz-Lazarowitz, R. (1980). A group investigation method of cooperative learning in the classroom. In S. Sharan, P. Hare, C. Webb, & R. Hertz-Lazarowitz (Eds.)., *Cooperation in education* (pp. 14–46). Provo, UT: Brigham Young University Press.

Sharan, S., & Hertz-Lazarowitz, R. (1982). Effects of an instructional change program on teachers' behavior, attitudes and perceptions. *Journal of Applied Behavioral Science, 18,* 185–201.

Sharan, Y., & Sharan, S. (1992). *Expanding cooperative learning through group investigation.* New York: Teachers College Press.

Slavin, R. (1983). *Cooperative learning.* New York: Longman.

Slavin, R. (1990). *Cooperative learning: Theory, research and practice.* Englewood Cliffs, NJ: Prentice-Hall.

Snell, M. E., & Farlow, L. J. (1993). Self-care skills. In M. E. Snell (Ed.), *Instruction of students with severe disabilities* (4th ed.) (pp. 380–441). New York: Charles E. Merrill.

Sobsey, D., & Wolf-Schein, E. G. (1991). Sensory impairments. In F. P. Orelove & D. Sobsey, *Educating children with multiple disabilities: A transdisciplinary approach* (2nd ed.) (pp. 119–153). Baltimore: Paul H. Brookes.

Thousand, J., Fox, T. J., Reid, R., Godek, J., Williams, W., & Fox, W. (1986). *The homecoming model.* Burlington, VT: Center for Developmental Disabilities.

Thousand, J. S., Villa, R. A., & Nevin, A. I. (1994). *Creativity and collaborative learning.* Baltimore: Paul H. Brookes.

Udvari-Solner, A. (1994). A decision-making model for curricular adaptations in cooperative groups. In J. S. Thousand, R. A.Villa, & A. I. Nevin (Eds.), *Creativity and collaborative learning: A practical guide to empowering students and teachers* (pp. 59–77). Baltimore: Paul H. Brookes.

Villa, R. A., & Thousand, J. S. (1993). Redefining the role of the special educator and other support personnel. In J. W. Putnam (Ed.), *Cooperative learning and strategies for inclusion: Celebrating diversity in the classroom* (pp. 57–91). Baltimore: Paul H. Brookes.

Villa, R. A., Udis, J., & Thousand, J. S. (1994). Responses for children experiencing behavioral and emotional challenges. In J. S.Thousand, R. A. Villa, & A. I. Nevin (Eds.), *Creativity and collaborative learning: A practical guide to empowering students and teachers* (pp. 369–390). Baltimore: Paul H. Brookes.

York, J., Doyle, M. B., & Kronberg, R. (1992). A curriculum development process for inclusive classrooms. *Focus on Exceptional Children, 25*(4).

York, J., & Rainforth, B. (1991). Developing instructional adaptations. In F. P. Orelove & D. Sobsey, *Educating children with multiple disabilities: A transdisciplinary approach* (2nd ed.) (pp. 259–295). Baltimore: Paul H. Brookes.

York, J., & Vandercook, T. (1991). Designing an integrated program for learners with severe disabilities. *Teaching Exceptional Children*, winter, 22–28.

7

INSTRUCTIONAL STRATEGIES FOR INCLUSIVE SETTINGS

SANDRA ALPER

Objectives

After completing this chapter the reader will be able to:

1. Define the term *best practice.*
2. Define operant behavior.
3. Define the basic components of the term *applied behavior analysis.*
4. Define and provide examples of how applied behavior analytic techniques may be used with students with disabilities in general education settings.
5. Discuss the importance of generalization training for students with disabilities.

Key Terms

Acquisition
Antecedent
Applied Behavior Analysis
Best Practices
Conditioned Response
Conditioned Stimulus
Consequent
Discriminative Stimulus
Extinction
Functional Analysis
Generalization

Learning
Maintenance
Modeling
Negative Reinforcement
Operant Behavior
Positive Reinforcement
Punishment
Respondent Conditioning
Shaping
Stimulus Control

A rich technology of instruction is available to educators for use with students with disabilities (as well as with students without disabilities) in a wide variety of settings. This instructional technology includes strategies that result in the acquisition of functional and age-appropriate skills as well as elimination of inappropriate behaviors. Also available are instructional strategies that result in maintenance of skills after instruction ends and generalization of skills learned in one setting to other, untrained settings in school, home, and the community. Instructional strategies that are effective in bringing about positive changes in the behavior of a wide variety of students are often referred to as "best practices" (Snell, 1993). Some examples include task analysis, the use of discrete cues, positive reinforcement, modeling, and the system of least prompts. Instructional strategies that are generally considered to be best practices have a basis in behavioral principles of human learning.

The scientific study of the behavior of individuals with and without disabilities and applications of that work to real world settings involves careful analysis of behavior within the environmental context in which it occurs (Williams, Howard, Williams, & McLaughlin, 1994). Specific behavior is operationally defined and systematically observed. Hypotheses are generated about stimuli in the environment that precede and follow the behavior and their effects on the frequency, duration, and intensity of the behavior. Changes in behavior are produced by manipulating environmental stimuli.

Williams et al. (1994) pointed out that behavioral scientists do not necessarily dismiss the genetic and biological bases of behavior. Behavioral scientists focus their attention, however, on the environmental stimuli that they are able to manipulate in order to bring about changes in behavior. For example, some cases of mental retardation are caused by genetic factors. A condition known as phenylketonuria (PKU) is the result of a missing enzyme necessary for the proper metabolism of protein found in human and cows' milk. Faulty cell division of the egg or sperm cells can result in Down syndrome. Other cases of retardation may be the result of the mother ingesting agents, such as alcohol or drugs, that are toxic to the developing fetus. In other instances, the cause of mental retardation is unknown. Behaviorists focus on how to teach individuals with mental retardation (or learning disabilities or behavioral disorders) new skills based on manipulating the antecedent events and consequences of specific behaviors. Thus, the instructional strategies are the same, regardless of the etiology, or cause, of the disability.

The instructional technology of teaching new behaviors through manipulation of environmental stimuli is referred to as "applied behavior analysis." Applied behavior analysis focuses on systematically and objectively analyzing the causes of observable and measurable behaviors in real world settings. In their classic article Baer, Wolf, and Risley (1968) wrote:

> *Analytical behavior application is the process of applying sometimes tentative principles of behavior to the improvement of specific behaviors, and simultaneously evaluating whether or not any changes noted are indeed attributable to the process of application—and if so, to what parts of that process (p. 91).*

Applied behavior analysis consists of several key components. First, a behavior must be observable and measurable (Baer et al., 1968; Ullmann & Krasner, 1965). According to Alberto and Troutman (1990), a behavior must be seen, heard, touched, or smelled in order to be observable. In addition, a behavior must be directly measured according to frequency, duration, amount, or intensity. According to these criteria, a student's failure to complete a homework assignment is an observable and measurable behavior, while "laziness" is not.

Second, a behavioral principle must be applied to a particular behavior that is socially relevant or valuable to consumers (Kazdin, 1982; Wolf, 1978). This requires educators of students with disabilities to target behaviors for instruction that are functional and age-appropriate. Behaviors used frequently in a variety of natural settings by persons without disabilities of the same chronological age are emphasized. Learning to purchase a soft drink from a vending machine is a functional skill. Learning to count change using simulated money is not.

Third, the behavioral intervention is implemented in an applied, or natural, setting rather than in a controlled laboratory setting. Behavioral interventions are implemented in schools, job sites, domestic residences, restaurants, recreational facilities, stores, and many other places that persons with and without disabilities frequent.

Fourth, the goal of the behaviorist is to demonstrate a functional relationship between the behavior and the intervention (Wolf et al., 1968). Empirical data must document that a particular change in behavior occurred as a result of the intervention rather than because of some external factor outside of the control of the behaviorist, such as maturation or previous learning history. *The Journal of Applied Behavior Analysis,* established in 1968, serves as a rich and scholarly source of accumulated evidence documenting the effectiveness of the application of learning principles to human behavior.

This chapter reviews basic applied behavior analytic principles of learning along with some examples of their applications in inclusive settings. First, the chapter includes a brief historical overview of applied behavior analysis and then the basic principles of instruction. There will be examples of how instructional strategies may be implemented in a variety of natural settings in school, home, and the community in order to bring about positive changes in the behavior of students with disabilities. This chapter does not include a comprehensive discussion of applied behavior analysis. For this the reader should consult textbooks by Alberto and Troutman (1990) and Schloss and Smith (1994).

Historical Overview

Alberto and Troutman (1990) pointed out that behavioral principles of learning have undoubtedly been in operation for as long as human beings have existed. Jewish people concentrate on obeying the Ten Commandments and the concept of reward and punishment while reciting the second paragraph of the Shema, taken from Deuteronomy 11:13–21.

And it will come to pass that if you continually harken to My commandments that I command you today, to love the Lord, your God, and to serve Him with all your heart and with all your soul—then I will provide rain for your land in its proper time . . . and you will eat and be satisfied. Beware, lest your heart be seduced and you turn astray and serve gods of others and bow to them. Then the wrath of the Lord will blaze against you. He will restrain the heaven so there will be no rain and the ground will not yield its produce.

Parents and teachers often use behavioral principles to change behaviors whether or not they are aware of them (Alberto & Troutman, 1990). Parents give children allowances in exchange for performing household chores. Teachers provide opportunities for free time, candy, and points that may be traded for rewards when students follow classroom rules. Some parents spank or send children to their room following inappropriate behavior.

One pioneer in the scientific study of behavior and its environmental influences was the Russian psychologist, Ivan Pavlov (Kazdin, 1978; Schultz, 1969). Pavlov studied the process of digestion in dogs. By chance, Pavlov observed that the mere sight of persons who usually fed his dogs in the laboratory, or the sight of food, resulted in salivation in his dogs. He knew that there was no physiological explanation of how the mere sight of food could bring about salivation. Pavlov hypothesized that the mere sight of food elicited salivation because it was always followed by the dogs being fed.

Pavlov designed a classic experiment. A tone (a neutral stimulus [NS] that normally did not elicit salivation) always preceded the presentation of food powder (an unconditioned stimulus [UCS] that normally brought about an unconditioned response [UCR] salivation in dogs). Gradually, the tone alone elicited salivation. The tone now served as a conditioned stimulus [CS] for a conditioned response [CR]. Over time, the process by which a previously UCS could become a CS that elicited a CR became known as respondent, or classical conditioning.

The work of Pavlov significantly influenced American psychologist, John Watson (1919). Watson brought the term *behaviorism* to the professional literature (Alberto & Troutman, 1990). He was opposed to psychological constructs popular at the time, such as "mind," "consciousness and the unconscience," and therapies that analyzed past experiences and dreams to result in "insight" about one's own feelings and behavior.

Watson and Rayner (1920) conducted a study in which a previously neutral stimulus, a white rat, was repeatedly paired with an unconditioned stimulus, a loud noise, and presented to Albert, an eleven-month-old child. Albert normally responded to loud noise with the UCRs of startling and crying. After only a few trials, presentation of the rat alone elicited the startle reflex and crying, now CRs, in Albert. The rat now served as a CS.

B. F. Skinner (1938, 1953) developed a model of human behavior known as operant conditioning. Skinner first described the distinction between operant behaviors, or behaviors that are under voluntary control, and respondent, or reflexive behaviors. Operant behaviors are voluntary behaviors that antecedent events and behavioral consequences may shape and control. Respondent behaviors, on the other hand, are usually reflexes that some stimulus elicits. Consequent events have no effect on whether a respondent behavior will or will not occur again.

Skinner focused much of his early work on modifying the responses of laboratory animals, such as rats and pigeons. He demonstrated that animal behaviors such as pecking, turning in circles, or pressing a lever could be controlled by the consequences following such responses. Few individuals anticipated the enormous impact this early work would have on American education and psychology. Applying principles of learning based on operant conditioning to human behavior, the term *behavior modification* came into being (Ullmann & Krasner, 1969).

Today, the preferred term *applied behavior analysis* refers to a vast body of research that has developed and successfully used basic principles of learning with students who differ widely in learning and behavioral characteristics. Instructional strategies based on these principles of learning are among the "best practices" available to special and general educators today. The following sections define basic principles of operant conditioning and provide examples of how they apply to students with disabilities in inclusive settings.

Operant Principles of Learning and Their Application in Inclusive Settings

Positive Reinforcement

Positive reinforcement consists of a functional relationship, or contingency, between a particular behavior, or response, and a stimulus that is a consequence of that behavior (Alberto & Troutman, 1990). Positive reinforcement occurs when a particular behavior is followed by a consequence that increases the probability of the behavior occurring again. For example, a student sits quietly in her chair and completes her assignment. The teacher then allows her to have 10 minutes of free time after which she returns to her desk and completes the next assignment. A parent gives money to a child for completing certain household chores, thereby increasing the likelihood that the child will continue to complete chores.

Williams et al. (1994) pointed out that a consequence is a positive reinforcer because of its effect on the future occurrence of the behavior and not because of any positive or pleasant perception. A consequence may be perceived as pleasant, but fail to result in an increase in the rate of a behavior. A parent might try to reinforce good grades with social praise. Even though the student might enjoy receiving the praise, if he or she does not earn high grades, the praise would not be a reinforcer.

Sometimes a stimulus that most persons would agree is unpleasant, or even painful, has the effect of increasing the rate of a particular response and, therefore, serves as a positive reinforcer. For example, a young child receives attention from a parent (spanking) only when the child misbehaves. The spanking may have the effect of increasing the likelihood of misbehavior to obtain attention from the parent.

Positive reinforcement is one of the easiest and most natural strategies to use with students with disabilities in inclusive settings. Students and teachers may effectively administer positive reinforcement. It often occurs spontaneously, as when students praise each other, or a teacher gives a student a pat on the back for good work.

There are three basic steps for using positive reinforcement. First, the particular behavior that a teacher wants to occur more frequently is defined in observable, measurable terms. Second, the consequence, or stimulus, that follows the behavior, is identified. Some examples include social praise, a smile, candy, free time, or opportunity to engage in an activity the student enjoys. Third, the teacher checks to make sure that the consequence is, in fact, resulting in an increased rate of the target behavior.

In an elementary classroom that includes a child with disabilities, the teacher developed a "menu" of fun things to do. Children select ten minutes of fun after appropriate behavior. The teacher determines for each student the specific target behaviors and how long each student must engage in them before receiving reinforcement. While some students without disabilities may have the ability to work for two hours without reinforcement, a student with behavior disorders may earn a reinforcer after each thirty-minute interval of on task behavior.

In a high-school program that includes youth with aggressive behaviors, each student with a disability has a daily calendar (Schloss, Smith, & Schloss, 1990). For each thirty-minute period, the student can earn points for remaining in an assigned area and completing the assigned task. At the end of four periods, or two hours, if the student has a positive number of points, he or she can then take a thirty-minute break and participate in a preferred activity.

Negative Reinforcement

In the use of negative reinforcement, the probability that a target behavior will occur again increases by following the behavior with the removal of an unpleasant stimulus. By performing the target behavior, the individual can escape or avoid some unpleasant stimulus condition. Most modern day automobiles contain some type of alarm that sounds unceasingly until the driver buckles the seat belt. Adults sometimes work during their lunch hour so that they can leave the workplace earlier.

Teachers of students with and without disabilities commonly use negative reinforcement. For example, many teachers encourage their students to finish their work so that they will not miss recess or some other preferred activity. In using negative reinforcement, it is important to place the emphasis on the appropriate behavior expected of the student rather than the threat of an unpleasant consequence for not performing the target behavior (e.g., "Go sit down at your desk and be quiet so that we can start the movie," rather than "You will not get to watch the movie with the rest of the class if you don't sit down").

Perhaps because of the word *negative*, negative reinforcement is sometimes confused with punishment. The use of both positive and negative reinforcement increase the probability that an appropriate behavior will occur again. Positive reinforcement accomplishes this goal by following the desired response with a pleasant consequence. In negative reinforcement, performing a desirable behavior allows the individual to escape or avoid some unpleasant stimulus. A student completes an assignment to avoid staying after school. Punishment decreases the frequency of an undesirable behavior by following the behavior with an unpleasant consequence. A student has to stay after school as a result of not completing assigned work during regular school hours.

Extinction

Extinction eliminates an inappropriate or undesirable behavior that was previously reinforced by withholding the reinforcer. Extinction is sometimes referred to as purposeful ignoring. A classic dilemma for new parents is what to do when the baby cries after being put to bed at night. It is very tempting to go back into the baby's room just to make sure the child is safe; but if the parents go back into the room every time the child cries, they reinforce the crying behavior. Baby soon learns that crying results in the parents returning to the room and will cry every time they leave. The parents must now steel themselves to extinguish the crying by ignoring this behavior (after making sure the child is safe, of course). Within a short time most babies learn that crying does not result in the desired outcome (parents in room).

Extinction has eliminated a number of inappropriate behaviors in school settings such as teasing, talking out of turn, and disrupting classmates. Students often engage in these behaviors because they can gain the attention of others. Students often attend to the disruptive student. When a teacher instructs classmates to ignore such behaviors, they often stop.

Discretion must determine whether or not one uses extinction to eliminate a particular behavior. In some cases, a phenomenon known as an "extinction burst" (Schloss, Smith, & Schloss, 1990; Williams et al., 1994) will occur. The student temporarily increases the frequency or intensity of the undesirable behavior in a stronger attempt to obtain reinforcement shortly after reinforcement is withdrawn. Teachers must anticipate that an extinction burst might occur and be prepared to deal with it if it does. The parent of the infant must prepare to listen to initially longer bouts of crying before the behavior extinguishes. Similarly, students who disrupt classmates or abuse themselves may increase the frequencies of these behaviors for a short time.

In some cases, extinction alone is not sufficient to eliminate an unwanted behavior. This is because the behavior may be maintained by some reinforcer other than the attention of others. A student who is disruptive, for example, may receive reinforcement by escaping work. In other cases, ignoring a particular maladaptive behavior (e.g., verbal threats to run away or engage in self-injury or aggression towards others) would present too great of a safety risk to be prudent or ethical.

Punishment

Punishment occurs when a particular behavior precedes a consequence or stimulus that results in a decrease in the rate at which the behavior occurs again. For example, a student fails to complete assigned work during math class and is made to complete the work during recess. The next day the student completes the work on time during the math class. A soccer coach makes a player run laps after a practice in which the player made fun of another team member. The teasing did not occur during the next practice. A teenager spends two to three hours on the telephone each night rather than working on homework. Grades fall. The parents take away telephone privileges until the grades improve.

Alberto and Troutman (1990) pointed out the term *punishment* should describe only those situations in which a specific consequence resulted in a decrease in the rate of the preceding behavior. Sometimes the term *punishment* is erroneously applied to a situation in which a specific consequence may be perceived as unpleasant by an individual but does not reduce the occurrence of the target behavior. Parents may believe they are punishing a child by spanking him each time the child says a naughty word. Even though the child loudly protests the spanking, punishment has actually occurred *only* if the occurrence of saying naughty words decreases. A functional relationship must be demonstrated between the consequence and the decrease in the rate of the behavior.

Williams et al. (1994) described the use of two forms of punishment. Punishment may involve either contingent presentation of a stimulus or contingent removal of a stimulus following an undesirable behavior. In the first case, an undesirable behavior (disrupting classmates) is followed by presentation of consequence (moving the student's desk away from others). In the second form of punishment, the disruption of classmates is followed by taking away the student's recess period. In both cases punishment has occurred only if the consequences following the inappropriate behavior result in a decrease in the rate of occurrence of that behavior.

Stimulus Control

Stimulus control refers to situations in which particular responses occur consistently after the presentation of a particular antecedent stimulus. The antecedent stimulus or event consistently evokes or cues a certain response. A response is more likely to occur in the presence of antecedent stimuli that were present when the response was reinforced in the past. A young child may smile and laugh whenever she sees Grandma coming because Grandma always hugs and kisses the child and then gives her a treat. In this case, the sight of Grandma serves as an antecedent stimulus, or cue, to the child that something pleasant will occur. A teacher may flick the lights on and off in her classroom as a cue for students to put away their materials and get ready to go home.

In stimulus-control procedures, antecedent stimuli may either set the occasion for a particular response or reduce the likelihood that the response will occur. A particular antecedent stimulus (S^D) is likely to cue a response that is consistently reinforced in the presence of that stimulus, as in the example of a young child and her grandmother. On the other hand, a response is likely to be suppressed when preceded by a particular stimulus (S^Δ) and then followed by withholding a reinforcer. If a student raises a hand in response to a teacher's question, but is never called on by the teacher, the student stops raising the hand. In this case, the teacher's question serves as an antecedent stimulus that cues the student that he is unlikely to obtain teacher attention by raising a hand.

In implementing stimulus-control procedures in the classroom, consistency is of the utmost importance. Many children quickly learn to manipulate situations in which there is inconsistency. Children learn to ask favors of the parent who is most likely to say yes. They often exhibit more inappropriate behaviors around those who are most tolerant and lenient. It is common for students to attempt to "bend the rules" with a substitute teacher or new student teacher. Inconsistency leads to confusion about the consequences of a particular response. We all know what to do when confronted with a red or green traffic light at an intersection. Further, most drivers understand the potential consequences of failure to respond appropriately to traffic signals. Imagine the confusion that would result if one day the traffic signal at the intersection changed from red to blue!

Students who do not follow the rules, fail to complete assigned work and who may be disruptive and/or aggressive are among the most difficult to include in general education settings. Many of these students come from home backgrounds that do not prepare them well for school. Many have met with repeated lack of success in school. For these students, the entire school environment may serve as a discriminative stimulus to exhibit maladaptive behaviors (Alberto & Troutman, 1990).

Teachers can use stimulus-control procedures in inclusive settings in determining the physical arrangement of the classroom, in providing verbal instructions and feedback, and in presenting instructional content. Here are some examples of how teachers can incorporate stimulus-control procedures into each of these components of the classroom environment.

The classroom can be arranged so that different physical features of the environment serve as discriminative stimuli. The teacher may place individual study carrels so that students are unable to observe each other. A class rule can state that seatwork is to be completed in the carrels with no talking. Students can raise their hands when finished or if they need teacher assistance. Other areas of the classroom may have a less formal arrangement. A sofa, table and chairs, or carpeted areas may be areas in which less formal behaviors such as quietly talking to peers, looking at magazines, or playing board games can occur. Many teachers use different areas, or stations, of the classroom for different instructional activities. A physical stimulus such as a timer or picture taped to the board may cue students that talking is or is not permitted.

The teacher may provide verbal instructions and feedback in such a way as to establish stimulus control. Verbal directions should be short, consistent, and specific. The teacher should specify what behavior is expected, under what conditions, and the consequences for compliance and noncompliance. An example would be, "Seth, sit at your desk and complete the math problems on page 42 of your book. If you finish before the period is over, you may play a computer game. If you don't finish the work, you will have to do it during your next break. Raise your hand if you need any help." This degree of specificity gives the student much more information about what is expected than, "Seth, get busy."

Finally, stimulus control may be established by instructional content. Schloss, Smith, and Schloss (1990) described a daily planner for use by students with disabilities. The planner included the assigned area and task for completion during each day. Such a device helps students to monitor their own time and performance. It is particularly useful with secondary-school-aged students because many adults use daily planners.

Many teachers present their students with instructional content in individualized folders. Folders may be color-coded to represent different academic subjects. The teacher may include task-analyzed instructions for assignments in the folders.

Alberto and Troutman (1990) suggested some novel ways for presenting instructional content. One example provided by these authors was to photocopy pages out of traditional texts and workbooks and then present them in smaller clusters or chunks of work. Many students find it easier to attend to and stay on task when smaller pieces of work are presented in this manner.

Modeling

One of the easiest and most natural instructional strategies to implement in inclusive settings is observational learning, or modeling. Modeling occurs when one learns new behavior by watching another person perform the behavior (Bandura, 1969, 1971, 1973). Many examples of modeling occur naturally in everyday life. A child watches her mother tie shoes and then tries to imitate the same steps. Students observe and try to imitate the behavior and dress of sports, music, and movie stars. A golfer watches a film of a professional to improve his swing.

There are some general guidelines for the use of modeling in the classroom. First, the teacher must specify the target behaviors to be taught through the use of modeling. Second, the teacher can arrange the instructional environment to facilitate modeling. Students who need to learn a new behavior may be grouped for instruction with those who have previously learned the behavior. Third, students should observe the models receiving reinforcement for appropriate behavior because modeling is strengthened when combined with reinforcement (Talkington & Hall, 1975). Fourth, a student should not observe another student achieving a desired outcome (e.g., escaping a nonpreferred task) through maladaptive behavior. A student can learn maladaptive, as well as adaptive, behaviors through modeling. Finally, the particular student selected to serve as the model should be highly regarded by the observer. The observer tends to imitate more the behavior of high-status models than the behavior of a model that the observer does not admire.

Generalization

Students with disabilities often have difficulty in generalizing responses to untrained situations. Teaching a student to use money at school, for example, is no guarantee that he will be able to use money in a store. The fact that a student has learned how to use a push button phone at home does not mean she can use any telephone encountered away from home.

Students with disabilities frequently demonstrate two types of difficulties in generalization. First, they often have deficiencies in stimulus generalization. Skills trained in isolation in school do not generalize to natural settings in the community because the stimulus characteristics vary between settings. The student who has learned how to cook macaroni and cheese at home cannot prepare the same dish at school. The cooking utensils, appliances, and physical arrangement of the two kitchens are different. Response generalization is another often observed deficiency in students with disabilities. Response generalization is the ability to perform related, but different, skills than those targeted for instruction (Stokes & Baer, 1977). For example, a student who learned to cook macaroni and cheese would then be able to prepare any similar boxed dinner even though not every type of boxed dinner was targeted for instruction.

Schloss, Smith, and Schloss (1987) recommended several strategies to promote generalization from school to community settings. First, stimulus materials, cues, and reinforcers used in school should be the same as those present in natural settings. In teaching money skills, for example, real money should be available to make actual purchases within the school. Functional sight words the student would encounter in natural settings (e.g., men, women, walk, poison, danger, exit) should be present in school exactly as they appear outside of school. Photographs can sometimes "recreate" the context in which a printed stimulus naturally occurs. The type of reinforcement and rate of reinforcement present in the natural setting may also be the same in the classroom.

Second, instruction can include multiple exemplars. Within this approach, the student learns stimuli and responses that are representative of the entire domain of skills in a particular area (Browder & Snell, 1993; Schloss, Alper, & Watkins, in press). The student who is learning to write her name can use a variety of writing utensils during instruction. She also learns to print and write in cursive. Teaching students to use the telephone to obtain information, dial for emergency help, or take messages can utilize several different telephone models. For cooking skills, the student receives instruction in the steps that one uses frequently in many different recipes.

Third, Schloss, Smith, and Schloss (1990) suggested that promoting the development of self-control skills enhances generalization from classroom to community settings. Teaching students to monitor and evaluate their own behavior facilitates independent functioning in the real world. Calendars, daily schedules, simple graphic displays, self-grading, and verbally discussing performance may all assist students in self-monitoring and evaluation.

Functional Analysis

O'Neill, Horner, Albin, Storey, and Sprague (1990) described an assessment process known as "functional analysis" that one may use to develop an effective behavioral intervention plan for students who exhibit challenging behaviors such as disruptive, aggressive, or self-injurious behaviors. Functional analysis has three major outcomes. First, an operational definition of the undesirable behavior is formulated. Second, the daily schedule is analyzed in an attempt to identify the times and situations in which the undesirable behavior is most likely to occur. Third, the function, or desired outcomes, obtained by the student as a result of exhibiting the maladaptive behavior are identified.

O'Neill et al. (1990) recommended several methods of collecting the information used to identify situational factors that are likely to produce challenging behavior. Talking to individuals directly involved in situations in which the challenging behavior occurs may yield information with which to identify consistent patterns of behavior. Systematic observations of behavior across several days and settings are important sources of information. Finally, the teacher may directly manipulate specific antecedent and consequent events (e.g., presenting difficult tasks, interrupting preferred activities, attention from specific individuals) in order to identify the conditions in which targeted behaviors are most likely to occur.

O'Neill et al. (1990) presented a functional analysis observation form for collecting this type of information. Using this form, teachers can record specific target behaviors and where and when they occur throughout the day, antecedent and consequent events, and the perceived functions of challenging behaviors (e.g., the maladaptive behavior allows the student to obtain a desired outcome or escape an undesired event).

Summary

The focus of this chapter has been on behavioral principles of learning. The chapter included a brief historical perspective of behaviorism, a discussion of applied behavior analysis, and a review of some basic principles of learning based on the behavioral perspective. Examples of how these principles may be applied to students with disabilities in inclusive education settings were provided.

Instructional strategies based on applied behavior analysis constitute an effective instructional technology. These strategies are effective with students with and without disabilities. They are often implemented naturally in day to day life and can be implemented by students as well as teachers. Teachers skilled in the use of these techniques are able to analyze the learning principles in operation in specific situations, reduce the occurrence of maladaptive behaviors, and teach more appropriate and functional prosocial responses.

References

Alberto, P. A., & Troutman, A. C. (1990). *Applied behavior analysis for teachers: Influencing student behavior* (3rd ed.). Columbus, OH: Charles E. Merrill.

Baer, D. M., Wolf, M. M., & Risley, T. R. (1968). Some current dimensions of applied behavior analysis. *Journal of Applied Behavior Analysis, 1,* 91–97.

Bandura, A. (1969). *Principles of behavior modification.* New York: Holt, Rinehart, & Winston.

Bandura, A. (1971). Analysis of modeling processes. In A. Bandura (Ed.), *Psychological modeling: Conflicting theories.* Chicago: Aldine-Atherton.

Bandura, A. (1973). *Aggression: A social learning analysis.* Englewood Cliffs, N.J.: Prentice-Hall.

Kazdin, A. E. (1978). *History of behavior modification: Experimental foundations of contemporary research.* Baltimore: University Park Press.

Kazdin, A. E. (1982). *Single-case research design: Methods for clinical and applied settings.* New York: Oxford Press.

O'Neill, R. E., Horner, R. H., Albin, R. W., Storey, K., & Sprague, J. R. (1990). *Functional analysis of problem behavior.* Sycamore, IL: Sycamore.

Schloss, P. J., & Smith, M. A. (1994). *Applied behavior analysis in the classroom.* Boston: Allyn & Bacon.

Schloss, P. J., Alper, S., & Watkins, C. (In press). A template approach for teaching cooking skills to youth with mental retardation. *Teaching Exceptional Children.*

Schloss, P. J., Smith, M., & Schloss, C. N. (1990). *Instructional methods for adolescents with learning and behavioral problems* (pp. 349–350). Boston: Allyn & Bacon.

Schultz, D. P. (1969). *A history of modern psychology.* New York: Academic Press.

Skinner, B. F. (1938). *The behavior of organisms.* New York: Appleton-Century-Crofts.

Skinner, B. F. (1953). *Science and human behavior.* New York: Macmillan.

Snell, M. E. (1993). *Instruction of students with severe disabilities.* New York: Macmillan.

Stokes, T. F., & Baer, D. M. (1977). An implicit technology of generalization. *Journal of Applied Behavior Analysis, 2,* 349–367.

Talkington, L. W., & Hall, S. M. (1975). Relative effects of response cost and reward on model on subsequent performance of EMRs. *The Journal of Developmental Disabilities, 1*(2), 23–27.

Ullmann, L. P., & Krasner, L. (1969). *A psychological approach to abnormal behavior.* Englewood Cliffs, N. J.: Prentice-Hall.

Ullmann, L. P., & Krasner, L. (Eds.). (1965). *Case studies in behavior modification.* New York: Holt, Rinehart & Winston.

Watson, J.B. (1919). *Psychology from the standpoint of a behaviorist.* Philadelphia: Lippincott.

Watson, J. B., & Rayner, R. (1920). Conditional emotional reactions. *Journal of Experimental Psychology, 3,* 1–14.

Williams, R. L., Howard, V. F., Williams, B. F., & McLaughlin, T. F. (1994). Basic principles of learning. In E. C. Cipani and F. Spooner (Eds.). *Curricular and instructional approaches for persons with severe disabilities.* Boston: Allyn & Bacon.

Wolf, M. M. (1978). Social validity: The case for subjective measurement or how applied behavior analysis is finding its heart. *Journal of Applied Behavior Analysis, 11,* 203–214.

8

INTERACTING WITH NONDISABLED PEERS

SANDRA ALPER

Chapter Objectives

After completing this chapter the reader will be able to:

1. Discuss the components of social integration
2. Define social skills
3. Define friendships
4. Describe why social interactions and friendships are important for students with disabilities
5. Define social validation and describe how to use it with skills targeted for instruction
6. Describe how to incorporate skills necessary for appropriate social interaction with students without disabilities into curriculum in inclusive school settings
7. Describe several strategies teachers in general education settings can use to promote social interaction skills.
8. Describe some approaches that promote friendships between students with and without disabilities in inclusive settings

Key Terms

Adaptive behavior
Buddy systems
Cooperative learning
Culture of the school
Friendship

Social skills
Social interaction
Social norms
Social skills training
Social supports

Natural supports   Social validation
Peer tutoring   Subjective evaluation
Social comparison

As more school districts attempt to implement full inclusion, teaching students with disabilities skills that enable them to interact and develop friendships with their nondisabled age peers becomes critical. The goal of social integration is to develop supports that allow students with disabilities to participate in the same activities, communicate with, and develop friendships with students without disabilities (Grenot-Scheyer, Coots, and Falvey, 1989a). Efforts toward full inclusion that fail to emphasize social integration can result in misunderstanding, erroneous assumptions about students with disabilities, and perpetuation of segregation within school buildings and classrooms (Alper & Ryndak, 1992).

Sailor, Gee, and Karasoff (1993) maintained that promoting interactions and friendships between students with disabilities and their peers without disabilities requires the following elements: (1) systematically structured times to participate together in academic and leisure activities, (2) providing students with assistance in appropriately initiating, maintaining, and terminating interactions, (3) strategies to include students with disabilities in activities in which those without disabilities are engaged, and (4) positive models of interaction and ongoing communication.

The emphasis in this chapter is on teaching social interaction skills and fostering friendships in inclusive settings. First, social skills and friendships will be defined. Second, the critical need for students with disabilities to learn these skills is discussed. Third, the curriculum-content identification process for inclusionary educational settings as applied to social skills and friendships is discussed. Finally, specific strategies for teaching appropriate social responses and some general guidelines for promoting friendships will be described.

Definition of Social Skills

Social skills include a wide array of specific responses required to appropriately initiate, maintain, and terminate interaction with others (Snell, 1993). Schloss, Smith, and Schloss (1990) noted that social skills also include the ability to adjust to varying demands of different social contexts. They observed that social skills are situation specific; that is, social skills requirements may change from one situation to another, as well as within the same setting. For example, the teacher in one classroom may require students to always raise their hands before speaking, while another teacher in the same school may expect students to raise their hands before speaking during some activities but not in others. A student may be describing the activities she engaged in over the weekend, but if she goes on too long, her listeners may lose interest. Thus, students must learn to modify their responses as the demand characteristics of the social situation dictate (Schloss et al., 1990).

Haring and Ryndak (1994) noted the reciprocal nature of social skills. Social skills are responses that affect the behavior of another. A response such as, "Hey, how are you doing? Did you watch the game last night?" increases the likelihood that another person will respond in a particular way. Many persons with moderate to severe disabilities have extremely limited social skill repertoires. They often lack the social skills required to initiate and maintain a social interaction with another individual.

Falvey (1989) recommended that skills in the following areas be part of a social skills curriculum for students with disabilities:

1. Ability to discriminate between assertive, passive, and aggressive behavior, language, and voice tone and knowing which is appropriate in a specific situation.
2. Making positive choices and demonstrating a good self-concept.
3. Respect for others.
4. Discriminating between strangers, acquaintances, and friends.
5. Initiating appropriate social interactions.
6. Sharing places, interests, activities, thoughts, and feelings. (p. 134)

Friendship

Grenot-Scheyer, Coots, and Falvey (1989b) characterized friendship as "a bond between two individuals characterized by mutual preference for one another, a positive affective style, an ability to engage in social interactions, and to have interactions that last over a period of time" (p. 348). These authors made the distinction between friendship and popularity. They characterized popularity as being liked by many peers. They pointed out that some children (similar to some adults who are in the public spotlight) may be popular but have few close friends.

Importance of Teaching Social Skills

While social skills and friendship are familiar to us all, they are, at the same time, difficult to define (Falvey, 1989). These concepts may represent different things to different individuals. Despite these definitional difficulties, few would argue with the critical need for students with disabilities to learn social competence.

Inappropriate social skills may account for many negative outcomes for students with disabilities. Social skills deficits repeatedly result in lowered achievement in school, unsuccessful integration in school and community, placement in more sheltered, restrictive environments in the community, and loss of competitive employment (Greenspan & Schultz, 1981; Hagner, 1992; Schloss & Schloss, 1987;

Schloss & Sedlak, 1986; Snell, 1993). Clearly, the social skills deficits of many students with disabilities are major obstacles to full participation in school and the community.

In addition to the devastating outcomes resulting from lack of social competence, lack of social skills interferes with the formation of friendships with others. Newton and Horner (1993) drew the following conclusions after reviewing literature on social interactions of individuals with moderate to severe disabilities living in the community: (1) they have few friends and commonly experience social isolation and loneliness, (2) their social interactions with persons other than family members are of short duration, and (3) paid staff may be the sole source of social support for many individuals who experience disabilities. Clearly, improving the ability of students with disabilities to interact with their peers who do not experience disabilities is of major concern in efforts directed toward inclusionary education.

Berry (1987), in an essay on community living, contended that all people need close relationships with others. There can be no sustained relationships, he argued, unless they have common ground in some experience. The people who ultimately become our friends are often initially met because they share some mutual activity, set of beliefs, or cause with us. Thus, many people meet those with whom they develop friendships at work, during leisure or recreational activities, at church or synagogue, during meetings of specific interest groups, and so on.

Extending Berry's ideas to inclusive schools, if students with disabilities are to have meaningful relationships with their peers who do not experience disabilities, they must share activities and experiences, spend time together, and develop "common ground." Developing basic social skills is a prerequisite to this process.

The next sections focus on teaching students with moderate to severe disabilities the skills they need to interact with their peers without disabilities. First, the application of the curriculum content identification process (detailed in Chapter 3) to the area of social skills is discussed. Then, specific instructional strategies found to be effective in teaching social skills and some general guidelines for promoting friendships will be presented.

Applying the Curriculum Content Identification Process to Social Skills

There are three major processes (see Chapter 3) for identifying appropriate curriculum content in the area of social skills. First, an ecological inventory approach (see Chapter 2) identifies the priority functional needs of the student. Second, the educational team gathers information to determine the general educational settings and curriculum objectives taught in those settings that allow the student to learn new skills needed to participate more fully with peers. Third, the educational team negotiates annual goals for instruction in general educational settings and in the community. These processes as they relate specifically to the area of social interaction skills are discussed below.

Identify Priority Functional Needs of the Student

The ecological inventory approach (Brown et al., 1979) identifies the functional social skill needs of the student (see Chapter 2). The team then identifies specific settings in which students with and without disabilities may have opportunities to interact. These might be school settings including general education classrooms, the cafeteria, gymnasium, and hallways and nonschool settings where students attending the same school are likely to frequent, such as a pizza parlor, playground, or video arcade.

The team analyzes each setting to determine the specific activities engaged in and social skills required in that setting. Social validation identifies specific social skills targeted for intervention within each training setting. Social validation is the process used to (1) assess the functional significance for the student of the skills targeted for training, (2) evaluate the appropriateness of the instructional strategies, and (3) determine that the outcomes of the intervention are important in the student's daily life (Kazdin & Matson, 1981; Wolf, 1978).

According to Schloss et al. (1990), within the context of teaching social skills to students with moderate to severe disabilities, social validation involves asking the following questions:

1. Will learning the social skills targeted for training enhance the student's ability to interact with nondisabled peers?

2. Is there documented evidence showing the instructional strategies as effective in teaching social skills to other students with disabilities? Are they the least restrictive training procedures for improving acquisition, maintenance, and generalization of social skills? Are these instructional strategies useful in a variety of natural settings in school and the community without drawing negative attention from persons without disabilities?

3. Are the outcomes of the training program likely to allow the student with disabilities to interact with a variety of persons in the school and community? Will the social skills targeted for training lead to the development of friendships?

Social comparison and subjective evaluation (Kazdin & Matson, 1981) are two procedures that may be useful in establishing social validity. Social comparison involves observing nondisabled age peers perform activities and targeted skills in natural settings. An observer might note the type and frequency of social interactions between students without disabilities that occur during different activities in general educational classrooms, in the cafeteria, during an assembly, and in the hallways. Using these observations, the educational team prioritizes the social interaction skills that are absolutely required and used frequently for instruction to students with disabilities.

It is very important to prioritize the observed skills that students without disabilities perform during social comparison, particularly in the area of social interactions. Social skills are very complex. Some are directly observable, measurable, and always necessary. For example, responding appropriately to another student's greeting, ("Hi, Seth, how ya doing? Did you see the Bears game last night on TV?") is necessary to avoid negative attention. Other social skills, however, are more subtle and arbitrary. They may not be absolute requisites for appropriate social interactions to occur between students with and without disabilities. Examples include certain facial expressions, shaking hands, and maintaining eye contact. In addition, the appropriateness of these skills varies across racial and cultural groups (Misra, 1994).

Subjective evaluation prioritizes social skills. Subjective evaluation involves obtaining "expert" opinion relative to skills and acceptable performance criteria. Within the context of the present discussion, "experts" include peers without disabilities, parents, teachers, school-bus drivers, school administrators, playground supervisors, and others in the community. Interviewing these individuals may be informal, or their opinions may be more formal using ecological inventory survey formats (see Chapter 3).

Subjective evaluation is an important step to complete for at least two reasons. First, as previously mentioned, although some skills are "nice to have" and may allow others to judge one as having impeccable manners, they are not absolute essentials for appropriate social interaction to occur between students with and without disabilities. Second, teachers often have difficulty second guessing what skills other groups of people in natural settings consider important. While many slang words and phrases may be unfamiliar or frowned upon by teachers and parents, students who do not know these words may be ostracized by their peers.

Preferences of the student with disabilities are worthy of consideration. What activities does the student prefer? In what settings does the student like to participate? In what activities and settings would the student like to be able to participate? There are a number of techniques for ascertaining answers to these questions. The teacher may determine which activities and settings the student with disabilities prefers through verbal responses, observing preferred activities the student initiates during free time, allowing the student to visit a number of settings and then indicate verbally or through pictures to which she would like to return, and so on.

Identify Priority General Education Needs

In addition to the functional and age-appropriate social skills the student needs, there is a survey of the general educational curriculum and settings. The purpose is to identify any goals and objectives in the general education curriculum that might require adaptation to meet the needs of the student with disabilities. In addition, the educational team identifies specific settings students without disabilities frequent. Students with disabilities might access these settings to facilitate social interactions. These places might include the lunchroom, playground, hallways, library, and gym, in addition to classroom settings.

One of the commonly cited advantages of inclusive education is that students with disabilities have more opportunities for social interaction and developing friendships. We have also pointed out that simply placing students with and without disabilities in the same educational settings does not guarantee that social interaction and friendships will develop.

Hagner (1992), in a discussion of social interactions of coworkers with and without disabilities in supported employment sites, discussed the "culture" of the job site.

> *Each workplace has its own customs, traditions, and shared meanings that develop over time as workers spend time at work together and produce some collective product or deliver a service. These customs are referred to as the organizational or workplace culture. (p. 217)*

Extrapolating from Hagner's work, there exists a "culture" of the school (see, for example, Nisbet, 1992). Each school building has its own mascot, school colors, school song, special holidays, traditions, customs, and routines. For example, in one elementary school, students typically pass through the hallways as they move from classroom to lunch in straight lines and with no talking. In another building, students have permission to speak to each other and to adults as they move about the halls. In one high school, teenagers typically socialize in the parking lot and at fast-food restaurants adjacent to the school grounds before and after school and during the lunch hour. In another high school, students may not leave campus between classes or during lunch. Students must understand and follow the rules, customs, and routines of the school.

It is particularly important in the area of social interactions to know and consider the culture of the school in identifying general education curriculum content. This is true because many opportunities for social interaction, sharing activities of mutual interest, participating in group activities, and communicating with peers exist outside of the formal written curriculum and are separate from any specialized services or programs. Rather, people without disabilities rely upon a variety of natural supports (Nisbet, 1992) in their school, work, and other community environments in order to meet people, engage in social activities, and develop friendships. These natural supports are an integral part of the school culture.

Nisbet defined natural supports for students with disabilities of school age as those elements of the school program typically available to students who do not have disabilities:

> *Natural supports for school-age children with disabilities are those components of an educational program—philosophy, policies, people, materials and technology, and curricula—that are used to enable all students to be fully participating members of regular classroom, school, and community life. Natural supports bring children closer together as friends and learning partners rather than isolating them. (p. 183)*

The following program description illustrates Nisbet's definition of natural supports. In a sixth-grade classroom, the tropical rain forest became the theme around which many learning activities developed. The entire class brainstormed with the teacher and developed a list of activities to be completed. These included decorating the room as a rain forest for an art project, studying the ecology of the rain forest including wildlife and weather, studying the products derived from the rain forest that are beneficial to human beings, visiting a zoo and observing animals and birds whose natural habitat is the rain forest, calculating the economic costs of destruction of rain forests, and hosting a party for parents and another class where food products of the rainforest were refreshments. Students who varied in ability were in cooperative learning groups, and each group worked on specific projects. Within each group, individual assignments ranged in difficulty from drawing and coloring room decorations to writing research reports on medicines derived from vegetation in the rain forest.

After identifying objectives and settings within the general curriculum, the teacher considers identifying modifications in the objectives, activities, instructional materials, or physical settings that might better accommodate the student with disabilities. In the example of the class project, curricular modifications included matching particular responsibilities to specific student abilities and interests. Thus, while some students had major responsibility in computing acres of rain forest lost per minute, others were responsible for purchasing items at the grocery store for the party.

Negotiate Annual Goals

The final phase of the curriculum content identification process is to negotiate annual goals. The educational team agrees on which social skills objectives are of highest priority for a particular student for the year. Objectives may be from the general education curriculum (e.g., writing thank-you notes after a field trip), consist of blended objectives (e.g., participating in a cooperative learning group to plan a class party), or consist entirely of functional skills objectives (e.g., responding appropriately when greeted). Then, the teacher decides on the specific settings in the school and community for instruction in these objectives. Because opportunities for social interactions occur in virtually all settings, a variety of school and community settings are likely selections for instruction. It is extremely important to target more than one setting for social skills instruction so that social interaction skills learned in the classroom generalize to other school, home, and community settings.

Instructional Strategies

A number of instructional strategies have been successful in teaching social interaction skills to students with disabilities. Two specific approaches are described. First, instructional strategies based on applied behavior analysis have been successful in teaching specific targeted responses that allow students with disabilities to interact with their peers. Second, general suggestions for promoting friendships between students with and without disabilities will be addressed.

Principles of Teaching Specific Social Skills

Many students with disabilities have extremely limited social interactions with others because they lack socially appropriate skills and often exhibit inappropriate behaviors. These social skill deficits can result from a variety of factors, including limited intellectual abilities, lack of consistent social skills training, few opportunities to observe appropriate models, or histories of reinforcement of maladaptive behaviors.

Sugai and Tindall (1993) offer the following general considerations in teaching social skills:

1. The same instructional strategies apply to teaching both social and academic skills. One learns both prosocial and maladaptive responses in the same manner as any other behavior.

2. In order to be effective, social skill instruction must be consistent and ongoing. Opportunities for students to observe, model, and receive feedback on social interaction skills should occur repeatedly throughout the course of the day. The student must use these skills for learning to be efficient.

3. Social skills training should occur within the real-life context that requires the skills. Due to the slow learning rates and difficulties in memory and generalization experienced by many students with disabilities, teaching social skills within the natural situations that require them is necessary.

It is important to keep in mind the dual goals of any social skills training program (Snell, 1993). One must teach new, socially appropriate skills and, at the same time, extinguish inappropriate responses. Students may perform inappropriate behaviors (e.g., disruptive behaviors, noncompliance with requests, crying, or aggressive responses) in order to achieve some outcome. Donnelan, Mirenda, Mesaros, and Fassbender (1984) speculated that disruptive behaviors may serve a communicative function for students who have very limited communication skills. Carr and Durand (1985) demonstrated that as students learn functional communication responses the frequency of their disruptive behavior decreases. It is imperative that we teach a student what to do as well as what not to do.

A variety of effective and easily implemented instructional strategies are available with which to teach appropriate social skills. These strategies include modeling, reinforcement, rehearsal, and feedback. Each of these instructional techniques is briefly described here.

Modeling

Modeling, or observational learning, occurs when an individual observes, and then imitates, the behavior of another person (Bandura, 1969). Research has repeatedly demonstrated that even students with severe levels of mental retardation are capable of learning new behaviors by observing others perform particular responses and then imitating those responses. Modeling can be a particularly potent instructional strategy when paired with positive reinforcement. Students with disabilities can acquire socially appropriate behaviors by observing others gain positive reinforcement for those behaviors (Mercer & Snell, 1977).

A student can learn both appropriate and inappropriate behaviors through modeling. Many individuals who were abused as children grow up to repeat the pattern of abuse with their own children. One of the arguments against depicting violence on television is that some children may be more likely to imitate the aggressive behaviors they repeatedly view.

Teachers in inclusive settings can use modeling as an effective strategy for teaching prosocial responses. Schloss et al. (1990) suggested that teachers arrange situations so that the student with disabilities is likely to observe peer models exhibit socially appropriate behaviors and obtain rewards as a consequence. Other suggestions by these authors are to use high-status peers as models and to avoid situations in which maladaptive behavior results in a student accomplishing a desired outcome. These suggestions have important implications for instructional grouping and seating arrangements in the classroom.

Reinforcement Strategies

Schloss et al. (1990) suggested that verbal praise ("Ben, I liked the way you shared that toy with Jose."), physical contact (pat on the back), and gestures (A-OK sign, a smile) can all be effective social reinforcement in social skills training programs. Social reinforcers have several advantages in teaching new social responses to students with disabilities. First, they are easy and efficient to administer. Second, a number of different individuals, including special and general education teachers, therapists, students with and without disabilities, parents, and others in the community can efficiently use social reinforcers. Third, they are often natural consequences of appropriate social responses in a variety of natural settings, and, therefore, facilitate generalization of skills across people and settings. Finally, the student may continually use some inappropriate responses because they result in positive outcomes. For example, a student may have a tantrum because she has learned that tantrums always result in attention from adults. Social reinforcement is a natural and efficient means of providing the student with the attention she seeks contingent on more appropriate social responses.

Rehearsal

Schloss et al. (1990) recommend that rehearsing appropriate social behaviors, or role-playing, can be effective in teaching students with disabilities the positive consequences of appropriate behavior and the unpleasant consequences of maladaptive behaviors. By practicing, or rehearsing a particular set of responses, the student can learn alternative prosocial responses. Rehearsing appropriate social responses to specific situations is particularly effective when combined with modeling and reinforcement. For students with verbal and cognitive abilities, verbally labeling the desired responses along with the antecedents and consequences, in addition to labeling the consequences for inappropriate behavior, can also be effective.

Feedback

Providing the student with clear and consistent information about his or her performance during training is referred to as feedback (Gold, 1980). Feedback consists of reminding the student of the expected standard, or criterion for performance, in a given situation and letting her know how she is performing relative to that standard. ("Claire, if you want to play with the doll, ask me and I will pass it to you. If you grab toys from me without asking, I won't play with you.") Feedback can often assist the individual in modifying his or her own behavior.

Feedback is an effective and easily implemented instructional strategy. Any number of different individuals can use feedback, and it occurs naturally in a variety of natural settings. Because peers with and without disabilities and adults can use this strategy, one may easily implement it in the general education setting.

Breen (1992) conducted an exhaustive review of the behavioral research literature in the areas of social interaction and social integration. She grouped instructional methods for improving social interaction skills of students with disabilities into three categories. First, within the area of direct instruction (i.e., instructional strategies such as modeling, prompting, shaping), students learn social interaction skills within the context of adult or peer tutoring. Peer tutoring strategies, in which one student serves as the instructor for another, have been used to teach a wide variety of social and academic skills. Both students with and without disabilities can take turns serving as the tutor (Haring & Ryndak, 1994).

The second group of instructional strategies Breen noted was contextual interventions. Contextual interventions involve manipulating some aspect, or stimulus condition, of the nonphysical context in which the social interaction occurs. According to Breen, examples of contextual interventions include increasing information about disabilities (e.g., LaTonya cannot speak. This is how she will use her communication board to talk with us.), targeting group behaviors for reinforcement (e.g., a class movie and pizza on Friday for appropriate behavior in math class during the week), and assigning roles of status or power (e.g., group leader, teacher assistant) to particular students.

The third group of instructional strategies Breen found to be effective in increasing social interaction skills was manipulation of the physical environment, including altering materials, seating arrangements, or the setting in which an activity usually occurs.

Based on her review, Breen (1992) drew the following conclusions:

1. Both adult mediated and peer mediated strategies are effective in teaching social interaction skills; however, peer mediated strategies are more likely to generalize to untrained situations.
2. Strategies that target social interactions that the peer tutee initiated rather than the peer tutor are more effective relative to frequency and duration of social interactions that occur between students with and without disabilities.
3. Alternating the role of tutor and tutee within student dyads is effective.
4. Conferring a role of power or status on a student with disabilities can improve social acceptance and facilitate social interaction.

5. Peer networks (e.g., a member of the pep club who has several friends is given responsibility for acting as a special friend to a student with disabilities) can be effective in improving social integration and social interaction skills of students with disabilities.
6. Successful manipulation of group contingencies improve social interaction between students with and without disabilities.
7. Providing access to interactive materials that the student prefers can facilitate social interactions.
8. Teachers who use combinations of strategies to increase social interaction between students with and without disabilities have the greatest success.

Fostering Friendships

In addition to specific instructional strategies for use in teaching discreet social skills, the literature contains a number of suggestions for fostering friendships between students with and without disabilities (Falvey, 1989; Falvey, Brown, Lyon, Baumgart, & Schroeder, 1980; Haring & Ryndak, 1994; Stainback & Stainback, 1987; Strully & Strully, 1985). As the number of persons with disabilities who live and go to school in their home communities increases, family members, as well as researchers, have become increasingly interested in promoting friendships between students with and without disabilities.

Friendships serve a number of important functions for all people (Grenot-Scheyer et al., 1989b). First, they provide opportunities to practice and refine social and communication skills. Second, friendships are a source of nurturance and support. Third, they allow interaction with persons who share similar attitudes and preferred activities. Finally, one can learn new skills and interests from friends.

Stainback and Stainback (1987) identified a number of skills that are often associated with friendships. They urged professionals to foster these skills in students with disabilities in order to maximize their potential for developing friends. The authors discussed the following skills: (1) laughing, smiling, a soft touch, and other displays of positive interaction, (2) ability to convey a message to another, (3) good listening skills, (4) sharing objects and feelings, and (5) ability to participate in a mutually enjoyable activity with another individual.

Grenot-Scheyer et al. (1989b) suggested two areas for consideration in any attempt to foster friendships between students with and without disabilities. First, these authors highlight the importance of utilizing natural and age-appropriate settings, materials, and activities. Naturally occurring social and recreational activities in which age peers without disabilities frequently participate are available in any community. Students with disabilities can be given access to those settings in which their age peers normally congregate. Examples might include playgrounds, parks, swimming pools, snack bars, basketball courts, and so on. Students with disabilities and their age peers without disabilities need frequent opportunities to be together within the context of naturally occurring activities.

Second, Grenot-Scheyer et al. pointed out that friendships are typically based on mutually shared characteristics or compatabilities. Our friends are often people with whom we share some personal or professional similarity. These authors suggested that professionals emphasize and build on the *similarities* between students with and without disabilities (e.g., Jeff and Matt both enjoy basketball) rather than their *differences* (Jeff has mental retardation and a seizure disorder and Matt does not).

Implications

Grenot-Scheyer et al. (1989a; 1989b) discussed a number of implications for service providers that stem from teaching students with disabilities the skills required to interact with nondisabled peers and develop friendships. First, there needs to be a strong emphasis on providing students with disabilities access to the natural settings in school and the community that their peers without disabilities frequent. These authors (1989b) pointed out that serving students with disabilities in settings separate from nondisabled peers conveys the message that "They don't belong." (p. 354)

Second, the structure and organization of extracurricular activities, as well as academic activities, in school may require modification. Organizations and events that include only students with disabilities will perpetuate segregation, even if they acquire new functional skills. Grenot-Scheyer et al. (1989a) argued that the acquisition of functional skills alone will not ensure that students with disabilities will be able to fully participate in their home, schools, and communities.

Third, these authors (1989b) suggest that we may need to reevaluate the concept of independence. Teaching students with disabilities to function as independently as possible has always been an emphasis in the field of special education. But Grenot-Scheyer et al. (1989b) maintain that in our efforts to teach students with disabilities skills to function more independently, we may have overlooked the fact that all people need support and assistance from others. We need to foster interdependence as well as independence. Peer tutoring, the use of peer networks, student support groups, and special friends and buddies are all methods that incorporate the idea of one person helping another. Although adults usually organize and structure these methods at first, they can evolve into true friendships between students with and without disabilities over time.

Summary

The emphasis of this chapter has been on teaching students with disabilities the social skills they need in order to interact with their nondisabled age peers and to develop friendships. The chapter discussed the devastating outcomes of limited socially appropriate skills and the curriculum content identification process applied to the area of social skills. Also included were several instructional strategies that have been used successfully in teaching social skills along with some general suggestions for promoting friendships between students with and without disabilities.

References

Alper, S., & Ryndak, D. L. (1992). Educating students with severe disabilities in regular classes. *Elementary School Journal, 92*(3), 373–387.

Bandura, A. (1969). *Principles of behavior modification.* New York: Holt, Rinehart, & Winston.

Berry, W. (1987). Men and women in search of common ground. *Home Economics,* (pp. 112–122). San Francisco: North Point Press.

Brown, L., Branston, M. B., Hamre-Nietupski, S., Pumpian, I., Certo, N., & Gruenewald, L. (1979). A strategy for developing chronological age appropriate and functional curricular content for severely handicapped adolescents and young adults. *Journal of Special Education, 13*(1), 81–90.

Carr, E., & Durand, M. (1985). Reducing behavior problems through functional communication training. *Journal of Applied Behavior Analysis, 18,* 111–126.

Donnelan, A. M., Mirenda, P. L., Mesaros, R. A., & Fassbender, L. L. (1984). Analyzing the communicative functions of aberrant behavior. *The Journal of the Association for Persons with Severe Handicaps, 9,* 201–202.

Falvey, M. (1989). *Community-based curriculum: Instructional strategies for students with severe handicaps.* Baltimore: Paul H. Brookes.

Falvey, M A., Brown, L., Lyon, S., Baumgart, D., & Schroeder, J. (1980). Strategies for using cues and correction procedures. In W. Sailor, B. Wilcox, & L. Brown (Eds.), *Methods of instruction for severely handicapped students* (pp. 109–133). Baltimore: Paul H. Brookes.

Gold, M. W. (1980). *Try another way training manual.* Champaign, IL: Research Press.

Greenspan, S., & Schultz, B. (1981). Why mentally retarded adults lose their jobs: Social competence as a factor in work adjustment. *Applied Research in Mental Retardation, 2,* 23–38.

Grenot-Scheyer, M., Coots, J. & Falvey, M. (1989a). Integration issues and strategies, (pp. 321–343). In M. Falvey, *Community-based curriculum: Instructional strategies for students with severe handicaps.* Baltimore: Paul H. Brookes.

Grenot-Scheyer, M., Coots, J., & Falvey, M. (1989b). Developing and fostering friendships, (pp. 345–358). In M. Falvey, *Community-based curriculum: Instructional strategies for students with severe handicaps.* Baltimore: Paul H. Brookes.

Hagner, D. C. (1992). The social interactions and job supports of supported employees (pp. 217–239). In J. Nisbet (Ed.), *Natural supports in school, at work, and in the community for persons with severe disabilities.* Baltimore: Paul H. Brookes.

Haring, T. & Ryndak, D. L. (1994). Strategies and instructional procedures to promote social interactions and relationships. In E. Cipani and F. Spooner (Eds.), *Curricular and instructional approaches for persons with severe disabilities* (pp. 289–321). Boston: Allyn & Bacon.

Kazdin, A. E., & Matson, J. L. (1981). Social validation in mental retardation. *Applied Research in Mental Retardation, 2,* 39–53.

Mercer, C. D. & Snell, M. E. (1977). *Learning theory research in mental retardation* (pp. 226–256) Columbus, OH: Charles E. Merrill.

Misra, A. (1994). Multicultural diversity in families of students with disabilities, (pp. 143–179). In Alper, S., Schloss, P. J., & Schloss, C. N. (Eds.), *Families of students with disabilities: Consultation and advocacy.* Boston: Allyn & Bacon.

Newton, J. S., & Horner, R. (1993). Using a social guide to improve social relationships of people with severe disabilities. *The Association for Person with Severe Handicaps, 18*(1), 36–45.

Nisbet, J. (1992). *Natural supports in school, at work, and in the community for persons with severe disabilities.* Baltimore: Paul H. Brookes.

Sailor, W., Gee., K., & Karasoff, P. (1993). Full inclusion and school restructuring (pp. 1–30). In M. E. Snell (Ed.), *Instruction of students with severe disabilities.* New York: Macmillan.

Schloss, P. J., & Schloss, C. N. (1987). A critical review of social skills research in mental retardation. In R. P. Barrett & J. L. Matson (Eds.), *Advances in developmental disorders.* Greenwich, CT: JAI Press.

Schloss, P. J., & Sedlak, R. A. (1986). *Instructional methods for students with learning and behavior problems.* Boston: Allyn & Bacon.

Schloss, P. J., Smith, M. A., & Schloss, C. N. (1990). *Instructional methods for adolescents with learning and behavioral problems.* Boston: Allyn & Bacon.

Snell, M. E. (1993). *Instruction of students with severe disabilities.* New York: Macmillan.

Stainback, W., & Stainback, S. (1987). Facilitating friendships. *Education and Training in Mental Retardation* pp. 18–25.

Strully, J., & Strully, C. (1985). Friendship and our children. *Journal of The Association for Persons with Severe Handicaps, 10*(4), 224–227.

Sugai, G. M., & Tindall, G. A. (1993). *Effective school consultation: An interactive approach.* Belmont, CA: Wadsworth.

Wolf, M. M. (1978). Social validity: The case for subjective measurement-or how applied behavior analysis is finding its heart. *Journal of Applied Behavior Analysis, 11*, 203–214.

9

APPLICATION OF THE PROCESS TO ECOLOGICAL DOMAINS

SANDRA ALPER

Chapter Objectives

After completing this chapter the reader will be able to:

1. Discuss parallels between the ecological curriculum domains and curriculum for students without disabilities.
2. Identify skills in the domestic, community access, vocational, and recreation/leisure domains in which the students may receive instruction in inclusive settings.
3. Describe three approaches to teaching recreation/leisure skills.
4. Apply the curriculum-content identification process to the functional skill domains.
5. Discuss options for providing instruction in natural settings in the school and community.

List of Key Terms

Community Access
Community-based Instruction
Criterion of Ultimate Functioning
Discrepancy Analysis
Domain
Domestic Skills
Ecological Domains

Job Analysis
Next Future Environment
Recreation/Leisure Domain
Supported Employment
Transition
Work Domain

Certain aspects of day-to-day life are shared by all persons. These include activities that occur at home, in the community, at work, and during free time. Brown et al. (1979) referred to these "areas" as ecological domains. They recommended a systematic analysis of these four basic life domains to develop functional curricula for students with disabilities, an approach that was described in detail in Chapter 2.

The purpose of this chapter is to discuss the development of curriculum for inclusive settings in the areas of domestic, community access, vocational, and recreation/leisure skills. First, each of the four ecological domains will be briefly reviewed with examples of skills included. Second, an explanation of the importance of teaching skills within each of these domains will be provided. Third, the curriculum content identification process will be applied to the recreation/leisure skills domain. Fourth, strategies for grouping students to facilitate community-based instruction will be discussed.

Ecological Domains Common to General and Special Education

Teaching skills that students with disabilities require to participate fully in the community (i.e., to live, work, enjoy leisure time, and have access to a variety of community settings) affords many opportunities for participation in the same activities with persons without disabilities. This is because the ecological domains have parallels within the general education curriculum. The general education curriculum often includes courses that emphasize job skills (e.g., vocational and industrial education classes). Students without disabilities may take courses in home economics that emphasize managing and maintaining a home, social-sexual information, and consumer skills. Many students are required or elect to take courses in physical education that emphasize skills used in leisure time such as sports activities. Finally, students without disabilities obtain information in a variety of different classes that enables them to be participating, contributing members of their community. For example, they acquire skills necessary to be informed consumers and good citizens.

While many students with and without disabilities learn skills that fall under the four broad life domains of home, community, work, and leisure, the specific skills match the individual needs of each student. Falvey (1989) suggests that there are several considerations for targeting skills for instruction. First, one should analyze the particular settings and skill requirements of the student's home community. This is necessary because skills necessary to maintain a home, obtain and maintain a job, or engage in some leisure time activity vary across settings within the same community, as well as across communities. Second, one should consider the individual strengths and weaknesses of the student. Any adaptations for skill performance or materials that a particular individual may require get special attention. Third, one should explore preferences of the parents and student. It is important for parents, teachers, and the student to agree on what skills become targets for instruction. Fourth, one should identify the skills that chronological age peers who do not experience disabilities perform in a number of natural settings. Fifth, one should carefully consider the question of what the student's next least restrictive environment might be and the skills necessary in that setting.

Domestic Skills

Traditionally, the curriculum in domestic skills for students with disabilities has emphasized grooming, dressing, self-feeding and toileting, and basic housecleaning tasks such as making a bed or washing dishes (Eshilian, Haney, & Falvey, 1989). As more and more persons with disabilities have prepared to live in the community in their natural homes, group homes, or foster homes, however, educators have become aware that a broader spectrum of skills is necessary to function successfully in domestic environments. Currently, the emphasis is on skill areas in the domestic domain including social–sexual skills, home management, home care, and personal health care and hygiene (Eshilian et. al., 1989; Snell, 1993). Figure 9.1 includes an array of skills typical in the domestic domain.

Educational programs designed to result in acquisition, maintenance, and generalization in domestic skills are important for all students. These programs are particularly critical for persons with disabilities for several reasons. First, if persons with disabilities grow up without competence in this area, they are very likely to place heavy burdens on their family members, or they may have to move to more restrictive and costly settings. This problem worsens in situations in which the person with disabilities is an adult for whom care is given by aging parents.

Second, competence in the domestic domain can maximize an individual's chances of not only living in his or her home community, but in the least restrictive domestic environment within that community. For example, a person with disabilities who cannot perform simple household chores, interact appropriately with roommates or neighborhoods, or completely care for all her own personal hygiene needs may live in a group home with several paid professional staff. An individual who has learned to care for all personal care needs and, in addition, can clean, shop, cook, and interact appropriately with others is far more likely to live more independently, have fewer supervisors, and exercise more choice in day-to-day activities.

Third, competence in the domestic domain projects a positive image of persons with disabilities to those who are not challenged by disabilities (Eshilian et al., 1989; Falvey, 1989). The more frequently persons with disabilities openly perform normal day-to-day activities in their homes and communities, the more capable they appear to the general public. Gold (1972) referred to this phenomenon as the competence-deviance hypothesis. Gold maintained that when an individual with disabilities is observed performing a functional, normalized activity competently,

Social Interaction	Home Care	Home Management
1. Family/Roomates appropriate greetings communication skills sharing space and appliances sharing responsibilities following house rules making decisions together respect of others belongings respect of privacy acknowledgement of personal space knowing emergency procedures social skills/manners 2. Neighbors/Visitors appropriate greetings respect of property and privacy social skills/manners acknowledgement of personal space communication skills borrowing and lending skills 3. Friends telephone skills communication skills invitations to come over, meet social skills/manners planning foods/activities transportation time skills 4. Service Providers social skills/manners communication skills acknowledging personal space money skills time skills	1. Meals planning what to eat purchasing locating items storage preparation clean up 2. Eating skills table manners social skills communication skills basic skills 3. House Cleaning appropriate usage of materials acceptable level of performance how to perform each given task (i.e. dust, make bed, vacuum) 4. Laundry storage of clean clothes storage of dirty clothes using washer using dryer sorting clothes use of detergents and bleach ironing skills 5. Clothing daily care storage (hang fold) choice of what to wear (matching) purchasing size sewing repair 6. Yard Maintenance basic care (i.e. mowing, trimming hedges) removal of trash knowing where to store keep clean trash-collection day 7. Household Appliances appropriate use of safety measures storage	1. Choices decision-making skills natural consequences 2. Schedules/Routines following a schedule following through on tasks: responsibility ownership cleaning/maintenance sequence total home vs. personal space (?) natural consequences 3. Time reference to schedule concept of use of management of 4. Materials appropriate use of and following directions purchase of storage of maintaining and replacing 5. Organizations location of items sharing responsibilities establishing routines following a determined schedule 6. Use of Home Space safety of placement of items accessibility personal taste

FIGURE 9.1   Sample Skills in Domestic Domain

the public tends to focus on that person's competence and deemphasize the disability.

Community Access Skills

Having learned skills that allow persons with disabilities to live in normalized homes in the community is a necessary, but not sufficient, condition to become fully participating members of the community. These individuals need to have access to the same resources, facilities, and programs as persons without disabilities.

Snell (1993) identified two major areas of community access skills: mobility around the community and the use of community facilities. Traveling from place to place around the community involves a number of different means of transportation, depending on the size of the community. Riding a bus, taxi, or subway, walking from one location to another, crossing intersections and obeying traffic signs, and riding a bicycle are all examples of activities that fall in the mobility skill category. In addition, students with disabilities need to know what to do in the event that they become lost, need to ask directions, or require some type of assistance.

The age of the individual dictates use of facilities in the community. In general, the objective is to teach the student with disabilities to use the same generic community facilities as do chronological age peers. These facilities include parks, playgrounds, restaurants, stores, banks, grocery and convenience stores, public transportation and health care services. Figure 9.2 lists many of the skills for which a student with disabilities requires instruction within the community access domain.

Teaching students with disabilities to utilize generic resources in the community is critical if they are to remain in the least restrictive setting. This is particularly important as more and more persons with disabilities either remain in their home communities or return to the community from institutional settings. Gothelf (1987) pointed out that "an important component of successful community living is a flexible network of community resources consisting of educational, social, vocational, medical, commercial, and recreational resources" (p. 146). In order for students to fully participate in their schools and communities, they must use the same facilities in the same ways as persons without disabilities.

The use of community resources is one indicator of participation in the neighborhood. Although use of generic community resources does not guarantee social integration with those who do not have disabilities, it is one measure of integration in the community (Sherman, Frenkel, and Newman, 1984).

Keul, Spooner, Grossi, and Heller (1987) described a program in North Carolina for teaching persons with mental retardation to use community resources. The Community Resources Training (CRT) program these researchers developed had three major components. These were instruction in skills necessary for independent living in the community, training persons with mental retardation to use generic resources in the community, and involvement of parents and other family

A. Mobility

Bus: routes, times, payment/money skills, social skills
Taxi: phone skills: dialing and telephone book skills, payment/money
Friends: social skills, phone skills

B. Usage of generic community resources

Skills used in all domains: communication, money, transportation, social, time
1. Physician's office
2. Dentist's office
3. Public library
4. Post office
5. Public school
6. Grocery store
7. Convenience store
8. Public telephone
9. Shopping mall
10. Public school bus
11. Restaurants
12. Hotels
13. Laundromat
14. Gymnasium
15. Swimming pool
16. Extracurricular activities
17. Theaters
18. Bowling alley
19. Gas stations

FIGURE 9.2   Sample Skills Included in Community Access Domain

members in the instructional program. The Assessment of Independent Living Skills (AILS) developed by Keuhl, Spooner, Test, Heller, & Grossi in 1985 is the basis of the curriculum of the CRT program. This scale consists of eight clusters of skills including appropriate public behavior, grooming, social skills, use of transportation, use of sources of information in the community, leisure, time and money management, and use of generic community resources.

Vocational Skills

A number of follow-up studies of students with disabilities who have graduated from special education have revealed disappointing results in terms of postschool outcomes (Frank & Sitlington, 1993; Frank, Sitlington & Carlson, 1992; Halpern, 1990; Halpern & Benz, 1987; Hasazi, Gordon, & Roe, 1985; Mithaug, Horiuchi, & Fanning, 1985). These studies indicated that the majority of special education graduates were not adequately prepared to successfully work and live in the community. Rather, they have moved from school to sheltered and restrictive settings with little contact with persons without disabilities. They experienced exceedingly low wages that foster dependence on welfare, long periods of inactivity, few friends, and little opportunity for training that could lead to less restrictive settings (Bishop & Falvey, 1989; Frank & Sitlington, 1993; Halpern & Benz, 1987).

Several researchers in special education and rehabilitation have developed models of transition to result in meaningful outcomes for special education graduates, including remunerative work in competitive employment (Rusch, 1986; Rusch, Destefano, Chadsey-Rusch, Phelps, & Szymanski, 1992; Wehman & Moon, 1988; Wehman, Moon, Everson, Wood, & Barcus, 1988). Meaningful work is a valued aspect of life for most adults (Turkel, 1972). Work provides the economic ability to acquire desired items, provides outlets for meeting people and developing social interactions, structures our daily lives, helps us to formulate self-concepts, and allows us to become contributing members of society (Rusch, 1986).

The goal of teaching students with disabilities vocational skills is the same as that for their peers without disabilities. Vocational skill training should lead to competitive employment. At least three factors drive the goal of employment in competitive, rather than sheltered, job sites for persons with disabilities according to Bishop and Falvey (1989). First, the results of follow-up studies, such as those cited previously, led many special educators to the conclusion that traditional sheltered employment was a costly "dead end," with few opportunities for productivity. Second, researchers in the 1970s demonstrated that students, including those with severe disabilities, were capable of learning complex vocational tasks when appropriately trained (Gold, 1972, 1976; Bellamy, Horner, & Inman, 1979). Third, the trends toward normalization, social integration, and full inclusion are consistent with competitive employment.

Supported employment is the service delivery model through which students with disabilities are trained in competitive jobs. The Office of Special Education and Rehabilitative Services in 1985 launched a federal initiative to make supported employment the primary job training model for persons with mental retardation. Since then persons with learning disabilities, closed head injuries, mental illness, physical disabilities, and hearing and visual impairments have received services from supported employment programs. Supported employment has the following features (Rusch, 1986; Wehman & Moon, 1988):

1. Work produces valued goods or services.
2. Remuneration for work is minimum wage or more.
3. The job site employs workers without disabilities.
4. Opportunities for advancement exist.
5. A job coach accompanies the student to the actual job site in the community and provides training and support services as needed.
6. Ongoing support is readily available for as long as needed.
7. Interagency collaboration between special education, employers, vocational rehabilitation, and other adult service providers (case managers) is crucial.
8. An emphasis is on parent and family involvement.

The following components are common to supported employment programs:

1. There is identification of potential employment options in the job market in the local community, including jobs that are likely to exist in a number of different locations and that have a demand for new workers.
2. Specific jobs are task analyzed into on-the-job skills, social skills, and any functional, academic, or other job-related skills necessary to obtain and maintain the job.
3. Community-based training sites open at the workplace. The student receives employment skills training from a job coach.
4. After training, the student works in either the training site or a similar job site.
5. The employee gets ongoing training and support to ensure that he or she maintains the job and learns any new skills that might be required if the demands of the job change in any way (e.g., new equipment changes the way in which the work is performed, a new supervisor has different standards and expectations of employees).

Implications for Inclusive Educational Settings

The emphasis on supported employment programs that result in competitive employment for students with disabilities has several implications for inclusive education settings. First, vocational curriculum has to be functional. The skills taught are those that workers actually perform on the job. The job analysis, or task analysis of a specific job provides the basis for the curriculum. Classroom skills must be functional and directly related to the demands of competitive employment. Figure 9.3 presents a sample job analysis format.

Second, community-based training sites are critical. Students with disabilities (and many individuals without disabilities) can most effectively learn job skills only at the actual job site. Community-based training should occur on a regular basis, preferably every day. In addition to job skills, the teaching of skills that involve shopping, banking, social interactions, and use of public transportation should occur in the community as frequently as possible.

Third, direct and systematic instruction is necessary for teaching on-the-job and job-related skills. This includes behavioral objectives that are task analyzed into measurable and observable responses, procedures for data collection, instructional strategies that include shaping, prompting, reinforcement, and correction procedures.

Fourth, and perhaps most importantly, the collaboration of professionals from a variety of disciplines is necessary, including those in general education. It is extremely unlikely that any one discipline can achieve the outcome of competitive employment for students with disabilities. Professionals must begin to plan collaboratively for effective vocational training for students with disabilities long before graduation. The expertise of general educators needed in this process should focus on the social, functional, academic, and other job-related skills necessary to maintain employment.

Job Tasks (in prioritized order)
1. Punch in at time clock in office
2. Get job list from supervisor

Pick Up Grounds Daily Routine
1. Get black trash bags from storage house
2. Place trash bags in hip pocket
3. Get pick from storage house
4. Begin at entrance gate to apartment complex
5. Pick up trash around buildings A–Z in order
6. Take full trash bag to nearest dumpster
7. Tie bag
8. Place in dumpster

Trim Bushes
1. Get trimming list from supervisor; will tell which buildings bushes need trimming
2. Get hedge trimmers from storage house
3. Get trash bags from storage house
4. Go to apartment building on list i.e., Building C ___
5. Place trash bags in a pile in the grass
6. Take trimmers and trim bush so that new growth is cut off—new growth will be a lighter green than rest of bush
7. Continue trimming until bush is completely finished
8. Place trimmers by trash bags on the ground
9. Pick up trash bag
10. Open trash bag
11. Place trimmings in bag
12. Fill trash bag with all trimmings until bag is full
13. Take out list given by supervisor
14. Check off tasks that have been completed i.e., Building C ___
15. If bag is full, tie and place on nearest dumpster
16. Continue trimming until all bushes on the given list are completed and checked off
17. Make sure that every building is completed and is checked off

FIGURE 9.3   Sample Job Analysis Format

Recreation and Leisure Skills

Recreation/leisure time has been one of the most neglected areas of curriculum for students with disabilities until recently. This area has been deemphasized for the following reasons. First, academic, social, and communication deficits of these students were of a much higher priority than lack of recreational skills. Some educators took the position that recreation/leisure skills would be part of the curriculum only if time permitted. Second, because some students with disabilities have physical and motor difficulties, educators often assumed them to be unable to participate in many sports activities students without disabilities enjoy. Third, during the years in which students with disabilities primarily attended separate schools and classes, there were few opportunities for recreation/leisure activities. The exception to this situation was the Special Olympics program that the Kennedy family originated in the 1960s. While this program has many advantages including numerous opportunities for students with disabilities to participate in sports, it has not included opportunities for the participation of many students without disabilities.

Recently, there has been increased recognition of the importance of teaching students with disabilities to participate in integrated recreation/leisure activities at school and in the community. This awareness has been the result of at least two factors according to Falvey and Coots (1989). First, researchers have established that students with severe disabilities are able to learn and participate in functional and age-appropriate recreational activities (Bates & Renzaglia, 1982; Datillo, 1991; Schleien & Meyer, 1988; Schloss, Smith, & Kiehl, 1986; Voeltz, Wuerch, & Wilcox, 1982). Second, there is value in teaching students with disabilities appropriate behaviors to replace inappropriate responses. Recreation/leisure skills can serve as acceptable replacement behaviors.

Schleien, Green, and Heyne (1993) recommended that recreation/leisure curricula have a basis in best professional practices. According to these authors, best practices in integrated recreation are "founded on the belief that every individual has the basic human right to be fully included in typical recreational activities. The community has been identified as the least restrictive environment for recreation participation" (p. 536). Recreational activities in the community afford students with disabilities opportunities for social interaction as well as development of recreation skills. The authors identified the following best professional practices:

1. Individual needs assessments
2. Individual preference assessments
3. Activity selection guidelines
4. Collateral skill development
5. Environmental analyses
6. Adaptations
7. Ability awareness orientations and friendship training
8. Cooperative grouping arrangements
9. Behavioral teaching methods
10. Program evaluation (p. 536)

Approaches to Recreation and Leisure Programs

Schleien and Green (1992) described three approaches to developing integrated, community-based recreation/leisure skills programs for students with disabilities. They contended that while recreation programs that serve only students with disabilities are preferable to no recreation/leisure program at all, the development of socially integrated programs is most desirable.

Integration of Generic Recreation Programs

Within this approach, a student who has disabilities indicates preferences for recreation activities from among the traditional, age-appropriate activities that already exist in the community. Next, special education and general education professionals work together to identify any discrepancies between the skill requirements and environmental constraints of the activity and the capabilities of the student. Finally, the educators develop and use strategies to accommodate student participation in the activity despite the skill deficits and environmental demands. Examples of such strategies are partial participation (i.e., the student participates in some but not all steps involved in the activity), adaptation of materials or equipment, peer tutoring, cooperative learning groups, or revision of the way in which the activity is performed.

The integration of generic recreation programs approach has several advantages over segregated programs according to Schleien, Green, and Heyne (1993). These include the opportunity for social contact, utilization of generic programs that exist within the community, and development of skills required for participation in age-appropriate recreation activities that by many students without disabilities enjoy. A major disadvantage is that the very strategies designed to enable the student with disabilities to participate in the activity may call undo attention to his or her differences and attract negative attention from others.

Reverse Mainstreaming

The second approach to developing integrated recreation programs in the community is reverse mainstreaming. Within this approach, which some Special Olympics programs have adopted, educators make efforts to attract students without disabilities to activities originally established for students with disabilities. First, they identify the needs and interests of students without disabilities relative to recreation/leisure activities. Then, they make modifications to the program to attract the interest of and maintain participation by individuals without disabilities.

Advantages of this approach include opportunities for social interactions and friendships. Students with disabilities stay in the same programs to which they may have grown accustomed and in which they feel comfortable. Schleien, Green, and Heyne (1993) noted several disadvantages to the reverse mainstream approach. Among these are the sporadic, rather than ongoing, nature of the program and the difficulty in attracting large numbers of students without disabilities into programs originally designed for those with disabilities.

Zero Exclusion

The newest approach to developing integrated, community recreation/leisure-time programs that serve all students is the zero exclusion approach (Schleien & Green, 1992). Within this approach, special and general education professionals collaborate to design, develop, and implement new programs that will attract and serve all interested students regardless of ability level. This is the most inclusionary of the three approaches Schleien and Green (1992) describe.

The zero exclusion approach to recreation programs requires a commitment from educators, as well as the larger community, to serve all students within one program. It avoids duplication of services often found in dual service delivery systems, that is, separate services for different groups of people, and can be cost-efficient as a result. The need for programs using this approach grows as more and more students with disabilities are enabled to live, go to school, and work in the same community settings as those without disabilities.

Schleien, Green, and Heyne (1993) observed that zero exclusion programs are not free of disadvantages. These programs typically have higher initial start-up costs. In addition, they may generate fears among some parents and professionals that segregated programs will be either eliminated or "watered down" as a result of decreasing revenues.

We have reviewed the areas of domestic, community access, vocational, and recreation/leisure skills, the ecological curriculum domains that have parallels in the general education curriculum. The content of each of these domains was described along with the critical need for these skills to be learned by students who have disabilities. A detailed description of specific instructional strategies for each curriculum domain is beyond the scope of this text. The interested reader is referred to the excellent and comprehensive discussions of teaching strategies found in Falvey (1989), Snell (1993), and Cipani and Spooner (1994). In the next section of this chapter, the curriculum content identification process is applied to the recreation/leisure skill domain.

Application of the Curriculum Content Identification Process to the Recreation and Leisure Domain

Several key characteristics of activities should be stressed when developing curriculum for students with disabilities in the recreation/leisure domain. First, activities must be functional. Schleien, Green, and Heyne (1993) recommended that to develop the palmar grasp, for example, the student should engage in functional activities such as riding a bicycle or throwing a Frisbee.

Second, recreational activities should be age-appropriate and attractive to peers without disabilities. As in all areas of curriculum for students with disabilities, there must be many opportunities for social interaction and friendship. The recreation/leisure domain offers many naturally occurring opportunities in which students with and without disabilities may share mutually enjoyable activities.

Third, recreational activities students with disabilities learn should be readily accessible and ongoing. Activities that occur infrequently (e.g., a skiing trip, a float trip) are enjoyable, but unlikely to be part of a regular routine due to cost or availability. If they are the only recreational activities available, there will be few opportunities for participating in recreation and interacting with peers.

Finally, selection of recreation/leisure activities should be based on the students' choice of activities. By definition, leisure time is freedom from activities of which the individual has little or no choice. Having the freedom to engage in the activity makes it enjoyable and increases the probability that it will become part of a regular routine. Some students with disabilities have limited choice repertoires due to lack of exposure or experience with certain activities. Nevertheless, educators should make every effort to allow students to express preferences for leisure pursuits.

The first step in the curriculum-content identification process is to gather information to identify functional recreation/leisure needs of the student. Information from a variety of sources, including community and family is necessary. Table 3.3 in Chapter 3 (Community Inventory Worksheet) is useful to survey the community and determine what generic recreational opportunities are available. Figure 9.4 illustrates how this format can assess the availability of community recreational activities for a twelve-year-old-student with mental retardation and challenging behaviors such as verbal and physical aggression.

A. Resource: Bowling Alley—Oakland Lanes
   Location   2116 Vandiver
   Activities: bowling, roller skating, pool tables, video games, snack bar
   Clientele: older adults, middle-aged adults, younger adults, college students,
                         teenagers, children
   Dress Code and Average Dress: shirt and shoes required, pants/shorts, socks, shoes (either
                                    own bowling shoes or rental for bowling participation
   Hours: M–F, Saturday, and Sunday hours
                         open 10:00 a.m., closed between hours of 11 p.m. and 2 a.m.
   Travel: approximately 15 miles round trip
   Accessibility: ramp to the door, level flooring, ramp to bowling lanes,
                         no automatic doors

B. Resource: Swimming pool—Albert-Oakland Pool
   Location: 1900 Blue Ridge Road
   Activities: swimming, diving boards, laying out in the sun, bring own
                         games from home, pool games (i.e., tag, Marco Polo)
   Costs: youth
                         teen
                         adult
   Clientele: high to low SES, older adults, middle-aged adults, younger adults,
                         college students, teenagers, youth, infants
   Dress Code and Average Dress: bathing suits, wraps, (change of) casual clothes, sandals or
                                    tennis shoes, bathing cap, goggles, floatation devices
   Hours: Monday—Sunday
   Travel: approximately 10 miles to and from
   Accessibility: ramps, level concrete to pool (has reservoir along edges), steps and ladders
                         to get in and out of pool from edge, ladders to reach diving board, changing
                         and shower and restroom area is accessible

Continued

FIGURE 9.4   Community Inventory Worksheet Domain: Leisure Skills

C. Resource: Gymnasium (Campus)
   Location: UMC campus
   Activities: indoor track for walking, jogging, running, wheelchair accessible, basketball, volleyball, racquetball, tennis, weight lifting, stationary bike and stepper, aerobics, mats available for exercise (i.e., sit ups, push ups, warm-up exercises, wall exercises), spectator area for sitting and watching games, badminton, paddle ball, handball
   Locker Rooms: showers, restrooms, saunas, lockers, changing area
   Cost: $5.00 for pass, student's enrolled use student I.D.
   Clientele: students, professors, teenagers, youths
   Dress Code and Average Dress: sweats, tee shirt, shorts, socks, tennis shoes
   Hours: 6:00 a.m.–12:00 midnight
   Travel: approximately 6 miles
   Accessibility: ramps, elevators, locker rooms, bathrooms, weight room

D. Resource: Nature Trail
   Location: Stadium Blvd.
   Activities: walking, jogging, running, biking
   Cost: free
   Clientele: older adults, middle-aged adults, younger adults, college students, teenagers, youths, infants
   Dress Code and Average Dress: Sweats, tee shirt, shorts, tennis shoes
   Hours: dawn till dusk (daylight)
   Travel: approximately 4.5 miles

E. Resource: Shopping mall
   Location: Stadium Blvd.
   Activities: using money skills to purchase goods, comparison shop, play video games, purchase food, walk, socialization, theater, restaurant
   Cost: variations in the items looked at (purchased or free) to free entertainment through socialization with peers
   Clientele: older adults, middle-aged adults, younger adults, college students, teenagers, youths, infants, high to low SES
   Dress Code and Average Dress: casual to formal dress
   Hours: 9:00 a.m. (mall-walkers) 10:00 A.M.–9:00 P.M.
   Travel: 2.5 miles
   Accessibility: easily accessible, ramps, even flooring, racks at even height, turn easily

F. Resource: Arcade
   Locations: Mall and downtown
   Activities: video games, pinball, SkeeBall, prize machine
   Cost: $0.25 tokens for arcade games, some games require $.50 in tokens
   Clientele: adults, college students, teenagers, youths
   Dress Code and Average Dress: casual dress, shirt and shoes required
   Hours: mall hours: 10:00 A.M.–9:00 P.M.
                      downtown: 10:00 A.M.–9:00 P.M.
   Travel: mall: 2.5 miles
                      downtown: 8 miles
   Accessibility: even flooring, may be difficult to maneuver a wheelchair when crowded, machines screen and buttons may not be accessible to all heights and types of wheelchairs, ability to walk to machines is possible, spacing is adequate to play machine without interference

FIGURE 9.4   *Continued*

The next step in the curriculum-content identification process is to gather information to identify general education curriculum needs. The General Education Curriculum Content Worksheet can be helpful here. The activities and objectives in the general education curriculum and other settings enter the inventory. An example of a completed worksheet for the twelve-year-old student is Figure 9.5.

After one identifies the functional and general education goals, a blending of both content areas may occur to establish the final annual goals and the education settings. Schleien (1993) described a discrepancy analysis procedure that blends functional and general education recreational skills content. This process analyzes recreational activities in which students without disabilities engage at school and in the community into the component steps necessary to complete the task. Then, one notes discrepancies in performance between students with and without disabilities. Finally, one identifies any necessary adaptations of the task or materials that will allow the student with disabilities to participate in the task. Figure 9.6 describes the completion of this procedure for a student with disabilities.

Facilitating Community-Based Instruction

This text emphasizes the importance of teaching functional skills in the settings in which they naturally occur. Teaching in natural settings is necessary because many students with disabilities have difficulties in performing skills learned in one setting in other, untrained settings. Because of these generalization difficulties, there is no guarantee that students will be able to perform skills learned in the classroom in any other setting.

The natural setting for many skills includes the classroom and other environments within the school. School settings provide many naturally occurring opportunities for students to perform social interaction skills; functional money, time, and measurement skills; and functional reading tasks. Many skills falling under the domestic, vocational, community-access, and recreation/leisure domains, however, normally occur outside of school settings. Educators are then faced with the need to provide instruction in nonschool settings, while at the same time, meeting the needs of students remaining in the classroom. Two examples follow.

Austin is a ten-year-old student with severe mental retardation. He is able to communicate verbally using short phrases and can feed himself. His mother is a working single parent who has two younger children. The family usually has dinner at a fast-food restaurant two nights each week. Austin's mother would like him to learn how to order his meal, find a place to sit down, and eat dinner without assistance.

Alicia is sixteen years old and has moderate mental retardation and a seizure disorder. Her family wants Alicia to be able to work in competitive employment. There is a job-training site for Alicia in the kitchen of the local hospital. Alicia will need to spend two hours each school day at the hospital kitchen with her job coach. The hospital is located approximately three miles from her school.

Expected Outcomes	Components Relevant	Settings and Activities for Application		
		General Education	Home	Community
Skill: Putting models together Integration: work with peers Can be an individual activity that gives them time to themselves Can be a small group or peer activity that can facilitate use of communication skills	Eye-hand coordination Age-appropriateness Shopping skills Money skills Social skills Communication skills Decision-making skills	Math skills Consumer skills	Communication skills with family, peers Time to spend by self Quiet leisure time Social skills	Interaction with peers without disabilities Shopping skills Money skills Social skills Transportation skills
Skill: Video/arcade games Integration: Interaction with peers without disabilities in the community Can be performed at home setting	Transportation to arcade in community Eye-hand coordination Money skills Social skills Communication skills Age-appropriate activity	Social skills Communication skills Money skills Problem solving techniques	Communication skills Social skills engaged individually or with family member	Interaction with peers without disabilities Social skills Money skills Communication skills
Skill: Swimming Integration: Lessons with peers without disabilities Activities performed and practiced in the community	Swimming skills learned and developed in swimming lessons: floating, kicking, armstrokes, breathing	Extracurricular activities Swim team	Communication with family and peers Exercise/fitness routine Parties (birthday)	Oakland Pool Twin Lakes Camping or float trips Vacationing

FIGURE 9.5   General Education Curriculum Content Worksheet

Targeting Settings for Instruction

Selecting appropriate settings for instruction is as important as identifying the necessary functional and age-appropriate skills. Instruction for some skills (e.g., writing a name) can be provided almost entirely within the classroom. Instruction in other skills may occur in both classroom and community settings. Austin may work on using money in the classroom and school cafeteria, as well as in fast food restaurants. Still other skills are appropriately taught only in the natural community setting in which they occur, as in the case of operating a dish washing machine in a hospital cafeteria. These skills are difficult or impossible to recreate or simulate in the school setting. In addition, the materials and persons (e.g., supervisors and coworkers) present in the work site will not be present at school.

Determining the Amount of Time Allotted for Community Training

Brown et al. (1979) and Sailor et al. (1986) argued that time spent in community-based training settings should increase as students with disabilities become older. This is because as chronological age increases, there is more emphasis on performing functional skills necessary to work and live in the community and less emphasis on academic skills. While elementary students may spend most or all of the school day in school, secondary students may be in community training sites for the majority of their instructional time.

In many secondary programs the goal is for students to be working full time in a competitive job site by the time they are high school seniors. This makes the transition from school to adult life in the community easier for students with disabilities and their families. Young adults with disabilities often require services that professionals from a variety of agencies offer. Many families find that these services are easier to access and coordinate while the student is still in school.

Shared Responsibilities

Community-based instruction requires teamwork and cooperation. All involved must meet simultaneously the needs of students remaining in the classroom and those receiving instruction in community sites. Educators must carefully consider how to group students for instruction in nonschool settings and who will provide instruction.

Most authorities agree that instruction in any one community-based setting should be provided to small groups of students or, in some cases, on an individual basis (Snell, 1993). Two to four students may receive instruction from one adult. Small, heterogeneous groups of students may be formed. One student who requires a great deal of the teacher's time may be part of a group in which all the oth-

Name: Jasper L.

Domain: Leisure

Environment: Community

Subenvironment: Skate town

Activity: Roller skating and appropriate interaction with people in the community

Directions: Read the steps in the ecological inventory on the left and use the System of Least Prompts to collect data on which steps can be done: I (Independently), M (through Modeling the behavior), V (with Verbal assistance), T (with a Tactile cue), or H (with Hand-over-Hand assistance). Mark the level of assistance needed to perform the step in the middle column. Identify a teaching procedure, adaptation, or strategy to increase the independence level or partial participation of the individual when performing that step in the right column.

1. Enter the skating rink.	I	1. No adaptations needed.
2. Wait in line to pay for admittance.	I	2. No adaptations needed.
3. Give the cashier the correct amount of money using the next dollar strategy.	V	3. Needs practice on using the next dollar strategy across all situations/settings.
4. Smile, use appropriate gestures and language with cashier and counter attendant.	I	4. Good greeting skills, needs practice saying "Thank you" and "excuse me" when necessary
5. Remove shoes, give to counter attendant, and state correct skate size.	V	5. Practice going to the skating rink more. Student was unfamiliar with the nature of the skating rink.
6. Take skates and find appropriate place to sit.	I	6. No adaptation needed.
7. Put on and lace up skates.	I	7. Motor problems make this time consuming, but he can still do independently.
8. Skate over to rink on carpet.	H	8. Just needs practice skating and prompting to let go of counters, walls, and staff.
9. Enter rink appropriately.	H	9. Needs practice entering rink, holds onto rails and staff.
10. Skate on rink appropriately.	H	10. Practice skating and encourage to let go of wall.
11. Remain calm during falls.	V	11. Stick to behavior plan, practice skating, leave rink, if necessary.
12. Interact appropriately with others.	V	12. Model and practice.
13. Get off skating rink appropriately.	H	13. Practice skating and getting off rink without staff assistance. Encourage to let go of wall, rails. This step becomes more difficult when he is angry.
14. Unlace skates and return to attendant. Receive shoes from attendant.	V	14. Practice routine to follow at rink. Follow behavior plan at all times.
15. Put on shoes.	I	15.
16. Exit skating rink.	I	16.
17. Follow staff instructions at all times.	V	17. Follow behavior plan, make clear to student that he will have to leave for inappropriate behavior.

FIGURE 9.6   Discrepancy Analysis

er students require less of the instructor's time. Many teachers stagger community-based instruction so that a few students are in the community with a teacher while another teacher or aide stays in the classroom.

A number of different individuals may provide instruction in community-based sites. Teachers, related services personnel such as physical therapists, paraprofessionals, peer tutors, volunteers, practicum students, and student teachers may provide instruction. Individuals without disabilities who are normally in the community setting (e.g., a coworker on a job site, a child in the playground, a clerk in a store) sometimes spontaneously provide assistance. It is extremely important to specify exactly who is responsible for providing instruction to the student before implementing community-based training.

Jorgensen (1992) presented a format for systematically analyzing instructional periods in inclusive schools and specifying activities that normally occur, what the student with disabilities is expected to do during the activity, and the exact responsibilities of any individual who provides support to the student. Jorgensen's format would be appropriate for use in community-based and school settings.

Transportation

The availability of reliable transportation is a major consideration in selecting training sites. Transportation between the school and community training sites may be provided in a number of different ways. Snell (1993) discussed the use of teachers' and paraprofessionals' private automobiles, assuming adequate insurance coverage, school bus or van, public transportation, and walking.

Safety Issues

Parents and school officials often express several concerns in the planning phases of community-based instruction. Concerns about students getting lost or kidnapped, insurance coverage in case of injury in the community, and how the general public will treat students with disabilities are common. Students can get instruction on what to do if lost or in need of assistance. Students with disabilities may receive training in how to ask for assistance, call 911, and show a laminated ID card. Staff involved in community-based instruction can get training in emergency medical procedures. Some teachers have "shadowed" their students in the community by having them unobtrusively observed by individuals unknown to the students. This can be a very effective method to periodically assess the degree of safety and capabilities of students in the community.

Snell (1993) suggested that school personnel check their insurance coverage before implementing instruction in the community. Parents must have complete information about community instruction, and they must give permission in writing.

While the general public may, at times, ridicule or tease students with disabilities the reverse situation is also true. Educators involved in community-based instruction often observe many individuals who are helpful and friendly to students with disabilities.

Summary

The emphasis in this chapter has been on developing curriculum content for students with disabilities in areas that parallel the general education curriculum. These areas, or domains, are domestic, community access, vocational, and recreation/leisure. These areas of the curriculum are important for several reasons. First, they include the functional skills that are necessary for students with disabilities to learn to live, work, and recreate in normal community-based settings. Second, they increase the level of competence of students with disabilities in many of the same life activities that all people perform. Viewing students with disabilities perform competently can result in more positive attitudes held by persons without disabilities. Finally, because these curriculum domains have parallels in general education, they offer increased opportunities for social interaction between students with and without disabilities.

References

Bates, P., & Renzaglia, A. (1982). Language instruction with a profoundly retarded adolescent: The use of a table game in the acquisition of verbal labeling skills. *Education and Treatment of Children, 5*(1), 13–22.

Bellamy, G. T., Horner, H., & Inman, D. (1979). *Vocational habilitation of severely retarded adults: A direct service technology.* Baltimore: University Park Press.

Bishop, K. D., & Falvey, M. A. (1989). Employment skills. In M. A. Falvey (Ed.), *Community-based curriculum: Instructional strategies for students with severe handicaps.* 2nd ed., (pp. 165–187). Baltimore, MD: Paul H. Brookes.

Brown, L., Branston, M., Hamre-Nietupski, S., Pumpian, I., Certo, N. & Gruenwald, L. (1979). A strategy for developing chronological age appropriate and functional curricular content for severely handicapped adolescents and young adults. *Journal of Special Education, 13*(1), 81–90.

Cipani, E. C., & Spooner, F. (1994). *Curricular approaches for persons with severe disabilities.* Boston: Allyn & Bacon.

Datillo, J. (1991). Mental retardation. In D. Austin & M. Crawford (Eds.), *Therapeutic recreation: An introduction* (pp. 163–188). Englewood Cliffs, NJ: Prentice-Hall.

Eshilian, L., Haney, M., & Falvey, M. A. (1989). Domestic skills. In M. A. Falvey (ed.), *Community-based curriculum: Instructional strategies for students with severe handicaps,* 2nd ed., (pp. 115–140). Baltimore: Paul H. Brookes.

Falvey, M. A., & Coots, J. (1989). Recreation skills. In M. A. Falvey (ed.), *Community-based curriculum: Instructional strategies for students with severe handicaps,* 2nd ed., (pp. 141–163). Baltimore, MD: Paul H. Brookes.

Falvey, M. A. (1989). Community-based curriculum: *Instructional strategies for students with severe handicaps,* (2nd ed.). Baltimore, MD: Paul H. Brookes.

Frank, A. R., & Sitlington, P. L. (1993). Graduates with mental disabilities: The story three years later. *Education and training in Mental Retardation, 28,* 30–37.

Frank, A., Sitlington, P., & Carson, R. (1992). Adult adjustment of persons with severe/profound mental disabilities: A longitudinal study. *Journal of Developmental and Physical Disabilities 4*, 37–50.

Gold, M. (1972). Stimulus factors in skill training of the retarded on a complex assembly task: Acquisition, transfer, and retention. *American Journal of Mental Deficiency, 76*, 516–526.

Gold, M. W. (1976). Task analysis of a complex assembly task by the retarded blind. *Exceptional Children, 43*, 78–84.

Gothelf, C. R. (1987). The availability of community resources to group homes in New York City. In R. F. Antonak & J. A. Mulick (Eds.), *Transitions in mental retardation: the community imperative revisited,* (Vol. 3, pp. 146–164). Norwood, N.J.: Ablex.

Halpern, A. (1990). A methodological review of follow-up and follow-along studies tracking school leavers from special education. *Career Development for Exceptional Individual, 13*(1), 13–27.

Halpern, A., & Benz, M. (1987). A statewide examination of secondary special education for students with mild disabilities: Implications for the high school curriculum. *Exceptional Children, 54*, 122–129.

Hasazi, S., Gordon, L., & Roe, C. (1985). Factors associated with the employment status of handicapped youth exiting high school from 1979 to 1983. *Exceptional Children, 51*, 455–469.

Jorgensen, C. M. (1992). Natural supports in inclusive schools. In: J. Nisbet (Ed.), *Natural supports in school, at work, and in the community for people with disabilities* (pp. 179–215). Baltimore: Paul H. Brookes.

Keul, P. K., Spooner, F., Grossi, T. A., & Heller, H. W. (1987). The community resources training program: A collaborative program between the University of North Carolina at Charlotte and Goodwill Industries of the Southern Piedmont. In R. F. Antonak & J. A. Mulick (Eds.), *Transitions in mental retardation: The community imperative revisited,* (Vol. 3, pp. 183–201). Norwood, N.J.: Ablex.

Keul, P. K., Spooner, F., Test, D. W., Heller, H. W., & Grossi, T. (1985). *Assessment of Independent Living Skills* (AILS). Unpublished manuscript, University of North Carolina at Charlotte, College of Education and Allied Professions, Charlotte, NC.

Mithaug, D., Horiuchi, C., & Fanning, P. (1985). A report on the Colorado statewide follow-up survey of special education students. *Exceptional Children, 51*, 397–404.

Rusch, F. R. (1986). *Competitive employment issues and strategies.* Baltimore, MD: Paul H. Brookes.

Rusch, F. R., Destefano, L., Chadsey-Rusch, J., Phelpes, L. A., & Szymanski, E. (1992). *Transition from school to adult life.* Sycamore, IL: Sycamore Publishing Co.

Sailor, W., Halvorsen, A., Anderson, J., Goetz, L., Gee, K., Doering, K., & Hunt, P. (1986). Community intensive instruction. In R. Horner, L. Meyer & B. Fredericks (Eds.), *Education of learners with severe handicaps* (pp. 251–288). Baltimore: Paul H. Brookes.

Schleien, S. J., Green, F. P., & Heyne, L. A. (1993). Integrated community recreation. In M. E. Snell (Ed.), *Instruction of students with severe disabilities,* 4th ed., (pp. 526–555). New York: Charles E. Merrill.

Schleien, S., & Green, F. (1992). Three approaches for integrating persons with disabilities into community recreation. *Journal of Park and Recreation Administration, 10*(2), 51–66.

Schleien, S., & Meyer, L. (1988). Community-based recreation programs for persons with severe developmental disabilities. In M. Powers (Ed.), *Expanding systems of service delivery for persons with developmental disabilities* (pp. 93–112). Baltimore: Paul H. Brookes.

Schloss, P. J., Smith, M. A., & Kiel, W. (1986). Rec Club: A community centered approach to recreational development for adults with mild to moderate retardation. *Education and Training of the Mentally Retarded, 21*(4), 282–288.

Sherman, S., Frenkel, E., & Newman, E. (1984). Foster family care for older persons who are mentally retarded. *Mental Retardation, 6,* 302–308.

Snell, M. E. (1993). *Instruction of students with severe disabilities* (4th ed.). New York: Charles E. Merrill.

Turkel, S. (1972). *Working.* New York: Pantheon.

Voeltz, L. M., Wuerch, B. B., & Wilcox, B. (1982). Leisure and recreation: Preparation for independence, integration, and self-fulfillment. In B. Wilcox, & G. T. Bellamy, *Design of high school programs for severely handicapped students* (pp. 175–209). Baltimore: Paul H. Brookes.

Wehman, P. & Moon, M. S. (1988). *Vocational rehabilitation and supported employment.* Baltimore, MD: Paul H. Brookes.

Wehman, P., Moon, M. S., Everson, J. M., Wood, M., & Barcus, M. (1988). *Transition from school to work: New challenges for youth with severe disabilities.* Baltimore: Paul H. Brookes.

Endnotes

1. The author acknowledges the contributions made by Nicole Werner and Michelle Meenahan in developing the figures presented in this chapter.

10

APPLICATION TO SPECIAL EDUCATION CURRICULUM AREAS WITH GENERAL EDUCATION PARALLELS

DIANE LEA RYNDAK　　　　*SARAH D. WEIDLER*

Objectives

After reading this chapter the reader will be able to:

1. Compare and contrast the content and curricular approach of traditional special education curricula and general education curricula in relation to oral and written language, motor skills, academic subjects, special subject areas, electives, and other special activities.
2. Define receptive and expressive communication, and give examples of each that students with moderate and severe disabilities demonstrate.
3. Describe how inappropriate or problematic behaviors of students with moderate or severe disabilities could have a communicative intent.
4. Define the differences between aided and unaided augmentative and alternative communication systems.
5. Describe the role of social interaction skills in curriculum content for students with moderate or severe disabilities.
6. Give two definitions of functional reading and writing.
7. Compare and contrast the constructivist and skills emphasis view of literacy attainment emphasizing how curricular content decisions would differ.
8. Describe the development of school discourse practices in general education in the areas of speaking, listening, reading, and writing.

9. Describe how general education teachers make curriculum content decisions in speaking, listening, reading, and writing.
10. Define and describe the content of adapted physical education, the content related to basic physical needs, and general education physical education programs.
11. Define and describe the mathematics, science, and social studies content traditionally included in special education curricula and in general education curricula.
12. Define and describe the special subject areas, electives, and other activities traditionally offered through general education programs versus special education programs, and explain why students with moderate or severe disabilities historically have not had access to these.
13. Provide examples of how, by using the curriculum content identification process discussed in Chapter 3, an education team can identify content from each of the general education curriculum areas that have parallels with special education curricula that is meaningful for a student with moderate or severe disabilities.
14. Provide examples of how an education team can identify functional activities for which a student with moderate or severe disabilities needs instruction, and how that instruction can occur within general education instructional activities across curriculum areas.

Key Terms

Adapted physical education	Institutional writing
Aided communication system	Language arts
Alternative communication system	Library/information use
Art education	Literacy
Augmentative communication system	Mathematics
Basic motor skills	Motor skills
Communication	Music education
Communication assessment	Nonsymbolic communication
Communicative intent	Oral and written language
Constructivism	Other activities
Electives	Physical education
Emergent literacy	Reading readiness
Explicit language	Receptive communication
Expressive communication	School discourse
Functional	Science
Functional reading	Social studies
Functional writing	Symbolic communication
Implicit language	Unaided communication system

Curriculum Areas with Parallels

There are a number of areas traditionally within special education curricula which have parallels within the general education curriculum. For instance, the majority of special education curricula include receptive and expressive language, writing, and reading (Ford, Schnorr, Davern, Black, & Kaiser, 1989b). These curricular areas are also in the general education curriculum but within the area of language arts (Vacca, Vacca, & Gove, 1991). This type of parallel can be drawn in relation to motor skills, academic areas, and special subject areas. This chapter describes curriculum content in areas for which parallels exist between traditional special education and general education curricula, and how curricular concerns in these areas can be addressed through the curriculum content identification process described in Chapter 3.

Oral and Written Language

According to Kaiser (1993) people communicate to share feelings, needs, or information. Oral and written language are the tools people use to communicate through either person-to-person interaction or written messages. Let's look at how educators traditionally have organized in special and general education curricula the skills a student requires to use oral and written language.

Traditional Special Education Content Related to Oral and Written Language

Because of the various needs of students with disabilities, educators traditionally have subdivided the skills oral and written language into numerous areas. While this division has been helpful when identifying the specific skills that a student either demonstrates or needs to develop, it frequently has led to fragmented instruction in isolated skills. One of the benefits of providing instruction within inclusive settings is the naturally occurring activities that demand the integration of instruction on communication skills, supporting either partial participation in, or independent completion of, general education activities.

Receptive and Expressive Communication
People interact through a combination of nonsymbolic and symbolic communication. According to Siegel-Causey and Wetherby (1993), communication is "a reciprocal interaction involving reception (i.e., understanding others' behavior) and expression (i.e., using behaviors to signal others)" (p. 296). When identifying curriculum content for a student with moderate or severe disabilities, education teams need an accurate picture of that student's abilities in relation to both recep-

tive (i.e., understanding of facial expressions, gestures, or verbalizations made by others), and expressive (i.e., effective use of facial expressions, gestures, or verbalizations to signal others) communication. Meaningful communication assessments, therefore, delineate the degree to which a student demonstrates both receptive and expressive communication skills. In addition Siegel-Causey and Wetherby (1993) state that meaningful communication assessments provide information on (1) the communicative forms used by a student, (2) the communicative functions of a student's behaviors, (3) the degree to which a student's behaviors are intentional, (4) the degree to which others read a student's signals, (5) the repair strategies a student uses, and (6) the capacity for symbols that the student demonstrates. Finally, a meaningful communication assessment describes and takes into consideration both the environments in which the education team completed the assessment and those in which the student has opportunities to interact with others.

In addition to behaviors that one typically interprets as attempts to communicate, students with moderate or severe disabilities sometimes exhibit problem behaviors that are not readily discernible as communicative in nature. Such behaviors may be (1) dangerous to the individual or to others, such as severe hitting; (2) mildly undesirable, such as drooling; or (3) functionally irrelevant, such as stereotypic behaviors (O'Neill, Horner, Albin, Storey, & Sprague, 1989). O'Neill et al. (1989) categorize the possible functions of problematic behaviors in two areas: (1) behaviors that obtain a desirable event or object, whether through internal stimulation or external stimuli, and (2) behaviors that allow avoidance of or escape from undesirable events, whether internal stimulation or external stimuli. Meyer and Evans (1989) categorize such problem behaviors as (1) social-communicative, (2) self-regulatory, and (3) self-entertainment or play. Regardless of how such behaviors are categorized, a meaningful communication assessment determines the communicative intent of each problem behavior (see O'Neill et al., 1989, for a detailed process for conducting a functional analysis of behaviors).

Traditional special education curricula emphasize skills needed to communicate more effectively in terms of both receptive and expressive communication. The scope and sequence of skills are in a developmental sequence through which students can demonstrate their understanding of others' signals and use behaviors to signal others. The main focus of current special education curricula is the development of receptive and expressive communication skills within functional situations (Mirenda & Smith-Lewis, 1989). This development occurs best through the use of communication within natural contexts, at times when communication is needed, and during activities during which communication is meaningful for a student (Halle, 1984; Kaiser, 1993; Siegel-Causey & Wetherby, 1993). Inclusive settings automatically provide meaningful activities, at naturally occurring times, in natural contexts, and with peers who have the receptive and expressive communication skills to interact effectively. Such settings, therefore, provide excellent opportunities for effective instruction of receptive and expressive communication skills.

Augmentative and Alternative Communication Systems
While most students communicate through verbal language, many students with moderate or severe disabilities require either augmentative or alternative systems to communicate effectively with others. According to Vanderheiden and Yoder (1986) augmentative communication systems use aids or techniques to supplement verbal communication skills, which a student already demonstrates. In contrast, alternative communication systems replace verbal communication for a student who does not demonstrate the capacity for verbal communication. According to Miller (1993) both augmentative and alternative communication systems can be either aided or unaided systems. An aided system requires the use of a device that is external to the individual and *aids* that person in communicating. An unaided system is one in which the individual does not use external devices but relies on the use of hand or body motions to supplant or supplement their vocal communication (see Table 10.1 for examples).

Because of the needs of some students with moderate or severe disabilities, special education curricula include the possible use of augmentative and alternative communication systems. A wealth of information is available on (1) deciding when an augmentative or alternative communication system is needed (Beukelman & Yorkston, 1989; Reichle, Mirenda, Locke, Piche, & Johnston, 1992), (2) identifying the best type of augmentative or alternative communication system (Miller, 1993; Reichle, 1991a), (3) determining the instructional sequence to follow when teaching the use of an augmentative or alternative communication system (Miller, 1993; Reichle, York, & Sigafoos, 1991), and (4) selecting effective instructional strategies to teach the use of an augmentative or alternative communication system (Miller, 1993; Siegel-Causey, & Wetherby, 1993; Sigafoos, Mustonen, De-Paepe, Reichle, & York, 1991). As with receptive and expressive communication, augmentative and alternative communication systems are most effectively taught within natural contexts, at times when communication is needed, and during activities in which communication is meaningful for a student (Kaiser, 1993; Siegel-Causey & Wetherby, 1993). Inclusive settings naturally provide these criteria (i.e.,

TABLE 10.1   Examples of Aided and Unaided Communication Systems

Aided Systems	Unaided Systems
Communication boards, books, or wallets	Facial expressions
Head light pointer	Gestures
Speech synthesizer	Pointing
Touch talker	Touching
Computer	Nodding or shaking head
	Sign language
	Speech

meaningful activities completed at meaningful times and in natural contexts) with peers who have the communication skills to interact with classmates who use an augmentative or alternative system.

Social Interaction

A second area into which oral and written language traditionally is subdivided in special education curricula is social interaction. Because receptive and expressive communication skills are not sufficient for socially acceptable interactions, special education curricula also have focused on the use of receptive and expressive communication skills during interactions. For example, there are skills and instructional strategies for (1) initiating, maintaining, and terminating interactions (Reichle, 1991b), (2) making spontaneous requests, informational statements, rejections, or communicative exchanges (Reichle & Sigafoos, 1991), and (3) interacting to build friendships (Schleien, Green, & Heyne, 1993; Snell & Brown, 1993).

Functional Reading: Receptive Written Communication

A third area into which special education curricula traditionally have subdivided oral and written language is functional reading, or the reception of written communication. Because of the learning characteristics of students with moderate or severe disabilities, reading complex written communication has not been seen as appropriate curriculum content. Instead, the emphasis has been placed on recognition of words considered to be "functional" for the student.

Special education curricula use the term *functional* in relation to reading in two ways. First, several curricula incorporate a list of words that are considered useful to most people (Gartland, 1990). Such lists may include: (1) signs found in the community (e.g., restroom, stop, walk, don't walk), (2) words found in the home (e.g., poison), (3) personal data (e.g., name, address, telephone number), and (4) words frequently used in written material (e.g., Dolch word list). A second interpretation of the term *functional* refers to the use of ecological inventories to determine the words that are most relevant and meaningful in an individual student's life, such as described in Chapter 2. In either case, the instruction of functional reading words traditionally has been separate from general education reading material and activities (Browder & Snell, 1993), instead of in conjunction with reading materials and activities for nondisabled peers.

Discussions about curriculum content for students with moderate or severe disabilities recently have begun to include such components as word attack skills, syllabication, comprehension, and word analysis (Browder & Snell, 1993). To date, however, these discussions have not related the curriculum content selected for instruction to the content being taught to nondisabled peers. When selecting reading skills to teach a student with moderate or severe disabilities in an inclusive setting, there should be strong consideration for the reading skills and vocabulary that the student's nondisabled classmates will be learning.

Functional Writing: Expressive Written Communication

The last area into which special education curricula traditionally have subdivided oral and written language is functional writing, or using written communication expressively. As with functional reading, functional writing also has two interpretations, with functional indicating either predetermined life skills that incorporate writing (e.g., completing job applications) or activities that are relevant and meaningful for a particular student's life (e.g., writing when the student has a specific purpose to write in relation to completing an activity) (Ford et al., 1989b). In addition, curricula for students with moderate or severe disabilities have begun to acknowledge the need for various modes of writing that allow students to communicate in written formats more independently (e.g., rubber stamp, typewriter, computer, touch talker with printed output) (Browder & Snell, 1993). Inclusive settings provide an endless array of activities during which a student with moderate or severe disabilities can respond meaningfully through written communication.

Traditional General Education Content Related to Oral and Written Language

In traditional general education curricula the skills necessary for effective oral and written language are within the area of language arts. No discussion of language arts, however, could commence without addressing and defining the underlying concept of literacy; that is, the ability to read and write. Literacy involves all the language arts—speaking, listening, reading, and writing. Along with thinking, these components of literacy all interrelate, developing simultaneously and interactively. Because of this, general educators do not teach the components of literacy as separate subjects. Students become literate through genuine opportunities to speak, listen, read, and write as opposed to completing contrived and isolated academic exercises.

This view of literacy reflects a "new view" of emergent literacy, in contrast to the "old view" of literacy as reading readiness (Strickland, 1990; Sulzby, 1985). Emergent literacy has no discrete beginning point, as it begins well before a child learns to read formally. Similarly, it has no discrete ending point. There is no hierarchy of skills to address because one assumes that speaking, listening, reading, and writing develop concurrently. On the other hand, proponents of the reading readiness view of literacy contend that a child must reach a certain level of mental, physical, and emotional maturity to profit from instruction. Most reading readiness programs assume that a hierarchy of reading skills exists and include activities to develop prerequisite skills, such as memory, and auditory and visual discrimination. Curriculum content and instruction, therefore, focus on "isolated skill development" in a predetermined sequence. For example, students master the smallest units of written language (i.e., letter recognition) before progressing to larger units (i.e., sight word recognition).

Teachers who follow a skill development model tend to be directive and view the learner as passively awaiting instruction. Learning becomes a teacher-to-student process, with the focus on teaching the building blocks of language arts. As a result there is a concentration on the *form* of language arts, such as letters, sounds, spelling, and punctuation, resulting in identification of curriculum content based on the developmental skills that students should acquire next in order to progress through the predetermined sequence of skills.

Recent research on literacy attainment, however, supports the view that reading readiness is not an appropriate way to conceptualize instruction for beginning readers and suggests emergent literacy as a developmentally appropriate view upon which to build instructional practice, curriculum development, and assessment (Teale & Sulzby, 1986). General education teachers who agree with the emergent literacy approach to language arts subscribe to a "constructivist" view of how literacy is attained and what curriculum content should be emphasized during language arts instruction to facilitate the development of literacy. Teachers who follow this constructivist model see learners essentially as active participants in learning; learners who are able to self-select tasks, and select and organize stimuli in order to accomplish those tasks. Learning, therefore, is a collaborative group process and emphasizes the effectiveness of a student's use of language (i.e., the ability to inform or persuade). Instruction in one area of language arts blends with instruction in the other areas because the goals of speaking, listening, reading, and writing overlap. Teachers who embrace such a holistic model view making decisions about what students should learn as an integral and natural part of instruction in which the routine activities of listening, speaking, reading, and writing serve as both instructional and assessment activities.

Effective teachers of language arts teach "school discourse" over and above a skills emphasis model which stresses the isolated, mechanical skills associated with speaking, listening, reading, and writing (Gee, 1985). The essence of special education instruction for students with moderate or severe disabilities is to assist in acquiring and using skills within real-life activities across settings and is consistent with the constructivist model of language arts instruction. General education classes, especially those whose teachers subscribe to constructivism and the concept of emergent literacy, provide numerous opportunities for effective instruction for students with moderate or severe disabilities through inclusion.

Listening and Speaking

Children begin life by expressing to parents meanings that arise out of immediate physical or psychological contexts. Such language is implicit because it relies on shared knowledge, feelings, opinions, and interpretation of emerging language. As children grow older, however, their audiences become more distant, less familiar, and less intimately connected with them. Their language must become more explicit if they are to make themselves understood to these less familiar audiences. Children must make clear their knowledge, desires, understanding of situations, intentions, reasons, and expectations of others.

School intensifies these communication demands. Students must learn to understand teachers speaking about topics unrelated to the immediate physical and psychological context of the classroom. As both a listener and a speaker, children must learn to deal with explicit language. In the middle and upper grades, "teacher talk" begins to take on the characteristics of prepared lectures, and students must deliver formal oral presentations. Such formal speech must be accurate, explicit, and concise.

Teachers help students make connections between listening and speaking by providing them opportunities to listen to language that is increasingly more explicit and to speak in situations where increasingly more explicit language is necessary for effective communication. Teacher-student conferences and students working cooperatively in groups on well-defined tasks offer excellent opportunities for the use of explicit language. When deciding what to teach in relation to listening and speaking, therefore, teachers must make effective communication the objective. By receiving feedback on their success in reaching this objective, students gain facility with the use of explicit language whether or not they are accustomed to hearing and using it outside of the school context. The emphasis general education teachers place on effective communication, while using increasingly more explicit language, is consistent with the instructional needs of students with moderate or severe disabilities. Inclusive settings that emphasize effective explicit language create unlimited opportunities for effective instruction of oral communication skills.

Reading and Writing

Children's involvement with written language follows a similar pattern as their involvement with oral language. Many children exhibit reading-like behavior long before entering school by recognizing print on familiar packages, advertising, or environmental symbols (e.g., McDonald's logo, the word *stop* on a stop sign). The first words that a child often recognizes are in books that parents share with their child dozens of times. Reading at this stage is recognizing print and relying entirely on context for the meaning of that print.

In the early grades, students learn that print has its own meaning. Parents and teachers provide early experiences with print where context suggests the correct meaning and supports word recognition. As students progress in school, the nature of the printed language they encounter changes with the context becoming less helpful and the topics less familiar. In the middle grades, written language takes on characteristics that one associates with published, edited writing, sometimes referred to as "institutional" writing (Stubbs, 1980).

As student readers encounter writing that is more institutional, their own writing develops the characteristics of institutional writing. Because writing and reading develop concurrently, students' writing experiences aid their reading comprehension. As both reading comprehension and writing skills develop, students learn that written language is accurate, explicit, and not redundant. When selecting curriculum content for reading and writing, effective general education teachers focus on the degree to which students demonstrate the ability to construct meaning from written language and to communicate effectively in writing. The degree to which students demonstrate these abilities dictate the curriculum objectives of instruction. This approach to identifying instructional objectives for reading and writing is consistent with the approach described in Chapter 3 for students with moderate or severe disabilities.

Essence of Teaching Language Arts

The essence of teaching language arts is not teaching isolated skills, such as diction in speech, auditory memory in listening, letter formation in writing, or print translation in reading. The essence of teaching language arts is helping students understand what they say, hear, read, and write, both to succeed in school and to communicate effectively throughout life. As such, the general education curriculum areas incorporated in language arts have the same focus as special education curriculum areas for oral and written language.

Motor Skills

Curriculum content related to the development of motor skills has the aim of teaching students to move effectively, feel comfortable in their movement, and enjoy movement during sports and leisure activities (Snell, 1993). Because of the delayed development of physical and motor skills that students with moderate or severe disabilities experience, the curriculum content incorporated into their instructional programs traditionally has been different from that of general education.

Traditional Special Education Content Related to Motor Skills

There are two types of programs through which educators traditionally expect students with moderate or severe disabilities to develop motor skills. The first type of program, adapted physical education, emphasizes participation in sports and leisure activities similar to, but markedly different from, those in the general education curriculum. The second type of program is rooted much more firmly in the physical therapy needs, occupational therapy needs, and physical development milestone discrepancies that each student demonstrates. While the purpose of each of these types of programs has been the development of physical skills for partial participation in activities, there has been little emphasis on participation with nondisabled peers in their naturally occurring activities.

Adapted Physical Education
The rules and regulations for PL 94-142 (reauthorized as the Individuals with Disabilities Act [IDEA] of 1990) in the *Federal Register* (1977) define *physical education* in the following manner:

> (i) *The term means the development of:*
>   (A) *Physical and motor fitness;*
>   (B) *Fundamental motor skills and patterns; and*
>   (C) *Skills in aquatics, dance, and individual and group games and sports (including intramural and lifetime sports)*
> (ii) *The term includes special physical education, adapted physical education, movement education, and motor development*

Students with disabilities traditionally have received physical education through segregated, adapted physical education programs (Winnick, 1990). Sherrill (1981) states that "all good physical education is adapted physical education" (p. 7) but goes on to define adapted physical education as a "comprehensive service delivery system designed to identify and ameliorate problems within the psychomotor domain" (p. 10) (i.e., motor and fitness performance). Winnick (1990) describes the curricular aim of an adapted physical education program as psychomotor development, with content goals including: (1) physical fitness, (2) motor development, (3) posture and body mechanics, and (4) community and sport-related activities.

Recent adapted physical education texts discuss both the implications of PL 94-142 (and IDEA) on the role of adapted physical education teachers and the option of providing consultant services to the general physical education teacher to meet the needs of students with disabilities within the general physical education class (Cratty, 1989; Sherrill, 1981; Winnick, 1990). These discussions, however, imply that consultant services, and the pursuant adaptations to curriculum and instructional methods, are appropriate only for students whose psychomotor needs can be totally met within that setting. The activities in these texts, therefore, still highlight segregated adapted physical education classes focusing on skill development and participation in sports. There is no clear discussion of the benefits of inclusion in general physical education classes for students with moderate or severe disabilities in these texts.

To date, the inclusion of students with moderate or severe disabilities in general physical education classes is occurring with collaboration and consultation for physical education teachers by special education teachers, physical therapists, and occupational therapists from a student's education team. The emphasis is on the student meeting his or her own objectives within general class activities. Those objectives focus on both functional objectives for the student (e.g., interaction with peers during activities, reach and grasp, range of motion) and some of the physical education objectives for the entire class. There should be no confusing, however, of participation in general physical education class with a student's needs and services in physical or occupational therapy.

Physical Development Needs
Many students with moderate or severe cognitive disabilities have concomitant physical disabilities which require physical therapy, occupational therapy, or concentration on basic motor movements that allow functional movement of body parts and mobility. According to Rainforth, Giangreco, and Dennis (1989) the development of motor skills follows specific sequences including: (1) head-to-foot (i.e., developing control progressively from the head, to the trunk, and then to the legs), (2) gross-to-fine (i.e., developing large body movements before refined body movements using fine motor control), (3) weightbearing-to-nonweightbearing (i.e., developing skills to prop up on arms before reaching and grasping), and (4) proximal-to-distal (i.e., development of control in the trunk before control in the limbs). These developmental sequences are critical to consider when helping students learn to move volitionally, to participate in functional activities such as feeding themselves or changing positions, to communicate, and to demonstrate cognitive skills through movement. For instance, any instructional activity, whether focusing on functional or general education curriculum content, must take into account a student's ability

in relation to trunk control, volitional movement, crossing midline, and reaching for, grasping, and releasing objects. If a student does not have the skills to perform such basic physical skills independently, then personal support or adapted equipment become essential for the student to participate in that instructional activity.

Traditional curriculum content for students with deficits in motor skills incorporates the development of basic motor skills through supported participation in functional and naturally occurring activities. Motor skills that are important for a student to acquire are those that help the student maintain good health and increase both immediate and future participation in inclusive environments (Rainforth et al., 1989). While conserving the focus on maintaining good health, curriculum content in inclusive settings must modify these emphases to increase participation with nondisabled classmates in general education activities in the classroom, school, and community.

Traditional General Education Content in Motor Skills

Physical education is concerned with teaching skills and knowledge, and developing attitudes, through human movement (Seaton, Schmottlach, Clayton, Leibee, & Messersmith, 1983). Sherrill (1981) stated that the

> *...major purpose of physical education instruction is to change psychomotor behaviors, thereby facilitating self-actualization, particularly as it relates to understanding and appreciation of the body (and the self) in motion and at rest.... it includes instruction in relaxation, opportunities for creative expression, practice in social interaction, and guidance in finding and developing one's leisure self. The outcome of such instruction should be a person who feels good about himself, has confidence in his movement abilities, and is self-actualizing in the psychomotor domain. (p. 9)*

To accomplish this outcome, Sherrill (1981) suggested that the physical education curriculum continuously adapt to meet the needs of each individual student, both with and without identified disabilities, to minimize failure and preserve ego strength. Williams (1989) supported this thought of fitting a physical education curriculum to the needs of the students during primary years.

The physical education program in elementary school curricula provides continuity in movement experiences for students through vigorous activity that uses large muscles for locomotor and nonlocomotor skills (Seaton et al., 1983) during play, exercise, games, sports, and dance. These experiences help students to (1) develop and maintain a suitable level of physical fitness, (2) become competent in management of the body and acquisition of useful physical skills, (3) acquire desirable social standards and ethical concepts, (4) acquire needed safety skills, (5) enjoy wholesome recreation, (6) acquire a desirable self-concept and effective self-image, and (7) derive personal and educational benefits from the program (Dauer & Pangrazi, 1975).

At the secondary level the physical education program should consist of health instruction, free and individual play activities, sports and games, relaxation, remedial and adapted activities, coeducational and corecreational activities, and, if possible, hiking, camping, and boating (Vannier & Fait, 1975). The American Alliance for Health, Physical Education, Recreation, and Dance (1978) stated that the most pressing problem for secondary programs to address was assisting students in developing the "skills and attitudes necessary for solving problems and coping with everyday stress." To help students develop these skills, many secondary programs have begun to emphasize more strongly life-long sports activities, such as cycling, camping, skiing, and golf (Seaton et al., 1983).

Throughout both elementary and secondary physical education programs the curriculum emphasis is consistent with the needs of students with moderate or severe disabilities. As the emphasis on the acquisition and application of skills within real activities with nondisabled peers increases, the importance of including students with moderate or severe disabilities in general physical education classes becomes clearer for immediate and life-long needs related to the development of physical abilities both in everyday activities and in sports and leisure activities.

Academic Subjects

Historically education programs have focused on the three Rs: reading, writing, and arithmetic. In more current history, education programs have added science and social studies to the basic academic subjects for every student. While some school districts consider other subject areas to be academic in nature, not all education programs agree, and not all students receive instruction in those subjects. For this reason, we do not include those subjects in this section. In addition, because there was a discussion of reading and writing in a previous section of this chapter, we will emphasize here mathematics, science, and social studies.

Traditional Special Education Content in Academic Subjects

As with general education programs, the cornerstone of academic content in special education programs historically has been reading, writing, and arithmetic. In a number of school districts, however, science and social studies have been added in a cursory or "watered down" fashion. The following sections describe the math, science, and social studies curriculum content found in traditional special education curricula.

Mathematics
Special education curricula consistently include the basic concepts of mathematics including: (1) grouping objects into sets, (2) ordering objects by characteristics (e.g., small to large), (3) counting by rote, (4) rational counting of objects, and (5) creating and comparing sets by using one-to-one correspondence (Browder &

Snell, 1993; Falvey, 1986; Ford, Davern, Schnorr, Black, & Kaiser, 1989a). When using a developmental approach to encourage mathematics skills, special education curricula focus on (1) numeral recognition and place value, encouraging movement to two, and possibly three, digit numbers; (2) addition and subtraction, encouraging sums to ten, and (3) estimation of quantities (Browder & Snell, 1993; Falvey, 1986; Ford et al., 1989a). These curricula suggest a combination of manipulatives and augmentative aides when students require such assistance, including manipulatives to count, a numberline, a calculator, place value cards, and computation sheets. Traditional special education curricula have two different foci, first on progressing a student as far as possible through the developmental sequence of mathematics skills (Resnick, Wang, & Kaplan, 1973; Spradlin, Cotter, Stevens, & Friedman, 1974), and second on assisting the student to function as independently as possible in situations where mathematics skills are necessary (Browder & Snell, 1993; Ford et al., 1989a).

A second area of mathematics that consistently is part of special education curricula is the identification and use of money (Browder & Snell, 1993; Ford et al., 1989a). For students who are unable to identify paper money and coins by name, curricula suggest match-to-sample strategies to facilitate independent completion of functional activities, such as purchasing items at a store, vending machine, or cafeteria. In addition, the use of adaptations (e.g., number line, calculator; money cards) are helpful in allowing students to be more independent during functional activities. As in other areas, the focus of instruction for students with moderate or severe disabilities is on the acquisition and use of money skills in naturally occurring situations that require those skills of a particular student. The more meaningful and motivating the situation is for a student, the more quickly the student will acquire new skills. In addition to using money to purchase items, several special education curricula include budgeting and banking skills. There is particular emphasis on these skills as students become older, with the emphasis focused on the skills they need to function as independently as possible in adult society. Budgeting the amount of a paycheck to ensure meeting all financial obligations and living needs becomes critical as a student enters the world of work and independent living. If the student does not acquire the skills for independent budgeting and banking, additional emphasis is necessary for developing adaptations, alternative strategies, and a support network to assist the student in functioning in the community (Ford et al., 1989a).

A third area of mathematics that consistently is part of special education curricula is time telling and time management. Ford et al. (1989a) recommended initial instruction on the use of environmental cues to signal the beginning and ending of routine activities, followed by the use of picture or symbol schedules for managing daily activities. As these skills develop, clock faces that represent the times when activities begin and end replace pictures and symbols on these daily schedules. Curriculum content on actual time telling progresses from telling time on the hour, to the half hour, to the quarter hour, to five minutes, and to the minute (Ford et al., 1989a; Snell, 1993). In addition, some special education curricula include functional use of a calendar (Snell, 1993). As with the basic math concepts, the focus of special education curricula is divided between following a specific developmental sequence and determining manners in which a student can function more independently in various environments.

Finally, some special education curricula include identification and use of telephone numbers. Basic mathematics skills of one-to-one correspondence and matching are critical for independent telephone use. The focus of instruction shifts, however, from these basic mathematics skills per se to their use during the functional activity of making a telephone call (Snell, 1993).

For each mathematics area included in special education curricula education teams identify the mathematics skills a student currently demonstrates, determine the mathematics skills that student needs to function more independently during specific activities, and consider that student's past learning rate and current chronological age. This information is used to balance the content of instruction between: (1) the next steps the student needs when following a development sequence and (2) the adaptations, supports, and augmentative aides that would allow the student to participate in activities more independently. Neither of these takes into account the curriculum content that is currently being taught to the student's nondisabled peers. Recent curriculum texts, however, have begun to discuss strategies for allowing students to partially participate with their nondisabled classmates during mathematics class (Schulz et al., 1991; Stainback & Stainback, 1992).

Science
Historically students with disabilities who receive services in general education rooms frequently either have gone to resource rooms during science class or have refrained from participating in science activities (Schulz, et al., 1991). One can assume, therefore, that students with moderate or severe disabilities have experienced little or no science education. For students with moderate or severe disabilities who have received services in self-contained rooms, the lack of science content in traditional special education curricula (Ford et al., 1989c; Snell, 1993) has done little, if anything, to encourage teachers to include science education in their instruction. Menhusen and Gromme (1976) hypothesized that teachers did not include students with disabilities in science education programs because they assumed that these students were not interested in science, that science was too difficult for them, and that they would break the equipment. With the advent of inclusion and instructional emphasis on manipulation of materials and participation with nondisabled classmates, special education texts on curriculum increasingly are providing suggestions for adapting both science education activities and instructional strategies (Schulz et al., 1991). Students with moderate or severe disabilities increasingly are receiving opportunities to acquire knowledge from science education curricula and to demonstrate other skills (e.g., social interaction, fine motor, organization) within science education activities.

Social Studies
As with science, social studies is a content area that has received limited emphasis in traditional special education curricula for students with moderate or severe dis-

abilities, though there has been some emphasis on social studies for students with mild disabilities. Instead, the belief that students with more significant disabilities need to know basic demographic information about themselves, their home, and their community has dictated the bulk of their social studies content. Specifically, focus has been on knowing facts such as their name, address, telephone number, birthdate, names of family members, and roles of key people at home, school, and in the community. Even this information has been part of other curriculum areas (e.g., functional writing, vocational skills, personal management). Little other social studies content has been part of the curricula for students with moderate or severe disabilities (Ford et al., 1989c; Snell, 1993), however, special education curriculum texts are beginning to include information on the adaptation of instructional activities and strategies in social studies (Schulz et al., 1991).

Traditional General Education Content in Academic Subjects

In addition to language arts, the other components general education curricula traditionally include are mathematics, science, and social studies. While there are a number of curriculum packages available in each of these areas, we address basic content across these curricula in the following sections.

Mathematics

The *Curriculum and Evaluation Standards for School Mathematics* (National Council of Teachers of Mathematics, 1989) established a broad framework meant to guide reform in school mathematics during the 1990s. This document has a theme of increased emphasis on conceptual development and mathematical reasoning at all grade levels and specifies that the mathematics curriculum should emphasize problem solving, communicating about mathematics, and making connections between math topics. The Council suggested that students (1) have hands-on experiences, (2) use manipulatives, calculators, and computers, and (3) work in cooperative groups. Figure 10.2 lists the content and curricular emphases recommended by the National Council of Teachers of Mathematics across grades kindergarten through four, five through eight, and nine through twelve.

Opportunities for instruction naturally occur for a student with moderate or severe disabilities when a general education mathematics teacher follows these guidelines and includes hands-on experiences, the use of manipulatives and computing tools, and cooperative groups throughout instructional activities. Such naturally occurring instructional opportunities are present across grade levels, regardless of the mathematical concept in the class activity.

Science

The goals of modern science education include the acquisition of knowledge, manipulative skills, intellectual skills, and investigative and objective attitudes. Science activities that employ techniques of inquiry and are activity-based help children to grow in oral communication, social studies, mathematics, and reading skills (Esler & Merritt, 1976; Lawson, Costenson & Cisneros, 1986). Additionally,

Grades Kindergarten through Four

Number

Number sense
Place-value concepts
Meaning of fractions and decimals
Estimation of quantities

Geometry and Measurement

Properties of geometric figures
Spatial sense
Process of measuring
Concepts on units of measurement
Estimation of measurements
Use of measurements
Use of geometry ideas

Operations and Computation

Meaning of operations
Operations sense
Mental computation
Estimation and reasonableness of answers
Selection of appropriate
   computational method
Use of calculator for complex computation
Thinking strategies for basic facts

Probability and Statistics

Collection and organization of data
Exploration of chance

Patterns and Relationships

Pattern recognition and description
Use of variables to express relationships

Instructional Practices

Use of manipulative materials
Cooperative work
Discussion of mathematics
Questioning
Justification of thinking
Writing about mathematics
Problem-solving approach to instruction
Content integration
Use of calculators and computers

Problem Solving

Word problems in a variety of structures
Use of everyday problems and applications
Study of patterns and relationships
Problem-solving strategies

Grades Five through Eight

Problem Solving

Pursuing open-ended problems and extended
   problem-solving projects
Investigating and formulating questions from
   problem situations
Representing situations verbally, numerically,
   graphically, or symbolically

Communication

Discussing, writing, reading and listening to
   mathematical ideas

Reasoning

Reasoning in spatial contexts
Reasoning with proportions
Reasoning from graphs
Reasoning inductively and deductively

Connections

Connecting mathematics to other subjects and the
   world outside the classroom

Connecting topics within mathematics
Applying mathematics

Numbers, Operations, and Computation

Developing number sense
Developing operation sense
Creating algorithms and procedures
Using estimation in solving problems and
   checking the reasonableness of results
Exploring relationships among representations of,
   and operations on, whole numbers, fractions,
   decimals, integers, and rational numbers
Developing an understanding of ratio, proportion,
   and percent

Patterns and Functions

Identifying and using functional relationships
Developing and using tables, graphs, and rules to
   describe situations
Interpreting among different mathematical
   representations

Continued

**FIGURE 10.2   Recommended Content and Curricular Emphases for Grade Levels
Kindergarten through Four, Five through Eight, and Nine through Twelve.**

Source: National Council of Teachers of Mathematics (1989) *Curriculum and evaluations standards for school mathematics*
(Report). Reston, VA: National Council of Teachers of Mathematics.

Algebra

Developing an understanding of variables, expressions, and equations
Using a variety of methods to solve linear equations and informally investigate inequalities and nonlinear equations

Statistics

Using statistical methods to describe, analyze, evaluate, and make decisions

Probability

Creating experimental and theoretical models of situations involving probabilities

Geometry

Developing understanding of geometric objects and relationships
Using geometry in solving problems

Grades Nine through Twelve

Algebra

Using real-world problems to apply theory
Using computer utilities to develop conceptual understanding
Solving equations and inequalities with computer utilities
Understanding the structure of number systems
Developing and applying matrices

Geometry

Integrating geometry across topics
Using coordinate and transformation approaches
Developing short sequences of theorems
Expressing deductive arguments orally and in sentence and paragraph form
Using computer-based explorations of two- and three-dimensional figures
Using three-dimensional geometry
Applying in real-world situations and modeling

Trigonometry

Using appropriate scientific calculators
Completing realistic applications and modeling
Understanding connections between right triangle ratios, trigonometric functions, and circular functions
Using graphing utilities for solving equations and inequalities

Functions

Integrating functions across topics
Understanding connections among a problem situation, its model as a function in symbolic form, and the graph of that function
Using function equations in standardized form as checks on the reasonableness of graphs
Constructing functions as models of real-world applications

FIGURE 10.2   *Continued*

students develop logical thinking about science processes, curiosity, and positive attitudes toward science.

Several science curricula have designs for addressing the present and future goals of science instruction. *Science and Technology for Children* (National Science Resource Center, 1987) is a curriculum package for grades one through six comprised of four units: (1) observing, measuring and identifying properties, (2) seeking evidence, and recognizing patterns and cycles, (3) identifying cause and effect and extending the senses, and (4) designing and conducting experiments. *Activities that Integrate Mathematics and Science* (AIMS) is a program meant to supplement and enrich already existing science curricula. It integrates mathematics and science in the elementary and middle school grades by involving children in activity-based problem-solving science activities. The instructional materials consist of paperback booklets, each containing at least twenty problem-solving activities that stress science and mathematics skills. *Project 2061* (American Association for the Advancement of Science, 1989) is a long-term effort designed to reform science education in grades K–12. Completion of this program was planned to occur in three phases. Phase I identified in their report *Science for All Americans* (American Association for the Advancement of Science, 1989) scientific literacy goals for all students in American schools (see Figure 10.3). The scientific literacy goals from Phase I now are providing the direction for the development of a specific curriculum during Phase II. Phase III then will involve experts in science education assisting school districts nationally to implement the new science curriculum in their schools.

While Phases II and III are near completion, many general education science teachers have incorporated the goals of modern science education (i.e., acquisition of knowledge, manipulative skills, and investigative and objective attitudes) into their science instruction. Science programs that include the use of manipulative activities are proving to be easily adaptable and especially effective for students with moderate or severe disabilities (Kartoaka & Patton, 1989). In addition, the emphasis on investigative attitudes provides numerous opportunities for instruction on problem-solving skills.

Social Studies

Traditionally, the social studies draw upon seven disciplines: history, geography, economics, political science, sociology, anthropology, and psychology. Students study people in the context of their environment in both the past and present. The combination of history, geography, and social sciences helps explain the events, individuals, and ideas that have produced both continuity and change in our world. Content from literature, art, music, and science also can stimulate social studies instruction (Barr, Barth, & Shermis, 1977; Jenness, 1990).

1. The Nature of Science
2. The Nature of Mathematics
3. The Nature of Technology
4. The Physical Setting
5. The Living Environment
6. The Human Organism
7. Human Society
8. The Designed World
9. The Mathematical World
10. Historical Perspectives
11. Common Themes
12. Habits of Mind

FIGURE 10.3   Recommended Science Literacy Goals for All Students

Source: American Association for the Advancement of Science (1989). *Science for all Americans: A project 2061 report on literacy goals in science, mathematics, and technology.* Washington, D.C.: American Association for the Advancement of Science.

There are three philosophical approaches to social studies instruction: (1) citizenship transmission, (2) social science, and (3) reflective inquiry. Although all three approaches emphasize the broad goal of citizenship education, they differ on how to achieve that end. When taught as citizenship transmission, social studies emphasizes the importance of instilling a basic commitment to the issues facing our country. When taught as a social science, it focuses on helping students understand the major concept of each social science discipline. When taught for reflective inquiry, social studies emphasizes the importance of motivating students to question, think, and evaluate information critically.

For the National Council for the Social Studies, Barr, Barth, and Shermir (1977) defined social studies as

> ...a basic subject of the K–12 curriculum that (1) derives its goals from the nature of citizenship in a democratic society that is closely linked to other nations and peoples of the world, (2) draws its content primarily from history, the social sciences, and, in some respects, from the humanities and science, and (3) is taught in ways that reflect an awareness of the personal, social, and cultural experiences and developmental levels of learners. (p. 251)

In 1989, however, the National Commission on Social Studies in the Schools called for reform in social studies education in their document *Charting a Course: Social Studies for the 21st Century.* Through this report the Commission recommended that history and geography be the center of social studies, without neglecting the other social sciences. In addition, the Commission recommended (1) a more challenging curriculum during the primary grades by adding more concepts, and (2) an inclusion of content across countries, rather than only the United States. Figure 10.4 summarizes the content recommended by the Commission for grades kindergarten through three, four through six, seven and eight, and nine through twelve.

As changes to social studies curricula occur, the philosophical orientation of every general education teacher will determine which philosophical approach will get emphasis in a given classroom (Barr et al., 1977). Regardless of the philosophy espoused by a general education social studies teacher and the degree to which the curriculum changes to reflect the Commission's recommendations, the goals of social studies instruction are consistent with the needs of students with moderate or severe disabilities. While students with moderate or severe disabilities do not require all the curriculum content, the education team can identify components of the curriculum that are relevant and meaningful for any specific student.

Special Subject Areas, Electives, and Other Activities

In addition to the basic academic subjects and physical education, most school districts offer some combination of special subjects, electives, and other activities. For example, in many elementary and middle schools all students receive instruction

Grades Kindergarten through Three

Introduce concepts from history and social
  sciences through concrete applications
    Time
    Space
    Family
    Community—first grade
    Change
    Location
    Diversity
    Power
    Trade-Offs
    Justice
    Holidays
Balance content about United States with equal
  content on other cultures & places

Grades Four through Six

United State history
World history
Geography

Grades Seven and Eight

Local history
Economics and political development of United
  States and changing relationships with other
  countries

Grades Nine through Twelve

World and American history and geography to
  1750
World and American history and geography
  1750–1900
World and American history and geography since
  1900
Two semesters in government, economics,
  sociology, or contemporary issues
Supervised experiences in community service

FIGURE 10.4   Recommended Social Studies Curriculum for Various Grade Levels.

Source: National Commission on Social Studies in the Schools (1989). *Charting a course: Social studies for the 21st century.* Washington, D.C.: National Commission on Social Studies in the Schools.

in art, music, and library/information use. As students progress through middle and high school, they increasingly may have access to elective subjects, such as wood shop, home and careers, auto shop, photography, drama, and keyboarding. In addition, many schools sponsor clubs (e.g., science club, chess club), projects (e.g., yearbook, student government, plays) and nonathletic extracurricular activities (e.g., trips, dances). Because the list of special subject areas, electives, and other activities offered by school districts could be endless, this section will cover only (1) those special subject areas that, when offered, traditionally are provided for every student, (2) a global category of electives, and (3) a global category of other activities.

Traditional Special Education Content in Special Subject Areas, Electives, and Other Activities

There are few special subject areas or electives that consistently have been part of traditional special education curricula for students with moderate or severe disabilities. Those that have been part of either written curricula or school programs are art, music, and library/information use. In addition, there have been few special events in which students with moderate or severe disabilities have participated systematically, other than segregated activities (e.g., school proms, special olympics).

Art

While including some form of art, special education programs historically have not incorporated an actual art education curriculum. Instead, Cox (1970) supports the use of arts and crafts activities as the most effective way to assist students with disabilities "adjust to learning situations," believing that participating in arts and crafts helps students feel good about themselves and their environment, and thus learn more during other activities. Krone (1978) believes that art is a means to communicate thoughts, feelings, wishes, and imaginings. As such, art-related activities encourage students with disabilities to express their thoughts or feelings, find enjoyment by being creative, and take pleasure in visual objects in their environment. In addition, special education programs traditionally have advocated that art-related activities assist students with disabilities (1) develop manual dexterity, hand-eye coordination, muscle control and patterns of movement, and perception, (2) learn to interact with others across settings by sharing materials and decision-making responsibilities, and discussing thoughts and feelings, (3) increase skills in concept development, problem solving, creative thinking, logical thinking, visual discrimination, and following complex directions, and (4) improve self-concept and control of their environment (Krone, 1978; Lindsay, 1972).

Art for students with disabilities more recently has progressed to the point of supporting the provision of instruction within general education art classes, rather than in special classes or in one-to-one sessions (Clements & Clements, 1984; Uhlin & De Chiara, 1984). In addition, the fields of art education therapy (i.e., use of art for remedial purposes for students with disabilities to improve the quality of their learning process) and art therapy (i.e., use of art for diagnostic purposes and assisting the student to meet emotional and psychological problems) have developed (Uhlin & De Chiara, 1984). Neither of these developments, however, have defined clearly an art education curriculum per se. Rather, they have described the use of techniques for adapting activities from the general art education program for students with various types of disabilities. Despite this lack of clarity of content, the National Committee on Arts for the Handicapped has been successful at drawing attention to art by individuals with disabilities through statewide Very Special Arts Festivals.

Music

As early as 1980 Graham and Beer advocated for the provision of music education for students with disabilities in general education classes with support from special education and related services. These authors state that only 15 percent of students with a disability received any type of music education at the time PL 94-142 was enacted and that only half of those students received music education from a certified music teacher. While these numbers have improved over the years, most research on the effectiveness of music education for students with disabilities focuses on students with mild-to-moderate disabilities (Schulz et al., 1991).

Music curricula for students with disabilities (Graham & Beer, 1980) traditionally have focused on using

> *...commercial "special education" recordings that directed the children through certain movements to music, usually at a rate of speed to which few students, handicapped or not, could accurately respond. The major part of all music education for the handicapped was on the elementary level, whereas handicapped children in the secondary grades were universally neglected or consciously excluded from music education experiences. (p. 13)*

While the majority of curricula for students with moderate or severe disabilities still do not include general education music content (Ford et al., 1989c; Snell, 1993), some curriculum textbooks for students with disabilities are beginning to provide instructional strategies and ideas for adapting activities to accommodate all students with disabilities in general education music classes. Schulz et al. (1991) suggested that all students with disabilities can benefit from inclusion in general education music classes across four areas: (1) music concepts, (2) mobility (i.e., gross motor skills), (3) related academic areas (e.g., language arts, listening, reading, communication, memory, fine motor), and (4) peer relations.

Library/Information Use

When reviewing curricula for students with moderate or severe disabilities it is apparent that the skills necessary for using a library or library information are not evident (Falvey, 1986; Ford et al., 1989c; Snell, 1993; Stainback & Stainback, 1992; Stainback, Stainback, & Forest, 1989). If considered, library/information use seems to be part of community-referenced instruction when it is a priority activity either during the student's leisure time or with family members, rather than part of the school-based curriculum. In addition, limited reference is made to the role of the librarian in educational programs for students with disabilities. When referenced, their role is limited to identifying high interest–low vocabulary reading material (Schulz et al., 1991), rather than either curriculum content itself or the instructional role of the librarian.

Electives and Other Activities

Historically, curricula for students with moderate or severe disabilities have not included courses that traditionally are electives for nondisabled students. For example, electives frequently offered in middle schools (e.g., home and careers, wood shop, computers) have not been available, especially on segregated campuses. In addition, the only special activities that segregated campuses have supported have been segregated special events, such as Special Olympics or prom. Because of the nature of the campuses, those who have attended these events historically have been either (1) only students with disabilities and adults from the school or (2) students and adults from the school and specific nondisabled peers invited for "reverse mainstreaming" purposes (i.e., bringing nondisabled students to segregated settings or activities specifically to provide opportunities for the students with disabilities to interact with nondisabled peers). No special education curriculum consistently has offered special activities such as those offered in the general education curriculum.

As students with moderate or severe disabilities moved into self-contained classes on general education campuses, few electives consistently have been options for them. This may have occurred either for safety reasons, lack of space and/or equipment, lack of prerequisite skills, or lack of consideration of the elective as a priority functional need. Additionally, few students with disabilities consistently have participated in special activities. As students with disabilities have been included in general education classes, however, their participation in electives and other special activities has increased, with education teams systematically considering each elective and activity for its potential benefit to a student.

Traditional General Education Content in Special Subject Areas, Electives, and Other Activities

There are three general education special subject areas that, when offered by a school district, are available to all students: art, music, and library/information use.

Art

The traditional general education art program has many purposes including: (1) promoting social, personal, and perceptual and conceptual development and (2) helping students understand and appreciate feelings, ideas, and values expressed through the major art forms (Clark & Zimmerman, 1981). Present art education programs follow the rationale that art is an essential and unique component of a complete general education curriculum and thus requires regularly scheduled instructional time and careful attention to curriculum content organized for cumulative learning. As students participate in instruction and engage in making art, they have opportunities to reflect on fundamental questions about art. Their art work becomes more sophisticated with each grade level as they gain knowledge and skills related to art production. The National Art Education Association (1986) recommends that art instruction integrate the study of aesthetics, art criticism, art history, and art production (see Figure 10.5). As with other curriculum areas, it is vital to evaluate student progress in art education and the effectiveness of the art education program (Bennett, 1988).

Music

The music-related benefits of an effective music education program include musical skills, knowledge, habits, attitudes, and understandings. In addition there are a number of extramusical benefits, such as development of a healthy self-concept, motor coordination, language skills, language arts skills, social skills, and content from other curricular areas in the content of songs (Reimer, 1989; Wilson, 1984). To assist students in developing both music-related and extramusical skills music education programs use various group activities to expose students to music that is appropriate to their developmental ages.

An important consideration in planning a music education curriculum is the recognition of how students acquire, retain, and apply knowledge at various stages of their physical, mental, and emotional development. Musical experiences en-

Making and using art to communicate and express ideas, and to convey feelings, has been a basic human activity throughout history.

Art is one of the most revealing of human activities. It is a rich source for understanding human societies.

Making art is central in the art education of all students.

Art objects are at the center of the study of art and understanding. A quality art education can be achieved when teachers and students explore the object through each of its four components: making art, responding to art, understanding its history, and making judgments about it.

An education of excellence must include a quality art education for all students.

FIGURE 10.5   National Art Education Association Statement on Quality Art Education

Source: National Art Education (1986). *Quality art education* (Report). Reston, VA: National Art Education.

courage growth in three areas of learning. First, they encourage growth in the psychomotor domain through physical movements used during performance. For example, students might move to music by dancing, playing instruments, playing song games, or experimenting with dramatization in music.

Second, musical experiences encourage growth in the cognitive domain through the acquisition of factual information, formation of concepts, generalization of information, and development of perceptual skills. For example, students might (1) identify pitch, rhythm, harmony, and instrumentation, (2) examine the same aspect of music in different compositions, or (3) identify similarities and differences between a stage play and an opera.

Finally, musical experiences encourage growth in the affective domain through music-related attitudes, feelings, values, and opinions. Enjoying music is a vital outcome in this domain, and teachers can encourage music enjoyment by giving students opportunities to experiment with musical instruments, encouraging attendance at concerts, and providing choices in musical activities.

Participants in the Music Educators National Conference (1986) identified music education goals for grades kindergarten through six. Figure 10.6 lists both musical and other subject matter goals the Conference identified for each grade.

Library/Information Use

The major purpose of library/information use is to produce students who are independent, effective, and lifelong users of information as well as fostering appreciation in the areas of reading, viewing, and listening. Program goals include: (1) identifying a wide range of information sources, (2) locating and selecting information sources to meet specific needs, (3) using bibliographic data to acknowledge information sources, (4) evaluating, analyzing, and synthesizing information for specific use, and (5) using information for problem solving, decision making, and communication (Virginia State Department of Education, 1985).

Ages Four through Five. By Completion of Kindergarten Students Will:

Performance and Reading

Utilize the singing voice versus speaking voice

Match pictures and sing in tune within their range most of the time

Show awareness of beat, tempo, dynamics, pitch, and similar versus different phrases through movement and playing instruments

Utilize pictures, shapes, and other symbols to represent pitch, durational patterns, and simple forms

Creating

Explore sound patterns on instruments

Improvise songs during classroom and play activities

Complete "answers" to unfinished melodic phrases by singing or playing instruments

Express ideas or moods using instruments or environmental and body sounds

Valuing

Demonstrate awareness of music as part of everyday life

Enjoy singing, moving to music, and playing instruments alone and with others

Respect music and musicians

Listening and Describing

Give attention to short musical selections

Listen attentively to an expanded repertoire of music

Respond to musical elements and styles through movement or playing instruments

Describe with movement or language similarities and differences in music (e.g., volume, speed)

Classify instruments by shape, size, pitch, and tone quality

Use a simple vocabulary of music terms to describe sounds

Grades One through Three. By Completion Of Grade Three Students Will:

Performing and Reading

Sing in tune alone or with group using clear, free tone

Sing from memory a repertoire of folk and composed songs

Sing with appropriate musical expression

Respond to beat by clapping, walking, running, or skipping

Play simple pitch patterns on melodic instruments (e.g., bells, xylophones)

Play simple rhythmic patterns on percussion instruments to accompany songs or activities

Sing a simple ostinato with a familiar song

Sing a part in a round while maintaining steady tempo

Interpret basic notational symbols for rhythm patterns (i.e., quarter, eighth, half notes, and rests) with movements, chanting, or instruments

Recognize basic features (e.g., melodic contour, expressive qualities) of unfamiliar songs by studying notation

Use correct notational symbols for pitch and expression

Use a system (e.g., syllables, numbers, letters) for reading notation

Creating

Create "answers" to unfinished melodic phrases by singing or playing instruments

Create short melodic patterns on instruments or by singing

Improvise songs and accompaniments to movement using instruments

Create short pieces consisting of nontraditional sounds in room or with body (e.g., snapping, rubbing)

In class, create new stanza to familiar melodies

Dramatize songs and stories

Valuing

Realize music is important part of everyday life

Feel a sense of respect for music, its performance, and creation

Display a sense of enjoyment when participating in music activities

Use music as a means of personal expression

FIGURE 10.6 Music Education Goals for Various Grade Levels.

Source: Music Educators National Conference (U.S.) (1986). *The school music program: Description and standards* (2nd ed.). Reston, VA: Music Educators National Conference.

Listening and Describing

Recognize differences in long/short sounds, repeated/contrasting phrases, slow/fast tempo, duple/triple meters, major/minor modes, etc.

Indicate recognition of high/low pitches by making hand movements following pitch

Recognize timbre of basic wind, string, and percussion instruments

Describe in simple terms the stylistic characteristics of some of the music listened to

Use musical terms and concepts to express thoughts about music (e.g., loud, short, high, melody, rhythm)

Use hand motions and other movements or graphic designs to indicate how portions of a musical work sound

Identify patterns of simple forms (e.g., AB, ABA)

Grades Four through Six. By Completion of Grade Six Students Will:

Performing and Reading

Sing song accurately and independently, reflecting understanding of tonal and rhythmic elements

Control voice to produce desired musical quality to communicate expressive intent

Perform basic tonal patterns, rhythmic patterns and simple songs on recorder, keyboard, synthesizer, and other instruments

Provide choral accompaniments with instrument (e.g., guitar, autoharp)

Conduct songs in two-, three-, and four-beat meter

Sing one part alone in thirds and sixths

Perform simple accompaniments by ear

Recognize tonal and rhythm patterns and musical forms from notation

Use systematic approach to music reading

Demonstrate growth in singing or playing music from notation

Creating

Make thoughtful alterations and variations in existing songs

Improvise simple ostinato-like accompaniments on pitched instruments

Improvise rhythmic accompaniments for songs

Create simple descants, introductions, and codas

Experiment with variations in tempo, timbre, dynamics, and phrasing for expressive purposes

Utilize diverse sound sources when improvising or composing

Valuing

Demonstrate increased awareness of music as part of everyday life

Participate in music through singing and playing instruments

Enjoy listening to most types of music

Discuss personal responses to works of art

Describe the musical phenomena on which their observations are based

Listening and Describing

Demonstrate understanding of rhythm through physical response or with instruments

Notate simple pitch and rhythm patterns presented aurally

Identify by listening a basic repertoire of orchestral and vocal compositions

Use correct terminology to discuss characteristics of a work (e.g., melody, rhythm, meter, key, form, style, and expressive qualities)

Discuss in own words the qualities of a work of music

Identify by listening most orchestral instruments, classification of voices, formal patterns and variations (e.g., AB, ABA, rondo, theme) and salient musical features (e.g., dynamic level, major/minor modes, meter, counterpoint, and types of music)

FIGURE 10.6 *Continued*

Electives and Other Activities

Traditional general education curricula include a plethora of electives from which students in middle and high schools can choose. Lists of electives are available from every school district and details can be obtained for each elective either through written curriculum guides or from general education teachers. For example, one elective traditionally offered through general education curricula is home economics, consisting of courses, activities, and units of instruction which provide learning experiences for personal, individual, family, and occupational needs of students. The intent of the program is to assist students in developing skills, knowledge, attitudes, and essential competencies which effect individual and family life management. Instruction typically includes (1) food and nutrition, (2) clothing and textiles, (3) child development, care, and guidance, (4) consumer education, (5) family living and parenthood, and (6) housing, home management, home furnishings, and equipment (Hayward Unified School District, 1984).

A second elective traditionally a part of general education curricula is industrial/vocational education. These curricula include both the study and safe use of tools, materials, processes, and products, and the study of occupations related to industry and technology. General goals for students enrolled in industrial/vocational education include: (1) application of math, science, and language skills in an industrial setting, (2) development of personal attributes regarding work ethics, (3) appreciation of, and a sense of responsibility for, satisfactory work, (4) experience with technological advances, (5) development of critical thinking and problem-solving skills, and (6) clarification, enrichment, and a broader understanding of career opportunities (Missoula School District, 1991).

In addition to electives, general education students from elementary through high school have a number of school-sponsored activities in which they can choose to participate. School-sponsored activities have overt purposes that are social (e.g., dances), sports-related (e.g., team sports), content-oriented (e.g., language club), service-oriented (e.g., school government, crossing guards), product-related (e.g., school newspaper, yearbook), and honorary (e.g., scholastic achievement club). Participation in school-sponsored activities is voluntary, and students may choose to participate in any combination of activities at any time of the year. In addition, students may select activities for their overt purpose or for other purposes (i.e, sports-related events may be selected for social purposes).

Using the Process with Parallel Subject Areas

The curriculum identification process described in Chapter 3 provides a mechanism for identifying relevant content for subject areas which have parallels between general and special education. The following sections describe how each step of the process relates to identifying meaningful curriculum content in parallel subject areas and examples.

Content Related to General Education Settings

The items listed in Figure 3.4 assist an education team in identifying factors related to general education settings which will influence a student's performance. For each of these factors the education team determines if the student with moderate or severe disabilities can participate in the same manner as nondisabled classmates, or whether modifications in the environment or instruction are required for the student to participate as independently as possible.

For instance, as described in the Student Profiles (see Appendix A) Tony's severe physical disabilities and volitional movement limit the degree to which he can access materials in the fifth-grade classroom and require personal support for him at all times. Because of this, the education team decided that modifying the general education settings per se would not increase his ability to participate in activities. Modifications in activities and materials, however, could allow Tony to participate more fully in class activities. For example, Tony's fifth-grade teacher frequently handed out papers to the class. During any class activity that required the distribution of papers Tony could participate with (1) a modification of the classroom routine (i.e., students approached Tony for their papers), (2) an adaptation (i.e., a wrist band with a sticky substance facing his wheelchair tray), and (3) instruction on the use of that adaptation (i.e., volitionally moving his arm up and down so the wrist band touched and raised one piece of paper for a classmate to grasp). In addition, instruction on this meaningful task would benefit Tony by creating opportunities for him to interact frequently with every classmate and by providing instruction on a skill that could be generalized to the use of switches during other activities.

Content Related to General Education Curriculum Content

To identify relevant general education curriculum content, education teams conduct an inventory of the content presented to the nondisabled students during the academic year. Education teams first identify the general education teacher's expected and desired outcomes for the entire class (see Table 3.5). From these outcomes, team members identify those that would be most meaningful for the student with moderate or severe disabilities either that year or in the future, would allow the student to participate in instructional activities in a valued way, and would increase opportunities for the student to interact with classmates. This information then helps identify the activities during which the student could receive instruction on that content across settings. The team then prioritizes the outcomes in preparation for comparing the relative importance of each outcome with the prioritized outcomes from the previous inventories (e.g., family, peer, community).

For instance, as described in Appendix B, Maureen's reading level and comprehension negated her ability to participate in a high school English class on Shakespeare in the same manner and with the same instructional expectations as her classmates (e.g., spontaneously reading aloud, completing unadapted unit exams). Her education team, however, decided she could benefit from the class and participate with modifications in expected outcomes, homework, class activities, and exams. For homework on a selected section of an assigned play she could listen to audio tapes, watch video productions, read commercially prepared study notes, and practice reading aloud. During class reading, she could read aloud the section she practiced. As a unit assignment, instead of writing an essay on the play, she could develop posters about Shakespeare and his plays. In addition to providing mechanisms for Maureen to participate in the class, these modifications would provide her instructional opportunities for other functional goals (e.g., asking for assistance when needed, finding and using required information, fine motor skills for cutting and pasting items, visual perception and organization, reading for meaning). Finally, these modifications would provide Maureen the experiences she needed to acquire the language and background information necessary to participate in discussions about Shakespeare outside of class with both peers and family members.

Content Related to Functional Curriculum Content

As discussed in Chapter 3, education teams identify the functional needs of a student with moderate or severe disabilities through a series of inventories focused on the student's family life, peers, community, related services assessments, records, and personal preferences. For each inventory, the education team again develops a prioritized list of the student's needs to use when negotiating IEP annual goals. While education teams frequently consider the student's potential use of a functional activity across settings when prioritizing the identified functional needs, some functional needs are so critical within one setting that the importance of the activity in other settings becomes irrelevant. Both the degree to which a need is critical in one setting and the number of settings in which a need is evident are reasons for selecting a functional need as a priority for instruction. Regardless of the reason for selecting functional curriculum content for instruction, an education team then focuses on how instruction on that need can blend into general education activities across the day.

For instance, as described in the Student Profiles (see Appendix A), Jason's behaviors with adults and classmates, during both instructional and noninstructional times, frequently were inappropriate (e.g., hugging, kissing), off-task (e.g., short attention span, refusal to complete tasks), and disruptive (e.g., throwing tantrums). In addition, his gross and fine motor delays frequently caused him to be fatigued after extended periods of work. His functional needs included (1) learning appropriate social interaction behaviors with peers and adults, (2) attending to class activities and completing his work, (3) acquiring the communication skills necessary to replace the disruptive behaviors that had communicative functions, (4) developing fine motor control and strength, and (5) developing gross motor strength and coordination. The education team determined that there would be instruction on each of these throughout the school day during general education activities. During language arts Jason would be asked questions about either his family life or his classroom work for which the correct answers were known. When answering, Jason would be required to (1) speak in three or four word sentences, (2) use new vocabulary words for the week, and (3) position himself as other students, without inappropriately touching the teacher. In relation to his physical needs, Jason would (1) receive reminders to sit with his head upright and his feet on the floor when working at his desk; (2) receive physical therapy support services during physical education class, with attention to abdominal muscle development, and (3) learn to use an electric typewriter to supplement his handwritten work. Each of these would become part of the general education activities across the day, regardless of the general education content being addressed.

Negotiating Annual Goals

When completing the steps discussed above, the intent of the education team is first to identify the most relevant instructional content for a student with moderate or severe disabilities in relation to both functional curriculum and the general education settings and curriculum for the relevant grade level. Second, the education team's intent is for each member to prioritize in one list the curriculum content identified as appropriate for the student, including both the general education and functional content. At this point, the education team meets and negotiates which of those priorities will become part of the final list of priorities on the student's IEP for that academic year (see Figure 3.6 in Chapter 3). For some students with moderate or severe disabilities the negotiation process will lead to annual goals that reflect only general education content, while for other students goals will reflect only functional content. For the majority of students, however, negotiated annual goals will reflect a combination of general education and functional content. The education team immediately involved with a student determines the percent of annual goals that reflect general education versus functional content and the relative importance they place on priorities identified through the curriculum process.

For example, Tony's education team (see Student Profiles, Appendix A) placed a great deal of emphasis on his functional needs but still allowed for the possibility that he would acquire some of the general education content through the use of yes/no responses to questions during general education activities. Conceivably, as Tony responded correctly to questions on concrete content, the team could modify the questions to reflect both more abstract and more general education content. In contrast, Maureen's education team (see Appendix B) placed a strong emphasis on her acquisition of general education content but determined how they also could address her functional needs through general education activities.

Determining Locations for Instruction

Once education teams have negotiated annual goals, they can address the issue of where they will provide instruction per goal. As indicated on Table 3.8 in Chapter 3, instruction can occur across general education settings (i.e., any setting in which the class participates) or functional activity settings in the classroom, building, field-trip settings, home, or community. The more critical it is to address generalization concerns for a student, the greater the number of settings selected for instruction.

For instance, because of his profound mental retardation, instruction for content in each of Tony's annual goals occurred whenever an opportunity presented itself across every setting (see Student Profiles, Appendix A). Because of Jason's severe mental retardation, instruction for content in his annual goals also occurred across settings (e.g., instruction on identifying and using coins occurred in general education activities when presented for other students, when preparing his money for lunch, when purchasing his lunch, and when shopping with family members in the community). In contrast, instruction on Maureen's general education content occurred only during general education activities, including homework assignments, while instruction on her functional needs occurred whenever opportunities were naturally present across settings (see Appendix B).

Underlying Issues

Underlying this entire process is the judgment that each education team member makes regarding the relative importance for any given student of some curriculum content in comparison with all other content. This becomes important not only when comparing one skill or piece of knowledge in a subject area with other skills or pieces of knowledge in that subject area (e.g., relative importance of single digit addition compared with use of money), but also when comparing general education curriculum content with functional content (e.g., relative importance of single digit addition completed as other students compared with systematic task completion with adaptations, or requesting assistance when needed). Each education team member struggles with questions like:

1. How long and to what skill level should we emphasize general education curriculum content for this student?

2. Will this student benefit more, both now and in the future, if instruction *this academic year* focuses on this general education content or this functional content?

3. To ensure that this student can function as an adult in inclusive living, working, leisure, and community settings, do we place more emphasis on functional activities in the community *this academic year* or on general education content? Should a shift occur at some stage in this student's educational career? If so, at what age?

In answering these questions, education team members focusing on inclusive settings frequently refer to two basic issues: first, maximizing the blending of instruction on both general education and functional curriculum content for this student to provide instruction on as much content as possible, thus trying to address the maximal number of future contingencies, and second, identifying the other instruction or experiences the student will miss if instruction focuses on functional needs, especially when those functional needs are addressed outside of general education activities. Given this identification, the education team then asks, "Which is more important—instruction on the functional need or what the student would be missing?"

Finally, when considering even momentary removal from general education activities for instruction on either a functional need or one-to-one attention on general education content, education team members ask (1) can instruction on this functional need take place during any general education activities and (2) is this functional or general education content *critical* for the student? If not, is instruction on this content really more important *this academic year* than the instruction and/ or experiences the student would be missing?

While there are no easy answers to any of these questions, education team members in inclusive settings assist each other in remaining focused on their overall purpose for providing instruction for a student with moderate or severe disabilities. That focus must be assisting the student to participate as fully and independently as possible with nondisabled peers across current and future settings, including where and how they live, work, spend leisure time, and access the community.

Summary

This chapter describes content in subject areas for which parallels exist between traditional general and special education curricula, and how content in these areas can blend into instruction during general education activities. To accomplish this, education team members need to be familiar with content most frequently included in both types of curriculum.

In relation to oral and written language, special education curricula traditionally address: (1) receptive and expressive communication, including augmentative and alternative communication systems, (2) social interaction, (3) functional reading, and (4) functional writing. On the other hand, in general education curricula oral and written skills are part of language arts (i.e., speaking, listening, reading, writing) which contribute to literacy when combined. Research supports a "constructivist" model of emergent literacy in which learning outcomes are an integral and natural part of instruction across grade levels and subject areas, with a student "constructing" literacy as interrelated skills develop in speaking, listening, reading, and writing. The constructivist model characterizes oral and written language attainment and instruction as a holistic journey in which students acquire the knowledge necessary for lifelong learning. This view is compatible with the traditional special education curricular emphasis on developing oral and written language skills in activities, settings, and times that are functional and meaningful for students with moderate or severe disabilities. This compatibility makes general education language arts classes ideal for instruction on oral and written language skills for included students.

Motor skills traditionally have been addressed in special education curricula through two types of programs: (1) adapted physical education, stressing participation in sports and leisure activities and (2) physical development needs, stressing a student's need for basic motor movement development, physical therapy, and occupational therapy. In contrast, general education curricula use human movement to teach the skills and knowledge required to be physically fit and help students develop positive attitudes about physical fitness and lifelong activities. In inclusive settings, general and special education teachers are recognizing that the goals of general physical education are consistent with the needs and lifelong goals of students with moderate or severe disabilities. With this recognition they are blending general physical education goals and functional goals during general physical education activities.

In mathematics, traditional special education curricula focus on two areas: (1) advancing a student through a developmental sequence of skills, including basic concepts and (2) helping a student function independently when using mathematic skills, money, time, and telephone numbers. General education curricula in mathematics emphasize the need for conceptual development, mathematical reasoning, and problem solving at all grade levels. These curricula recommend that students have opportunities for (1) hands-on experiences; (2) use of manipulatives, calculators, and computers; and (3) cooperative group work. These instructional adaptations provide a natural opportunity for the inclusion of students with moderate or severe disabilities in general education classes, and a blending of instruction on functional and general education content.

Historically, students with moderate or severe disabilities placed in self-contained classes have received little or no instruction in science or social studies content. In general education curricula, science goals include the acquisition of (1) knowledge, (2) manipulative skills, (3) intellectual skills, (4) investigative and objective attitudes, (5) techniques of inquiry, and (6) problem solving. Social studies curricula emphasize the broad goal of citizenship education. Both the increased emphasis on inquiry, problem solving, and use of manipulatives in science, and the focus on citizenship in social studies are consistent with the needs of students with moderate or severe disabilities. Because of this, it is possible to blend instruction on general education and functional content during activities in science and social studies classes.

Of the three special subject areas typically part of special education curricula (i.e., art; music; library/information use), only general education art curricula describe techniques for adapting activities for students with moderate or severe disabilities in inclusive settings. The fields of art education therapy and art therapy have provided additional support for these suggestions for adaptations. Goals of general education music education curricula include growth in psychomotor skills, cognitive skills, and affective skills. Goals of library/information use curricula stress the need for students to become lifelong users of information.

Courses that traditionally are electives in general education curricula (e.g., home economics, industrial and vocational education, foreign language) seldom have been available to students with moderate or severe disabilities. With the advent of inclusion, education teams are reexamining the benefits of electives for students with moderate or severe disabilities, resulting in an increase in their inclusion.

Across each of these subject areas parallels are found between general and special education curricula. The overlap creates natural opportunities for education teams to identify general education content that is relevant for a student with moderate or severe disabilities. In addition, education teams are able to identify how a student with moderate or severe disabilities can receive instruction on functional needs while partially participating in general education activities. This allows the student access to (1) nondisabled peers, (2) general education vocabulary and activities for both structured and incidental learning, and (3) meaningful opportunities to practice and use functional skills.

References

AIMS Education Foundation (undated). *Project AIMS (Activities that integrate mathematics and science)*. Fresno, CA: Author.

American Alliance for Health, Physical Education, Recreation, and Dance (1978). *Guidelines for secondary school physical education*. Washington, D.C.: Author.

American Association for the Advancement of Science (1989). *Science for all Americans: A project 2061 report on literacy goals in science, mathematics, and technology*. Washington, D.C.: Author.

Barr, D., Barth, J., & Shermis, S. (1977). *Defining the social studies*, Bulletin 51. Washington, D.C.: National Council for the Social Studies.

Bennett, W. (1988). Why the arts are essential. *Educational Leadership, 45*(4), 4.

Beukelman, D., & Yorkston, K. (1989). Augmentative and alternative communication application for persons with severe acquired communication disorders: An introduction. *Augmentative and Alternative Communication, 5*, 42–48.

Browder, D. M., & Snell, M. E. (1993). Functional academics. In M. E. Snell (Ed.). *Instruction of students with severe disabilities* (pp. 442–479). New York: Macmillan.

Clark, G., & Zimmerman, E. (1981). Toward a discipline of art education. *Phi Delta Kappan, 63*(1), 53–56.

Clements, C., & Clements, R. (1984). *Art and mainstreaming: Art instruction for exceptional children in regular school classes*. Springfield, IL: Charles C. Thomas.

Cox, A. (1970). *Arts and crafts are more than fun in special education*. Danville, IL: Interstate Publishers.

Cratty, B. (1989). *Adapted physical education in the mainstream* (2nd ed.). Denver: Love.

Dauer, V., & Pangrazi, R. (1975). *Dynamic physical education for elementary school children* (5th ed.). Minneapolis, MN: Burgess.

Esler, W., & Merritt, Jr., K. (1976). Teaching reading through science experience stories. *School Science and Mathematics, 24*(2), 203–206.

Falvey, M. A. (1989). *Community-based curriculum: Instructional strategies for students with severe handicaps* (2nd ed.). Baltimore: Paul H. Brookes.

Federal Register 42 (August 23,1977): 42474–98

Ford, A., Davern, L., Schnorr, R., Black, J., & Kaiser, K. (1989a). Money handling. In A. Ford, R. Schnorr, L. Meyer, L. Davern, J. Black, & P. Dempsey (Eds.). *The Syracuse community-referenced curriculum guide for students with moderate and severe disabilities* (pp. 117–148). Baltimore: Paul H. Brookes.

Ford, A., Schnorr, R., Davern, L., Black, J., & Kaiser, K. (1989b). Reading and writing. In A. Ford, R. Schnorr, L. Meyer, L. Davern, J. Black, & P. Dempsey (Eds.). *The Syracuse community-referenced curriculum guide for students with moderate and severe disabilities* (pp. 93–116). Baltimore: Paul H. Brookes.

Ford, A., Schnorr, R., Meyer, L., Davern, L., Black, J., & Dempsey P. (Eds.) (1989c). *The Syracuse community-referenced curriculum guide for students with moderate and severe disabilities.* Baltimore: Paul H. Brookes.

Gartland, D. (1990). Reading instruction. In P. J. Schloss, M. A. Smith, & C. N. Schloss (Eds.), *Instructional methods for adolescents with learning and behavior problems* (pp. 243–256). Boston: Allyn & Bacon.

Gee, J. (1985). The narrativization of experience in the oral style. *Journal of Education, 167*(1), 9–35.

Graham, R., & Beer, A. (1980). *Teaching music to the exceptional child.* Englewood Cliffs, NJ: Prentice-Hall, Inc.

Halle, J. (1984). Arranging the natural environment to occasion language: Giving severely language-delayed children reason to communicate. *Seminars in Speech and Language, 5*(3), 185–197.

Hayward Unified School District (1984). *High school curriculum guide in home economics.* Hayward, CA: Author.

Jenness, D. (1990). *Making sense of social studies.* New York: Macmillan.

Kaiser, A. (1993). Functional language. In M. Snell (Ed.). *Instruction of students with severe disabilities* (pp.348–379). New York: Macmillan.

Kartoaka, J., & Patton, J. (1989). Teaching exceptional learners: An integrated approach. *Science and Children, 27*(1), 48–51.

Krone, A. (1978). *Art instruction for handicapped children.* Denver: Love.

Lawson, A., Costenson, K., & Cisneros, R. (1986). A summary of research in science education. *Science Education, 70*(3), 213–221.

Lindsay, Z. (1972). *Art and the handicapped child.* New York: Van Nostrand Reinhold.

Menhusen, B., & Gromme, R. (1976). Science for handicapped children—Why? *Science and Children,* March, 35–38.

Meyer, L. H., & Evans, I. M. (1989). *Nonaversive intervention for behavior problems.* Baltimore: Paul H. Brookes .

Miller, J. (1993). Augmentative and alternative communication. In M. Snell (Ed.). *Instruction of students with severe disabilities* (pp.319–346). New York: Macmillan.

Mirenda, P., & Smith-Lewis, M. (1989). Communication skills. In A. Ford, R. Schnorr, L. Meyer, L. Davern, J. Black, & P. Dempsey (Eds.). *The Syracuse community-referenced curriculum guide for students with moderate and severe disabilities* (pp. 189–210). Baltimore: Paul H. Brookes.

Missoula County School District (1991). *Industrial arts/vocational education curriculum.* Missoula, Montana: Author.

Music Educators National Conference (U.S.) (1986). *The school music program: Description and standards* (2nd ed.). Reston, VA: Author.

National Art Education Association (1986). *Quality art education* (report). Reston, VA: Author.

National Commission on Social Studies in the Schools (1989). *Charting a course: Social studies for the 21st century.* Washington, D.C.: Author.

National Council of Teachers of Mathematics (1989). *Curriculum and evaluations standards for school mathematics* (Report). Reston, VA: Author.

National Science Resources Center (1987). *Science and technology for children.* Burlington, NC: Carolina Biological Supply.

O'Neill, R. E., Horner, R. H., Albin, R. W., Storey, K., & Sprague, J. R. (1989). *Functional analysis: A practical assessment guide*. Unpublished manuscript. Eugene: University of Oregon, Research & Training Center on Community-Referenced, Nonaversive Behavior Management.

Rainforth, B., Giangreco, M., & Dennis, R. (1989). Motor skills. In A. Ford, R. Schnorr, L. Meyer, L. Davern, J. Black, & P. Dempsey (Eds.). *The Syracuse community-referenced curriculum guide for students with moderate and severe disabilities*. Baltimore: Paul H. Brookes.

Reichle, J. (1991a). Defining the decisions involved in designing and implementing augmentative and alternative communication systems. In J. Reichle, J. York, & J. Sigafoos (Eds.). *Implementing augmentative and alternative communication: Strategies for learners with severe disabilities* (pp. 39–60). Baltimore: Paul H. Brookes.

Reichle, J. (1991b). Developing communicative exchanges. In J. Reichle, J. York, & J. Sigafoos (Eds.). *Implementing augmentative and alternative communication: Strategies for learners with severe disabilities* (pp. 133–156). Baltimore: Paul H. Brookes.

Reichle, J., Mirenda, P., Locke, P., Piche, L., & Johnston, S. (1992). Beginning augmentative communication systems. In S. Warren & J. Reichle (Eds.). *Causes and effects in communication and language intervention* (Vol. 1). (pp. 131–156). Baltimore: Paul H. Brookes.

Reichle, J., & Sigafoos, J. (1991). Establishing spontaneity and generalization. In J. Reichle, J. York, & J. Sigafoos (Eds.). *Implementing augmentative and alternative communication: Strategies for learners with severe disabilities* (pp. 157–172). Baltimore: Paul H. Brookes.

Reichle, J., York, J., & Sigafoos, J. (Eds.) (1991). *Implementing augmentative and alternative communication: Strategies for learners with severe disabilities*. Baltimore: Paul H. Brookes.

Reimer, B. (1989). Music education and aesthetic education: Past and present. *Music Education Journal*, February, 22–28.

Resnick, L. B., Wang, M. C., & Kaplan, J. (1973). Task analysis in curriculum design: A hierarchically sequenced introductory mathematics curriculum. *Journal of Applied Behavior Analysis, 6*, 697–710.

Schleien, S. J., Green, F. G., & Heyne, L. A. (1993). Integrated community recreation. In M. Snell (Ed.). *Instruction of students with severe disabilities* (pp. 526–555). New York: Macmillan.

Schulz, J., Carpenter, C. D., & Turnbull, A. (1991). *Mainstreaming exceptional students: A guide for classroom teachers* (3rd ed.). Boston: Allyn & Bacon.

Seaton, D., Schmottlach, N., Clayton, I., Leibee, H., & Messersmith, L. (1983). *Physical Education Handbook* (7th ed.). Englewood Cliffs, NJ: Prentice-Hall.

Sherrill, C. (1981). *Adapted physical education and recreation*. Dubuque: Wm. C. Brown.

Siegel-Causey, E., & Wetherby, A. (1993). Nonsymbolic communication. In M. Snell (Ed.). *Instruction of students with severe disabilities* (pp. 290–318). New York: Macmillan.

Sigafoos, J., Mustonen, T., DePaepe, P., Reichles, J., & York, J. (1991). Defining the array of instructional prompts for teaching communication skills. In J. Reichle, J. York, & J. Sigafoos, *Implementing augmentative and alternative communication: Strategies for learners with severe disabilities* (pp. 173–192). Baltimore: Paul H. Brookes.

Snell, M. E. (Ed.) (1993). *Instruction of students with severe disabilities*. New York: Macmillan.

Snell, M. E., & Brown, F. (1993). Instructional planning and implementation. In M. E. Snell (Ed.). *Instruction of students with severe disabilities* (pp.99–183). New York: Macmillan.

Spradlin, J. E., Cotter, C. W., Stevens, C. M., & Friedman, M. (1974). Performance of mentally retarded children on prearithmetic tasks. *American Journal of Mental Deficiency, 78*, (397–403).

Stainback, S., & Stainback, W. (Eds.). (1992). *Curriculum considerations in inclusive classrooms: Facilitating learning for all students*. Baltimore: Paul H. Brookes.

Stainback, S., Stainback, W., & Forest, M. (1989). *Educating all students in the mainstream of regular education.* Baltimore: Paul H. Brookes.

Strickland, D. S. (1990). Emergent literacy: How young children learn to read and write. *Educational Leadership, 47*(6), 18–23.

Stubbs, M. (1990). *Language and literacy.* Boston: Routledge and Kegan Paul.

Sulzby, E. (1985). Kindergartners as writers and readers. In M. Farr (Ed.), *Advances in writing research* (Vol. 1). Norwood, NJ: Ablex.

Teale, W., & Sulzby, E. (1986). *Emergent literacy: Writing and reading.* Norwood, NJ: Ablex.

Uhlin, D., & De Chiara, E. (1984). *Art for exceptional children* (3rd ed). Dubuque: Wm. C. Brown.

Vacca, J. L., Vacca, R. T., & Gove, M. K. (1991). *Reading and learning to read.* New York: Harper Collins.

Vanderheiden, G., & Yoder, D. (1986). Overview. In S. W. Blackstone (Ed.). *Augmentative communication: An introduction* (pp. 1–28). Rockville, MD: American Speech-Language-Hearing Association.

Vannier, M., & Fait, H. (1975). *Teaching physical education in secondary schools* (4th ed.). Philadelphia: W. B. Saunders.

Virginia State Department of Education. (1985). *Standards of learning objectives for library/information use.* Richmond, VA: Author.

Williams, A. (Ed.) (1989). *Issues in physical education for the primary years.* Philadelphia: Falmer Press, Taylor & Francis.

Wilson, F. R. (1984). The full development of the individual through music. *Update,* Spring, 3–7.

Winnick, J. (1990). *Adapted physical education and sport.* Champaign, IL: Human Kinetics Books.

11

APPLICATION TO SPECIAL EDUCATION CURRICULAR AREAS WITH NO GENERAL EDUCATION PARALLELS

SANDRA ALPER

ROBERT D. McMULLEN

VICTORIA McMULLEN

PATRICIA J. MILLER

Chapter Objectives

After completing this chapter the reader will be able to:

1. Identify self-help skills that students may learn in inclusive settings.
2. Define self-determination.
3. Describe strategies for teaching students with disabilities to make appropriate choices.
4. Discuss the rationale behind the circle of friends.
5. Discuss the implementation of the concept of circle of friends in inclusive settings.

Key Terms

Circle of friends
Personal management
Self-care skills
Self-determination

Self-empowerment
Self-help skills
Socialization
Traditional curriculum areas

Students with disabilities have some unique instructional needs and considerations. These include the need to learn self-help skills, social skills, and self-determination skills. The first two areas were part of some of the earliest attempts to educate students with disabilities, beginning with the classic work of Itard (Cited in Humphrey & Humphrey, 1962) in the late eighteenth century. The self-determination area focuses on skills that enable students with disabilities to make prudent choices. This area gained a great deal of attention more recently due to the self-advocacy and self-empowerment movement (Alper, Schloss, & Schloss, 1994) and the belief that persons with disabilities have the right to make choices about their own lives (Schloss, Alper, & Jayne, 1994).

This chapter addresses the curriculum areas of self-help and self-determination skills and the critical need for students with disabilities to learn these skills. Teaching these skills within inclusive settings, even though they are not typically part of the general education curricula, will also be a topic in this chapter. We will apply the curriculum content identification process to socialization skills covered in detail in Chapter 8.

Self-Help Skills

Toileting, eating, and dressing are the most critical self-care skills (Snell, 1993). These skills are necessary for maintaining basic health care needs of the individual, being accepted by peers, and gaining access to a variety of integrated settings in the school and community at large. Acquisition of these skills also represents increasing independence from parents and other care givers.

While most children begin to learn self-help skills at an early age, some students with disabilities will acquire these skills only through direct and systematic instruction. Intellectual disabilities, physical disabilities such as cerebral palsy, lack of motor skills, vision and hearing impairments, and disruptive behaviors are all obstacles to independence in toileting, eating, and dressing. For students with moderate to severe disabilities, lack of independent toileting skills can limit access to a number of natural settings, reduce the amount of teacher time available to train other skills, and make the student less pleasant for others to be around. Of course, all these problems are exacerbated as the student grows older (Snell, 1993).

Toileting and Consideration for General Education Settings

The vast majority of students without disabilities learn toileting skills in a predictable developmental sequence. Most children learn daytime bladder control before nighttime control. Bowel movements may come under control before urination, although independence in both is often achieved simultaneously (Snell, 1993). A child must acquire toileting-related skills such as undressing, wiping, and dressing for total independence.

Snell (1987, pp. 338–339) identified three basic indicators of readiness for toilet training. These characteristics, probably related to maturity of the central nervous system and the ability to control sphincter muscles, are (1) a stable pattern of elimination, (2) daily stable periods of dryness, and (3) a chronological age of at least two and one half to three years of age. The design of special adaptations is necessary in the instructional program for students who use wheelchairs, do not indicate the need to use the bathroom, do not appear to respond to the sensation of being wet, or who have aggressive behaviors that interfere with toileting procedures.

Snell (1987, 1993) summarized the instructional decisions the teacher will need to make in teaching toileting skills. These decisions are:

1. What toys, activities, foods, or social events are reinforcing to the student, age-appropriate, and suitable for use in general education settings?

2. What specific training objectives will the teacher prioritize? Will emphasis be on daytime or nighttime control? Will the teacher target for instruction bladder or bowel control? Will related skills such as undressing or washing hands be part of the toileting skills instruction sequence?

3. Will training occur at home as well as in school?

4. When and how often will training occur? It is extremely important that training occur immediately before the student is likely to need to eliminate. Ready access to toileting facilities is important.

5. What instructional strategies will the teacher use to teach the objectives? The teacher might consider specific techniques such as shaping, backward chaining, dry pants check, positive practice, and systematic prompting. Snell (1993) provided an excellent review of training techniques found to be effective in teaching students with disabilities independence in toileting.

Opportunities for teaching toileting skills exist throughout the school day in general education settings. Several considerations are important for students with disabilities in these settings. First, the teacher should schedule toilet training sessions carefully and on an individual basis. Students without disabilities commonly have regularly scheduled periods during which they may use the restroom. It is important to schedule toilet training around all meal and snack periods, upon arrival at school, and shortly before dismissal. Some students with disabilities may need opportunities to use the bathroom at more frequent intervals.

Second, the educational team should clearly specify the person or persons responsible for toilet training. The special education teacher, general educator, related services personnel, aide, and, in some cases, other students can provide assistance in basic toileting procedures. One should not assume, however, that whomever is present will automatically handle toilet training as needed, particularly in the case of older students with disabilities.

Third, the student should learn some verbal, manual, or gestural cue so that he or she may have a reliable means to indicate to others the need to use the bathroom.

Indicating the need to eliminate can be the first step written into the toileting procedure.

Finally, the teacher should write down each of the steps the student is to perform during toileting along with the specific verbal or gestural cue the trainer will use to signal the student to perform each step. The student and teacher, respectively, should then perform these steps and use discreet cues consistently each and every time toileting occurs.

Eating and Considerations for General Education Settings

Meal and snack times provide many opportunities for learning a variety of skills. Food is a primary and natural reinforcer for many students. Instructional programs built around eating and related skills are often highly motivating for students. The act of eating provides opportunities to emphasize related skills such as ordering a meal at a fast-food restaurant, paying for the purchase, and socializing appropriately while dining. Cafeterias, restaurants and snack bars are settings that students without disabilities frequent. They provide opportunities for students with and without disabilities to interact while participating in a naturally occurring and reinforcing activity. Finally, an expansion of the area of eating skills may include meal planning and preparation and nutrition and shopping. These are skills that are extremely important as students with disabilities grow older and live independently in the community.

Falvey (1989) identified several critical skills in this area including choice of what, when, and where to eat, eating a nutritionally balanced diet, purchasing food, meal preparation, clean-up after mealtimes, basic eating skills, and manners. Snell (1993) discussed basic eating skills for students with severe disabilities such as eating finger foods, drinking from a cup, using a knife, fork, and spoon, and eating at a socially acceptable rate. She also provided task analyses of these skills along with recommendations for adaptations necessary for students with physical disabilities.

Reid-Arnold, Doherty, Schloss, Alper, and Green (manuscript submitted for publication) designed a meal planning and preparation program for youths with mental retardation and physical aggression. Before implementation of the program, the youths were typically eating unbalanced meals that were high in calories and fat. They would often choose to eat the same foods day after day. One youth who participated in this program was a fragile diabetic for whom a poor diet could pose a life-threatening situation.

Skills targeted for training were (1) using the four basic food groups to plan all meals and snacks for three days at a time, (2) developing shopping lists from these menus, (3) purchasing the food, (4) meal preparation, and (5) clean-up. Instructional strategies included the use of picture cue cards to plan menus based on the four food groups, task analyses, and the system of least prompts. All training occurred in natural settings within home and grocery stores. Results indicated that students learned to plan, purchase, and prepare nutritious meals and snacks that included

100 percent of the required daily minimum amounts of seven essential vitamins and minerals. In addition, Reid-Arnold et al. demonstrated that the caloric intake met standards recommended for age, sex, and height of the participating youths.

Instructional strategies for teaching eating and related skills typically consist of a careful task analysis of the skills. The teacher may use shaping, modeling, verbal, gestural, and physical prompting. It is important to schedule training around the times in which these activities normally occur within school, home, and community settings. Teaching eating skills, like toileting, dressing and grooming skills is most effective across the settings in which they naturally occur. For this reason it is extremely important to gain information from the family as to routines and preferences.

Social validation procedures (see Chapter 8) may determine socially acceptable standards for eating. For example, the teacher or parent will have to make decisions about using a napkin, use of fingers to pick up certain foods, and rate of eating. While rules of etiquette apply, it is also true that many persons without disabilities use their fingers to eat, do not always use a napkin, and eat while standing up, particularly while in the privacy of their own homes.

We recommend that standards for eating behaviors be set at a level at which the student with disabilities may *eat without drawing negative attention.* Through subjective evaluation, same age peers without disabilities can be observed eating in a variety of settings, and their use of manners and rate of eating noted. The same performance standards can then apply to students with disabilities.

General education settings offer many natural opportunities in which to practice eating skills. These include breakfast and lunch, parties, and snacks between classes and during extracurricular activities. Many teachers have found it helpful to ask a student without disabilities to volunteer to assist a student with disabilities during specific eating times.

Dressing and Grooming and Considerations for General Education Settings

Like acquisition of toileting and eating skills, developing competence in dressing and grooming skills can result in increased independence from caretakers, greater access to natural settings that persons without disabilities frequent, and acceptance by peers. Dressing and grooming is another area, similar to eating and toileting, on which parents and teachers typically place a very high priority for training.

This skill area for students with disabilities typically includes dressing and undressing, taking a bath or shower, washing hair, brushing hair and teeth, and menstrual care. Selecting clean clothes that match and fit well and paying some attention to clothing styles and make-up are also often part of this curriculum area.

There is wide variability in the skills in this area of the curriculum based on the age and ability level of the student. For many students with mild disabilities, dressing and grooming may be of no more concern than for children without disabilities. Students with severe and multiple disabilities, however, will often have to focus on the most rudimentary skills of dressing and basic hygiene.

There is a wide variety of strategies for teaching dressing and grooming skills to students with disabilities. Much of the research has focused on students with severe disabilities, although the instructional strategies are equally applicable to persons with mild disabilities. These instructional strategies have included the following:

1. *Task analysis.* The educational team performs a task analysis of the specific skill, breaking it into its component observable and measurable responses according to the sequence in which the student performs them. Each step of the task analysis is stated as directly and succinctly as possible, often using a verb-noun format (e.g., "Pull pants up to waist"). Instruction in virtually every area of the curriculum for students with severe disabilities will utilize task analysis.

2. *Prompts.* Some type of verbal, modeled, or physical prompt, or cue instructs the student to complete each step of the task analysis. It is important to use clear, simple prompts consistently. Some teachers have used pictures or photographs of each step in the task for the student to follow.

3. *System of Least Prompts.* The teacher gives the verbal command to complete the task and waits for a specified number of seconds to see if the student will respond without assistance. If the student makes no response, the teacher provides the least intrusive prompt, usually a verbal instruction. If, after a certain time delay, there is still no response, the teacher will use the next level of prompt, such as modeling the task or a gesture. The teacher repeats this procedure until the student has received enough assistance to complete the task.

4. *Physical Guidance.* The teacher physically assists the student through the task by placing her hands on the hands of the student. This procedure would be used only in the event that less intensive forms of assistance had failed to result in the student performing a response.

5. *Time Delay.* Teachers have used time delay to fade prompts. In this procedure, the time between the stimulus (e.g., a verbal cue to complete a response) and the prompt gradually lengthens to increase the student's chances of independent performance (Snell, 1993).

6. *Shaping.* The instructor rewards a student's successive approximations to the targeted response. A student may not have learned to completely perform a particular skill, as when a young child can pull a shirt over his head but not pull the shirt down straight and tuck it in. The teacher will reinforce behaviors that resemble the target behavior.

7. *Forward Chaining.* The first step of the task is taught, then the first and second steps, then the first, second, and third steps, and so on, until the student has performed all steps in the task.

8. *Backward Chaining.* Sometimes, the last steps in a task are easier to perform than the first steps. This is true of many dressing tasks. For example, pulling up slacks from the knees to the waist is easier for most students than putting the right foot into the right pant leg. In backward chaining, the last step is taught first, then the next to the last step is taught, and so on.

9. *Reinforcement.* The instructor combines all of the above procedures with reinforcement of correct responses or follows a correct response (or completion of the entire task) with a pleasant consequence such as a stroke or pat on the back, verbal praise, or preferred activity. Because dressing and undressing or taking a bath may not be intrinsically motivating for many students, reinforcement is especially important.

These instructional strategies are not unique to the areas of dressing and grooming. They may be useful in teaching a wide array of skills to students with disabilities.

Dressing and grooming offer fewer natural opportunities for occurrence at school than other areas of the curriculum for students with disabilities. Snell (1993) recommended that scheduled training in these areas might coincide with arrival and getting ready to leave school, before and after recess, during physical education activities, and during toileting routines. Instructors might schedule other opportunities for grooming, use of cosmetics, selection of clothing, and care of menstrual needs into home economics classes. Even if opportunities to teach these skills are not frequently available in inclusive settings, teachers should make the time to address this important area.

Snell (1993) cautioned that teachers should avoid training procedures that are not socially acceptable to persons without disabilities or that could draw negative attention to the student with disabilities. She also reminds teachers to avoid training procedures that show disregard for an individual's privacy and personal feelings.

Self-Determination Skills and Considerations for General Education Settings

Self-determination refers to the freedom and ability to weigh options and make choices regarding one's own day-to-day life. Many persons with disabilities have been denied the freedom to make choices because of professional attitudes and lowered expectations of ability. The ability to consider options and make choices does not occur automatically (Falvey, 1989). Rather, instructors must teach students with disabilities self-determination skills using the same systematic and direct instructional strategies that they use to teach any other area of the curriculum.

Schloss, Alper, and Jayne (1994) identified three reasons why educators are placing increased emphasis on teaching self-determination skills to students with disabilities. First, the professional literature indicates quality of life is associated with the ability to make choices (Blatt, 1987; Kishi, Teelucksingh, Zollers, Park-Lee, & Meyer, 1988). Second, data indicate that persons with the most severe disabilities are capable of learning to make choices (e.g., Realon, Favell, & Lowerre, 1990). Making even the most basic choices in daily life such as what to eat for breakfast can enhance the quality of life. Third, students with disabilities often have great difficulty in making a successful transition from school to work and adult life in the community. Impairments in the ability to make appropriate decisions in regard to appropriate behavior at work, how to budget money, how to spend leisure time, and how to respond when frustrated or angry often exacerbate these difficulties.

Schloss, Alper, and Jayne (1994) presented a three-dimensional decision model that a teacher may use to expand the range of choices of students with disabilities. They base their model on a careful consideration of the benefits of increased freedom of choice balanced with the potential for risk to the student. The three dimensions considered are: (1) degree of input the student with disabilities has in the decision, (2) degree of physical, emotional, or economic risk involved if the decision is wrong, and (3) degree to which the student with disabilities must accept the input of others in decision making.

Educators can provide students with disabilities many opportunities to learn to make appropriate choices in general education settings. Initially, the choices can be relatively simple and risk-free (e.g., choice of food in the cafeteria, choice of activity during recess or free time). The choice options available can gradually expand depending on the age of the student, ability, and past record of making prudent decisions. The student can make decisions such as whom to sit next to, how to spend money, and what elective subjects to take in school. Older students may have some or total input into decisions regarding what job they would like training on and where they might like to live as an adult. The choice options available to the student can be expanded or restricted based on degree of risk and past student performance at any point in time.

Schloss, Alper, and Jayne (1994) recommended that teaching strategies for self-determination skills consist of managing prompts, that is, providing only the degree of assistance needed by the student to make an appropriate choice. Using the minimal amount of prompts, or input from the trainer, in naturally occurring choice situations throughout the school day should enable the student with disabilities to exert an increasing degree of choice and control over his or her own life.

Simulations may be useful for teaching self-determination skills in two kinds of situations (Schloss, Alper, & Jayne, 1994). First, the teacher may decide to simulate an activity that naturally occurs only infrequently and, therefore, provides few opportunities to practice. Examples of such an activity might include interviewing for a job or selecting holiday gifts for the family. Second, simulations are necessary in training for situations in which making the wrong choice carries a high degree of risk. What to do when alone with a member of the opposite sex and how to respond if approached by a stranger are examples.

Social Skills and Considerations for General Education Settings

The final curriculum area we will discuss in this chapter is social skills. Because Chapter 8 covered this topic in detail, we will provide an example of how teachers used the curriculum identification process to promote social skills and friendships between students with and without disabilities who were attending an inclusive school setting for the first time.

The following is a description of a program aimed at creating circles of friends (Forest & Lusthaus, 1989) for students with and without disabilities entering junior high from a variety of general and special education settings.

When students with disabilities are included in general education settings for the first time during the junior high years, many people involved may feel uncomfortable. Parents, general and special education teachers, administrators, and the students themselves are not sure what to expect. Involvement in extracurricular activities for students who are entering the general education setting for the first time may alleviate some of these feelings and promote socialization among all students. Many of the students entering middle school may not know each other as a result of coming from different elementary schools. A circle of friends club may allow for the forging of supportive friendships in this new setting.

If extracurricular clubs are already a part of the school program, interested parties may choose to sponsor such a club. The group should advertise its formation in whatever way other groups typically advertise their existence. The emphasis in describing the group should be on making new friends, talking with friends, playing games, and having fun.

A number of students may show up at the first meeting just to see what it is about. Games in which all participants can be successful are great icebreakers. A brainstorming session at this first meeting may help identify goals and interests of the group.

Establishing routines and symbols that are associated with the group may help develop a sense of membership. Samples might include choosing a group name, a signal or sign, and a mascot. Members should set up a routine meeting schedule that includes a variety of different types of activities (opening agenda, large and small cooperative groups, snacks). Activities that randomly assign students to cooperative groups and allow all students to interact and get to know each other are a preliminary step to facilitating the establishment of friendships.

A Case Study: John F. Kennedy Middle School

This situation involved a group of students with moderate to severe disabilities entering a culturally diverse suburban middle school for seventh, eighth, and ninth graders. Everyone directly involved with the program was new to the setting. Both the faculty and the student body of the school approached the situation with apprehension. Administrators integrated the students with disabilities into lunch and physical education initially. Their schedules gradually included more inclusionary classes as the year progressed. Yet, opportunities for socialization were minimal.

One of the advantages the school had to offer its students without disabilities was a previously established after-school activity program. The special educator decided to form a "Circle of Friends" club as a way to implement activities that would focus on the strengths and interests of students with and without disabilities in a fun and supportive environment. The school administration was highly supportive of the idea.

Prospective members of the club included students the teachers selected, individuals the counselors and principal suggested, members of the student council, and anyone who expressed an interest in the club. The special educator presented the club as a way to add to the acquaintance and friendship circles of all who joined.

Before each of the three nine-week sessions, the school distributed flyers describing the various after-school activities. The first description of "Circle of Friends" said, "Selected students will explore and develop friendships through group discussions and activities requiring team work and socialization skills." This changed for the later two sessions to read, "Talk with peers, play lots of games, and celebrate friendship." Initially, the school sent notes to parents of interested persons describing the purpose of the organization in detail. Also, the school used posters and buttons to spark interest. Throughout the year, members of the Circle of Friends club received little notes (with candy, buttons, etc. attached) containing reminders of their value to the club.

The Circle of Friends club held meetings once a week for one hour. The number in attendance fluctuated but was typically fifteen to twenty students. The school administration did not require special education paraprofessionals to participate in the club because it met after school hours; however, they joined in with enthusiasm. The school asked parents of the students to attend each meeting to assist the teachers. As an added benefit, the parents had the opportunity to develop their own friendships with people who might share similar experiences and concerns.

Generally, meetings followed a format similar to this one:

I. Introduction (approximately ten minutes)
    A. Review the posted rules
        1. Follow directions
        2. Use and pay attention to the "Quiet Sign" (peace sign)
        3. Treat others as you would like to be treated
        4. Be positive and have fun
    B. Announce upcoming events
    C. Discuss questions and concerns
II. Large group activity (approximately 10 minutes)
    "Energizers" for the purpose of meeting new people.
    "People Bingo" (available from Quest Books) is an example of such a game where members must find names to put in spaces that request some aspect like, "Has a pet," and "Sleeps past 10 a.m. on Saturdays."
III. Small group activity (approximately 20 minutes)
    This included making posters and buttons for the club, preparing small skits, playing games like UNO and Sorry, trimming Campbell Soup labels as a service project, making pizzas, etc.

IV. Refreshments (approximately 15 minutes)

The associated parents provided chips, cookies, soda, etc. on a rotating schedule. Students remained in their small groups, and teachers encouraged them to exchange phone numbers during this time.

V. Closure (approximately 5 minutes)

This provides a time set aside to express thoughts about the club, friendship, or other topics. A group hug or a song was the last activity on the agenda so the meeting would have an upbeat ending.

Several field trips took the place of meetings. These included games at the bowling alley and an end-of-the-session party at a local restaurant owned by one member's father. Parents and teachers provided the transportation.

A brainstorm session early in the year helped the group define some common goals to accomplish as a team. Teachers asked everyone to suggest ways that they could be friends to the school. As a result, the students planted flowers in front of the school and participated in the Campbell's Labels for Education program to gain educational and athletic equipment. The members generally treated disruptive behavior during the meetings as a communicative attempt. They handled such behavior accordingly in each situation. "Time out" situations were rare. The members felt encouraged to cheer for ideas and the accomplishments of others.

Summary

In this chapter, we addressed areas of the curriculum necessary for students with disabilities that are not typically a part of the general education curriculum. Proficiency in self-care, self-determination, and socialization skills are all critical for students with disabilities. Lack of competence in these areas leads to dependence on others, lack of meaningful contact with persons without disabilities, and restricted access to inclusive settings in school and the community.

Although teachers do not typically provide instruction in these areas of the curriculum to the majority of students without disabilities, opportunities for instruction exist within general education settings. Moreover, because students without disabilities have typically mastered many of these skills, they can often serve as peer tutors, coaches, special friends or buddies, or they can work with students with disabilities in cooperative learning groups.

References

Alper, S., Schloss, P. J., & Schloss, C. N. (Eds.) (1994). *Families of persons with disabilities: Consultation and advocacy.* Boston: Allyn and Bacon.

Blatt, B. (1987). The community imperative and human values. In R. F. Antonak & J. A. Mulick (Eds.), *Transition in mental retardation: The community imperative revisited* (pp. 236–247). Norwood, NJ: Ablex.

Falvey, M. A. (1989). Community-based curriculum: *Instructional strategies for students with severe handicaps,* (2nd ed.). Baltimore: Paul H. Brookes.

Forest, M., & Lusthaus, E. (1989). Promoting educational equality for all students: Circles and maps. In S. Stainback, W. Stainback, & M. Forest (Eds.), *Educating all students in the mainstream of regular education.* Baltimore: Paul H. Brookes, pp. 43–57.

Itard, J. M. G. (1962). *Wild boy of Aveyron.* (G. Humphrey & M. Humphrey, Eds. and trans.). New York: Appleton-Century-Crofts. (Original work published 1801).

Kishi, G., Teelucksingh, B., Zollers, N., Park-Lee, S., & Meyer, L. (1988). Daily decision-making in community residences: A social comparison of adults with and without mental retardation. *American Journal on Mental Retardation, 92,* 430–435.

Realon, R. E., Favell, J. E., & Lowerre, A. (1990). The effects of making choices on engagement levels with persons who are profoundly multiply handicapped. *Education and Training in Mental Retardation, 25,* 299–305.

Reid-Arnold, G., Doherty, R., Schloss, P. J., Alper, S., & Green, C. *Meal planning and preparation for youth with mental retardation and mental illness.* (Manuscript submitted for publication.)

Schloss, P. J., Alper, S., & Jayne, D. (1994). Self-determination for persons with disabilities: Choice, risk, and dignity. *Exceptional Children, 60* (3), 215–225.

Snell, M. E. (1987). *Instruction of students with severe disabilities* (3rd ed.). New York: Charles E. Merrill.

Snell, M. E. (1993). *Instruction of students with severe disabilities* (4th ed.). New York: Charles E. Merrill.

12

MANAGEMENT OF EXCESS BEHAVIOR IN INCLUSIVE SETTINGS

JAMES CHARLES GREEN   *SHERI L. MENSCHER*

Objectives

After completing this chapter the reader will be able to:

1. Define excessive behavior, and give examples in each of three categories.
2. Describe the progression from aversive to nonaversive behavior management strategies.
3. Describe the purposes and communicative intent of behavior.
4. Define and describe functional analysis and functional assessment.
5. Outline and describe how teachers should prepare for behavioral interventions.
6. Outline and describe the steps taken in implementing a behavioral intervention strategy.

Key Terms

Aggression
Antecedent
Aversive
Behavior management
Consequence
Dangerous behavior
Destructive behavior
Disruptive behavior
Excess behavior

Functional analysis
Functional assessment
Inclusion
Intervention
Performance periods
Reinforcement
Replacement behavior
Social-communicative hypothesis
Target behavior

During the latter half of the 1980s, individuals with disabilities began to gain opportunities for inclusion in schools, classes, and other types of communities. As this movement grew, individuals with severe cognitive and physical disabilities began to gain access to previously denied environments. If one examined this movement, however, a trend began to emerge. This trend was one of exclusion from these same environments for one group of individuals—those who display excessive, challenging behaviors. Many of these individuals have cognitive or physical characteristics that are similar to those of their peers without disabilities. The most common justification for their assignment to restrictive environments is difficulty in the management of the challenging behavior.

This chapter will present a discussion of the management of excess behaviors. Because individuals who display excess behaviors have demonstrated that they are able to learn how to get what they want, a philosophy of teaching more appropriate ways to gain the same result will be presented. The chapter will begin with a definition of those behaviors we classify as excessive. A review of typical management techniques that teachers employ to manage challenging behaviors will follow. The progression toward a focus of nonaversive management strategies will be highlighted as the chapter reviews the communicative intent of challenging behaviors. Functional analysis and functional assessment procedures will be discussed. Finally, the chapter will present a management system for working with teens and young adults who demonstrate excess behaviors.

Definitions of Excess Behavior

Individuals who display severe behaviors are usually among the last in consideration for inclusion. Even after these individuals have the opportunity to move into another environment, they are often limited in access or participation. Often, school authorities return them to the previous environment or send them to an even more restrictive site (Elmquist, 1989; Janney & Meyer, 1990; Mayeda & Sutter, 1981; Meyer & Evans, 1986; Singer, Close, Irvin, Gersten & Sailor, 1984).

When excess behaviors become targets for intervention, they typically fall into three levels (Voeltz, Evans, Derer, and Hanashiro, 1983). The lowest of these levels is disruptive behavior, or excess behavior reflecting normal deviance (Meyer and Evans, 1986). Specific behaviors that might fall within this level include (1) refusals, (2) bumping into people and objects, (3) pounding surfaces, (4) throwing or tearing items, (5) spitting, (6) crying, and (7) lying on the floor. The next level of challenging behavior is destructive. Destructive behaviors are those that are serious and require formal considerations. There is some subjectivity involved when making the distinction between behaviors that are distracting and those destructive. This is due to individual interventionist tolerance levels and the variability in distraction levels of classmates and community members. Behaviors that might be destructive are those that interfere with attention to assigned task or activity. Some examples are (1) screaming, (2) tantrums, (3) pulling on people, (4) throwing and tearing work materials, and (5) any physically aggressive behaviors to self or others that do *not* result in tissue damage. Dangerous behaviors are health or life-threatening and include physical aggressions that result in tissue damage such as (1) hitting, (2) kicking, (3) biting, (4) scratching, (5) head banging, and (6) eye poking. Running from the school or group while in the community might also be classified as dangerous behavior.

Working with individuals who display excessive levels of challenging behaviors requires systematic, intensive, and comprehensive intervention. Because most individuals who display behaviors of this intensity once had to attend segregated schools or community centers and often lived in institutional settings, many of the strategies for working with the challenging behaviors were based upon research conducted in laboratory or clinical treatment settings. The next section will examine these interventions for addressing challenging behaviors.

Progression from Aversive to Nonaversive Management Strategies

Typically, management of severe behaviors employed a strict behavior modification approach that used contingencies so as to decrease or eliminate the behavior. Often, these excessive behaviors had been part of the individual's behavioral repertoire for many years. Even with a continuum of interventions, such as (1) contingent reinforcement, (2) ignoring, and (3) reduction of demands, the behaviors did not decrease to desired levels. Often, teachers employed more intrusive strategies such as (1) contingent physical restraint, (2) exclusionary time out, and (3) response cost. Teacher, and caregivers have used a continuum of strategies from least intrusive to most intrusive for many years in schools, community, and residential settings. The administration of noxious solutions such as Tabasco sauce, lemon juice, and ammonia spray was also a management technique.

Many professionals who work with individuals who have severe disabilities began criticizing these management strategies and advocating for teaching appropriate behaviors to replace challenging behaviors (Durand, 1990; Evans & Meyer, 1985; LaVigna & Donnellan, 1990; Meyer & Evans, 1989). These criticisms came to the forefront with the publication of an article by Linscheid, Iwata, Ricketts, Williams, and Griffin (1990) on the use of the electric shock device, the Self-Injurious Behavior Inhibiting System (SIBIS).

In addition to the controversy over the use of punishment, a debate continues among professionals as to what the term *aversive* actually means. Horner et al. (1990b) define *aversive* as "... a class of stimuli that are followed by escape or avoidance responses" (p. 126). Turnbull et al. (1986) define *aversive procedures* as "... any intervention that is applied as a result of a person's behaving in certain disapproved ways, and that is intended to have or has the effect of providing physical or emotional pain or discomfort" (p. 176). In calling for the ban or restriction of aversive behavior procedures, some researchers categorize interventions that

(1) deliver physical pain, (2) result in harm that requires medical attention, or (3) are disrespectful or dehumanizing, as aversive (Iwata, 1988; Matson & Taras, 1989).

Contributing to the impetus for the abolishment of aversive procedures were resolutions by professional organizations such as Association for Persons with Severe Handicaps (TASH), and the American Association of Mental Retardation (AAMR). Numerous states have regulations or laws banning usage of aversive procedures.

Thompson (1990) reiterates how the term *aversive* has been used subjectively and, therefore, makes it difficult to clearly classify interventions. He further points out that aversive must be viewed within the context of the individual and the intervention. Meyer and Evans (1989) presented removing a food tray when a tantrum occurs as nonaversive. Thompson (1990) identifies this intervention as a time-out procedure.

The precise definition of aversive procedures will, most likely, continue to be debated by professionals who bring differing perspectives and philosophies to the field of working with individuals who display excess behaviors. Durand (1990a) characterizes the controversy and debate over this conversion to a nonaversive approach of managing challenging behaviors by stating "The question is no longer whether these procedures should be used, nor is it when these procedures should be used. Instead, the real question is how best to use positive behavioral interventions to facilitate the changes suggested...." (p. 141)

Whether strictly nonaversive procedures produce clinically significant changes in challenging behaviors is currently under scrutiny. Differential reinforcement of other behaviors (DRO) and differential reinforcement of incompatible behaviors (DRI) are frequently studied methods. Friman (1990) concludes that "research on DRO/DRI used on high-rate behavior problems in children with severe disabilities has produced mixed results" (p. 64). He reviewed comparative experiments that suggest the superiority of overcorrection and contingent restraint over nonaversive procedures. Other research suggests that DRO/DRI methods are effective when combined with reprimands, restraint, or time-out. Friman's review included two examples of research support for the solitary use of DRO/DRI.

Proponents of nonaversive management strategies advocate for an emphasis on the analysis of learning principles. Behavior and its communicative intent are the focus of this approach.

The Communicative Intent of Behavior

Carr (1977) and Carr and Durand (1985a) discuss the social-communicative hypothesis of behavior as a reciprocal function. These authors explain that an individual may acquire and maintain certain behaviors because of the social consequences that they produce. When looking at behavior as purposeful for communication, Meyer and Janney (1989) state "behaviors are emitted by the student to achieve some purpose..." (p. 263). Numerous studies support the social-communicative function of behavior (Carr & Durand, 1985b; Durand & Carr, 1987; Durand & Crimmins, 1987). Behaviors the individual displays to (1) gain attention, (2) escape or avoid, or (3) obtain something further categorizes this social-communicative intent. Meyer and Evans (1986) further classify some excess behaviors as intents for purposes other than communication. These authors identify self-regulatory behaviors that allow the individuals to adjust energy, arousal, and/or attention levels. The behaviors are dependent upon different stimulus conditions and, therefore, may vary. Behaviors that were previously considered "self-stimulatory" may serve a self-regulatory purpose. Self-stimulatory behaviors can also function as play or self-entertainment. A way to help discriminate self-regulatory behaviors from play behaviors is to observe the individual's task attention. Self-regulatory behaviors do not interfere with the individual's task attention. Play behaviors distract the individual and interfere with completion of task.

Proponents of functional behavior also ascribe to careful analysis and assessment of the behavior. Meyer and Janney (1989) state "if such behaviors do have specific functions, the most effective intervention strategy would logically involve teaching the appropriate positive replacement skills to students..." (p. 263). Teaching of appropriate skills is often part of positive programming or behavioral support.

Functional Analysis and Functional Assessment

Not only is it helpful to analyze behaviors to determine their function, it is important to gather assessment information to identify more appropriate behaviors that will serve as a functional equivalent for the challenging behavior. Functional analysis is a component of functional assessment. A functional assessment not only identifies variables, but also develops a hypothesis about the behavior.

Functional Analysis

Traditionally, functional analysis deals with the ABCs of behavior—the antecedent, the behavior, and the consequences of the behavior (Alberto & Troutman, 1990; Snell, 1987). Manipulation of consequences are planned to increase or decrease behavior. Functional analysis typically analyzes all events that happen before the behavior occurs. Characteristics of the behavior such as (1) complexity, (2) functional nature, (3) criteria, and (4) appropriateness are studied (Brown, 1991). An important component in functional analysis is the direct observation of changes in the targeted behavior. Determinations regarding the purpose of the behavior are made through functional analysis. A functional analysis usually follows certain steps (O'Neill, Horner, Albin, Storey & Sprague, 1990):

1. Describe the behavior.
2. Define potential ecological events that may affect the behavior(s).
3. Define events and situations that predict occurrences of the behavior(s).
4. Identify the "function" of the undesirable behavior(s). What consequences maintain the behavior(s)?
5. Define the efficiency of the undesirable behavior(s).
6. Define the primary method(s) the person uses to communicate.
7. What events, actions, and objects does the person perceive as positive?
8. What "functional alternative" behaviors does the person know?
9. Provide a history of the undesirable behaviors and the programs that caregivers or teachers have attempted.

Functional Assessment

Karsh and Repp (1991) highlight the importance of functional assessment. These authors note that functional assessment (1) guides the decision making process, (2) identifies the functional relationship between problem behavior and conditions or events in the environment, (3) leads to hypothesis driven interventions that address the function of the behavior, and (4) focuses on nonaversive interventions that teach efficient, appropriate responses to replace the problem behavior. Lennox and Miltenberger (1989) encourage interventionists to conduct a functional assessment prior to attempting to teach the individual positive replacement behaviors. Possible risks associated with the omission of a functional assessment include: (1) a delay in effective treatment procedures, (2) counter-therapeutic effects, and (3) unnecessary exposure to aversive and restrictive procedures.

There are a variety of methods for conducting a functional assessment. The first category of methods are informal and include: (1) behavioral interviews, (2) rating scales, (3) checklists, and (4) questionnaires. The next category involves direct observation similar to an antecedent-behavioral-consequence assessment. The last type deals with manipulation or functional analysis of the hypothetical reasons, functions, or purposes for the challenging behavior.

Foster-Johnson and Dunlap (1993) presented a comprehensive functional assessment and the resultant behavioral intervention plan to manage head hitting as an effort to escape undesired activities. Redmond, Bennett, Wiggert, and McLean (1993) summarized their use of a functional assessment to support a teen in the community. The challenging behaviors were attempts to tear or shred clothing. Another example that included a functional assessment (Cooper, Peck, Wacker, and Millard, 1993) supported the simultaneous use of functional assessment and behavioral intervention.

Meyer and Janney (1989) encourage interventionists to look for evidence that "the outcomes associated with their efforts are meaningful for the student" (p. 269). They caution that meaningful outcomes should be the driving force behind helping students learn alternatives for challenging behaviors. Horner et al. (1990a) encourage practitioners to assist in the "development of effective procedures for (a) prevention, (b) assessment, (c) intervention, (d) training, and (e) systems development so as to make it unnecessary to use procedures that involve pain, tissue damage or humiliation" (p. 146). The remaining portion of this chapter will detail an intervention system used with teens and young adults who display excess behaviors.

Suggested Guidelines for the Management of Excess Behavior

Teachers, parents, and other caregivers may be more interested in the results of a behavioral change program than the theories behind it. Daily interactions with children or adults whose behavior is antisocial is a continuous source of stress. Frustrating attempts to decrease inappropriate behavior replace precious instructional time. Professionals must recognize that a student who is in constant need of teacher intervention to correct maladaptive behaviors actually is displaying a desperate need for instruction in the skill areas that should serve as replacements for the problem behaviors in the repertoire. Following are general guidelines with specific examples for successful classroom management of students who display excessive behaviors. The first sections describe the preparations the teacher must make prior to the introduction of the intervention strategy.

Teacher Preparation for Intervention

To appropriately prepare to successfully bring about a significant positive behavior change in a student, the teacher must answer the following questions.

Exactly What Is the Behavior Targeted for Change?
It is common to hear teachers say that a child is simply "out of control". Almost anyone can create an image in their mind as to what the teacher means. This is certainly enough information when used in an informal discussion but is insufficient should the teacher be asking for answers to a specific classroom problem. The first step in helping a child manage excess behavior is to identify and define those behaviors that need to change. This provides a better understanding of what both the teacher and the student can expect.

Perhaps the best method for the initial gathering of data regarding problem behaviors is simple anecdotal recording. The teacher can easily do this by writing brief descriptions of behaviors immediately after an incident. The teacher should examine this information to determine exactly what led to the undesirable behavior (antecedent), the discrete characteristics of the behavior, and what occurred immediately following the incident (consequences). For practical reasons, descriptions should be short and to the point. They must, however, include enough information for the teacher or a consultant to determine the characteristics surrounding the display of behavior.

What Should I Teach as a Replacement Behavior?

Once the teacher has determined the characteristics of the target behavior (the behavior the teacher wishes to replace), he or she must identify a replacement behavior. For example, one might seek to teach a student to raise a hand to be called upon (replacement behavior) rather than to talk out without permission (target behavior). The teacher should thoughtfully examine the possibilities and choose the most age-appropriate substitute behavior within the child's abilities.

What is Reinforcing to This Child?

All teachers have a reinforcement "menu" in their heads. The teacher knows that he or she will have to be ready to provide numerous rewards throughout the day. These rewards are the natural consequences of socially appropriate behavior. A smile, a pat on the back, or verbal praise are all items on the teacher's menu of reinforcers. When dealing with children who display excessive behaviors it is important to realize that natural reinforcers for appropriate behavior have probably been in place for quite a while with no substantial effect. For this reason it is sometimes necessary to pair a contrived reinforcer, such as edibles or special activities, with a natural reinforcer at the beginning of the behavioral intervention. As the student displays the appropriate behavior to the satisfaction of the teacher, the contrived reinforcer may be faded and the natural ones maintained.

Teachers may use past experience with the child to determine what would best motivate him or her, or the teacher may experiment with several reinforcers to see which one is the most motivating to that particular student. The most powerful reinforcer could already be available to the student on a noncontingent basis. Should this be the case, the teacher should not hesitate to make that reinforcer contingent upon the appropriate display of the replacement behavior he or she is trying to teach the student.

How Often Is the Reinforcer Provided?

Once the teacher has determined what the expected replacement behavior is to be, he or she must determine when to present the reinforcer. When dealing with behaviors previously described in this chapter, it is most effective to ask for the child to display the appropriate behavior for as long a period as possible. This period will correlate closely with the student's attention span and age. The longer the student is able to attend to task, the less often the reinforcer would need to be presented.

In a school setting, it may be wise to structure these performance periods around the normal school schedule. If school periods are fifty minutes each, the reinforcement performance periods might be twenty-five, giving the student an opportunity to earn two reinforcers in each period. For example, if a student uses appropriate terms (replacement behavior) to address peers and the teacher rather than using profanity and racial slurs (target behavior) for the first half of the math period, that student would receive five minutes of computer time to play a video game. The teacher can shorten or lengthen these periods as needed to adjust to the individual student. It is wise for teachers to initially set the periods at a length that will ensure at least moderate success. This will allow students to associate the reinforcer with the replacement behavior.

How Do I Adapt Natural Consequences to My Classroom?

Rules are useless if they are not followed. It would be nice if everyone would follow the rules simply because it is the right thing to do. However, some individuals need a little more encouragement. This encouragement comes in the form of consequences. Some consequences are natural, while others are contrived. We all know that driving a car over the speed limit is dangerous. One is much more likely to have an accident (natural consequence) at a high rate of speed. This natural consequence would seem to be enough of an incentive for drivers to slow down and obey the law, but is it? If the highway patrol stopped writing tickets for speeding (contrived consequence) today, would drivers continue to obey the speed limit to the extent that they now do?

Two things are important to remember when deciding upon consequences. First, the severity of the consequence must fit the severity of the behavior. For example, the consequence for chewing gum in class would certainly not be as severe as the consequence for striking another classmate. Just as problem behaviors range from disruptive to dangerous, consequences should also be on a continuum.

Second, consequences should fall within guidelines for behavior management that the school district and the building principal have set forth and approved. Administrators should be aware that educational interventions in special education are individualized and may need to occasionally deviate from normal school policy. The use of profanity by a child may warrant a suspension in some schools. What if a child receiving services for an emotional disturbance has a problem with using profanity, and that problem is a result of a disability? Would it then be appropriate, or legal, to dismiss that child for using profanity? A close working relationship with building administrators is important when dealing with excess behaviors, as they must have input into these decisions.

Perhaps the most important thing to remember about consequences is that the teacher must consistently implement them. If the teacher has determined that the consequence for using profanity is losing the privilege of speaking to peers for the rest of the day, then under no circumstances should the teacher allow the student to speak with peers. The teacher might want to ensure this by engaging the student in an activity that would not be conducive to conversation. Any inconsistencies in the delivery of consequences will signal to the student that there is a flaw in the system and he or she need only to learn how to exploit it. This "learning" will take the form of increases in display of the target behavior and will inhibit the student's ability to focus on the more appropriate replacement behavior.

How Do I Return the Student to My Regular Classroom Environment?

Although the teacher should be pleased when a student begins to have success at displaying the replacement behavior instead of the excessive one, some intervention procedures are too intrusive to be implemented over long periods of time. The teacher must begin to "fade" the intervention once the student has become successful. There are several methods of fading that will enable the student to maintain the appropriate behavior. One is to gradually increase the performance period for receiving the reinforcer. Students would need to display the replacement behavior for the entire math period, rather than just half, to earn an opportunity to play a computer game. Computer time could eventually fade until the entire day's performance determined whether the student earned it.

From Theory to Practice

Teachers want to spend the majority of time taking action, rather than planning for it. The following is a task analysis for teachers for dealing with excessive behaviors. Although directions and examples are for dealing with one student, the task analysis easily applies to groups.

Operationally Define the Behavior Change to the Student
Sit with the student in a distraction free setting and explain, using discrete and age-appropriate terms, the behavior you wish to reduce as well as the one with which you want to replace it. This step is very important as it may save the student from spending time searching for the correct response. It may help to have the student repeat the definitions to ensure understanding.

Describe Reinforcers and Consequences
The teacher should use general terms to identify reinforcers and seek to have the student associate them with the replacement behavior. The teacher can strengthen the reinforcing effect by having the student (with guidance) select reinforcers and consequences. The teacher should define the consequences resulting from performance of the target behavior and associate them with the behavior that will bring them about.

Set Length of Performance Periods
The teacher should make clear to the student the amount of time in which the student must perform the replacement behavior in order to receive the reinforcer. This period should ideally match the student's estimated attention span. Should the student lack the ability to tell time, the teacher may use other standards of measure. This may provide an excellent opportunity for the teacher to present time-telling skills in conjunction with the behavior management plan. For example, the teacher may say to the student, "If you can speak in a normal tone of voice for fifteen minutes, you may play with your puzzle. Fifteen minutes is how long story-time lasts, and that is what we are going to do now".

Explain the Procedure to the Student
Again being careful to use terms that the student can understand, outline the steps to be taken in the behavior management procedure. Have the student verbalize, if able, each step in proper order. The teacher should clearly explain the contingencies involved and have the student demonstrate an understanding of them. Particular emphasis should be placed on "if/then" statements from the student. For example, "If I keep my hands to myself for the entire period, then I will earn a re-

inforcer" or "If I use profanity during math, then I will miss recess." It is important to note that should the student be unable to verbalize understanding of these or any previous steps, more intrusive teaching procedures can explain the procedure. If the contingencies are consistently applied, students learn to associate behaviors and their consequences.

Implement Procedure

The initial trials in implementation may be most important. Consistency is imperative. The first few days of any behavioral intervention are when the student will most likely "test" the teacher's commitment to the procedure. The teacher must be physically and emotionally prepared to implement the procedure regardless of the student's actions. The student may display behaviors that are more antisocial than the one to be replaced at this point in order to manipulate the situation.

No intervention procedure is foolproof. Teachers must be ready and willing to "mend" the holes in the program as the student finds them. However, the teacher must use caution to ensure that changes made in the procedure do not result in the student being reinforced for maladaptive behaviors. It may be necessary to adapt intervention procedures to address problems that occur as a result of the student suddenly being held accountable for his or her actions.

Evaluate and Provide Feedback

The teacher should have a clear and systematic method for evaluating the student's performance with regard to the desired behavior change. We recommend that teachers use charts or graphs to display performance data. Charts should not be for public display. Having a personal chart on the wall for everyone to see could serve as an inadvertent reinforcer for displaying inappropriate behaviors. It could also be a violation of the student's privacy. Using a folder to organize data in chart or graph form is a better idea. The teacher can set aside a few minutes at the end of the day to review the student's performance with him or her. If the reinforcement schedule calls for a reward at the end of the day, this is a good opportunity for the student to self-evaluate and determine if he or she earned the reward.

Begin Fading Procedure

Once the student has met criteria for acceptable behavior, the teacher should begin to fade the intervention. It is important for the teacher to fully explain to the student how and why this is taking place. The teacher should thoughtfully plan the fading procedure prior to implementation. Teachers can expect a small fluctuation in the student's behavior as primary reinforcers are faded and replaced with social reinforcement. If consequences for the exhibition of the target behavior remain in place and are implemented with the same consistency as before, the student's behavior should return to established criteria for success. This is an excellent opportunity for the teacher to promote any new activities that the student may participate in due to positive behavior change. These might include participation of the student in group activities and games for which he or she was previously ineligible due to maladaptive behaviors.

Aggression

Ideally, all students would respond enthusiastically to behavioral interventions as we have outlined them. Many will do so after some initial tests of wills with the teacher, but there are always some who will pull out all of the stops to win this battle. Special and general education teachers must be prepared to successfully deal with these students. The student's most intrusive form of maladaptive behavior is generally aggression. The student may direct this behavior at either the teacher or other students in the classroom. Students know that no one will ignore aggressive behavior. They may use aggression to avoid nonpreferred activities.

It is important for the teacher to be completely familiar with district and building policies towards student aggression. Many schools require an immediate suspension of any student who shows aggressive behavior toward a teacher. Some students are exceptions to this policy due to their specific disability. If this is the case, a written and approved plan for dealing with aggression should be on file with the proper school authorities. Should the teacher expect to deal with aggressive students, he or she must know district and building policy related to physically touching a student. The following guidelines will be helpful in formulating a plan for teachers dealing with aggressive students.

1. The aggressive student should be isolated from other students as soon as possible, preferably without any physical guidance.
2. Physical guidance of the student should only be used to ensure the safety of the student and others. School personnel should not touch the student merely to force compliance with directions unless noncompliance places the student or others in danger.
3. Counseling or negotiating with an aggressive student who is in an agitated state should be discouraged.
4. All school personnel who are expected to deal with an historically aggressive student should be trained in the proper use of physical guidance and management.
5. Aggressive incidents should be well documented with particular emphasis on events immediately prior to the display of aggression.
6. Particular care should be taken to ensure that aggression is not rewarded by allowing the student to avoid an unpleasant situation. The student should re-enter the activity when he or she is in a relaxed condition and all consequences have been introduced.
7. The student should be required to provide some form of restitution for any physical or emotional damage done to objects or individuals.

It is important to remember that this information is intended as a guide, not a blueprint to managing excessive behaviors. Each student, teacher, and school has individual characteristics that the teacher who is attempting to work with a child with maladaptive behaviors should always carefully consider.

Summary

This chapter focused on the management of excessive behaviors. Excessive behavior was defined and classified as disruptive, destructive, and dangerous. A review and discussion of the trend toward nonaversive management strategies was included. This review discussed the changing definition of the term *aversive*.

It has been emphasized that students displaying excessive behaviors can learn more appropriate responses. Systematic, and direct intervention strategies were described as the most appropriate method for addressing these behaviors. Finally, a description of behavior management principles for successful management of excessive behavior was provided.

References

Alberto, P. A., & Troutman, A. C. (1990). *Applied behavior analysis for teachers* (3rd ed.). Columbus, OH: Charles E. Merrill.

Brown, F. (1991). Creative daily scheduling: A nonintrusive approach to challenging behaviors in community residences. *Journal of the Association for Persons with Severe Handicaps, 16*(2), 75–84.

Carr, E. G. (1977). The motivation of self-injurious behavior: A review of some hypotheses. *Psychological Bulletin, 84,* 800–816.

Carr, E. G., & Durand, V. M. (1985a). The social-communicative basis of severe behavior problems in children. In S. Reiss & R. Bootzin (Eds.), *Theoretical issues in behavior therapy* (pp. 219–254). New York: Academic Press.

Carr, E. G., & Durand, V. M. (1985b). Reducing behavior problems through functional communication training. *Journal of Applied Behavioral Analysis, 18,* 111–126.

Cooper, L. J., Peck, S., Wacker, D. P., & Millard, T. (1993). Functional assessment for a student with a mild mental disability and persistent behavior problems. *Teaching Exceptional Children, 25*(3), 56–57.

Durand, V. M. (1990a). The "aversives" debate is over: And now the work begins. *Journal of the Association for Persons with Severe Handicaps, 15*(3), 140–141.

Durand, V. M. (1990b). *Severe behavior problems: A functional communication approach.* New York: Guilford.

Durand, V. M., & Carr, E. G. (1987). Social influences on "self-stimulatory" behavior: Analysis and treatment application. *Journal of Applied Behavior Analysis, 20,* 119–132.

Durand, V. M., & Crimmins, D. B. (1987). Assessment and treatment of psychotic speech in an autistic child. *Journal of Autism and Developmental Disorders, 17,* 17–28.

Evans, I. M., & Meyer, L. H. (1985). *An educative approach to behavior problems: A practical decision model for interventions with severely handicapped learners.* Baltimore: Paul H. Brookes.

Elmquist, D. L. (1989). *Features of effectiveness of residential treatment centers for adolescents with behavioral disorders: A literature review.* Logan: Utah State University Department of Special Education.

Foster-Johnson, L., & Dunlap, G. (1993). Using functional assessment to develop effective, individualized interventions for challenging behaviors. *Teaching Exceptional Children, 25*(3), 44–50.

Friman, P. C. (1990). Nonaversive treatment of high rate disruption: Child and provider effects. *Exceptional Children, 57*(1), 64–69.

Horner, R. H., Dunlap, G., Koegel, R. L., Carr, E. G., Sailor, W., Anderson, J., Albin, R. W., & O'Neil, R. E. (1990a). In support of integration for people with severe problem behaviors: A response to four commentaries. *Journal of the Association for Persons with Severe Handicaps, 15*(3), 145–147.

Horner, R. H., Dunlap, G., Koegel, R. L., Carr, E. G., Sailor, W., Anderson, J., Albin, R. W., & O'Neil, R. E. (1990b). Toward a technology of "nonaversive" behavioral support. *Journal of the Association for Persons with Severe Handicaps, 15*(3), 125–132.

Iwata, B. A. (1988). The development and adoption of controversial default technologies. *The Behavior Analyst, 11*, 149–157.

Janney, R. E., & Meyer, L. H. (1990). A consultation model to support integrated education services for students with severe disabilities and challenging behaviors. *Journal of the Association for Persons with Severe Handicaps, 15*(3), 186–199.

Karsh, K. G., & Repp, A. C. (1991). *Functional assessment of problem behaviors in educational settings.* Address to the Association for Persons with Severe Handicaps conference. Washington, D.C.

LaVigna, G. W., & Donnellan, A. M. (1986). *Alternatives to punishment: Solving behavior problems with nonaversive strategies.* New York: Irvington.

Lennox, D. B., & Miltenberger, R. G. (1989). Conducting a functional assessment of problem behavior in applied settings. *Journal of the Association for Persons with Severe Handicaps, 14*(4), 304–311.

Linscheid, T. R., Iwata, B. A., Ricketts, R. W., Williams, D. E., & Griffin, J. C. (1990). Clinical evaluation of the self-injurious behavior inhibiting system (SIBIS). *Journal of Applied Behavior Analysis, 23*, 53–78.

Matson, J. L., & Taras, M. E. (1989). A 20-year review of punishment and alternative methods to treat problem behaviors in developmentally delayed persons. *Research in Developmental Disabilities, 10*, 85–104.

Mayeda, T., & Sutter, P. (1981). Deinstitutionalization: Phase II. In R. H. Bruininks, C. E. Meyers, B. B. Sigford, & K. C. Lakin (Eds.), *Deinstitutionalization and community adjustment of mentally retarded people* (pp. 375–381). Washington, DC: American Association on Mental Deficiency.

Meyer, L. H., & Evans, I. M. (1989). Modification of excess behavior: An adaptive and functional approach for educational and community contexts. In R. H. Horner, L. H. Meyer, & H. D. Fredericks (Eds.), *Education of learners with severe handicaps: Exemplary service strategies* (pp. 315–350). Baltimore: Paul H. Brookes.

Meyer, L. H., & Janney, R. E. (1989). User-friendly measures of meaningful outcomes: Evaluating behavioral interventions. *Journal of the Association for Persons with Severe Handicaps, 14*(4), 263–270.

O'Neill, R. E., Horner, R. H., Albin, R. W., Storey, K., & Sprague, J. R. (1990). *Functional analysis of problem behavior: A practical assessment guide.* Sycamore, IL: Sycamore Press.

Redmond, N. B., Bennett, C., Wiggert, J., & McLean, B. (1993). Using functional assessment to support a student with severe disabilities in the community. *Teaching Exceptional Children, 25*(3), 51–52.

Singer, G. H. S., Close, D. W., Irvin, L. K., Gersten, R., & Sailor, W. (1984). An alternative to the institution for young people with severely handicapping conditions in a rural community. *Journal of the Association for Persons with Severe Handicaps, 9*, 251–261.

Snell, M. E. (1987). *Systematic instruction of persons with severe handicaps* (3rd ed.). Columbus, OH: Charles E. Merrill.

Thompson, T. (1990). The Humpty Dumpty world of "aversive" interventions. *Journal of the Association for Persons with Severe Handicaps, 15*(3), 136–139.

Turnbull, H. R., III, Guess, D., Backus, L. H., Barber, P. A., Fiedler, C. R., Helmsetter, E., & Summers, J. A. (1986). A model for analyzing the moral aspects of special education and behavioral interventions: The moral aspects of aversive procedures. In P. R. Dokecki & R. M. Zaner (Eds.), *Ethics in dealing with persons with severe handicaps: Toward a research agenda* (pp. 167–210). Baltimore: Paul H. Brookes.

Voeltz, L. M., Evans, I. M., Derer, K. R., & Hanashiro, R. (1983). Targeting excess behavior for change: A clinical decision model for selecting priority goals in educational contexts. *Child and Family Behavior Therapy, 5,* 17–35.

13

MANAGING THE NEEDS OF STUDENTS WITH PHYSICAL AND HEALTH CHALLENGES IN INCLUSIVE SETTINGS

LECH WISNIEWSKI   *ROBERTA ANDERSON*

Objectives

After completing this chapter the reader will be able to:

1. Identify the attitudes and concerns of teachers, parents, and nondisabled peers for the placement of students with physical or health challenges within inclusive environments.
2. Identify strategies for modifying the attitudes of nondisabled peers and teachers.
3. State the concerns of students with physical or health challenges for inclusive placement.
4. Identify programmatic changes that address the concerns for students with physical and health challenges.
5. State common characteristics of students with physical and health challenges.
6. Identify relevant antecedents for learning involving students with physical and health challenges.
7. State the importance of positioning, seating, standing, floor seating, and foot stability for students with physical disabilities.
8. Identify relevant accommodations that can be made to a student's class schedule.
9. List and discuss the following scheduling accommodations: daily schedules, absences, recess, and medication schedules.
10. Outline relevant curricular and instructional modifications for students with physical and health challenges.

11. Identify specific classroom modifications that can accommodate the needs of students with physical and health challenges.
12. List and discuss the following classroom accommodations: room arrangements, individual seating, classroom appliances, work surfaces, class discussions, note taking, seat work, homework, completing assignments, workbooks and worksheets, writing tools, stabilizing and using educational materials, and taking tests.
13. Differentiate the various roles of assistive-device technologies; to prevent, rehabilitate, augment, and facilitate normalcy.
14. Describe relevant high and light technologies for students with physical and health challenges.
15. Outline the use of assistive-devices to facilitate communication, achieve environmental control, increase mobility, and gain access to microcomputer technologies.

Key terms

Assistive-device and microcomputer technologies
Augmentative and alternative communication systems
Bibliotherapy
Cerebral palsy
Communication aids
Consultant services
Consultant teachers
Consultation
Curricular modifications
Cystic fibrosis

Environmental control
High technologies
HIV positive
Least restrictive environment
Light technologies
Medically fragile
Muscular dystrophy
Nonelectronic and electronic aids
Orthotic and prosthetic devices
Physical and health challenges
Semantic compaction
Spina bifida

Relevant legislation, a society that embraces the inclusion of all its members, and a continuing and evolving concept of a free and appropriate education provide students with special needs, equal educational opportunities within a least restrictive setting (e.g., Brady, McDougall, & Bennis, 1989; Kauffman, 1989; Turnbull, Ellis, Boggs, Brooks, & Biklen, 1981; Wang, Reynolds, & Walberg, 1986). As numerous school systems are including students with varying disabilities in inclusive settings, school personnel have developed comprehensive models for the delivery of educational services for students with physical or health challenges[1] (Dove,

---

[1]Impairments include spina bifida and cerebral palsy—the most frequently occurring conditions—to muscular dystrophy, orthopededic impairments, chronic bowel disorders, being HIV positive, arthopryposis, Still's disease, cystic fibrosis, and having severe poly-drug affection and allergies. Impairment also includes the necessity for close supervision to monitor a range of health conditions or medically fragility, often requiring specialized medication or medical equipment. Table 13.1 lists the more common impairments and their underlying characteristics.

Holder, Richards, & Wheller, 1984; Jones, 1983). Educational teams have developed specific curricular adaptations to include these students in art education (Blandy, 1989), business education (Beaverton School District 48, 1984; Burrow & Hill, 1983; Karjala, 1983), consumer education (Nemeth & DelRogers, 1981a), driver education (Oklahoma Curriculum Improvement Commission, 1973), home economics (Redick & Hughes, 1981), outdoor education (Tetlow, 1981), recreation/ leisure education (American Alliance for Health, Physical Education, Recreation and Dance, 1991; Christie, 1985, Cooney, Emes, Ford, & Wasson, 1985; Greaves & Richmond, 1982; Hutchinson & Lord, 1983; Jambor & Gargiulo, 1987; McAnaney, 1989; Roice, 1981; Wolfson, 1991), and science education (Jones, Lynn, Topping, Elliot, & Dempsey, 1984; Keller, Pauley, Starcher, & Proctor, 1983). Guidelines facilitate the inclusion of these students within (1) pre-school settings (Capper Foundation for Crippled Children, 1990; Heekin & Mengel, 1983), (2) special education transition programs (i.e., vocational education, employment, and independent living) (Shackelford & Henak, 1982), (3) a variety of settings that lead to independence (Boothroyd, Mack, & Mahan, 1989; DeJong, 1984; Leavitt & Terrell, 1984), and (4) career and guidance counseling (Lombana, 1982; Patette & Hourcade, 1984). In addition, guidelines have been developed that consider the unique needs of young women (Linda & Rousso, 1991).

These inclusive settings provide practitioners with practical "how-to" information and specific guidelines that lead to the inclusion of students with physical and health challenges. In this chapter, the specific needs of students with physical and health challenges who receive special and related services within inclusive settings are discussed. This discussion begins with an examination of the attitudes and concerns of teachers, nondisabled students, and students with physical and health challenges. In the next section, the discussion focuses on specific curricular adaptations and the role of assistive and microcomputer technologies in managing the needs of students with physical and health challenges.

Attitudes and Concerns

One obstacle to the inclusion of students with physical and health challenges is the attitudes and concerns of peers, teachers, and the larger social community. Teachers and other allied professionals, nondisabled peers, and community members often do not have the experience to structure and maintain a social and learning environment that facilitates positive social relationships and human growth for these students. These social relations are critical in a process through which students develop self-expectations, feel valued, and understand their ability to become independent and productive citizens. Self-expectations, in turn, become determinants of personal behavior (Gibb & Flavahan, 1987).

Attitudes and Concerns of Teachers

The attitudes and concerns that teachers have toward students with physical and health challenges influence students' interpersonal relationships. Moorman (1980)

TABLE 13.1   Characteristics of Students with Physical and Health Challenges.

Disorder	Abbreviation	Fatigue	Mobility	Weakness	Flaccid Paralysis	Movement Tight Inaccurate	Movement Uncontrolled Inaccurate
Amputations							
arm(s)				l			
leg(s)			n				
Asthma		l					
Arthritis—Juvenile Rheumatoid	JRA	n	l	n			
Blood Disorders							
Hemophilia		l	s				
Sickle Cell Disease		l	s	s	s		
Burns		s	s				
Cardiac Disorders		n		l			
Childhood Cancers							
Bone		s	s				
Brain		l	s	s			
Leukemia		n		n			
Others		l					
Cerebral Palsy	CP						
Ataxia		s	l	l			l
Athetoid		l	n				n
Spastic		l	l	s		n	
Tremor			s				s
Mixed		l	l			l	l
Cystic Fibrosis	CF	l		l			
Diabetes		l		s			
Muscular Dystrophies	MD	n	n	n	n		
Spina Bifida		s	n		n		
Spinal Muscular Atrophy	SMA	n	n	n	n		
Spinal Cord Injury							
Cervical		n	n		n	s	
Thoracic		n	n		n	s	
Lumbar		n	n		n	s	
Traumatic Brain Injury	TBI	n	s	s		s	s

S = some children may exhibit these characteristics   l = many children   = most children

Limited Range of Motion	Emergency Protocol Needed	Frequent Absence	Medication Influences on Learning Behavior	Psycho-social Needs	Behavioral Needs	Perceptual Learning Needs	Organization and/or Attending Deficits
l				s			
				s			
	n	l	l	s	s		
l		s	l	l	s		
	n	s		s			
	n	l		s			
s		s		n	s		
	n	n		s			
s		s	s	n			
s	s	l	s	n		l	l
	s	l	s	n			
s	s	s	s	n			
	s			s		l	l
	s			s	s	l	l
n	s		s	s	s	l	l
s	s		s	s	s	s	s
l	s	s	s	s	s	l	l
	l	l	s	l	s		
	s	l	l	l			
n	n	l		l		s	s
s		s		s		l	s
n	s	l		l		s	
n	n	l		n	s		
n	n	l		n	s		
	s	s		n	s		
		s	s	n	n	n	n

reported that some vocational educators have little confidence in teaching students with physical challenges. These authors reported that while vocational educators did not hold negative attitudes, the teachers are concerned about their ability to provide a quality instruction within an inclusive setting because of their general lack of training and experience with students with physical challenges. More recently, Phillips, Allred, Brulle, and Shank (1990) reported that general educators viewed themselves as more capable and willing to instruct physically challenged students than any other category of exceptionality. As the severity of the learning, behavioral, or other concomitant impairments increased, however, general educators reported that their support for inclusion would wane. Their major concern is the lack of skills and training in providing a quality education in the absence of special materials, classroom aides, and consultant services.

In the classroom, general educators' attitudes and concerns may lead to inequitable treatment. Among educators who had and those who did not have experiences with physically challenged students (Frith & Edwards, 1981), educators without the prerequisite experience reported that they were most concerned with dispensing medication, addressing toileting needs, and increased paperwork associated with the individualized education program (IEP) process. Both groups of educators shared similar concerns for the lack of relevant classroom materials and the disproportionate amount of time perceived necessary to successfully include these students within the least restrictive environment. In a follow-up study, Brulle, Barton, Barton, and Wharton (1983) reported that general educators did spend more time attending to the needs of students with physical challenges. While the amount of time was statistically significant, this time was comparable to the amount of time spent meeting the needs of other nondisabled students. The ninety seconds per student average is not an unrealistic request of educators for including students with physical challenges within the mainstream.

Finally, the attitudes and concerns that teachers have for inclusion may create unrealistic teacher expectations. Expectations are a powerful force that shape students' learning and behavior (Gibb & Flavahan, 1987). These expectations may also lead to more serious problems (Rich, Linor, & Shalev, 1984). Campbell, Dobson, and Bost (1985) reported that teachers viewed the behavioral problems of students with physical challenges to be more serious than those of students labeled mentally retarded. These teacher reactions may be attributable to teacher bias or unrealistic expectations. Without intervention or support services, these behavioral problems may lead teachers to question the appropriateness of educational placements.

The attitudes and concerns of teachers are modifiable. In general, a teacher may modify an attitude by gaining positive experiences with students who have physical and health challenges and by gaining information about their abilities. Various strategies have produced such an attitudinal shift, including: (1) gaining an understanding of the legislative basis, (2) developing necessary pedagogic skills, and (3) developing systems of classroom support (see Horne, 1985). Additionally, Minner & Knutson (1980) suggested improving teacher attitudes through (1) developing an understanding of students and their characteristics, (2) streamlining the intake process, and (3) increasing teacher participation and perception of ownership of the special education placement.

Teachers will set aside their biases, become active participants, and adopt innovative practices when their perceptions lead them to believe that their pedagogic skills will enhance the learning outcomes of their students (Berman & McLaughlin, 1978). When positive experiences and classroom support occur (Horne, 1985; Mallory & Herrick, 1986; Stainback & Stainback, 1988; Stainback, Stainback, Strathe, & Redrick, 1983) teachers' initial concerns and uncertainties will often change, and they will support the innovation (Hall, 1979). Rainforth and York (1987) detail two specific strategies of classroom support—skill clustering and integrated therapy. These strategies support the teaching of interrelated communication, social, and motor skills within a functional skill sequence. In addition, they detail the delivery of related services within situations that functionally determine skills and meaningfully base performance upon individual needs.

Other strategies may include the use of special educators who serve as consultant teachers (Falvey, Coots, Bishop, & Grenot-Scheyer, 1989). In this strategy, students with disabilities are in age-appropriate general education classes and have consultant services. General educators, as well as special educators, can get consultant services to meet the needs of their students (see Alper, Schloss, & Schloss, 1994; Wood, 1992).

Attitudes and Concerns of Nondisabled Classmates

The attitudes of nondisabled classmates will also affect the quality of the learning and social environment and influence the educational experience for students with physical and health challenges (Allsop, 1980; Gresham, 1982; Horne, 1985). These attitudes will not only influence academic performance but also social status. Positive attitudes are essential in the development of interpersonal relationships and a healthy self-concept. Anecdotal reports by general educators and parents often voice concerns that students without disabilities will be openly cruel and hostile toward students with physical and health challenges. Randolph and Harrington (1981) found the reverse. They reported that fifth graders did not reject those peers who had a physical challenge. Rather, they found strong feelings of pity and sorrow, as well as a strong desire to reach out and help less fortunate peers. Fifth graders did report, however, concern for inclusion in situations that involved play and shared learning activities. This concern tended to focus upon standards of interaction.

Among high school students, Gillies and Shackley (1988) reported that nondisabled adolescents (fourteen-year-olds) tended to view students with physical challenges more positively in inclusive school settings. Nondisabled students were more likely to report that their peers with a disability were friendly, capable in domestic situations, and approachable in social circumstances. Inclusion made a significant contribution toward social acceptance. Similarly, students with physical challenges were more independent and better able to relate with authority figures than nondisabled students (DeApodaca, Watson, Mueller, & Isaacson-Kailes, 1985).

The attitudes and concerns of students without disabilities are also modifiable (Riester & Bessette, 1986). Guidelines for modifying the attitudes and concerns of general educators are, in general, applicable to nondisabled students. Essentially, these include gaining experiences and providing structure in learning and play activities. The greatest change occurs when nondisabled students develop empathy; examine their personal attitudes, feelings, and actions; and have positive experiences (McKalip, 1979; Riester & Bessette, 1986). Additional strategies include bibliotherapy (Ferguson, 1981; Glimps, 1983), structured learning and play activities (Spiegel-McGill, 1989), collaborative learning (Madden & Slavin, 1982), and curricular materials (see Table 13.2).

In summary, students without disabilities share the concerns of general educators for including students with physical or health challenges within general education classrooms. These concerns influence both the quality of learning and social environments which, in turn, influence human development. For teachers, gaining experience (Gillies & Shackley, 1988), information, and having ongoing classroom support modifies their views. Nondisabled students can modify their attitudes through experience, structured play, and learning activities.

Students with Physical or Health Challenges and Their Attitudes and Concerns

The attitudes and concerns that students with physical or health challenges have for their placements within inclusive settings also effects the quality of their educational and social experiences. Students with health impairment had a dim view of their school's resources. Recent graduates reported the need for more intensive guidance and counseling during their high school years. They also reported concerns relative to the transition services to a postsecondary setting. Specifically, they reported the need for improved job-skill training, knowledge of community transportation systems, and access to social and recreational programs during the transition to adulthood (Liebert, Lutsky, & Gottieb, 1990). Additionally, Nemeth and DelRogers (1981b) reported the need for improved consumer education (i.e., housing, ways to increase participation in activities outside of the home, and attendant care information). Teachers might consider developing a teen booklet (e.g., Center for Independent Living, 1981) that would address these issues for students with physical or health challenges.

Curriculum and Instructional Modifications

The visibility of an impairment neither correlates with one's learning potential nor predicts success in an inclusive setting. A student with a mild physical disability may have greater difficulty learning and require more resources than a student with severe motor impairment. Educational team members must remain open-minded and not make generalizations based on a student's physical appearance or on preconceived stereotypes. Students with a physical or health challenge, first

TABLE 13.2   Children's Literature and Curricular Materials to Modify Student Attitudes.

Children's Literature Dealing with Students with Physical and Health Challenges

Aiello, B. & Schuman, J. (1988). *It's your turn at bat!* Twenty-First Century Books.

Aiello, B. (1988). *Friends for life.* Twenty-First Century Books. (AIDS).

Amadeo, D. M. (1989). *There's a little bit of me in Jamey.* Albert Whitman.

Bergman, T. (1989). *Children living with leukemia.* Gareth Stevens.

Bergman, T. (1989). *On our own terms: Children living with physical disabilities.* Gareth Stevens.

Brown, T. (1984). *Someone special just like you.* Holt, Rinehart and Winston.

Fassler, J. (1975) *Howie helps himself.* Dutton.

Gaes, J. (1987). *My book for kids with cancer.* Melius and Paterson.

Killilea, M. (1960). *Karen.* Dell.

Kubler-Ross, E. (1982). *Remember the secret.* Celestial Arts.

Little, J. (1962). *Mine for Keeps.* Little, Brown and Co.

Mack, N. (1976). *Tracy.* Raintree.

Mellonie, B. & Ingten, R. (1983). *Lifetimes.* Bantam Books.

Rabe, B. (1981). *The Balancing Girl.* Dutton.

Roy, R. (1987). *Move over wheelchairs coming through.* Clarion.

Stein, S. B. (1974). *About handicaps.* Walker and Co.

Wolf, B. (1975). *Don't feel sorry for Paul.* Lippincott.

Materials for Teaching Nondisabled Students about Students with Physical and Health Challenges

Barriers: The Access Game, Indianapolis: Message Management Consultants.

Everybody is Somebody Special (coloring book). Developmental Disabilities Advocacy Network.

Every Kid is Special (filmstrip series, 6 animated filmstrips). Educational Enrichment Materials, Teaching Resource Films, 1977.

Feeling Free Series (film series, 6 films), Syracuse, NY: Human Policy Press.

 Feeling Free Books (book series; 4 books)

 Feeling Free: An Invitation to Teachers. (teachers guide to films)

 Feeling Free: Activities and Stories Book

 Feeling Free: Classroom Unit (includes all of above except films)

Hello Everybody (film series; 6 film strips). Santa Monica, CA: James Stanfield Film Associates.

I Am, I Can, I Will (multimedia presentation), Mister Roger's Program, Englewood Cliffs, NJ: Hubbard.

Keep on Walking (film), New York: National Foundation—March of Dimes.

Kids Come in Special Flavors (teaching kit: guidebook, cassette tape and materials for 16 action simulations of various handicaps), Dayton, OH: Special Flavors.

The Kids on the Block (puppet show), Barbara Aiello. Contact local school district.

Like You Like Me (film series), Chicago: Encyclopedia Britannica Educational Corporation.

Mainstreaming: What Every Child Needs to Know About Disabilities (book), The Meeting Street School Curriculum for Grades 1–4, Susan Bookbinder, 1976. Exceptional Parent Press.

My New Friend: Introducing the Special Child (filmstrips), P. T. Hancock, Eye Gate Media, 1977.

Not Just a Spectator (film), Town and Country Productions, New York: RehabFilm.

Our Record (stereo record) Tom Hunter, Human Policy Press.

The People You Never See (film), New York: Filmmakers Library.

Special Delivery (film series, 5 films), Mendocino, CA: Lawren Productions.

What Do You Do When Your Wheelchair Gets a Flat? Questions and Answers About Disabilities (book), Douglas Biklen and Michelle Sokoloff, Syracuse, NY: Human Policy Press.

What's the Difference (guide), Ellen Barnes, Carol Berrigan and Douglas Biklen, Syracuse, NY: Human Policy Press.

and foremost, are students. Each student is unique and few generalizations are available for planning services in inclusive settings.

The general educator need not fear the physically challenged student, nor fear that they may do something "wrong" when attempting to adapt or modify an activity, lesson, or the environment. Teachers should not fear trying different strategies. If one approach or adaptation does not work well, they can seek the input and advice of support services. The classroom teacher is not alone and isolated from support and aid. Inclusion is a team effort. These accommodations have a basis in an educational program that begins with an examination of the student's strengths and weaknesses. Simply asking the student may provide relevant information or new insights into potential solutions. In other instances, formal assessment with medical specialists are necessary to develop a plan that accommodates inclusion. The goal of a student's program is to develop accommodations that aid student learning within inclusive settings.

Variables to be Considered Prior to Instruction

Before discussing specific curricular adaptations, educators will need to consider the following variables: positioning; scheduling, including daily schedules, absences, recess and medication schedules; and classroom modifications, including arrangement of the classroom, individual student seating, access to classroom appliances, and work surfaces.

Positioning

Proper positioning of students with physical challenges is essential, because it decreases strain and fatigue while providing skeletal stability for the upper body. Skeletal support also maximizes the student's use of the head, neck, arms, and hands. All are essential antecedents to successful school performance (Bigge, 1991). Additionally, some students with neurological disorders, such as cerebral palsy, must utilize positioning strategies to "break up" primitive reflexes which interfere with normal motor functioning.

Seating

Seating is an essential component in proper positioning. Customized seating supports prevent tissue breakdown, sores, or ulcers. A student's wheelchair may have adaptations or customizations to facilitate the desired positioning while providing necessary skeletal support. Seating specialists or physical therapists can adapt existing school furniture by adding head or neck supports, pummels, padding, foam inserts, and safety and support belts or harness, insuring that the furniture is stable and sturdy. General educators and therapists may consult to design and provide specific recommendations that meet the student's needs.

Educators should provide opportunities for students who use wheelchairs to spend a portion of the day out of their wheelchairs. There are several alternatives that facilitate proper positioning. A prone stander or standing table provides such an opportunity. Some students can use beanbag chairs and sturdy wooden chairs with arms for short periods of time.

Using wedges or bolster cushions, teachers may place young students on the floor. Placing the student on his or her tummy draped over a wedge provides support to the trunk and yet freedom to use the hands and arms. A wide variety of specialized furniture such as floor sitters and corner chairs can be purchased and used in many classroom settings. The additional space some pieces of furniture require may make them unpopular with some teachers. If specialized furniture is necessary, the teacher should make every effort to accommodate its use. Often the only accommodation necessary is a little house cleaning and rearranging of furniture. The school can obtain or have made less expensive and cumbersome alternatives by utilizing community resources and the expertise of a seating specialist.

Important to the comfort of the student is the positioning of the feet. Feet must be flat on a surface and well supported. Adjusting the legs of the chair, adding foot rests, or putting a large wooden block or box under the student's feet can achieve this. Thick catalogs or phone books are temporarily adequate until something sturdier is obtained. Some students may require ankle straps that secure their feet in the desired position. In addition, some physical conditions cause tissue breakdown due to chafing and rubbing. Pads can be used to prevent these additional complications.

Scheduling Considerations

Another variable to consider before looking at the curriculum is scheduling. Classroom scheduling must be flexible and take into consideration a student's impairment, the effects of medication, and other treatment protocols. A student who has had an asthma attack, a seizure, or who is undergoing chemotherapy may fatigue easily. For some, personal care, such as getting ready for school, may require several hours of preparation. Homework, therapy, and social functions will also be parts of an already demanding schedule, not to mention the student's requirement for rest. Suggestions for daily schedules, dealing with student absences, the need for recess, and dispensing medications follow.

Daily Schedules

Teachers should be sensitive to a student's daily pattern of stamina, energy, and fatigue. The student's parents, physician, special educators, and school nurse can provide relevant information. The educational team should plan instructional activities so that the student can conserve energy and produce assignments as best as possible. Alternating restful with more active lessons is an obvious option.

Absences

Frequent absences is another issue that requires flexibility from administrators and educators. The educational team needs to work cooperatively with parents and support personnel to insure that students have the necessary educational materials to keep up with classmates. Policies regarding absences may require adjustment so that students with physical and health challenges are not penalized. These policies become particularly troublesome for those students who require frequent hospitalization. Secondary schools, in which attendance requirements are used in determining successful course completion, will need to review and modify their policies.

Recess

Students with physical and health challenges, not unlike other students, need the opportunity to socialize and develop friendships during free play and recess. Because playground equipment often is not suitable for students with physical and health challenges (c.f. Jambor & Gargiulo, 1987), teachers may need to plan structured activities as an alternative. With a little creative thinking, teachers can modify or adapt typical recess games and activities to meet a student's needs. For those who cannot go outside for recess, educators can design and develop alternative activities to include nondisabled classmates. Socialization is critical to human development— recess is one key to that development.

Medication

Each school district generally has a policy governing the dispensing of medications. Students who require medication should take responsibility for this as soon as they are able to do so. Certainly, educators or the school nurse will monitor and work with the student to develop strategies that facilitate self-regulation of medications. Small clocks with medication times taped on the corner of the student's desk are often helpful. Timers, wrist watches with alarms, and the like may offer other solutions. Physicians can often alter medication schedules so that the student with a physical or health challenge does not have to take medication while at school. Moreover, communicating with the family physician may lead to the development of other alternatives.

Classroom Modifications

Still another variable that teachers will want to consider before they look at curricular modification is the physical layout of the classroom. Occasionally, simple changes can make a dramatic difference. The following considerations involving classroom arrangements, student seating, accessing classroom appliances, and work surfaces may be helpful.

Arranging the Classroom

Classroom arrangements can effectively accommodate wheelchairs, walkers, crutches, and other ambulatory devices. A change in classroom traffic patterns can facilitate participation in classroom activities (e.g., learning and activities centers, game tables, science and lab experiments), personal self-care (e.g., drinking fountains, sink, and rest room fixtures), and personal safety (e.g., room exit and emergency procedures).

Individualizing Student Seating

Once the education team has determined the overall physical arrangement of the classroom, they must address evaluation of a student's physical placement within the classroom. This will depend on the format or style that the teacher uses (e.g., traditional lecture—rows of seats, learning centers—hands-on activities or stations, or student pods—cooperative learning, peer teaching). From the student's perspective, a desk or table should be at a convenient vantage point that allows the student to see and interact in all classroom activities. In addition, the student should have access to peers, access to classroom materials and equipment, and access to those resources necessary for inclusion. While some students with physical challenges may sit in the front of the classroom, this is often the exception rather than the rule. It is critical that seating arrangements facilitate inclusion rather than isolate.

Accessing Classroom and School Appliances

Most classrooms have been built and designed for students without disabilities. Many built-in classroom fixtures do not readily facilitate the needs of students with physical and health challenges. Problems may occur in the rest room, where stalls may not be large enough or may have doors. Lavatories, sinks, towel dispensers, mirrors, door knobs and latches, light switches, and drinking fountains are often at inappropriate heights. Unique toileting needs require privacy for the student or a paraprofessional to change diapers or empty a collection bag. Catheterization will also require special arrangements. Some adaptive devices can remedy problems encountered by doorknobs, switches, and dispensers; but, others will require retrofitting (e.g., in installation of mirrors, lavatories, sinks, and drinking fountains) with specially designed fixtures. Using a drinking cup or glass, rather than the fountain, can offer a temporary solution.

Blackboards, easels, and bulletin boards are often too high. If adjustments or replacements are not viable options, the teacher who writes extensively on the blackboard may want to consider using alternatives, including overhead projectors, easels with posters, and the like. If the height of classroom sinks, counter tops, or work areas is not acceptable, simply removing the cabinet doors or removing the base plate allows students with wheelchairs access.

Using Work Surfaces

Those students with coordination problems may benefit from the placement of educational material directly upon table-top surfaces. Additional alternatives to secure worksheets may include placing student materials within a large lid (sides two inches in depth), which is attached to a desk top-surface. The student may also use magnetized surfaces.

Curriculum Modifications

Students with physical or health challenges exhibit a wide range of abilities, have innumerable strengths and weaknesses, and may have an impairment that is multifaceted and multidimensional. These students have no generalizable style of learning or learning characteristics. It may be necessary for the teacher to modify current instructional approaches and curriculum to meet their physical and health needs. To do so, teachers should feel free to take risks and realize that these modifications may also benefit other at-risk students (e.g., Wood, 1992). Working closely with support staff, solutions to issues that concern teachers are readily available.

Many curriculum options exist which facilitate learning for all students. When the existing curriculum is inappropriate, vague, or absent, teachers sometimes feel at a loss. A student's IEP should provide a foundation from which to work; however, it is important that the student's educational program have continuity throughout the school career and have goals of specific outcomes. Outcome-based curricula work equally well for students with special needs and their nondisabled peers, because educational outcomes are essentially the same for all students. Cooperative and interactive learning provides an effective avenue for including the student with a physical challenge. It not only enhances academic learning but facilitates social learning and fosters positive social learning, peer relationships, and self-esteem. Teachers can implement parallel curricula for students who exhibit educational performance lags or learning deficits. Students with physical challenges can gain experience, knowledge, and competence in those skills relative to their disabilities (e.g., health-care management, technology, access, self-advocacy, resource management) while completing the academic requirements of the general curricula. Teachers need to consider inclusive curriculum in class discussions, note taking, presenting materials, homework assignments, test taking, and science experiments.

Including Students in Classroom Discussions

Students may achieve verbal interaction through alternative and augmentative communication systems. Augmentative communication devices offer the best solution for those whose speech is unintelligible. Because students with severe physical limitations can access the communication aid through an interface, communication or language boards are inexpensive alternatives. Both high and low technologies use either a message element or keyboard to "spell" out the desired message. Communication or language boards can attach to a surface such as a desk top or gerri chair. They can also become part of a posterboard, placed within acetate sleeves within a notebook or made into a flip book.

Some students, who can produce intelligible speech, may have distracting speech patterns. Speech may be slow and labored. Patience and additional time are critical. Teachers and service providers should not ignore, trivialize, or repeatedly guess what the student is trying to communicate. Initially, the teacher may have to facilitate interactions between a student with physical challenges and nondisabled peers, especially when speech communication is labored or difficult to understand.

Taking Notes

Information that a student must copy from the blackboard, from an overhead, or from a lecture can present a problem. Someone can photocopy or copy onto index cards this information from teachers' notes. A classmate can use carbon paper while taking notes, or the student can photocopy the notes. Finally, the student with disabilities can tape record the lecture.

Presenting Educational Materials

The teacher should present educational materials and manipulatives at desk-top or eye level. Objects should be large and easily accessible. After presenting an item or material to the whole class, the teacher can give it to the student for examination.

Some students with limited physical mobility may require physical assistance to manipulate and examine items being presented. Students with poor head, neck, and trunk control and those with diminished tactile sensation will benefit from descriptive dialog while viewing or examining items or materials. Teachers will need to be cognizant that some students with neurological impairments may experience hypersensitive tactile stimulation. They may retreat from activities involving physical contact. Some tactile-sensitive students may prefer to examine objects using body surfaces such as their arms or face rather than their hands. Allowing students with physical challenges additional time to view and gain experience with materials being presented may be the only modification necessary. The extra time will vary from student to student. Teachers may elect to involve one's nondisabled classmates to provide a descriptive narrative.

Completing Written Homework and Assignments

A number of student characteristics (e.g., lack of coordination, fatigue, and body movements that are slow and labored) hamper a student's ability to produce required assignments. Teachers must be flexible when requiring written assignments and other student products. The teacher must ask, how much must a student produce to demonstrate mastery of the concept or process. Must the product be written? Typed? Taped? Dictated? Does the student need to complete fifty problems (taking three hours) or will fifteen problems accomplish the task (taking one hour)? Can the student complete an assignment in an outline format rather than as a narrative? Can the student use shorthand rather than the longer and more complete formal prose? Can the student present a report orally rather than in writing, or can the student tape-record the assignment? Are there other ways in which the student can demonstrate mastery? The teacher can accommodate the student by providing sufficient time to complete a written task. Teachers need to keep in mind the instructional goal of an assignment and be open to alternatives.

Completing Workbooks and Worksheets

Using a copy machine that enlarges the content on the page may provide additional space to complete assignments. At the same time, this may make the task easier to read and focus one's attention. Black and white worksheets are preferable to blue ditto papers because they are easier to read and generally clear. Worksheet items can be put into a multiple choice format either on paper or using index cards so that the student can "select" the desired responses.

Using Writing Tools

Some students with physical disabilities may be able to write, but the legibility, time, and energy required to complete written assignments may make them impractical. For those who can write, adding commercially available pencil grippers can adapt pencils. Pushing the pencil through foam, a wiffle ball, a rubber or foam ball, or clay can increase the gripping surface the student needs. T-shaped pencil holders, plasticine, pencil gloves, and a variety of other commercially made products are also available. Finally, teachers can weight pencils by inserting them into PVC pipe or a cardboard tube filled with bird shot or beebees. Some students with physical and health challenges do better when the writing instrument is changed. A larger contact point such as those on large soft-lead pencils, felt tip markers, or wide-point ball point pens may improve penmanship.

Students with considerable hand or arm weakness need pens that are light and glide easily. Roller ball pens may work well for these students. Students with severe motor involvement may be more efficient using a mouth or head stick. Head sticks can attach to pencils, paintbrushes, and crayons. Some students may be adept at using their feet and toes in place of their hands and fingers. At times, the tools the student uses need little or no adaptation.

The computer can also act as a prosthesis for the student who is unable to control a pen or pencil. Many will never develop the fine motor control necessary for acceptable handwriting. Teaching keyboarding skills is a viable alternative. For some, an electric typewriter is useful. Both machines accommodate key guards and key protectors. The key guard supports the hand if necessary and facilitates the use of a single finger, stylus, head or mouth stick, the eraser end of a pencil, or a piece of dowel. Key protectors cut down on the selection of inappropriate keys.

Stabilizing Desk Top Items

To stabilize and secure objects in place, use Dycem (available commercially) or attach suction cups. Taping paper to the desk top, using drafting or masking tape, or using a clipboard can stabilize student materials. Select heavy paper that can withstand abuse and moisture. A string or curly cord can attach pens, pencils, or other small items to the desk. With a magnetized strip attached to a student's desk top, additional magnets can anchor items. Using one or two pound exercise weight cuffs around the student's wrists sometimes minimizes excessive movement, which in turn may reduce the need to stabilize items.

Accessing Books

Handling and turning pages in a book can be a very challenging task. It becomes additionally difficult to read and focus a student's attention if the student has poor head and neck control. Teachers may consider the use of large print books. General educators may also consider placing the book on a slanted, eye-level book stand.

When the pages of a book do not lay flat, break the binding or cut or tear the pages out and use a loose leaf ring binder. Acetate sleeves can offer protection of the materials from hard student use, ensuring long-term availability. If the student can effectively use the book but has difficulty turning pages, attach small quarter-inch-thick pieces of foam, sponge, or felt to the upper right hand corner of the pages. The student can then slide a hand, a pencil with eraser, or other object between the pages to turn them. Commercially made electronic page turners are also available. Finally, using a classmate as a buddy is another option.

Talking books, tapes, and computers with text-to-speech capability can also be useful. Most texts and a large literature collection are available from the American Printing House for the Blind or the Library of Congress (Services for the Blind and Physically Impaired). Local or regional libraries and service agencies for citizens with disabilities provide additional resources.

When a great deal of reading is expected, the student may follow along in a book while listening to a tape or talking book. This is especially helpful in content subjects and for secondary students who must read much in relatively short periods of time. When required readings are not available on tape, readers are generally available.

Taking Tests

Test taking is a major concern of general educators, particularly at the secondary level. A variety of alternatives exist that do not compromise the integrity of the test. Regardless of what alternatives the teacher uses, additional time is almost always necessary. Electronic tests are good alternatives for traditional paper-and-pencil examinations. The student may also record test answers on audio tape or complete the test orally with the teacher, aid, or another student. The multiple choice format allows the student to indicate the selection by pointing, using a mouth pointer, looking at, or indicating in some other way the correct answer. Essay tests sometimes pose a difficult problem. The use of a computer or tape recorder may present a strategy for taking essay tests. Alternative exam times may also be necessary to adequately accommodate the student with a physical or health challenge.

Science Experiments and Other Scary Activities

Certainly some students with physical and health challenges will be unable to complete all classroom activities for either physical or safety reasons. Pairing these students with a classmate or working in small groups on defined tasks generally works well in these instances. The student with a physical or health challenge must be permitted to participate as fully as possible, and the general educator must develop strategies that allow the student to be a contributing member of the group. Possibly the student can monitor parts of the activity, record data, summarize information, or direct others through the activity. General educators must be careful not to relegate the student with a physical or health challenge to a passive role. In some instances the teacher, aid, or classmate can physically assist the student in participating in the class activity.

Assistive-Devices and Microcomputer Technologies

Students with physical and health challenges are a diverse group. As the severity of the impairment increases, these students are more likely to have concomitant disorders. They are more likely to experience increased difficulty communicating, gaining control over their environment, and achieving some degree of mobility.

Assistive-device and microcomputer technologies are allowing students with physical and other health challenges greater opportunities to participate more fully in school and society (Enders, 1984; Hall & Porter, 1983). Historically, special education has been concerned with accommodating and adapting the environment. These changes lead individuals with disabilities to greater independence and interactions with their environments. Assistive-devices are specialized tools that accomplish desired skills or tasks that a nondisabled individual can perform unaided. Assistive-devices can (1) facilitate normalcy, (2) augment current levels of functioning, (3) prevent the occurrence of other disabilities, or (4) rehabilitate the cause of the impairment, thereby eliminating the cause of the disability (see Wisniewski & Sedlak, 1992). A wide range of technologies are available. These range from high-tech devices to the use of low (or light) technologies. For students with physical or health challenges, high technologies may involve the stimulation of the central nervous system to regain movement of their arms or legs. It also may involve the use of bionic limb replacement or complex and sophisticated talking computers, wheel chairs, or environmental control systems. Light technologies may involve the use of (1) modified eating utensils, clothing, or personal hygiene and self-care products, and (2) curb cuts or architectural modifications to home or classroom. Both forms of technologies are equally important for students with physical and health challenges.

This range of aids allows students with physical and health challenges access to new settings and participation in new activities. For example, with new prosthetic aids and advances in orthotics, students can now more fully participate in sports and recreation, lunch and assemblies, field trips, extracurricular events, and other general social activities that occur at school. Advances in medical technologies allow students with health challenges or who are medically fragile access to their neighborhood schools. Communication aids are permitting greater social interaction with the nondisabled. These technologies allow students with physical and health challenges greater control over their environment, independence in living and learning, and new options for adulthood.

Communication

For those whose physical challenge makes them unable to communicate fluently, a variety of assistive-device technologies are available to augment or provide an alternative to natural communication (Gorenflo & Gorenflo, 1991; Goossens & Kraat, 1985). Some of these employ light technologies, while others employ complicated computer devices that provide more than speech and language. Selection becomes increasingly difficult given the diversity of sensory, physical, and cognitive impairments, the range of available options, and the variety of inclusive environments where the student will interact. General educators will need to consider a broad array of options. Other considerations include long-term use, criteria for selecting the message elements (direct selection, scanning, multisignal), levels of implementation (such as fully independent and portable aids), flexibility, cost, speed, reliability, and maintenance of the device (see Hooper & Hasselbring, 1985; Vanderheiden, 1984). Within these considerations, a myriad collection of aids, techniques, and strategies exist.

In the classroom, general educators have several options (see Bigge, 1991). One option is the use of aided communication systems. Two systems are available for consideration—nonelectronic and electronic aids. Nonelectronic language aids include language boards in their various forms. Using this system, speech and language therapists and general educators construct a chart that represents the student's language in a form that maximizes the ability to produce the desired message. For example, the chart may consist of letters and commonly used words. The student may simply point, spelling the desired words to formulate the message. As the severity of the physical and cognitive impairment increases, however, the message element needs to change to better facilitate language production. Pictures or objects may replace letters and words. These vocabulary elements are organized according to the user's semantic syntax in order to maximize language production.

Portability is an important consideration for any communication device. The challenge becomes one of creating a device that is portable and yet contains present and future vocabulary elements. For those students whose language needs cannot be fully met by nonelectronic aids, the selection of an electronic aid may provide this potential. Electronic aids are an extension of nonelectronic aids with several additional features. One such feature is semantic compaction. Semantic compaction is a technique that compacts meaning contained within a message element, allowing students greater capacity for language production. Individual words and pictures are replaced by icons. An icon is a symbol that has meaning. As a student forms a message, an icon's meaning may change based upon its syntax within the sentence. Semantic compaction allows the user to access a much larger vocabulary from which to produce language.

Electronic aids also have other features that may facilitate the student's needs. Students are able to produce and store oral messages and written communication. When appropriately interfaced (a device that mediates between the user and assistive device), the device has still other features. A number of mechanical, electromagnetic, and biopotential switches achieve access (see Evans & Henry, 1989; Shell, Horn, & Severs, 1989; Sicoli, 1991). Some electronic aids are microcomputer-based systems that access learning machines, access other aids and devices, or control one's environment.

Environmental Control

Numerous aids are available to facilitate control over one's environment (Wisniewski & Sedlak, 1992). High-tech, multi-task systems produce more than speech and language. For example, voice commands may replace cumbersome key stokes. Intelligible speech is not a requirement of these voice recognition systems, rather consistent speech production is. Voice commands can be used to access distant learning resources and materials, to control appliances within one's "smart" home or classroom, or to complete classroom tasks and assignments.

Light technologies may also help students with physical disabilities perform a variety of tasks associated with daily living and cooking chores (Gendreau, 1980), caring for one's hygiene, and modifying and adapting ready-to-wear clothing (Kennedy, 1981). These aids may also improve the livability of the home and classroom environment and maximize a student's ability to participate in the general education classroom (Chasin, 1977; Lowell & Finkelstein, 1989). For example, these aids can facilitate the use of home appliances (e.g., cooking appliances, TV and radio) and school materials and equipment (e.g., microcomputer, books, writing tasks).

Mobility

The goal of any mobility aid is to provide a means of movement. The wheelchair has been the primary method for achieving some degree of independence. Lightweight metals, design improvements, and the introduction of new materials have increased consumer satisfaction. The introduction of electric, sport, and alternative-power wheelchairs allows students greater access to a wider variety of settings. Little (1991) provides general guidelines for teachers and parents that ensure proper care and maintenance.

In the classroom, electric wheelchairs allow even the most debilitated student mobility and access. Sport and alternative-power wheelchairs are available, allowing greater participation in school and community-based activities. For example, sport wheelchairs allow participation in physical education and general sport programs. Limited and restricted hand control can be augmented by mechanical or biopotential access switches. A hand-operated joystick, a chin and head positioner, or a "sip-and-puff" allows students considerable control.

Improvements to orthotic and prosthetic devices have also increased mobility. These improvements have provided additional opportunities for participation in community events and recreational activities. Guidelines are available to help teachers understand the nature and use of orthotic and prosthetic appliances. Several authors report on the formulation of classroom observations that help teachers to monitor and adjust the appliance (Fredrick & Fletcher, 1985; Minnes & Stack, 1990).

Microcomputers

Computer technology can provide numerous options for independence. This technology allows students greater independence in learning. The computer can facilitate the classroom teacher's lesson plans through computer-assisted instruction (e.g., drill and practice, tutorials, instructional games) and other software tools (e.g., word processing, telecommunication). The computer can also increase student access to a wider social and physical environment (Evans & Henry, 1989).

TABLE 13.3 Case Study—Anna.

Anna, a 9-year-old, has above average intellectual abilities and is friendly and outgoing. She is in the third grade. She is severely motorically involved and has cerebral palsy. She is unable to speak intelligibly, dress, feed, or bathe herself. She is able to communicate by using an augmentative communication device. She is also able to access a classroom computer through a single switch.

In order to successfully include Anna within a general education setting, the classroom teacher raised several reservations and concerns. Recognizing these issues, the special education consultant sought the help of building and other district personnel.

Given the restrictions placed upon her ability to communicate, Anna is able to participate only partially in those school activities in which oral communication is necessary. To address these concerns, the consultant employed the talents of the building's speech and language therapist. The therapist provides guidance to the classroom teacher, insuring that oral language does not become labored and exhaustive for both communicant and communicator. On a regular basis, the therapist conducts oral-language training sessions for both Anna's teacher and classmates. Currently, the focus of these training sessions is for participants to understand how to maximize communication patterns between Anna and others. Participants get instruction in several pragmatic communication patterns that are intended to elicit responses that are concise for Anna, thereby preventing labored use of the communication device.

The general educator had other concerns. Class activities, such as experiments and other manipulative activities, present a considerable challenge for the general education teacher. Through her communication device, however, Anna is able to direct and guide classmates through the physical tasks necessary to accomplish the activity. Her communication device allows her to participate in short discussions, hypothesize, summarize, and form conclusions.

There were also other concerns, such as completing worksheets and written assignments, taking exams, and other in-class tasks. The consultant thought it best to visit the classroom and conduct an initial needs assessment and environmental analysis necessary to make specific recommendations. The consultant and teacher easily remedied some of their concerns. For example, Anna could complete some written assignments and exams using a tape recorder. She could accomplish other assignments by a using a peer tutor to record responses or to provide individual instruction. The needs assessment indicated that special friendships could address other needs. The environmental assessment would also provide other suggestions relative to the physical arrangement of the classroom.

To address Anna's hygiene, eating, mobility, and other basic needs, a paraprofessional comes in occasionally throughout the school day. The paraprofessional assists Anna in her bathroom needs and assists her in eating and dressing. Anna's bathroom needs are scheduled at regular intervals during the day. The paraprofessional also must assist Anna as she arrives and departs school; however, the paraprofessional does not need—at this time—to assist Anna with other in-class activities.

Anna's needs are extreme. There are many more students with physical challenges whose needs are not as intense as Anna's. In this case study, however, Anna's needs can be met within an inclusive setting. The school district is fortunate to have a school consultant who has training, experience and technical skills necessary to work with students who have physical challenges. More importantly, the consultant is able to systematically address concerns that present obstacles for inclusion.

Computer work stations allow even the most severely debilitated student a source of employment. Telecommunication allows students to socialize with peers or to gain access to teachers during periods of extensive hospitalization. Electronic bulletin boards are available, linking a student to other students with and without disabilities. Computer games provide opportunities for leisure and socialization. Finally, the computer can augment a student's ability to gain control over a variety of daily living tasks. With the appropriate software, students can reduce dependence on others to write, manage money, and control their environment.

Summary

Inclusion is our current understanding of best practices for students with special needs. There have been a number of successful efforts to include students with varying disabilities. Inclusion requires the commitment and collaboration of administrators, teachers, and parents. In this chapter, the discussion focused on the specific needs of students with physical and health challenges who receive special education and related services within inclusive settings. This discussion began with an examination of the attitudes and concerns of teachers, classmates without disabilities, and students with physical and health challenges. Finally, specific curricular adaptations and the role of assistive and microcomputer technologies to manage the needs of students with physical and health challenges within inclusive settings were addressed.

References

Allsop, J. (1980). Mainstreaming physically handicapped students. *Journal of Research and Development in Education, 13,* 37–44.

Alper, S. K., Schloss, P. J., & Schloss, C. N. (1994). *Families of students with disabilities: Consultation and advocacy.* Boston: Allyn & Bacon.

American Alliance for Health, Physical Education, Recreation and Dance. (1991). *Sports instruction for individuals with disabilities. The best of practical pointers.* (ERIC Document Reproduction Service No. ED 331 802)

Beaverton School District 48, Oregon. (1984). *Accounting cluster demonstration program at Aloha High School. Final Report.* (ERIC Document Reproduction Service No. ED 248 330)

Berman, P., & McLaughlin, M. W. (1978). *Federal programs supporting educational change. Vol. VIII: Implementing and sustaining innovations.* Santa Monica, CA: Rand Corporation.

Bigge, J. (1991). Augmentative communication. *Teaching individuals with physical and multiple disabilities.* New York: Charles E. Merrill.

Blandy, D. (1989). Ecological and normalizing approaches to disabled students and art education. *Art Education, 42*(3), 7–11.

Boothroyd, P., Mack, R., & Mahan, P. (1989). *Housing for the physically disabled: A commentary, resource guide and selected bibliography.* (ERIC Document Reproduction Service No. ED 324 863)

Brady, M. P., McDougall, D., & Bennis, H. F. (1989). The schools, the courts, and the integration of students with severe handicaps. *Journal of Special Education, 23,* 43–58.

Brulle, A. R., Barton, L. E., Barton, C. L., & Wharton, D. (1983). A comparison of teacher time spent with physically handicapped and able-bodied students. *Exceptional Children, 49,* 543–545.

Burrow, E., & Hill, P. (1983). *Special needs adaptations for office education teachers.* (ERIC Document Reproduction Service No. ED 240 369)

Campbell, N. J., Dobson, J. E., & Bost, J. M. (1985). Educator perceptions of behavior problems of mainstreamed students. *Exceptional Children, 51,* 298–303.

Capper Foundation for Crippled Children. (1990). *Project Kidlink: Bringing together disabled and nondisabled preschoolers.* (ERIC Document Reproduction Service No. ED 322 682)

Center for Independent Living, Inc. (1981). *Taking charge of your life: A guide to independence for teens with physical disabilities.* (ERIC Document Reproduction Service No. ED 209 793)

Chasin, J. (1977). *Home in a wheelchair: House design ideas for easier wheelchair living.* (ERIC Document Reproduction Service No. ED 150 795)

Christie, I. (1985). Aquatics for the handicapped—A review of literature. *Physical Educator, 42,* 24–33.

Cooney, D., Emes, C., Ford, M. A., & Wasson, D. (1985). *Integrating physically disabled students into physical education.* (ERIC Document Reproduction Service No. ED 268 748)

DeApodaca R. F., Watson, J. D., Mueller, J., & Isaacson-Kailes, J. (1985). A sociometric comparison of mainstreamed, orthopedically handicapped high school students and nonhandicapped classmates. *Psychology in the Schools, 22,* 95–101.

DeJong, G. (1984). *Independent living and disability policy in the Netherlands: Three models of residential care and independent living. Monograph number twenty-seven.* (ERIC Document Reproduction Service No. ED 250 893)

Dove, S., Holder, J., Richards, B., & Wheller, S. (1984). Wheelchairs in a primary school. *Special Education Forward Trends, 11*(1), 18–21.

Enders, A. (1984). *Technology for independent living: Sourcebook.* (ERIC Document Reproduction Service No. ED 313 820)

Evans, C. D., & Henry, J. S. (1989). Keyboarding for the special needs student. *Business Education Forum, 43,* 23–25.

Falvey, M., Coots, J., Bishop, K., & Grenot-Scheyer, M. (1989). Educational and curricular adaptations. In S. Stainback, W. Stainback, & M. Forest (Eds.), *Educating all students in the mainstream of regular education* (pp. 143–158). Baltimore: Paul H. Brookes.

Ferguson, A. M. (1981). *Children's literature—For all handicapped children.* (ERIC Document Reproduction Service No. ED 234 541)

Fredrick, J., & Fletcher, D. (1985). Facilitating children's adjustment to orthotic and prosthetic appliances. *Teaching Exceptional Children, 17,* 228–30.

Frith, G. H., & Edwards, R. (1981). Misconceptions of regular classroom teachers about physically handicapped students. *Exceptional Children, 48,* 182–184.

Gendreau, J. C. (1980). *Making mealtime manageable.* (ERIC Document Reproduction Service No. ED 072 608)

Gibb, C. D., & Flavahan, R. P. (1987). "What distinguishes interpreted and segregated physically disabled pupils?" *Educational Research, 29,* 3–11.

Gillies, P., & Shackley, T. (1988). Adolescents' views of their physically handicapped peers—A comparative study. *Educational Research, 30,* 104–109.

Glimps, B. E. (1983). Books can make mainstreaming easier. *PTA Today, 8*(6), 23–24.

Goossens, C, & Kraat, A. (1985). Technology as a tool for conversation and language learning for the physically disabled. *Topics in Language Disorders, 6,* 56–70.

Gorenflo, C. W., & Gorenflo, D. W. (1991). The effects of information and augmentative communication technique on attitudes toward nonspeaking individuals. *Journal of Speech and Hearing Research, 34,* 19–26.

Greaves, E. R., & Richmond, A. (1982). *Involvement and participation. National Conference on Physical Activity for the Exceptional Individual.* (ERIC Document Reproduction Service No. ED 230 487)

Gresham, F. (1982). Misguided mainstreaming: The case for social skills training with handicapped children. *Exceptional Children, 48,* 422–433.

Hall, C. D., & Porter, P. (1983). School intervention for the neuromuscularly handicapped child. *Journal of Pediatrics, 102,* 210–14.

Heekin, S., & Mengel, P. (1983). *New friends: Mainstreaming activities to help young children understand and accept individual differences.* (ERIC Document Reproduction Service No. ED 242 131)

Hooper, E. H., & Hasselbring, T. S. (1985). Electronic augmentative communication aids for the nonreading student: Selection criteria. *Journal of Special Education Technology, 7,* 39–49.

Horne, M. D. (1985). *Attitudes toward handicapped students: Professional, peer, and parent reactions.* Hillsdale, NJ: Lawrence Erlbaum Associates.

Hutchinson, M. L., & Lord, J. (1983). Recreation integration. *Recreation Canada, 43,* 22–25.

Jambor, T., & Gargiulo, R. (1987). The playground: A social entity for mainstreaming. *Journal of Physical Education, Recreation, and Dance, 58*(8), 18–23.

Jones, A. V., Lynn, J., Topping, A., Elliot, K., & Dempsey, T. (1984). Science with handicapped pupils. *Physics Education, 19,* 6–10.

Jones, N. (1983). Integrating the Ormerod Children. *Special Education Forward Trends, 10*(2), 14–16.

Karjala, J. A. (1983). Typewriting for the special needs students. *Business Education Forum, 37*(5), 17–18.

Kauffman, J. M. (1989). The Regular Education Initiative as Reagan-Bush education policy: A trickle-down theory of education of the hard-to-teach. *Journal of Special Education, 23,* 256–278.

Keller, E. C., Pauley, T. K., Starcher, E., & Proctor, B. (1983). *Teaching the physically disabled in the mainstream science class at the secondary and college levels. Resource Book.* (ERIC Document Reproduction Service No. ED 253 393)

Kennedy, E. S. (1981). *Dressing with pride. Volume One: Clothing changes for special needs.* (ERIC Document Reproduction Service No. ED 215 092)

Leavitt, K. J., & Terrell, G. J. (1984). *Discover the world of independent living: An independent living skills curriculum and a guide to the implementation of the curriculum.* (ERIC Document Reproduction Service No. ED 256 102)

Liebert, D., Lutsky, L., & Gottieb, A. (1990). Postsecondary experiences of young adults with severe physical disabilities. *Exceptional Children, 57,* 56–63.

Linda, M., & Rousso, H. (1991). *Barrier free: Serving young women with disabilities.* (ERIC Document Reproduction Service No. ED 333 644.)

Little, J. (1991). Taking control of purchasing a wheelchair: Tips for parents about mobility equipment. *Exceptional Parent, 21,* 36–38, 46, 50.

Lombana, J. H. (1982). *Success for physically disabled students. Sources to upgrade career counseling and employment of special students.* (ERIC Document Reproduction Service No. ED 232 035)

Lowell, H, & Finkelstein, S. (1989). ABLE: The future of mechanical aids. *Exceptional Parent, 19,* 22–27.

Madden, N., & Slavin, R. (1982). *Count me in: Academic achievement and social outcomes of mainstreaming.* Baltimore: Johns Hopkins University.

Mallory, B., & Herrick, S. C. (1986). *Ramps are not enough: The movement of children with mental retardation from institutional to community-based care. (ERIC Document Reproduction Service No. ED 274 118)*

McAnaney, K. D. (1989). A camping we will go. *Exceptional Parent, 19,* 50–53.

McKalip, K. J. (1979). Developing acceptance toward the handicapped. *School Counselor, 26,* 293–298.

Minner, S., & Knutson. R. (1980). Improving vocational education attitudes toward mainstreaming. *Career Development for Exceptional Individuals, 2,* 93–100.

Minnes, P. M., & Stack, D. M. (1990). Research and practice with congenital amputees: Making the whole greater than the sum of its parts. *International Journal of Rehabilitation Research, 13,* 151–160.

Nemeth, C., & DelRogers, J. (1981a). *Consumer education for disabled persons.* (ERIC Document Reproduction Service No. ED 231 161)

Nemeth, C., & DelRogers, J. (1981b). *Analysis of the consumer needs of disabled persons.* (ERIC Document Reproduction Service No. ED 231 160)

Oklahoma Curriculum Improvement Commission. (1973). *Oklahoma curriculum guide for teaching driver education to the handicapped.* (ERIC Document Reproduction Service No. ED 217 122)

Patette, H. P., & Hourcade, J. J. (1984). The student with cerebral palsy and the public schools: Implications for the counselor. *Elementary School Guidance and Counseling, 19,* 141–146.

Phillips, W. L., Allred, K., Brulle, A. R., & Shank, K. S. (1990). The Regular Education Initiative: The will and skill of regular educators. *Teacher Education and Special Education, 13,* 182–186.

Rainforth, B., & York, J. (1987). Integrating related services in community instruction. *Journal of the Association of Persons with Severe Handicaps, 12,* 190–198.

Randolph, A. H., & Harrington, R. M. (1981). Fifth graders' projected responses to a physically handicapped classmate. *Elementary School Guidance Counseling, 16,* 31–35.

Redick, S. S., & Hughes, R. P. (1981). Characteristics of teachers implementing home economics programs for physically handicapped students. *Home Economics Research Journal, 10,* 32–39.

Rich, Y., Linor, M., & Shalev, M. (1984). Perceptions of school life among physically disabled mainstreamed pupils. *Educational Research, 26,* 27–32.

Riester, A. E., & Bessette, K. M. (1986). Preparing the peer group for mainstreaming exceptional children. *Pointer, 31,* 12–20.

Roice, G. R. (1981). *Teaching handicapped students physical education: A resource handbook for k-12 teachers.* (ERIC Document Reproduction Service No. ED 213 219).

Shackelford, R., & Henak, R. (1982). *Making industrial education facilities accessible to the physically disabled: A professional monograph.* (ERIC Document Reproduction Service No. ED 224 988)

Shell, D. F., Horn, C., & Severs, M. (1989). Computer-based compensatory augmentative communications technology for physically disabled, visually impaired, and speech impaired students. *Journal of Special Education Technology, 10,* 29–43.

Sicoli, T. R. (1991). What's new in software? Bringing computer technology and remedial help for learning disability to the alternate access user. *Journal of Reading Writing and Learning Disabilities International, 7,* 271–277.

Spiegel-McGill, P. (1989). Microcomputers as social facilitators in integrated preschools. *Journal of Early Intervention, 13,* 249–60.

Stainback, S., & Stainback, W. (1988). Educating students with severe disabilities. *Teaching Exceptional Children, 21,* 16–19.

Stainback, S., Stainback, W., Strathe, M., & Redrick, C. (1983). Preparing regular classroom teachers for the integration of severely handicapped students: An experimental study. *Education and Training of the Mentally Retarded, 18,* 204–209.

Tetlow, W. (1981). *Proceedings of the special needs conference.* (ERIC Document Reproduction Service No. ED 211 387)

Turnbull, H. R., Ellis, J., Boggs, E., Brooks, P., & Biklen, D. (1981). *The least restrictive alternative: Principles and practices.* Washington, DC: American Association of Mental Deficiency.

Vanderheiden, G. C. (1984). High and low technology approaches in the development of communication systems for severely physically handicapped persons. *Exceptional Education Quarterly, 4,* 40–56.

Wang, M. C., Reynolds, M. C., & Walberg, H. J. (1986). Rethinking special education. *Educational Leadership, 44,* 26–31.

Wisniewski, L. A., & Sedlak, R. A. (1992). Assistive-device technologies for students with disabilities. *The Elementary School Journal, 92*(3), 393–410.

Wolfson, P. L. (1991). Preparing for the mainstream. *Exceptional Parent, 21*(4), 24–26.

Wood, J. W. (1992). *Adapting instruction for mainstreamed and at-risk students.* New York: Macmillan.

14

ADDRESSING MEDICAL AND EMERGENCY PROCEDURES IN INCLUSIVE SETTINGS

GRACE CROSS   *MARILYN JEAN JONES*

Objectives

After completing this chapter the reader will be able to:

1. Discriminate between complex and noncomplex medical conditions.
2. Discuss current legislation and court rulings as they apply to students with special health care needs.
3. Define the term "related services" as opposed to "medical service" when determining the services a school is required to supply.
4. Discuss common health care procedures.
5. Identify the five "Rs" of medication.
6. Describe the actions one must take in the event a student should have a seizure.
7. Discuss tube feeding procedures.
8. Explain the rationale for careful documentation of health care services.
9. Describe the composition and function of a health care team.
10. Generate a basic health care plan.

Key Terms

Americans with Disabilities
   Act (ADA) (PL 101-336)
Atypical elimination

Clean intermittent
   catheterization (CIC)
Colostomy

Complex and noncomplex	Medical services
medical conditions	Nasogastric tube
Cardiopulmonary	Ostomy
resuscitation (CPR)	Pressure sores
Decubitus ulcers	Reasonable benefit
Education of All Handicapped	Related services
Children Act (PL94-142) (EHA)	Section 504
First aid	Seizure disorder
Gastronomy	Shunt
Individuals with Disabilities	Stoma
Education Act (IDEA) (1990)	Tracheostomy
Medically fragile	

Students with medical conditions present a wide variety of needs during instruction in inclusive settings. They form a heterogeneous group. (In fact, many such students are never considered—by themselves, peers, or teachers—to be special education students at all.) Their needs may be mild, moderate, or severe, but no matter what level of assistance they require, they will need an understanding teacher who is willing to make allowances and remembers that the effects of medication, fatigue, and pain may interrupt learning (Hill, 1991).

Students with health care needs may form two distinct subpopulations—those with *complex* and *noncomplex* medical conditions. Students with complex medical conditions may be medically unstable, exhibiting unpredictable responses to medication or treatment. They may need care requiring professional judgment, and there may be necessary procedures that a physician cannot delegate to others. A licensed medical professional should manage complex medical conditions. Students with noncomplex medical conditions may require procedures that a delegated, properly trained care giver can perform safely with no alterations requiring medical judgment. Most students will fall into this category, and one may easily learn most of the required procedures and techniques.

This chapter will briefly review the legislation and court cases involving health care needs. Some of the more common treatments and procedures involved in meeting special health care needs will be described. Guidelines for developing a plan to manage health care in inclusive instructional settings will be presented.

Legislation and Litigation

According to the *Eighth Annual Report to Congress on the Implementation of the Education of the Handicapped Act* (1986) there were approximately 234,000 students with low incidence disabilities in need of some type of health care or related services to allow them to benefit from an educational program and 68,000 students with other health impairments in special education services in American schools. Although the numbers vary based on identification criteria, the extent of the need for inclusive education of medically fragile students and those with health care needs is clearly significant. Modern medical technology has increased the numbers of children surviving with medical conditions and has provided the technology to assist families and schools to serve them in natural settings. The legislature and the courts have clearly and consistently upheld and clarified these students' right to a free and appropriate public education in the least restrictive environment.

As early as 1958, the enactment of Public Law (PL) 85–926 provided funds for direct grants to states and to institutions of higher education to train teachers of students with mental disabilities. Section 504 of the Rehabilitation Act of 1973 provided that:

> *No otherwise qualified individual with handicaps in the United States . . . shall, solely by reason of her or his handicap, be excluded from the participation in, be denied the benefits of, or be subjected to discrimination under any program or activity receiving Federal assistance . . ."*

This legislation set the stage for the Education of All Handicapped Children Act (EHA) of 1975 (PL 94–142). This landmark legislation established the rights and privileges of a free, appropriate public education in the least restrictive environment to all children with educational disabilities regardless of handicapping condition. The Education of the Handicapped Act Amendments of 1986 (PL 99–457) extended educational and related services to three-, four- and five-year-old children with disabilities. In order to receive federal funds for education, each must provide a plan to the federal government outlining how the State Department of Education will guarantee the mandated services to students with disabilities. In turn, each district must develop and make available to the public a compliance plan listing those policies and procedures that fulfill their local responsibilities.

The 101st Congress changed EHA to the Individuals with Disabilities Education Act (IDEA) of 1990. The new name places the individual first and changes handicaps to disabilities. IDEA extends the protection of PL 94–142 to individuals with autism and traumatic brain injury, requires more extensive and effective transportation services for those requiring these services, and includes rehabilitation counseling and social work as related services. The Americans with Disabilities Act of 1990 (PL 101–336), while primarily addressing adult needs, sets the goal of a more complete integration of disabled persons into the mainstream through equal opportunity, full participation, independent living, and economic self-sufficiency.

Litigation through due process is one vehicle that assures students with disabilities their rights under IDEA guidelines. No legislation can cover all contingencies and even good faith on the part of two parties does not guarantee agreement or compliance with established precedent. Some cases that have had significant impact upon the provision of health care in public schools are described in the following sections.

Wyatt v. Stickney 344 F. Supp. 373 (1972)

This decision in a class action suit brought on behalf of patients confined in Alabama mental institutions, protects patients from "unnecessary or excessive medication." It requires that "no medication shall be administered except at the written order of a physician" and mandates that "medication shall not be used as punishment, for the convenience of staff, as a substitute for program or in quantities that interfere with the patients treatment program." It limits coercive measures and restraints to emergency situations and establishes minimum guidelines for care.

Welsh v. Likins 373 F. Supp. 487 (1974)

This case was a class action suit in Minnesota and affirms the constitutional right of confined patients to a treatment program, not mere custodial care. It requires caregivers monitor and evaluate medication in a systematic manner and established procedural safeguards to ensure the well-being of students.

Board of Education of the Hendrick Hudson Central School District v. Amy Rowley 458 U.S. 176 (1982)

This case involves the provision of a sign-language interpreter to a student with hearing impairment who was already making above average progress with alternative and less expensive services. Although the lower court ruled that the school district provide such an interpreter as part of a "free and appropriate public education," the Supreme Court overturned the ruling and limited the right to educational services to those "reasonably calculated to enable the child...to receive educational benefits." It further stipulated that while there is no single test of "reasonable benefit" the "achievement of passing marks and advancement from grade to grade will be one important factor." The ruling does not require school districts to maximize the potential of a student, however worthy that goal, but only to provide necessary and "reasonable services."

Smith v. Robinson 468 U.S. 992 (1984)

This case allows parents or other plaintiffs the right to obtain legal fees and expenses from school districts when they win court actions against public schools. This is an extremely important decision because it makes due process under IDEA and other legislation available to all families regardless of their financial resources. Litigation is not only time-consuming and complicated, it is expensive. The threat of due process (and the high cost of losing) encourages both compliance with existing law and sincere negotiation on valid issues in dispute.

Irving v. Tatro 468 U.S. 883 (1984)

This case brought into question the school's obligation to provide clean intermittent catheterization (CIC) as a "related service" so that an eight-year-old girl with spina bifida could attend school. The court expanded the interpretation of "related services" to include procedures such as CIC that are necessary for a student to benefit from special education and that do not require the supervision of a physician. While on the surface it may appear that this ruling is opposite to that in the Rowley case—awarding rather than denying services—they actually both affirm the necessity of providing those services necessary for a student to achieve educational benefits.

Responsibilities of the School

In determining the services a school must provide for children with health care needs, it is important to distinguish between those related services necessary for the child to benefit from the educational process (which it *is* obligated to provide) and medical services (which it is *not*.) According to McCarthy (1991), the judiciary has interpreted medical services as those that a physician must provide or that require licensed health care professionals for constant monitoring. Greisman (1990) reviewed court cases and offered guidelines to assist school districts in identifying a particular service as a related health care service or a medical service. The distinction between the two areas is often unclear and one must evaluate each case on its own merits.

While the American Academy of Pediatrics (1988) views medical inputs as "essential not only to assist in making diagnosis for children with chronic disabilities but also to help determine the most appropriate therapeutic measures," in practice physicians are rarely able to attend committee meetings to determine the services needed. According to a report (1988) issued by the American Academy of Pediatrics, in only fourteen percent of all special education cases does the physician contact the school. Teachers have limited knowledge about health status, medical management, and the side-effects of medication. In determining the services necessary for a specific student, it is essential that the school personnel collaborate with parents, student, and medical professionals. This does not mean that the physician must attend all meetings but that a system for obtaining his or her input must be in place and utilized.

The Holmes Group (1990) recommended the utilization of a consultive service system, especially to small or geographically isolated school systems with a small population of children with health care needs and limited access to medical professionals. Kendell (1991) identified areas where students with health care needs may require adaptations, modifications, or related services. These areas include academics, specialized curriculum, self-help skills, adaptive devices, psychological support, mobility, transportation, physical education, recreation, vocational preparation, and transition skills. The consultant can provide training, technical assistance, and expertise in developing integrated programs while potentially reducing the financial burden for these services.

The transportation of children with special health care needs is a new field for many school districts with few standards and guidelines. Basically, transportation care providers must have training to provide services required en route and to meet emergencies—the same as building care providers (Richards 1989). A student may not be denied transportation essential to allow participation in the educational process.

Health Care Needs—Treatment and Procedures

This section includes procedures and techniques involved in caring for students with special health care needs. Figure 14.1 is a noninclusive list of some of the more common diagnoses encountered in the school setting. While each diagnosis is serious, the gravity and disabling conditions will vary greatly from case to case. A diagnosis is not necessarily the prerequisite for a specific health need. For example, a child diagnosed as having cerebral palsy may need positioning similar to a child with a broken leg. Both are in need of the same assistance in order to benefit from the educational process, assure safety, maintain dignity, and prevent further deterioration of the muscles. Some students with a label of "other health impaired" will require virtually no intervention beyond a notation in their records and, of course, monitoring. Others will require daily, regulated health care interventions. National organizations are a valuable resource for teachers and caregivers when dealing with a disability. Pamphlets, videos, lists of resources, and other valuable materials can help provide a greater understanding of condition as well as improved access to resources and services. Another valuable resource for teachers and caregivers is:

National Organization for Rare Disorders (NORD)
P.O. Box 8923
New Fairfield, CT 06812-8923
1-800-999-NORD

A teacher should consult state health care guidelines when dealing with health care issues in an individual applied setting. The Guidelines for Special Health Care Procedures in Missouri Schools (1990) defines health care procedures based on the services required rather than diagnosis.

Most health care needs can be met in an inclusive setting and require minimal training. While a registered nurse will need to perform the more complex tasks, a teacher or other caregiver can be delegated to provide other health services. When determining the assignment of a service to a caregiver, the team should consider the following factors:

1. The stability of the student's condition
2. The complexity of the task
3. The level of judgment and skill necessary to proceed from one step to the next or to alter standard procedure based on student needs

Acquired Immune Deficiency 　Syndrome (AIDS)	Fetal Alcohol Syndrome
Allergies	Heart Disease
Anemia	Hemophilia
Asthma	Hydrocephalus
Attention Deficit and Hyperactivity	Kidney Disease
Disorder (ADAHD)	Lead Poisoning
Atypical Elimination	Muscular Dystrophy Seizure Disorder
Cancer	Respiratory Disorders
Cerebral Palsy	Rheumatoid Arthritis
Cystic Fibrosis	Sickle Cell Anemia
Diabetes	Spina Bifida
Down Syndrome	Spinal Cord Injury
	Traumatic Head Injury

FIGURE 14.1　Common Diagnoses Encountered in School Settings

4. The ability of the student to assist with or perform part or all of the task independently
5. The concerns and wishes of the parents. Parents have usually learned to perform these procedures at home, and the education team should encourage them to participate in the selection and training of caregivers.
6. The need of the student to maintain privacy and dignity.

A case study follows that illustrates these points:

Shawnese returned to her first grade class in the fall following surgery that left her with limited functioning in her lower body. Although able to walk with braces, she was unsteady and unable to manage the stairs in the building. An assigned aide helped her on the stairs, on the playground, and in the restroom. When repeated urinary tract infections indicated the need for clean intermittent catheterization (CIC), the school authorities originally delegated the school nurse to perform the service. Shawnese and her mother, however, felt that this singled her out and made her disability more visible. They requested that the aide perform the CIC. The aide could perform the CIC in the girls' restroom while returning from physical education, art, etc. Because Shawnese took more time to return to class than other students in any case, this afforded her more privacy than would have been available in the nurse's office. The aide learned to perform CIC (at first under the supervision of the nurse) in less than half an hour total instructional time. Shawnese, her mother, and the aide all felt comfortable with the decision and the procedure worked smoothly. In fact, the greatest difficulty the aide has ever experienced has been convincing Shawnese to drink the cranberry juice that is a daily part of her treatment plan.

The purpose of this section is not to provide step-by-step instructions for the following procedures. There is no substitute for on-site training. The purpose is to provide an overview of common health care needs, to familiarize, and, thereby, to allay anxiety about their provision.

Common Classroom Health Care Procedures

Handwashing

Handwashing is the first and best defense against infection and disease. Everyone should do it, including the student with disabilities, before and after any physical contact, any medical or first-aid procedure, before and after handling procedural equipment, eating, going to the restroom, and even before and after wearing disposable gloves.

Remember to always remove any jewelry, use a liquid antiseptic soap, lather, and thoroughly clean nails, knuckles, entire hand, and at least two inches above the wrist. Rinse hand thoroughly and dry with disposable paper towels.

Disposable Gloves

One should always wear disposable gloves whenever handling body fluids or whenever carrying out any health care procedure with an open sore on the hand. Remove gloves and rewash hands after each procedure. Remove gloves by grasping the cuff and stripping it off inside out. Discard gloves in a plastic lined waste container.

Hepatitis B and AIDS are the most well-publicized transmissible infections, but contaminated hands transmit infections such as influenza, mononucleosis, common colds, and salmonellosis.

Medication

Dispensing medication at school is often a necessary part of a health care plan. Each district should have a written policy regarding both prescription and over-the-counter (OTC) medications. This policy should include obtaining the written authorization of a physician and the written consent of the parent, proper storage, delegated administration, and a log sheet for documentation. All medication, whether prescription or OTC, must come to school in the original, labeled container with written instructions for administration on the label. Always be sure of the "Five Rights" of medication: the right student, the right medication, the right dosage, the right time, and the right route (by mouth, inhaler, injection, etc.) (Wagner 1983). It is especially necessary when dealing with students with severe disabilities to be aware of possible side effects of medications (Table 14.1). The care giver should monitor the student's condition before and after receiving medication and document on a medication form (Figure 14.2) any concerns as the student may not be able to communicate these. A desk reference such as *The Essential Guide to Prescription Drugs* by James W. Long, M. D. is a useful reference on medications.

TABLE 14.1   Some Possible Side Effects of Common Medications.

Medication	Possible Side Effects
Amoxil Amoxicillin–antiboitic	Stomach cramps, diarrhea, fever, thirst, nausea, vomiting, tiredness or weakness, skin rash or itching.
Aspirin Salicylates–analgesic	Not to be given to children because of its association with Reye syndrome. Nausea, stomach pain, shortness of breath, hives or itching, tiredness or weakness.
Bactrim Sulfonamide–antibiotic	Itching, skin rash, aching of joint and muscles, difficulty in swallowing, fever, sore throat, redness, blistering, peeling or loosening of the skin, unusual tiredness or weakness, blood in urine, lower back pain, pain or burning while urinating, swelling of the front of the neck.
Benadryl; diphenhydramine Antitussive–respiratory tract medication	Sore throat, fever, unusual tiredness or weakness.
Dilantin; Pentytion Hydontion–anticonvulsant	Gingivival hyperplasia, uncontrolled movements, confusion, dizziness, ataxia, drowsiness, constipation, anorexia, nausea, vomiting.
Maalox; aluminum and magnesium Antacid–gastric medication	Mood or mental changes, swelling of wrist or ankles, constipation, unusual loss of weight, unusual tiredness or weakness.
Prednisone *Glucocorticoid*–anti-inflamatory	Decreased or blurred vision, decreased growth, frequent urination, increased thirst, hallucinations, skin rash or hives, burning or pain at place of injection, mental depression or other mood or mental changes.
Ritalin Methylphenidate–central nervous system stimulant	Rapid heartbeat, chest pain, uncontrolled movements of the body, bruising, fever, joint pain, skin rash or hives, blurred vision, convulsions, sore throat, fever, unusual tiredness or weakness.
Synthroid; Levothyroxine Thyroid modifier–hormone	Severe headache, skin rash or hives.
Tagamet; Cimetidine Antacid–gastric medication	Sore throat, fever, unusual bleeding or bruising, unusual tiredness or weakness.
Tylenol Acetaminophen–Analgesic	Difficult or painful urination, sudden increase in amount of urine, skin rash, hives or itching, unexplained sore throat and fever, unusual tiredness or weakness.

Adapted from Ault, M. M., Guy, B., Guess, D., and Rues, J. (1991) *Medication Information Guidelines*. Lawrence, KS: Project ABLE, Dept. of Education, University of Kansas.

_____ has received _____
                Student Name   Medication Name

prescribed by _____ beginning _____
                        Doctor's Name   Permit Date

Possible Side Effects:

_____

_____

_____

Other Medications Being Administered Concurrently:

_____

_____

_____

Possible Interaction Effects:

_____

_____

_____

Date	Time	Dosage	Administered by Signature	Date	Time	Dosage	Administered by Signature

FIGURE 14.2   A Sample Medication Treatment Form

Seizure Management

The purposes of seizure management are twofold: first, to protect a child during a seizure and second, to observe and document antecedent, seizure, and postseizure behaviors to aid in preventative treatment. There is nothing that can be done to stop a seizure, but several things can or should be done for the safety of the student. First, gently lower him to the ground and turn him on his side or stomach to prevent choking and keep his airway breathing open. Do *not* place anything in the student's mouth. Loosen tight clothing and cushion his head to prevent injury during spasms. Monitor his breathing. After the seizure has ended, check the student for incontinence or injury. Reassure and make him comfortable, then allow him to rest or sleep if he wishes. Note the time the seizure began and ended as well as the general characteristics of the seizure (i.e., where did the seizure begin, was the student limp or rigid, what were the type of body movements, etc.). Document any special antecedent behavior or activity and postseizure condition and activity. Report the occurrence to the school nurse or administrator and to the parent. Seizures can become an emergency matter that requires immediate medical care if the student should stop breathing or if the seizure should continue for more than five to ten minutes; but, that is rarely the case.

First Aid and Cardiopulmonary Resuscitation

Every person who deals with students is well advised to acquire and maintain first aid and cardiopulmonary resuscitation (CPR) certification from the American Red Cross or other agency. First aid is appropriate for minor injuries such as stings, cuts, or burns. Stings and bites should be treated by careful cleaning and should be left open. In case of stings, monitor the student for a possible allergic reaction. If the student is known to be allergic, an emergency kit containing epinephrine should be readily available. Treat burns by cooling with clean water then covering lightly with gauze. Treat cuts or scrapes with careful washing and mild antiseptic. If you suspect a bone fracture, immobilize the area and apply cold packs to reduce swelling until medical help arrives. Always wear disposable gloves to protect yourself and the student.

Cardiopulmonary resuscitation is an emergency response to a life threatening situation. In the event that CPR should be necessary, first call or send for assistance, then follow the *ABCs* of CPR. First gently try to rouse the student. Ask, "Are you all right?" Listen to the chest to determine if the student is breathing, then check the *Airway* for a blockage. Do *not* begin CPR for a blocked airway. Use a finger sweep to dislodge the object or apply the Heimlich maneuver. Restore *Breathing*. Place the student on his back and tilt the head back, lifting the chin to open the airway. Give two breaths into the student's mouth while holding nostrils closed, and watch to be sure the chest rises. Restore *Circulation*. Check for a pulse. Do *not* begin chest compressions if a pulse is present. Give five chest compressions for each breath. Continue to check for pulse or spontaneous breathing. Repeat the cycle until the pulse returns and the student starts to breath on his own or until the paramedics or emergency medical services (EMS) team arrives.

Positioning and the Prevention of Decubitus Ulcers

For wheelchair bound students and those with limited mobility, pressure sores (decubitus ulcers) are a persistent concern (Donovan 1981). They are easier to prevented than to treat. There are three stages in the progression of a sore. The first involves a reddened area of skin that does not blanch when touched. This can develop after only two to six hours of unrelieved pressure and may take up to thirysix hours to clear. The second stage involves a hard red area or scab. This indicates that tissue is dying. The third stage is the hole or ulcer formed after the tissue dies. Decubitus ulcers are more than painful, they may require hospitalization and, in the presence of other conditions, may even be life threatening. Pressure sores are easily reversible at stage one. It is essential that the student's skin is kept clean and dry and that his position is changed frequently, at least every two hours to relieve pressure. Flotation rings or pads, fleeces, and water-filled seats are very helpful. Keep all pads and clothing free of wrinkles when positioning, and be sure all adaptive and assistive devices are well fitting. Check the condition of the student's skin at natural pressure points (hips, buttocks, knees, elbows, etc.) and folds of the skin for signs of redness. Gentle massage and a moisturizing lotion will aid in maintaining healthy skin.

Fluids and Nourishment

Because some students with severe disabilities have difficulty chewing or swallowing, have special nutritional needs, or may require nonoral feeding methods, nourishment may be an important part of the health care plan.

It may be important to document the kinds and amounts of food and drink the student takes, to assist in self-feeding by means of cutting food or special utensils, to monitor the student for proper chewing and swallowing behaviors, to feed the student, or to assist with nonoral feeding methods. Gastronomy (abdomen) and nasogastic (nasal) feeding at school will involve a tube already in place. Specific instructions on amount of formula, a pump, feeding bag or syringe, and the time allotted for feeding will vary with the student. The procedure should be conducted in a private setting. Position the student appropriately. Check for proper placement of the tube, and attach the syringe or feeding bag and infusion pump. Feeding by the gravity method will take about twenty to forty-five minutes. Provide oral stimulation if possible. Stop the feeding if vomiting or distress occurs. End the feeding with the prescribed amount of clear water. Check the tube and resecure it in place. If the gastronomy tube should come out of the stoma, cover the stoma with gauze and notify the person delegated to replace it. Document the feeding time and amounts and any irritation of the stoma.

Darnell was a student with maple syrup urine disease, an inherited condition of protein intolerance. His parents and teachers had to rigorously monitor his protein intake, and they had to document everything he ate. They allowed him a maximum of ten grams of protein per day. Too much protein could result in projectile vomiting and convulsions and, perhaps, could even result in hospitalization. Parents and teachers kept careful records at home and school. He liked to eat cafeteria food with the other students, so his mother would send a marked menu to school, listing the items and amounts he could have for each day. The kitchen staff measured his allotted portion each day.

This did not hold up the line or place any special burden on anyone. Darnell was a sweet-natured child, well accepted by his peers, and all of the supervising staff knew of his condition so no sharing of undocumented food would take place. When he became ill one night after school, this careful documentation allowed his mother to eventually determine that the small amount of protein in the antibiotic he was taking was the cause of the problem. Neither the physician nor pharmacist had informed her that the medication contained a small amount of protein. Thereafter, she included this amount in his protein total and averted future problems.

Respiratory Care—Tracheostomy Care

A tracheostomy is a surgical opening into the trachea through the neck to facilitate breathing. A tube is inserted through the stoma, or opening, and held in place with ties around the neck. With a tracheostomy, it is important to keep the airway clear and free of secretions, to minimize the danger of infection, and to protect the area around the stoma from irritation. The tracheostomy is usually kept covered with a gauze pad that helps to retain expired moisture, remoistens inhaled air, and filters out dust particles.

Suctioning to remove secretions may occur on a regular basis, or it may be necessary only occasionally when there is a buildup in the tube indicated by gurgly or labored breathing, complexion changes, restlessness, or sleepiness. To suction a tracheostomy requires a suction machine, suction catheter, and suction tubing. Have all materials ready at the student's side. Wash your hands and wear disposable gloves. Have the student take some deep breaths and remove the gauze pad. Introduce the catheter through the tube opening. Do *not* suction while inserting the catheter. Apply suction intermittently while withdrawing the catheter. Do not have the catheter in the tube for more than five seconds at a time because it blocks the airway. Repeat suctioning the prescribed number of times or until the tube is clear of secretions. Suctioning should generally not take more than three to five minutes including rest periods for the student. If the student should cough spontaneously, gently clean the area with a gauze pad dampened with peroxide. Reattach the student's oxygen or ventilator if they were removed or recover with a gauze pad.

Parents usually change the tracheostomy tube and ties at home, but these tasks and CPR techniques should be part of the tracheostomy student's emergency plan.

Atypical Elimination

Clean intermittent catheterization decreases the frequency of urinary tract infections in students who are unable to thoroughly empty the bladder or to assist students with limited bladder control. This is usually done every three to four hours.

First, have the student attempt to void, then have the student sit on the toilet on an absorbent pad. Wearing gloves, gently cleanse the area around the opening of the urethra. Lubricate the tip of the catheter and gently insert it into the urethra until the urine begins to flow. Leave it in place until the urine ceases to flow. Too rapid draining of an overfull bladder can result in hemorrhage. The standard maximum of 500 ml of urine will not necessarily apply when the caregiver is not measuring the flow or in a young student. It is safest to cease the CIC if the flow seems unusually heavy. Remove the catheter. Clean and rinse and dry the area thoroughly. Document the CIC. Immediately report any signs of infection, unusual volume, bleeding, pain or difficulty in inserting the catheter.

Ostomy and Stoma Care

Many medical conditions that interfere with normal bowel elimination are treatable with an operation that closes the normal route of body wastes and opens a new route called a stoma. The procedure may be temporary or permanent. Body wastes go into a collection bag, which the wearer must change periodically. The wearer usually does this at home as the bags usually last longer than the school day. Should it be necessary to change the bag at school because of leakage, excessive gas, diarrhea, or other concerns, special care must be taken to keep the stoma and surrounding skin in good condition.

Be sure to wash hands thoroughly and wear disposable gloves. Arrange for privacy, and be aware that a student may need to lie down for part of the procedure. Gently remove the ostomy bag. Cover the stoma with a small wad of tissue to prevent leakage. Empty the contents, rinse, and empty again. Discard a disposable bag, or wrap up a reusable bag for a student to take home. Gently cleanse, rinse and dry the stoma and surrounding skin, being sure to remove any remaining adhesive.

Six-year-old Maria's consistent bowel problems had left her incontinent. Although she and her parents made every effort to keep her clean, she was taunted by classmates for wearing a diaper. They would refuse to sit next to her because of the odor her bowel movements caused and there were occasionally problems with leakage. She was shy, withdrawn, and sometimes tearful. Her physician and parents made the decision to have an ostomy operation over Christmas break. Maria tolerated the surgery well and returned to school. With her improved health and improved social relationships, her new personality blossomed. By the time she returned to school again in the following fall, she had become a smiling, happy child. Her operation was neither kept secret nor publicized, which allowed Maria to talk about it when she chose. The surgery did not limit her in normal primary-age activities.

Carefully examine the skin for any sign of breakdown, infection, or irritation. Apply the skin barrier or skin protector in use. Center and replace the new bag over the stoma. Seal and secure the bag according to the directions for that specific bag. Be sure both the student and yourself wash hands thoroughly.

Many of the problems in dealing with special health care needs arise because school administrators, teachers, and caregivers have inadequate information about the provision of services. It is helpful to reinforce the following:

1. A licensed medical professional will always perform complex medical procedures.
2. The medical procedures that do occur at school are usually quite simple. Parents, siblings, babysitters, and others with no significant medical background or training have mastered and performed them at home.
3. Before performing any medical procedure, the caregiver will have received thorough training. Just be sure to ask all the questions you may have. While there is an element of risk when dealing with health care needs, there is also risk in driving on a freeway and taking a shower.
4. When considering all aspects of providing health care needs, the two most critical are handwashing and documentation. Do them thoroughly and the rest will follow.
5. Maintain an open relationship with the parents. They are your best resource. They are the supreme experts on their child, and they have a vested interest in your success!

The Health Care Plan

Once an educational team determines that a student has health care needs to be met at school, the team, parents, medical personnel, school staff, and, if possible, the student should meet to develop the health care plan. This is a written document that will specifically identify the services, the delivery service system, the delegated care providers, the documentation procedures, and an emergency plan. Although, as previously mentioned, the student's physician will rarely be present at the team meetings, it is essential that the doctor's recommendations and input be part of the plan and that there be open, continuing communication.

The priority of the health care plan is to maintain the student's health and vitality and maximize her ability to benefit from the educational process. The dignity of the student (Perske, 1988) must remain intact, and decisions may need to balance benefits and safety against the risks in the goals of opportunity, normalization, and personal fulfillment. Health care needs do not alter the ultimate goal, which according to Rainforth, York, and MacDonald (1992) is to participate in a variety of home, school, and community activities with a variety of people using the supports and cues that occur naturally in those settings. Taylor's (1988) philosophy to ensure normalization—only as special as necessary—applies to the health care plan as in all other aspects of the IEP.

The selection of caregivers and the delegation of specific responsibilities should be a collaborative decision of the team members. The student's specific characteristics and developmental level (Griffith, 1992) will determine her level of responsibility for her own health care.

The documentation of the services provided to students is essential. In effect, if it is not written down, dated, and signed, it did not happen. Documentation of health care services is especially important because it can prevent minor health issues from becoming major health crises. The team should develop forms for documentation of specific information (Figure 14.3).

An important aspect of the health care plan is the emergency plan. Often an emergency is an unforeseen crisis, but for the purposes of the health care plan, the definition of "emergency" should include any combination of circumstances that calls for immediate action and the need for assistance and relief. Some components of emergency planning that apply to all students include:

1. The definition of a medical emergency for this particular student. During the team meeting talk to the parents and if possible the physician. Be aware of what may cause an emergency, time lines for occurrences, possible triggers, and any symptoms or behaviors that may serve as a warning. A good type of question to ask is, "Under what circumstances should I become concerned?"

2. The specific activities and actions one should take in each situation. This will include delegating and training some caregivers to provide specific services and others to care for the remaining students during the emergency. Include the location of any equipment, medication, etc. that may be necessary.

3. Emergency transportation procedures including who will determine the necessity to transport the student.

4. A list of persons to notify. This part of the plan should include who will notify the designated persons, what information to include, and when and how to notify them—immediately by phone, by note at the end of the day, or just at the next conference time.

5. The correct documentation for the emergency (Figure 14.4). When evaluating the health care needs, specific information about the event and its antecedents and consequences will be just as important as knowing when and where it occurred.

Summary

Schools are to provide for the health care needs of students when necessary to enable the student to reasonably benefit from the educational program. A trained delegated caregiver without a medical background can usually perform the necessary services. A medical professional, such as a registered nurse, can assume care of complex health needs.

Student Name　　　　　Date of Birth　　　　　Date

Information provided by _____

Primary caregiver(s) _____
　　　　　　　　　　　　　　Name(s) and Phone Numbers

Primary Physician _____|_____
　　　　　　　　　　　　Name and Phone Number　　　　　Date last seen

Specialists _____|_____
　　　　　　　　　　　　Name and Phone Number　　　　　Date last seen

　　　　　　_____|_____
　　　　　　　　　　　　Name and Phone Number　　　　　Date last seen

　　　　　　_____|_____
　　　　　　　　　　　　Name and Phone Number　　　　　Date last seen

Baseline Health Status _____　_____　_____　_____　_____
　　　　　　　　　　　　　Temp.　Blood pressure　Respiration　Height　Weight

Summary of Medical History:

_____

_____

_____

_____

_____

Special Health Care Needs and Procedures:

_____

_____

_____

_____

Assessment of Current Health Status:

_____

_____

_____

_____

FIGURE 14.3   A Sample Significant Health Information Form

_____   _____
Student Name   Date

_____   A copy should by filled out by or given
                             to each caregiver who works with the
                             student and kept in each classroom or
                             on the bus.

In case of emergency _____ will stay with the

student and _____ will call the nurse or EMS.

Under these circumstances:

Take these actions:

The delegated person to order transportation for this student is _____.

Phone Numbers:

Emergency Medical Services _____ Primary Physician _____

Specialist _____ Local Physician _____ Fire _____

Police _____ Preferred Hospital _____ Local Emergency Room _____

Mother's Work _____ Home _____

Father's Work _____ Home _____

Alternate Guardian's Work _____ Home _____

FIGURE 14.4   A Sample Emergency Form

The health care plan is a vital document that specifies in detail the services to be provided as well as when, where, and by whom. An emergency plan is an important part of the total plan. Documentation is exceptionally important in meeting health care needs.

References

American Academy of Pediatrics. *Special Report,* (1988).

Americans with Disabilities Act of 1990 (PL 101–336). July 26, 1990. 42 U.S.C. 1201, et seq.: *Federal Register,* 56 (144), 35544–35756.

Ault, M. M., Guy, B., Guess, D., & Rues, J. (1991) *Medication Information Guidelines.* Lawrence, KS: Project ABLE, Dept. of Special Education, University of Kansas.

Board of Education of the Hendrick Hudson Central School District v. Amy Rowley (458 U.S. 176) 1982.

Donovan, W. H.(1989). Spinal cord injury. In W. C. Stolov, & M. R.Clowers, *Handbook of Severe Disability.* Washington, DC: U.S. Dept. of Education & Rehabilitation Services Administration.

Education of All Handicapped Children Act of 1975. (PL 94–142) 20 U.S.C. Sections 1400–1461.

Education of the Handicapped Act Amendment of 1986. 20 U.S.C. 1471 et seq. and 1419 et seq.

Eighth Annual Report to Congress on the Implementation of the Education of the Handicapped Act (1986). Washington, DC: United States Government Printing Office.

Greisman, Z. (1990, September). Medically fragile children. *West's Education Law Reporter,* *61*(2), 403–08.

Griffith, D. R.(1992, September). Prenatal exposure to cocaine and other drugs: Developmental and educational prognoses. *Phi Delta Kappan,* pp. 30–34.

Guidelines for special health care procedures in Missouri schools. (1990, July). Jefferson City, MO: Missouri Department of Secondary and Elementary Education, Division of Special Education in cooperation with Missouri Department of Health.

Hill, J. L.(1991). *Accommodating a student with a disability: Suggestions for faculty.* Victoria, British Columbia, Canada: University of Victoria.

Holmes Group. (1990). *Tomorrow's schools: Principles for the design of professional development schools.* East Lansing, MI: Holmes Group.

Individuals with Disabilities Education Act of 1990. 20 U.S.C. Sec. 1400–1485.

Irving v. Tatro (468 U.S. 883) 1984.

Kendell, R. M. (1991). Unique educational needs of learners with physical and other health impairments. Monograph.

Long, J. W. *Essential Guide to Prescription Drugs* New York: Harper and Row.

McCarthy, M. M.(1991, September). Judicial interpretation of medical severely disabled children: Who pays? *Phi Delta Kappan,* pp. 66–71.

Perske, R. (1988). *A circle of friends.* Nashville, TN: Abingdon Press.

Rainforth, B., York, J., & MacDonald, C. (1992). *Collaborative teams for students with severe disabilities: Integrating therapy and educational services.* Baltimore: Paul H. Brookes.

Rehabilitation Act of 1973 (Section 504) 29 U.S.C. Section 794.

Research and Training Center on Independent Living. Bureau of Child Research. *Guidelines for reporting and writing about people with disabilities* (3rd ed.). (1990). Lawrence, KS: University of Kansas.

Smith v. Robinson (68 U.S. 992) 1984.

Taylor, S. J. (1988). Caught in the continuum: A critical analysis of the principles of the least restrictive environment. *Journal of The Association for Persons with Severe Handicaps, 13,* 41–53.

Wagner, M. (Ed.). (1983) *Nurse Reference Library. "Drugs."* Springhouse, PA: Intermed Communications.

Welsch v. Likins (373 F. Supp 487) 1974.

Wyatt v. Stickney (344 F. Supp 373) 1972.

For Further Reading

AdHoc Committee on the Medically Fragile (1988). *Report of the Council for Exceptional Children's Ad Hoc Committee on Medically Fragile Students,* Council for Exceptional Children. Reston, VA: Ad Hoc Committee on the Medically Fragile.

Ekstrand, R. E.(1982, May/June). Doctors do you make (school) house calls? *Children Today, 11,* 2–4, 37.

Ellinwood, B. W.(1990, April). The successful integration of the severely handicapped in a regular education elementary school—least restrictive environment. Arlington, VA: Educational Research Service.

Giangreco, M. F., York, J., & Rainforth, B. (1989). Providing related services to learners with severe handicaps in educational settings: Pursuing the least restrictive option. *Pediatric Physical Therapy, 1,* 55–63.

Greenlee, K. M. (1983). *An annotated bibliography of identifying and meeting the needs of the student with chronic health problems.* Project directed by C. R.DuVall. Indiana University at South Bend.

Haynie, M., Porter, S. M., & Palfrey, J. S.(1989). *Children assisted by medical technology in educational settings: Guidelines for care.* Boston: The Children's Hospital.

Health services for the school-age child. 1989 [and] supplement. Salem, OR: Oregon State Department of Education.

Long, R. (1959, April). *Second Missouri Conference: Aid for the multiply handicapped,* pp. 43–66. Jefferson City, MO: MO Health Council and Nemours Foundation of Delaware.

Lunden, Janet (Ed.). (1990). *Guidelines and procedures for meeting the specialized physical health care needs of pupils.* Sacramento, CA: Department of Education.

Nader, P., & Mahan, J. M.(1989). Measurement of social behavior and performance of chronically ill children. In *Chronic childhood illness: Assessment of outcome.* U.S. Government Printing Office, DHEW Pub. No. (NIH) 876–877.

Robert Wood Johnson Foundation, (1988). *Serving handicapped children: A special report,* (No. 1). Princeton, NJ.

Rotatori, A. F., & Fox, R. A.(1989). *Understanding individuals with low incidence handicaps: Categorical and noncategorical perspectives.* Springfield, IL: Charles C. Thomas.

Sirvis, B. (1989). *Students with specialized health care needs.* Reston, VA: Council of Exceptional Children.

Wood, S. P., Walker, D. K., Gardner, J. (1986). School health practices for children with complex medical needs. *Journal of School Health, 56*(6), 215–217.

15

PLANNING FOR TRANSITION ACROSS AGES AND SETTINGS

JENNIFER R. BUTTERWORTH   *DIANE LEA RYNDAK*

Objectives

After completing this chapter the reader will be able to:

1. Define transition.
2. List potential members of various types of transition teams.
3. Describe the purpose of a transition team and how the team effectively accomplishes transition planning across ages and between programs.
4. Define interagency agreement.
5. Describe how to develop an individualized transition plan.
6. Describe various types of employment services for adults and the benefits and disadvantages of each.
7. Describe options related to residential support available for adults with disabilities.
8. Discuss legal issues to consider during transition for adults with disabilities.
9. Describe supplemental security income.
10. Discuss why it is critical to consider medical expenses when an individual with disabilities transitions to adulthood.

Key Terms

Commensurate wages
Community, home, &
    job site instruction
Fair Labor Standards Act (FLSA)

Division of Rehabilitation
    Services (DRS)
Extended evaluation
Postschool services

Guardianship
Individualized family
  service plan (IFSP)
Individualized transition
  plan (ITP)
Individualized written
  rehabilitation plan (IWRP)
Infant and toddler services
Interagency agreement
Job Training Partnership
  ACT (JTPA)
Long-term advocacy
Medicare
Ongoing services
On-the-job training (OJT)
Plan for Achieving
  Self-Support (PASS)
PL 99–457
PL 101–476

Preschool services
Private nonprofit employment agency
Rehabilitation counselor
Residential options
School-age programs
Situational vocational assessment
Social security administration (SSA)
Supplemental security income (SSI)
Supplemental security disability
  insurance (SSDI)
Supported employment services
Supported work
Time-limited services
Transition
Transition team
Vocational assessments
Vocational rehabilitation
Work adjustment
Work training services

Definition of Transition

According to Neufeldt and Guralnik (1994) transition is "(a) passing from one condition, form, stage, activity, place, etc. to another (b) the period of such passing." Within special education, transition refers to a coordinated set of actions that facilitate a student's movement from one group of settings to another group. Students continually make transitions during their school careers, with major transitions occurring between agencies (e.g., preschool to school and school to postschool settings), grade levels, and schools (e.g., elementary to middle school). Each transition entails unfamiliar events, settings, and people. Most importantly, however, relationships that have been built on trust end, and new relationships with unfamiliar people under different circumstances are developed. Planning for a transition can facilitate the development of such relationships, as well as familiarity with new settings and routines. Accomplishing these prior to the actual change in services or placement can reduce fears about the change that students, their parents, and service providers experience. As with all students, those with moderate or severe disabilities experience changes when transitioning between agencies, grade levels, and schools. Because of the nature of their disabilities, however, students with moderate or severe disabilities have many needs that the education team can meet more effectively when they address them during transition.

While the process of transition planning includes the activities Chapter 3 described in the curriculum identification process, modifications in how these steps are carried out may be necessary, depending upon the type of transition occurring for a student. For instance, a student may transition from (1) a segregated setting to an inclusive setting, (2) one year of inclusive services to another year within the same service provider and building, (3) one building to another building within the same service provider (e.g., home middle school to home high school), (4) one service provider to another service provider (e.g., infant to preschool program, preschool to school-age programs, school-age to postschool services), or (5) combinations of transitions (e.g., segregated class in home elementary school to inclusive services in home middle school, high school to inclusive college). The manner in which the activities in the curriculum identification process are implemented will vary across these types of transition. For example, the individuals who complete the general education curriculum inventory and how they complete it will differ if a student is transitioning between years of inclusive services within one building versus transitioning from a segregated preschool to an inclusive elementary school.

Across types of transition, however, effective planning can serve four functions:

1. It can provide a systematic approach to identifying and accessing relevant services in the settings to which a student is transitioning.
2. It can facilitate carryover of effective services and support strategies from current settings to future settings.
3. It can decrease any fear of change the student, the parents or guardians, and both current and future service providers experience.
4. It can empower students and their families by providing them choices about the settings and services they access in the future.

Effective transition planning more readily occurs when both the sending and receiving service providers have the same inclusive philosophy, effective inclusive programs, a willingness to participate in transition planning and implementation, and the logistical and administrative support to participate in transition planning and implementation. The key to effective services, after all, is bridging the void that can exist when a student transitions between agencies, grade levels, and schools.

With each type of transition a student experiences, a different set of people constitute the team that plans and implements the transition. The responsibility for assembling a student's transition team and coordinating the development of that student's individualized transition plan (ITP), however, rests with the student's school district and current education team, whether the receiving service provider is the same school district, a different school district, or a different agency. Given coordination by the sending school district and education team, the responsibility for actually planning and implementing the student's transition plan does not rest with any single agency; rather, it rests with the coordinated efforts of the members of that student's transition team. A student's transition team always includes: (1) the student who is transitioning, their parents, and other relevant natural support network (Yancey, 1993) members, (2) current education team members, and (3) future education team members *or* future adult service providers (e.g., rehabilitation counselor, employer, employment and residential service providers). In addition, depending on the type of transition, a student's transition team could include representatives from (1) nonschool service providers (e.g., day care provider), (2) advocacy organizations, (3) local community facilities (e.g., community sports leagues, church), (4) the local social security office, and (5) health and medical services.

This chapter describes the main types of transition students with moderate or severe disabilities experience. It briefly describes why the transition process is critical for each type of transition and how each transition team functions. In addition, because of the complexity of transitioning from school-age to postschool services, the chapter provides information related to this transition.

Transitions within One Service Provider

The majority of transitions students with moderate or severe disabilities make are from one year of services to another year of services by the same provider. The provider of inclusive educational services is the student's home school district, in which three types of transitions occur. First, a student transitions from *one grade level to the next* with nondisabled classmates. This is the simplest type of transition and is planned and implemented effectively through the curriculum identification process in Chapter 3. During this transition information is necessary about the general education settings in which the student will participate the following year to determine the most meaningful general education and functional curriculum content for the student. This should include both content the education team will teach toward the end of the current academic year to prepare the student for the next set of general education settings and content for the student's individualized education program (IEP) for the next academic year. Without this information an education team cannot ensure that the content of their instruction, and the instruction they foresee for the following year, will meet the student's needs.

In addition to identifying relevant curriculum content for the student, however, the transition process has three benefits. First, it provides members of the student's education team for the next year opportunities to learn about the student's (1) instructional and physical management needs, (2) interaction style with peers and adults during both instructional and noninstructional times, and (3) requirements for adapted, alternative, or augmentative equipment and materials. Second, it allows new education team members, the student, and the student's family to meet and begin to establish relationships based on trust. Third, it provides the sending education team opportunities to share with the receiving team information that they believe is critical for the student's success next year. Transition activities may include: (1) the receiving team members observing the student in current general education settings, (2) the student and family members visiting the receiving general education settings to acclimate to the environments and people, and (3) meetings between sending and receiving team members to share information both on the student and logistics of teaming, as well as to plan instruction for next year.

The second most frequent type of transition that occurs within the same educational service provider is from *one school building to another* (i.e., elementary to middle school, middle to high school). The curriculum content identification process can again help plan and implement effectively this type of transition, though additional care is necessary to involve the appropriate individuals from both the sending and receiving buildings. Involvement of administrative personnel and those responsible for implementing the student's education program, both currently in the sending building and next year in the receiving building, is necessary to ensure a smooth and effective transition. For example, in Tony's district all fourth graders transition to the middle school for fifth grade. To ensure a smooth transition for Tony, the middle school principal and assistant principal became familiar with his needs (see Student Profiles in Appendix A) and provided opportunities for the fifth-grade teachers to observe Tony and other students with special needs in the fourth-grade classes. After these observations, the principal asked the fifth-grade teachers if they preferred certain student(s) with special needs for inclusion in their classes. Tony then was placed on the class roster for the fifth-grade teacher who most strongly preferred to provide instruction for him. During the remainder of the school year, that teacher participated with the fourth-grade education team in planning both a smooth transition and Tony's curriculum content for next year. The assistant principal also participated in this process to ensure that any building needs (e.g., architectural barriers, training of other building personnel) would be addressed prior to Tony's arrival.

A third type of transition that occurs within the same service provider is from *a segregated setting to inclusive settings.* If planned and implemented effectively, this type of transition occurs only once in the educational career of a student, but it usually causes the highest level of anxiety among district personnel and parents. Extra care should insure that the resources and support are in place for a student to succeed and for the education team to function appropriately. Prior to the move, adaptive equipment and instructional materials are in place, and the education team has developed plans in case the student requires unforeseen adaptations or supports, displays previously seen or new inappropriate behaviors, or experiences a medical emergency. The team must consider all the possibilities to insure that the general education teacher has support in any situation for which he or she is unprepared or uncomfortable. For example, when Michael moved from a segregated class into general education high school classes, he frequently refused to follow the general education teachers' directions, using learned responses with which he previously had been able to escape from work. The education team decided that if Michael refused to work in a class, either the general education teacher or the special education support person in the room at that time would say that was fine, but that he then would have to go to the guidance counselor's office and drop the class because he was unable to do the work. Because Michael was so motivated to be with his nondisabled peers and excited to be in "real" classes, the team believed that this strategy would eliminate his refusals. They were right! Within one week Michael stopped refusing to work, and completed his adapted work with minimal support.

Transitions between Service Providers

Transitions that occur between service providers are more complex than those that occur between settings of the same service provider and require more extensive participation of administrators. In addition, teams involved in these transitions require detailed information about the services other agencies provide. The following sections describe the types of transitions that occur between service providers and information related to transition from school-age to postschool services.

Types of Transitions

There are two types of situations in which a student transitions between service providers. First, when a student is no longer eligible for current services because of age, that student must transition to services provided for students in the new age bracket. This occurs between (1) infant and preschool services, (2) preschool and school-age services, and (3) school-age and postschool services. In addition, a student transitions between service providers when a family moves between districts.

Infant to Preschool Programs
The Education of the Handicapped Act Amendments of 1986 (PL 99–457) provide incentive monies for states to develop and implement services for infants and toddlers with disabilities and their families (Hallahan & Kaufman, 1994; Heward & Orlansky, 1992). According to this legislation, infants and toddlers with disabilities are children from birth to age two, inclusive, who require special education or related services through early intervention because they (1) are experiencing developmental delays in cognitive development, physical development, language and speech development, psychosocial development, or self-help skills, (2) have a diagnosed physical or mental condition which has a high probability of resulting in developmental delay, or (3) if a state chooses, are at risk of having substantial delay if they do not receive early intervention services (Section 672). In addition to services for children, this legislation focuses on family-centered intervention through the development of an Individualized Family Service Plan (IFSP). Similar to an IEP for school-age children, the IFSP consists of (1) the child's present performance levels, (2) major outcomes for the child and a projected timeline, (3) specific early intervention services necessary to meet the child's needs, and (4) projected dates for starting and ending services. The IFSP, however, also includes: (1) the *family's* resources, concerns, and priorities for the child, (2) major outcomes for the *family* and a projected timeline, (3) specific services needed to meet the *family's* need, (4) name

of a case manager, and (5) steps to ensure the child's smooth and effective transition to a preschool program. Possibly because of their demonstrated effectiveness, all 50 states have elected to provide early intervention services for infants and toddlers (Turnbull & Turnbull, 1990).

In contrast to providing incentives to states for early intervention services, PL 99–457 *mandates* preschool services for all children with disabilities between three and five years of age and their families, including special education, related services, and IFSPs (Hallahan & Kaufman, 1994; Heward & Orlansky, 1992). The provision of both early intervention and preschool programs within a state, and the development and use of the IFSP by both types of programs, facilitates transitions between the two programs. This is especially the case with the transition plan incorporated into the IFSP.

The complexity of transitions from early intervention to preschool programs most frequently is due to the manner in which services are provided by the two programs. The location of services (e.g., a center, the child's home, combination of both) and the focus of services (e.g., the child, the child's family) vary with early intervention programs (Heward & Orlansky, 1992; Karnes & Stayton, 1988). In contrast, preschool programs are centered-based, with an increasing number of preschool programs providing services both for children with disabilities and their nondisabled peers. The possible differences between early intervention and preschool programs, and the change in administering agencies, necessitate early interactions between the programs to prepare the child and the family to adapt best to the new services. The establishment of new relationships based on trust particularly is critical with families who are still adjusting to the child with disabilities, learning about effective services for their child, and discovering how to access and benefit from available services.

Preschool to School-Age Programs

As noted above, PL 99–457 mandates the inclusion of the transition plan in the IFSP for all preschool programs to facilitate the child's and family's transition from preschool to school-age programs. This transition, however, can be very complex. While it again incorporates a change of administering agencies, location, and manner of providing services, it also brings the child into a category of services with which families are familiar—school. In many ways families and service providers will struggle with determining how to best meet the student's needs within a general education context, which is significantly different from all the contexts in which the child and family have previously received services. The focus now will be on the student alone, rather than on the child and family. The setting now will be very formal, and one that already exists for all students of the same age, rather than specifically designed for children with disabilities.

The use of the curriculum content identification process insures that transition teams focus on the settings to which a student is transitioning and identify the activities in which the student will need to participate. While this assists in identifying skills that the student at least should begin to acquire prior to the actual change in services, it does not assist the student in adapting to a major change in services.

Most early intervention and preschool programs are teacher-directed; that is, a student's behaviors most often are in response to a teacher's direct instruction or cue. In most general education school-age settings, however, activities are student-centered; that is, a student's behaviors most often are in response to interactions between students or between students and their instructional materials. While in response to directions from a teacher, those directions are less direct, less immediate, and more focused on full activities rather than individual responses. The necessity for preparation for this major change in type of activities suggests that the transition process includes such activities as (1) the preschool education team observing the school-age settings and adjusting their own activities to more closely approximate the student-centered activities in school-age settings, and (2) the student participating in school-age activities for part of the day with the percent of time increasing slowly. Such activities require the participation of the education teams from the preschool and school-age programs, as well as administrators from both programs. The administrators may focus on (1) facilitating the transition activities the transition team identifies; and (2) meeting any building requirements the team identifies (e.g., barriers to access, inservice training).

School-Age to School-Age Programs

Transitions occurring between districts can be very simple or extremely complex depending upon the degree to which the philosophy of education and services provided in the two districts are similar. When the sending and receiving districts both have an inclusive philosophy and provide inclusive services, it may be expected that (1) student assessment information reflects performance in real situations, thereby providing information that is more helpful to the new education team, (2) current services are comparable to those at the receiving district, thereby providing a model to follow, and (3) the adaptations and support utilized in the general education settings have been effective, thereby being transferable to the receiving building. In this situation, the transition process may follow the same procedures outlined for transitions between buildings, with particular attention given to the administrative needs of both districts. Both administrative and building personnel participate in this type of transition process.

When the sending district does not embrace a philosophy of inclusion, the receiving inclusive district may find little assistance in the student's assessment information, current service format, and current adaptations and support. This precipitates the need for the receiving district to expend more time and energy on determining the student's level of performance, physical and management needs, and instructional needs. The receiving district will need additional time to observe the student, preferably both at school and in the community (e.g., with the family, with peers), to determine performance levels across settings and individuals. Information from these observations supplement any information from the sending district and provide information that is extremely useful when developing educational services for a student in inclusive settings. While the student's new education team will provide the majority of the additional time and effort, their administrative personnel continue to be involved to deal with any building adaptations that may be necessary.

School-Age to Postschool Services

Part B of the Individuals with Disabilities Education Act (IDEA) of 1990 (PL 101–476) mandates transition planning from school to postschool settings. IDEA defines transition from school to postschool settings as:

> ...a coordinated set of activities for a student, designed within an outcome-oriented process, which promotes movement from school to post-school activities, including post-secondary education, vocational training, integrated employment (including supported employment), continuing and adult education, adult services, independent living, and/or community participation. The coordinated set of activities shall be based upon the student's preferences and interests, and shall include instruction, community experiences, the development of employment and other post-school adult living objectives, and when appropriate, acquisition of daily living skills and functional vocational evaluation. (20 U.S.C. 1401[a][19–20])

IDEA requires an ITP for each student with disabilities age 16 and older, and age 14 if the student's education team thinks it is appropriate for the student (Section 602[a]).

Interagency Agreements and Local Postschool Transition Teams

Services that facilitate smooth transitions of students with moderate or severe disabilities to inclusive postschool settings typically are necessary at varying times during the transition process and for differing lengths of time, as determined by the needs of each student. Because effective transitions for young adults with disabilities from school to postschool services require coordinated efforts of a number of different agencies, each providing specific services and each under different regulations, this type of transition is a complex task. The division of authority and responsibility between school-age and postschool services has resulted in a number of students with moderate or severe disabilities receiving insufficient, inappropriate, delayed, or no services upon aging out of educational programs. Interagency coordination, therefore, is critical to effective transition activities to postschool services (Bates, Bronkema, Ames, & Hess, 1992; Berkell, 1988; Coerson, 1993; Everson & McNulty, 1992, 1995; Wehman, 1992; Wehman, Moon, Everson, Wood, & Barcus, 1988).

To facilitate this transition, states have developed interagency agreements that outline the roles and responsibilities of each agency during the transition process. Because local needs and availability of services vary, however, state interagency agreements frequently have lacked the specifics necessary to implement smooth transitions of *individual* students into postschool inclusive adult living, leisure, and work settings (Smith, Belcher, & Fuhrs, 1995). As a result, local postschool transition teams were formed to serve four functions. First, they provide other service providers current information on services available to adults with moderate or severe disabilities. Second, they identify the steps necessary for students to access local postschool services and the activities necessary to effect smooth transitions to those services in inclusive settings. Third, they develop a timeline for completion of these steps and activities, resulting in local action plans that lead to specific outcomes for a student after transition (see Figure 15.1). Fourth, they routinely evaluate the local action plans and assess the level of effectiveness of the transition process by identifying both facilitators and barriers to effective transitions, and by revising action plans accordingly.

Postschool Student Transition Team

In addition to the types of education team members that participate in other transitions, a student's postschool transition team must include representatives from services which the student *may* access, such as: (1) rehabilitation services, (2) public health, (3) agencies providing ongoing, extended, supported employment and supported living services, (4) current or prospective employers, and (5) the local social security office (Minnesota Educational Services, 1994). As other transition teams, a student's postschool transition team (1) identifies future settings and important instructional content related to those settings, (2) develops goals and objectives for that content, (3) determines the location and relative amounts of instructional time at each location, (4) identifies supports the student will need, and (5) identifies how and when the student will get these supports (Minnesota Educational Services, 1994). The focus of the postschool transition team, however, is on inclusive postschool settings and services. This focus requires a wealth of specialized information that other transition teams do not need. This focus entails activities such as observing the student across instructional settings, assessing for postschool service eligibility, and meeting the student's long-term adult needs.

High School Services that Support Postschool Transitions

The ultimate goal for each student is to (1) be a valued, respected, and active member in inclusive home, work, leisure, and community settings, and (2) have meaningful relationships and a support network of family members, friends, coworkers, and intimates. High school services that facilitate transition into postschool settings include instruction on functional curriculum content in the student's community. Instruction must focus on activities that are meaningful, functional, and valued in the inclusive postschool settings identified for a student (Bates, Renzaglia, & Wehman, 1981; Wilcox & Bellamy, 1987). In addition, instruction in the student's natural settings (i.e., home; work; leisure environments; community) is effective for teaching students with moderate or severe disabilities (Ford et al.,

FIGURE 15.1   **Sample Local Action Plan Related to Transitioning to Supported Employment**

Action	Agency or Party Responsible	Projected Date
1. Develop personal futures plan	LEA coordinates per student's transition team:	Annually
2. Provide family information on postschool services (e.g., DMH/MR services, DRS, social security, JTPA, PASS)	a. LEA coordinates program for families and students of at least eighth grade b. LEA sponsors inservice for teachers c. SSA presents inservice to students, families, and teachers; LEA invites participants d. LEA provides families of students in at least eighth grade brochure of postschool services e. DRS provides inservice to students, families, and teachers on supported employment; LEA invites participants	Annually in summer Annually in fall Annually at transition team meetings from 8th grade Annually in spring
3. Attend meetings and/or gather information on postschool services	Students and their families or guardians	As offered by LEA and agencies
4. Ensure student has social security number	LEA notifies families; families apply	As student enters school, then annually
5. Apply for entitlement programs (e.g., SSI, Medicaid)	Families apply; transition team encourages through use of lead sheet (from SSA)	At transition team meetings
Inform families that SSI benefits are reevaluated at age eighteen.	If student already receives benefits, SSA notifies student and family. If not receiving benefits, teacher notifies students and families of reevaluation—student becomes "family of one" and may be eligible at this time	At least 2 months *before* student turns eighteen
If applying for social security benefits, collect: a. Medical report or medical questionnaire (SSA 3820) b. Psychological evaluation. c. Proof of income and resources of student d. Supplemental questionnaire (SSA 3881) e. Lead sheet (from SSA) f. Authorization for medical release of information	SSA sends lead sheet to LEA; transition uses	
6. Address guardianship issues, wills, trusts	ARC provides *Family Handbook on Futures Planning* to LEA; LEA shares information with families; transition teams address issues per student and advises introduction of lawyer into process	Annually, or as appropriate, through transition teams
Register to vote	Student with parents or guardians	When student turns eighteen
Register for draft	Student with parents or guardians	When student turns eighteen

continued

FIGURE 15.1 *Continued*

Action	Agency or Party Responsible	Projected Date
7. Address long-term advocacy issues	LEA invites advocates to transition team meetings	Annually at transition team meetings from age of eighteen
	Families and students informed of options and importance	
8. Address medical issues.	Transition team raises issues with families	Year before student exits school
a. Transportation to and from routine medical and dental appointments	Transition team	
b. Insurance coverage	Families	
c. Medication and self-medicating procedures	Transition team	
	Transition team; families through lawyers (guardianship)	Prior to turning eighteen
d. Management of emergencies		
9. Visit adult employment services	LEA sponsors trips to agencies	As student enters high school
Apply for services when appropriate	Students and families	Last year of high school
10. Visit adult service providers	LEA notifies families of options and sponsors trips	As student enters high school
Apply for services when appropriate	Students and families	As available last year of high school
11. Obtain routine job assessment and training for community employment	LEA provides at least two job experiences per year, with attempts to secure paid jobs whenever possible	Annually as student enters high school
	Families apply for JTPA summer programs	Annually
12. Teach activities and skills as necessary for postschool success	LEA through IEP process	
a. Supported living option		Annually
b. Community access and use		Annually
c. Establishing and maintaining meaningful relationships		Annually
13. Alert adult service providers (e.g., DRS, DMH/MR) of graduation date	LEA and transition team	Three years before student exits schools, then annually
Provide report of service needs		Two years before student exits schools
Secure authorizations for release of information to adult service providers		Two years before student exits schools
14. Ensure psychological report(s) document student eligibility for adult services	LEA with transition team support	As student enters high school
15. Address finance management issues (e.g., SSI/SSDI, checking accounts)	Transition team	Prior to turning eighteen, then annually
16. Apply for DRS services	Students and families; DRS reviews for eligibility	One year before student exits school
	LEA provides vocational assessment summaries to DRS	Reports for last two years of training

FIGURE 15.1   *Continued*

Action	Agency or Party Responsible	Projected Date
17. Secure full-time job in community business	LEA confirms timeline with rehabilitation counselor	Two to three months before job is needed
a. Continue job training	DRS/LEA and/or employer	As needed during last year of school and/or as adult meets eligibility criteria
b. Build support network at work	DRS/employer and/or student/family	
c. Consider a PASS per student	Adult service providers with family/student	LEA when income and resources exceed $85 per month
d. Arrange transportation	LEA coordinates with service providers and families	Prior to job placement
18. Transfer student information to adult service providers (e.g., DRS, living option)	LEA coordinates with "next" service providers	Two to three months prior to exiting school
19. Continue job training and network development until a. Adult is reliably independent b. Adult meets IWRP goals and/or c. Time-limited services end	DRS and/or employer	After exiting school or upon exiting rehabilitation facility
20. Begin supported community living option	DMH/MR	Upon eligibility
21. Continue building afterwork support network	LEA and parents coordinate with community resources	Before exiting school
22. Alert agencies responsible for extended employment services that rehabilitation services are ending	DRS counselor	As time-limited services run out
23. Transfer support and training information to new adult service providers	DRS counselor	Two to three months before time-limited services run out
24. Begin extended and ongoing supported employment services	Supported employment service provider	Two to three months before time-limited DRS run out
25. Provide ongoing support to maintain job, living option, and relationships	Supported employment service provider, families, DMH/MR	Ongoing after exiting school

ARC = Association for Retarded Citizens
DMH = Department of Mental Health
DRS = Division of Rehabilitation Services
IEP = Individualized education program
JPTA = Job Training Partnership Act
LEA = Local Education Agency
MR = Mental Retardation
PASS = Plan for Achieving Self-Support
SSA = Social Security Administration
SSDI = Supplemental Security Disability Insurance
SSI = Supplemental Security Income

1989). The closer a student is to exiting school and entering postschool settings, the more instructional emphasis and time the team places on those settings to accommodate any difficulty the student may have with generalizing from instructional to noninstructional settings.

Job Site Instruction

Job site instruction is one strategy for preparing students with moderate or severe disabilities for employment upon exiting school. Instruction occurs across a variety of job sites that sample the array of job clusters available in a student's community (McDonnell, Hardman, & Hightower, 1989). This variety (1) presents numerous training exemplars that contribute to a student's general work habits and skills typical of most jobs (e.g., timely attendance, working with distractions, communicating need for supplies or materials, receipt of supervisor directions), and job-specific activities (e.g., operating office equipment, assembling diesel parts, painting cabinets), (2) allows employment options when a student exits school, (3) assists an education team in assessing a student's strengths, weaknesses, preferences, and supports necessary to maintain employment, and (4) provides a student with a greater number of options from which to choose employment.

The Fair Labor Standards Act (FLSA), which specifies both payment requirements and conditions under which school-age youth and adults legally may work (U.S. Department of Labor, 1962), requires payment for work performed during job site instruction. If an employer–employee relationship exists, by law a student must receive commensurate wages (i.e., wages that take into account wages earned by persons without disabilities performing the same job) for the work performed. When a student does not complete the entire job responsibility of a position, such wages are "subminimum wages" and must have the approval of the Department of Labor (DOL). If there is no employer–employee relationship during job site instruction, then the business is not legally bound to pay a student. The FLSA specifies, however, six criteria for a business to demonstrate there is no employer–employee relationship.

In addition, the U.S. Departments of Education and Labor have jointly developed guidelines "that detail the criteria to be met by educational agencies to ensure that the U.S. Department of Labor will *not* assert an employment relationship for purposes of the FLSA." While clarifying the six FLSA criteria, these guidelines also specify limitations on the number of hours per job experience for vocational exploration, assessment, and training. Figure 15.2 provides an example of a possible job site instructional history for one student. For many adults with moderate or severe disabilities, job site instruction has been an effective strategy to prepare for supported employment services. According to PL 99–506, supported employment is

> *. . . competitive work in integrated work settings for: (a) individuals with severe [disabilities] for whom competitive employment has not traditionally occurred; or (b) individuals for whom competitive employment has been interrupted or inter-*

mittent as a result of severe [disabilities], and who, because of their [disability],
need on-going support services to perform such work. (Title I, Sec. 103, i).

Home Site Instruction

Adults with moderate or severe disabilities must perform a number of meaningful, functional activities in order to live in the community with dignity and respect. Effective high-school instruction focuses on those activities and skills necessary for an individual to maximize self-management, personal hygiene, time management, care of belongings, and finance management. As young adults approach the time to exit school, there is an increasing amount of instructional time delivered for such activities, preferably in the student's targeted postschool home setting to increase the likelihood that the student will use in those settings the skills learned through educational services (Brown et al., 1983). Inclusive postschool home settings typically include shared apartments or homes, family homes, foster homes, and group homes.

Community Instruction

As students age, their immediate community expands. By the time students are ready to exit public schools, their communities should be comparable to those available to age-similar peers without disabilities. As with home site instruction, instruction in each student's home community is essential for ensuring effective transition to postschool life.

Potential Services and Programs for Adults

There are a variety of services and programs that may be accessible to high school students with moderate or severe disabilities who are exiting education programs, depending upon the resources available in local areas. Employment-related services are provided for either limited amounts of time (i.e., time-limited services) or as long as the services are needed (i.e., ongoing services). The agencies that provide these and services for inclusive living options are described below.

Division of Rehabilitation Services

A state's Division of Rehabilitation Services (DRS) is a federally funded agency that functions as a branch of the Rehabilitation Services Administration (RSA), a division under the U.S. Department of Education. The procedures for, and availability of, services from DRS vary both across states and within a state, depending on the DRS office and local rehabilitation counselor. The DRS provides time-limited services to assist eligible persons in obtaining and maintaining employment. A rehabilitation counselor determines DRS eligibility locally based on a person (1) being of work age, (2) possessing a physical or mental disability that prevents or seriously interferes with efforts to work, (3) being capable of performing meaningful work, and (4) possessing a reasonable possibility that rehabilitation services will result in employment (Hasazi, Collins, & Cobb, 1988; Menchetti & Rusch, 1988; Stout, 1983). The counselor largely determines eligibility with information from the potential consumer, his or her education program, any vocational evaluations conducted by private adult agencies, and his or her parents. In addition, however, DRS may obtain assessments (e.g., medical, physical, psychological, vocational) or an extended evaluation from one or more vendors over a period that does not exceed eighteen months. Once determined eligible, the consumer and rehabilitation counselor establish a vocational goal and objectives included in an Individualized Written Rehabilitation Plan (IWRP).

Unfortunately, many potential consumers with moderate or severe disabilities historically have been denied eligibility for DRS services based on the results of their vocational assessments. Vocational assessments traditionally have included both norm-referenced assessments (e.g., VALPAR, APTICOM) and informal assessments, usually conducted at sheltered workshops or rehabilitation training centers. These assessments, however, have questionable or nonexistent validity measures in terms of meaningful employment, especially for this population (Berkell, 1987; Browning & Irvin, 1981; Menchetti & Rusch, 1988; Menchetti, Rusch, & Owens, 1983). Through these assessments many potential consumers with moderate or severe disabilities have been labeled as being incapable of obtaining and maintaining employment in community businesses, thereby being (1) ineligible for DRS services, and (2) considered appropriate only for further training, work adjustment, employment at sheltered workshops, or other adult day programs serving persons with disabilities.

Increasingly, however, situational vocational assessments are being completed (Moon, Inge, Wehman, Brooke, & Barcus, 1990). These involve direct observations of a potential consumer with moderate or severe disabilities during training to identify (1) generic work habits, skills, and attitudes, (2) job-specific skills, (3) requirements for support to obtain and maintain employment on that job, and (4) preferences for jobs that have diverse characteristics (Moon et al., 1990; Revell, Kriloff, & Sarkees, 1980; Winking, O'Reilly, & Moon, 1993). The situational assessments then summarize these observations across job sites (see Figure 15.2 for a sample summary form). Situational assessments also may include feedback from employers on their level of satisfaction with the potential consumer's performance and their willingness to hire him or her. Compared with traditional assessments, situational assessments provide more accurate depictions of the abilities of people with moderate or severe disabilities to obtain and maintain meaningful employment (Moon et al., 1990). Again, if eligible for DRS services, the consumer and respective rehabilitation counselor develop an IWRP.

Once eligible, DRS provides a variety of services and employment-related goods (e.g., adaptive equipment, prosthetic devices, rehabilitation technology) from which a consumer could benefit. These are described here.

Work Training Services

There are four major types of work training services that the DRS provides. First, *work adjustment* provides opportunities for the consumer to acquire the generic

Job Site	Duties	Did Student Like The Job?	Job Cluster (a)	Job Format (b)	Primary Supervisor (c)	Level of Support (d)	Age	Wages?	Hours/ Week	Days/ Week
Johnson's Manufacturing	Lamp assembly	Yes	7	2	T	O	16	No	6	4
Burger King	Salad bar preparation; cook french fries	No	5	2	T	O	16	No	6	4
Board of Education	Light clerical— filing, phone answering	Yes	8	1	C	P/RE	17	No	6	4
Floyd's Nursery	Weeding, watering plants, light cleaning, planting seedlings	No	1	2	T	O	17	No	6	4
Maintown Motel	Housekeeping	No	4	1	T	O	18	No	8	5
Maintown Bank	Light clerical copying, filing	Yes	8	1	C	P/RE	18	Yes	8	5
Clean Car Wash	Wiping cars, cleaning inside	No	9	3	C	O	19	No	10	5
Maintown Groceries	Stocking, shelving, pricing	No	3	1	T	P	19	Yes	10	5
Doctor's office	Receptionist	Yes	6	1	C	P/RE	20	Yes	15	5
Maintown Hospital	Laundary	No	4	1	T	P	20	Yes	13	5
Dentist's office	Clerical	Yes	6	1	J/C	P/RE	21	Yes	20	5

(a) Job Cluster

1. Agriculture, nature, resources, animals
2. Construction
3. Distribution
4. Domestic and building services
5. Food preparation services
6. Health occupations and human services
7. Manufacturing and machine operations
8. Office and building services
9. Other

(b) Job Format

1. Individual
2. Enclave
3. Work crew
4. Facility based

(c) Primary Supervisor

T = Teacher or School job coach
J = DRS job coach
B = Business supervisor
C = Coworker
V = Vocational coordinator
P = Peer tutor

(d) Level of Support

O = Ongoing
P = Periodic checks
RE = Regular employees or Natural Supports

FIGURE 15.2 Sample Vocational Training History

DRS = Division of Rehabilitation Services

work habits and skills necessary across a number of community businesses over a period not to exceed eighteen months (Powell & Moore, 1992). Community businesses, sheltered workshops, and rehabilitation training centers may provide work adjustment services.

Second, *supported work* is time-limited training (i.e., 300 hours with 100 additional hours upon approval of the rehabilitation counselor supervisor) to prepare a consumer for a specific competitive job in the community for which employment is guaranteed upon successful training. Job coaches, who could be coworkers at the job site or persons external to the job site who are hired through a contractual arrangement with DRS, provide supported work services.

Third, *on-the-job training* (OJT) provides subsidies for the consumer's wages for a period of three to six months or until the consumer stabilizes on the job. This period may extend beyond six months, however, with special approval. OJT is intended to offset the employer's cost of training the employee, and occurs only if the employer is committed to hiring the subsidized employee upon acceptable work performance. Because of the wage subsidies, however, it also may serve as an incentive to potential employers.

Fourth, the Rehabilitation Act Amendments of 1986 in Title VI, Part C, and amended in 1992 (*Federal Register,* June 24, 1992), authorizes the *supported employment services program.* According to this Act, supported employment:

1. is meant for consumers with a severe (disability) to employment who either have not worked competitively or have a history of interrupted competitive employment.
2. must occur in integrated job sites providing daily contact with other employees and/or the general public who are not disabled and having no more than eight employees with disabilities clustered.
3. is full-time or part-time competitive employment for commensurate wages (see FLSA section of this chapter).
4. includes the provision of ongoing supports needed to obtain and maintain the supported employment placement, throughout the term of that employment, where ongoing supports include (1) a minimum of contact with the consumer twice monthly at the job site to assess job stability or off-site monitoring of at least two face-to-face meetings with the consumer and (2) one employer contact monthly.
5. includes the provision of extended services which a private agency other than DRS typically provides in the form of ongoing supports after time-limited DRS services end, consisting of the services necessary to maintain the supported employment placement. (Note. Sources other than Titles I, VIC, IIIC or IIID of the Federal Rehabilitation Act fund extended services.)

For an eligible person to access supported employment services, the transition team must identify providers of extended services in the consumer's local area. Typically, extended services are provided through contractual arrangements with adult service providers, other than DRS, but they also may be provided through a well-documented plan for the use of natural supports (e.g., employer and coworker agreements, family commitments).

Job Development and Placement Services
Job development and placement services include the (1) identification of an appropriate match between the consumer and the demands of a job and (2) placement and initial training on the job that best matches the consumer's skills and preferences (Winking et al., 1993). The consumer's rehabilitation counselor or a private adult service agency with which DRS has a contract may perform these services.

Job Training and Partnership Act Programs

The Department of Labor manages the Job Training and Partnership Act (JTPA) of 1983 (PL 97–300) which creates programs to better prepare youth and adults for competitive jobs. Eligible youth and adults are those who are economically disadvantaged, at risk of dropping out of high school, dependent on welfare, homeless, displaced, disabled, or otherwise facing major barriers to employment. Programs that JTPA authorizes include:

1. assessment and counseling
2. job search assistance
3. training referral
4. basic skills training (e.g., remedial education, literacy training, English as a second language instruction)
5. job development and placement
6. preparation for a high school diploma
7. scholarships for vocational education
8. on-site, industry-specific job training
9. retraining
10. time-limited, follow-up services.

There are two programs particularly relevant to students with moderate or severe disabilities. First, the Summer Youth Employment and Training Program (Title II-B) provides eligible youth exposure to the world of work. Second, the Youth Training Program (Title II-C) has the objective of improving transition from school to work.

Private Nonprofit Employment Agencies

Each state has one or more department(s) that fund private programs to provide a variety of services to adults with moderate or severe disabilities based on local needs assessments. While eligibility for these services varies across states, in most states eligibility depends on the results of psychological and vocational assessments.

Most states' delivery systems have evolved based on a presumed continuum of services intended to prepare, and eventually assist, adults with disabilities in obtaining and maintaining employment. This continuum was meant to move an adult from day activity and habilitation programs, to work activity, to sheltered work, and, finally, to supported or unsupported competitive employment. Despite the fact that day treatment, sheltered work adjustment programs, and sheltered workshops continue to be the primary service systems for persons with moderate or severe disabilities (Schutz & Rusch, 1982), there is increasing recognition of the fiscal, ethical, and clinical lack of soundness of this service delivery system (Browder & Belfiore, 1991; Menchetti & Flynn, 1990; Parent, Sherron, & Groah, 1992; Rusch & Hughes, 1990; Wehman, Sale, & Parent, 1992). In addition, as students with moderate or severe disabilities receive educational services in inclusive settings, fewer students, families, and other education team members are willing to consider any option other than supported or unsupported competitive employment. This is, after all, the only service option that maintains the student in inclusive work settings as an adult. While conversion to a delivery system based on supported employment outcomes is difficult, there are at least twenty-seven states currently receiving grant funds for systems-change efforts focusing on supported employment outcomes (Szymanski, Hanley-Maxwell, Schaller, Parker, & Kidder, 1992).

Residential Options

Until the mid 1980s adults with moderate or severe disabilities had few options for places to live. While dominated by group homes, other options included living at home with parents or guardians, sheltered or shared apartments, and state institutions. During the 1990s such congregate living options have become viewed as lacking the characteristics of homes in which adults demonstrate self-direction, control, and personal choice. Instead, congregate living options are characterized by issues that are central to agency-run facilities (e.g., licensure, staff and staffing patterns, funding based on congregate needs versus needs of individuals, classification based on level of supervision provided for residents, individual support limited to the facility's functions).

The recognition of these characteristics has brought a shift away from congregate living options and increased attention to, and planning for, living options that separate housing from support. Racino, Walker, O'Connor, and Taylor (1993) identified eight elements that distinguish this "housing and support" approach from the traditional congregate living approach (e.g., focus on people versus facility; separation of housing and support; choice in housing, location, roommates and support providers; individualized and flexible support that build on natural networks). Within this new approach, housing options include owning or renting a home, living with parents or guardians, sharing a home, and living in a cooperative. Support options include personal attendants, paid roommates, paid neighbors, unpaid family or friends, agency-supplied staff supports, and technical adaptations. The determination of appropriate options is made on an individual basis and takes into consideration the type of housing option the individual with disabilities prefers.

Legal Concerns for Adults

Long-Term Advocacy

Most adults with moderate or severe disabilities need long-term support to participate successfully and fully within inclusive communities. While family members most often are advocates and provide this support, other concerned individuals also may be advocates (e.g., close friend, member of the clergy, representative from a self-advocacy association). The need for a long-term advocate often presents itself before a student exits high school. Securing a long-term advocate, particularly if a student has needs and desires that parents or guardians oppose, is a difficult and important task that needs a well-planned and tactful approach. Transition team members can assist in securing a long-term advocate for a student with moderate or severe disabilities by facilitating the student's contact with advocacy agencies.

Guardianship

All young adults, typically at age eighteen, are presumed to be legally competent to make decisions concerning their own personal lives and property, unless they are adjudicated otherwise. Legal competence assumes that an individual is able to make informed decisions by evaluating the available choices and understanding the consequences of selecting each choice. If a young adult is unable to make informed decisions, then guardianship must be considered.

Each state has different types of guardianship, including full, limited, and temporary. Full guardianship implies that an individual is unable to make an *informed* decision in relation to *any* aspect of personal life and property. Limited guardianship implies that an individual is unable to make *informed* decisions concerning *certain aspects* of personal life or property. For example, limited guardianship may be obtained in relation to management of personal finances or medical needs, while guardianship is not obtained in relation to other aspects of personal life and property. Temporary guardianship typically is available when an individual has a *time-limited inability* to make *informed* decisions concerning personal life or property (e.g., drug use, temporary mental illness, emergency situations).

Many parents of students with moderate or severe disabilities are unaware that when their child with disabilities reaches the age of eighteen, that child is presumed legally competent, and the parents are no longer legally able to make decisions for that child. Because of this, the issue of guardianship frequently does not come up until parents retire or become disabled, a primary caregiver dies, or a medical emergency occurs. Transition teams, however, can guarantee dissemination of guardianship information to parents of students with moderate or severe disabilities through the transition process.

Wills and Trusts

Planning for the transition of students with moderate or severe disabilities from school-age to postschool inclusive settings provides a natural opportunity for parents to consider their child's financial security. Wills and trusts are tools through which parents can provide financial security for their child. Parents often overlook these tools, however, until a crisis situation arises or a primary caregiver dies. Transition teams again can guarantee dissemination of information on wills and trusts to parents as part of the transition process. During transition planning and implementation, the team can encourage parents to seek legal advice, as well as consult with other agencies (e.g., the Social Security Administration) concerning the effect that the content of a will or trust will have on other benefits (Berkobien, 1991).

Financial Concerns for Adults with Disabilities

In addition to potential income from work, a student's individual transition team considers other financial issues of importance to adults with disabilities. For instance, there are financial benefits available from the Social Security Administration (SSA) for which a student may be eligible, both as a student and as an adult. These benefits, however, depend on the family's income when the individual is a student and on the individual's income when over age eighteen. Because of this, a transition team considers the student's (1) potential employment, and the income that employment will generate, (2) income from wills and trusts, (3) potential benefits from SSA, and (4) medical and insurance needs. The transition team must plan how these, in combination, will insure a high quality of adult life through employment, maximized benefits for health care, and maximized income.

Social Security Administration

The SSA is a federally funded agency that provides financial assistance through a number of different programs to eligible persons with severe disabilities. The SSA defines disability for a person under the age of eighteen as a physical or mental impairment that limits "the child's ability to function like other children of the same age to such a degree that the impairment is comparable to one which would make an adult disabled" (U. S. Department of Health and Human Services [USDHHS], 1993a, pp. 7–8). An adult is considered disabled if the physical or mental impairment "is expected to keep her/him from doing any 'substantial' work for at least a year or is expected to result in death" (pp. 12). The SSA considers "substantial" income to be $500 or more per month. A person might be eligible for SSA benefits if he or she (1) has or comes from a home with limited income or resources, or (2) is on the record of a parent who is collecting retirement or disability benefits, or has died after contributing to social security (pp. 3–4).

A student and her or his parents apply for SSA benefits at their local social security office. In determining disability status, it is common for social security officers to request assessment information from the schools in areas such as cognition, communication, motor abilities, social skills, behavioral skills, and vocational skills.

Whether or not a student is eligible for SSA benefits as a child, a re-evaluation of eligibility and services occurs just prior to the student turning eighteen. If a student receives SSA benefits before turning eighteen, the SSA automatically initiates these re-evaluation procedures. If prior to age eighteen a student had not applied for or been denied SSA benefits, however, he or she may reapply alone, because the student is considered legally competent to make informed decisions, or with his or her parents if guardianship has been adjudicated. The SSA considers an individual of age eighteen or older a "family of one," regardless of whether that person is living with family members (USDHHS, 1993a, p. 6). Because it is not uncommon for young adults with moderate or severe disabilities to be eligible for one or more SSA service, reapplication at age eighteen is highly recommended.

Supplemental Security Income
Supplemental security income (SSI) is one of the benefits the SSA administers with general US tax revenues. SSI benefits are paid to low-income persons who are elderly, blind, or have another disability (e.g., physical, mental, emotional). Both children and adults are eligible for SSI depending on their overall eligibility for SSA benefits (Braddock & Fugiura, 1988).

Social Security Disability Insurance for Adult Disabled Children
Social security disability insurance (SSDI) is a second benefit that the SSA administers. It is funded, however, through taxes paid by employees and their employers. It consists of benefits paid to individuals with disabilities who have contributed to social security in the past and individuals with disabilities whose deceased parents had contributed to social security (Braddock & Fugiura, 1988).

Medicare
Medicare is a third benefit the SSA administers. It is medical insurance for persons who (1) have received SSDI for at least twenty-four months, (2) are receiving SSI benefits, (3) are over the age of sixty-five, or (4) have In-State Renal Disease (USDHHS, 1993b).

Plan for Achieving Self Support
A fourth benefit the SSA administers is the Plan for Achieving Self Support (PASS). This program addresses the support an individual with moderate or severe disabilities requires to obtain and maintain employment. PASS provides funds to the individual in the amount of the monetary value of the goods and services necessary to obtain and maintain employment. This amount adjusts the individual's gross income, which then is used to determine the resultant effects on that individual's SSA benefits. With PASS, it is possible for individuals with disabilities to earn income from meaningful employment but continue to receive other SSA benefits, depending upon the total income that individual earns. It must be remembered, however, that if an individual's total income exceeds a specific dollar amount, they no longer are eligible for SSA benefits (USDHHS, 1991).

Medical Issues

The transition team considers four major medical issues during the process of transitioning from school-age to inclusive postschool settings. First, the student's individual transition team may assist the family in considering and obtaining the life and health insurance necessary to insure that the student consistently will have access to the services needed to attain and maintain optimal health. For example, many supported living programs (e.g., group homes) require residents to have medical insurance. As a child, many students with moderate or severe disabilities are covered by their parents' insurance plans, but this coverage usually ends at specified ages. While many of these students will receive social security benefits and be eligible for medicaid insurance as adults, early determination of eligibility for such benefits would assist the transition team in identifying any additional insurance needs for the student.

Second, the student's transition team determines the procedures to be followed during medical emergencies which may occur during adulthood. In addition, if the transition team does not consider the student capable of making informed decisions about medical issues, they must address the issue of guardianship to prevent the possibility of either tardiness or refusal of medical treatment when needed.

Third, the student's transition team determines the procedures to be followed when the student needs to receive medication as an adult. These procedures should address (1) obtaining a prescription, (2) getting medication from a pharmacy, (3) ensuring the lack of harmful side effects or interactions with other drugs, (4) consuming medication as directed, and (5) monitoring the use and desired effects of medication.

Fourth, the student's transition team determines procedures for the student to maintain a routine of physical check-ups as an adult to insure optimal health. These procedures should address arranging appointments with medical personnel, scheduling and using transportation to and from appointments, and paying for medical services.

Summary

The transition process consists of a coordinated set of actions that facilitate a student's movement from one group of settings to another group. Transitions occur from segregated to inclusive settings, within school-age service providers, and across service providers. For students with moderate or severe disabilities, planning a transition can have multiple benefits resulting in the provision of effective services more immediately after the change in services. A student's transition team, which is comprised of the student, members of his or her family and support network, and service providers from both the sending and receiving programs, plans the student's transition.

The most complex transition occurs as a student exits school-age programs and enters the adult services system because of the variety of services available under a number of programs. Because each program has its own administering agency, definitions of consumers, eligibility requirements, time frames for applying for and receiving services, and ramifications on eligibility for other services, postschool transition teams require a wealth of specialized information from their own state departments. Postschool transition teams are *encouraged* to contact their State Departments of Vocational Rehabilitation and Mental Health early, and are *mandated* to develop transition plans as a student turns sixteen. Individualized transition plans should consider a student's future employment, living options, medical and financial needs, and legal status.

References

Bates, P. E., Bronkema, J., Ames, T., & Hess, C. (1992). State-level interagency planning models. In F. R. Rusch, L. Destefano, J. Chadsey-Rusch, L. A. Phelps, & E. Szymancki (Eds.), *Transition from school to adult life: Models, linkages, and policy* (pp. 115–129). Sycamore, IL: Sycamore.

Bates, P., Renzaglia, A., & Wehman, P. (1981). Characteristics of appropriate education for the severely and profoundly handicapped. *Education and Training of the Mentally Retarded, 16*(2), 142–149.

Berkell, D. E. (1988). Identifying programming goals for productive employment. In B. L. Ludlow, A. P. Turnbull, & R. Luckasson (Eds.), *Transitions to adult life for people with mental retardation: Principles and practices* (pp. 159–176). Baltimore: Paul H. Brookes.

Berkell, D. E. (1987). Vocational assessment of students with severe handicaps: A review of the literature. *Career Development of Exceptional Individuals, 10*(2), 61–75.

Berkobien, R. (1991). *A family handbook on future planning.* Arlington, TX: Association for Retarded Citizens of the United States.

Braddock, D., & Fugiura, G. (1988). Federal foundations for transitions to adulthood. In B. L. Ludlow, A. P. Turnbull, & R. Luckasson (Eds.), *Transitions to adult life for people with mental retardation: Principles and practices* (pp. 257–274). Baltimore: Paul H. Brookes.

Browder, D. M., & Belfiore, P. J. (1991). Assessment in and for the community. In D. Browder (Ed.), *Assessment of individuals with severe disabilities,* (pp. 177–212). Baltimore: Paul H. Brookes.

Brown, L., Nisbet, J., Ford, A., Sweet, M., Shiraga, B., York, J., & Loomis, R. (1983). The critical need for nonschool instruction in educational programs for severely handicapped students. *The Journal of The Association for Persons with Severe Handicaps, 8*(3), 71–77.

Browning, P., & Irvin, L. K. (1981). Vocational evaluation, training, and placement of mentally retarded persons. *Rehabilitation Counseling Bulletin, 24*(5), 374–408.

Everson, J. M. (1993). *Youth with disabilities: Strategies for interagency transition programs.* Stoneham, MA: Butterworth-Heinemann.

Everson, J. M., & McNulty, K. (1992). Interagency teams: Building local transition programs through parental and professional partnerships. In F. R. Rusch, L. Destefano, J. Chadsey-Rusch, L. A. Phelps, & E. Szymanski (Eds.), *Transition from school to adult life* (pp. 341–352). Sycamore, IL: Sycamore Publishing.

Everson, J. M., & McNulty, K. (1995). What happens when children who are deaf-blind grow up?: An overview of transition services. In J. M. Everson (Ed.), *Supporting Young adults who are deaf-blind in their communities: A transition planning guide for service providers, families, and friends* (pp. 5–20). Baltimore: Paul H. Brookes.

Federal Register, June 24, 1992.

Ford, A., Black, J., Rogan, P., Schnorr, R., Meyer, L., Davern, L., & Dempsey, P. (1989). Vocational domain. In A. Ford, R. Schnorr, L. Meyer, L. Davern, J. Black, & P. Dempsey (Eds.), *The Syracuse community-referenced curriculum guide* (pp. 45–63). Baltimore: Paul H. Brookes.

Hallahan, D. P., & Kaufman, J. M. (1994). Early intervention. In *Exceptional Children: Introduction to special education* (6th ed.) (pp. 44–85). Boston: Allyn & Bacon.

Harris, J., Dansky, H., & Zimmerman, B. (1985). *APTICOM.* Philadelphia: Jewish Employment and Vocational Services.

Hasazi, S. B., Collins, M., & Cobbs, R. B. (1988). Implementing transition programs for productive employment. In B. L. Ludlow, A. P. Turnbull, & R. Luckasson (Eds.), *Transitions to adult life for people with mental retardation: Principles and practices* (pp. 159–175). Baltimore: Paul H. Brookes.

Heward, W. L., & Orlansky, M. D. (1992). Early intervention. In *Exceptional children* (4th ed.) (pp. 573–613). New York: Macmillan.

Karnes, M. B., & Stayton, V. D. (1988). Model programs for infants and toddlers with handicaps. In J. B. Jordan, J. J. Gallagher, P. L. Hutinger, & M. B. Karnes (Eds.), *Early childhood special education: Birth to three* (pp. 67–108). Reston, VA: Council for Exceptional Children.

McDonnell, J., Hardman, M., & Hightower, J. (1989). Employment preparation for high school students with severe handicaps. *Mental Retardation, 27*(6), 396–404.

Menchetti, B. M., & Flynn, C. C. (1990). Vocational evaluation. In F. R. Rusch (Ed.), *Supported employment: Models, methods, and issues* (pp. 79–90). Sycamore, IL: Sycamore Publishing.

Menchetti, B. M., & Rusch, F. R. (1988). Vocational evaluation and eligibility for rehabilitation services. In P. Wehman & M. S. Moon (Eds.), *Vocational rehabilitation and supported employment* (pp. 79–90). Baltimore: Paul H. Brookes.

Menchetti, B. M., Rusch, F. R., & Owens, D. M. (1983). Vocational training. In J. L. Matson & S. E. Breuning (Eds.), *Assessing the mentally retarded* (pp. 247–284). New York: Grune & Stratton.

Minnesota Educational Services (1994). *Making the transition team work.* Little Canada, MN: Minnesota Educational Services.

Moon, M. S., Inge, K. J., Wehman, P., Brooke, V., & Barcus, J. M. (1990). *Helping persons with severe mental retardation get and keep employment* (pp. 67–90). Baltimore: Paul H. Brookes.

Neufeldt, V., & Guralnik, D. B. (Eds.) (1994). *Webster's New World Dictionary of American English.* New York: Prentice Hall.

Parent, W. S., Sherron, P., & Groah, C. (1992). Consumer assessment, job development, and job placement. In P. Wehman, P. Sale, & W. Parent (Eds.), *Supported employment: Strategies for integration of workers with disabilities* (pp. 105–148). Boston: Andover Medical Publishers.

Powell, T. H. & Moore, S. C. (1992). Benefits and incentives for students entering supported employment. *Teaching Exceptional Children, 24*(3), 16–19.

Racino, J. A., Walker, P., O'Connor, S., & Taylor, S. J. (1993). *Housing, support, and community: Choices and strategies for adults with disabilities.* Baltimore: Paul H. Brookes.

Rehabilitation Act Amendments of 1986. 29 U.S.C., 701.

Revell, W. G., Kriloff, L., & Sarkees, M. (1980). Vocational evaluation. In P. Wehman & P. McLaughlin (Eds.), *Vocational curriculum for developmentally disabled persons* (pp. 73–93). Baltimore: University Park Press.

Rusch, R. F., & Hughes, C. (1990). Historical overview of supported employment. In F. R. Rusch (Ed.), *Supported employment: Models, methods, and issues* (pp. 5–14). Sycamore, IL: Sycamore Publishing.

Schutz, R. P., & Rusch, F. R. (1982). Competitive employment: Toward employment integration for mentally retarded persons. In K. P. Lynch, W. E., Kiernan, & J. A. Stark (Eds.), *Prevocational and vocational education for special needs youth: A blueprint for the 1980's* (pp. 133–159). Baltimore: Paul H. Brookes.

Smith, M. D., Belcher, R. G., & Fuhrs, P. D. (1995). *A guide to successful employment for individuals with autism.* Baltimore: Paul H. Brookes.

Stout, N. L. (1983). Vocational rehabilitation services: A postsecondary student consumer's guide. *Rehabilitation Literature, 44*(7–8), 214–216.

Szymanski, E. M., Hanley-Maxwell, C., Schaller, J. L., Parker, R. M., & Kidder, S. (1992). Impact of a systems-change initiative on supported employment in Wisconsin. *Rehabilitation Counseling Bulletin, 35*(4), 210–217.

Turnbull, A. P., & Turnbull, H. R. (1990). *Families, professionals, and exceptionality: A special partnership* (2nd ed.). Columbus, OH: Charles E. Merrill.

United States Department of Education (Sept. 21, 1992). Departmental memo.

United States Department of Health and Human Services (1991). *Working while disabled: A guide to plans for achieving self-support while receiving supplemental security income.* Social Administration, Publication No. 05-11017.

United States Department of Health and Human Services (1993a). *Social security benefits and SSI benefits for children with disabilities.* Social Administration, Publication No. 05-10026.

United States Department of Health and Human Services (1993b). *Understanding social security.* Social Administration, Publication No. 05-10024.

United States Department of Labor (1962). *Field operations handbook,* (6/21/62-10b10–10b11). Washington, DC: United States Department of Labor.

Valpar Corporation (1980). *The VALPAR component work sample series.* Tucson, AZ: Valpar Corporation.

Wehman, P. (1992). *Life beyond the classroom: Transition strategies for young people with disabilities.* Baltimore: Paul H. Brookes.

Wehman, P., Moon, M. S., Everson, J. M., Wood, W., & Barcus, J. M. (1988). *Transition from school to work: New challenges for youth with severe disabilities* (pp. 97–130). Baltimore: Paul H. Brookes.

Wehman, P., Sale, P., & Parent, W. (1992). Job-site interventions. In P. Wehman, P. Sale, & W. Parent (Eds.), *Supported employment: Strategies for integration of workers with disabilities* (pp. 149–175). Boston: Andover Medical Publishers.

Wilcox, B., & Bellamy, G. T. (1987). *A comprehensive guide to the activities catalogue: An alternative curriculum for youth and adults with severe disabilities.* Baltimore: Paul H. Brookes.

Winking, D. L., O'Reilly, B., & Moon, M. S. (1993). Preference: The missing link in the job match process for individuals without functional communication skills. *Journal of Vocational Rehabilitation, 3*(3), 27–42.

Yancey, G. (1993). Importance of families in transition from school to adult life: A rehabilitation practitioner's perspective. *Journal of Vocational Rehabilitation, 3*(2), 5–8.

APPENDIX **A**

STUDENT PROFILES

DIANE LEA RYNDAK

Including Mark in Kindergarten

Student Description Before Inclusion in Kindergarten

Mark, a five year old boy with severe autistic behaviors, had been in a self-contained preschool program for three years. At the end of his preschool experiences Mark was described as avoiding physical contact with others, especially resisting any contact adults made to assist him in participating in structured activities. He preferred to play alone, usually looking at picture books or manipulating objects in a stereotypic manner. Mark tended to continue the same activity until repeatedly given directions to change activities. During attempts to interact, Mark avoided eye contact with both adults and peers. While he was capable of verbal communication in one word utterances, Mark expressed his wants and needs through gesturing and pointing. When asked a question, Mark either gave no response or repeated the last phrase he heard. At times, Mark attended well to some classroom activities, particularly coloring and music. Mark's family seldom took him into the community because of his inappropriate behavior, lack of attending to directions, and resistance to physical guidance to ensure appropriate and safe behaviors.

Upon transitioning from preschool services to kindergarten, the education team decided that he would be included in an all day general education kindergarten with assistance from a classroom aide, as well as special education and related services support. The team completed the curriculum content identification process and yielded the following results.

Prioritized Results from Inventories

Family Inventory

1. Allow for physical contact when in need of assistance
2. Initiate activities of preference instead of waiting for parental cues
3. Increase use of current verbal communication skills, and expand both vocabulary and use of new skills
4. Increase the time attending to tasks the instructor identified
5. Use the toilet independently instead of needing occasional assistance
6. Express feelings verbally or in an appropriate physical manner

Community Inventory

The education team looked only at the school and Mark's home environments when completing the community inventory. The education team wanted to focus initial instruction on school and home environments because (1) five year old children spend the majority of their day and week in those environments, and (2) Mark's family life limited his current interaction with other community environments. The team hoped that demonstration of skill acquisition at school and home would result in a higher probability of his family allowing him to interact with the community.

1. Increase expression of needs and wants across environments through verbal language, rather than pointing and gesturing
2. Initiate play across environments and play with peers in school
3. Across environments, verbalize to an adult his need to use the bathroom and use it independently

Peer Inventory

1. Interact with classmates throughout the day
2. Initiate and engage in conversation with peers, teachers, and significant others
3. Listen to the kindergarten teacher when she is reading a story
4. Socialize after school with friends

General Education Settings Inventory

1. Attend to instructional activities with reminders when in large (more than ten) and small (less than ten) groups
2. Perform a classroom job (e.g., take attendance to the office, clean erasers)
3. Go through the lunch line, select desired items, pay, and sit with friends in the cafeteria

General Education Curriculum Inventory

1. Speak in complete sentences
2. Cut, color, and paste when given step-by-step instruction

3. Write, pronounce, and say the sounds associated with letters of the alphabet
4. Write and name the numerals zero through ten

Goals Derived from Inventories

Goal 1   Mark will increase communication skills *from* the use of gestures and one-word utterances *to* verbally expressing himself in complete sentences across kindergarten activities.

Goal 2   Mark will increase social interaction skills across kindergarten activities *from* (1) avoiding eye contact, (2) not responding, and (3) resisting physical assistance *to* (1) initiating interactions, (2) responding to directions and questions, and (3) participating in activities with adults and peers.

Goal 3   Mark will increase toileting skills *from* occasionally wetting himself *to* using bathrooms independently during waking hours.

Summary of Progress on Goals During First Year of Inclusion

Goal 1   Increase communication skills
          Mark uses fragmented sentences in response to peer and adult conversation during structured and unstructured classroom activities.

Goal 2   Increase social interaction skills
          Mark reaches for the hand of an adult or peer when he needs assistance. He sings with the class, makes cards for classmates' birthdays, and performs assigned classroom jobs with peer partners. When an adult or peer initiates interaction with him, Mark usually makes eye contact and responds appropriately to the interaction.

Goal 3   Independent toileting skills
          Mark uses the bathroom during scheduled times throughout the school day, rarely having toileting accidents.

Student Description After Inclusion in Kindergarten

After completion of kindergarten, Mark often interacts independently with his peers during lessons and free time. Mark has begun to express his desires without prompting and to respond to questions using short phrases or fragmented sentences, although a large amount of his communication still involves gesturing and pointing. He initiates physical contact with others in a socially appropriate manner and does not resist when teachers and peers who are known to him make purposeful physical contact. When he needs assistance, Mark reaches for the hand of an adult or peer. He continues to attend to classroom activities, and he has increased dramatically his active participation in those activities. Because of his more appropriate behaviors, increase in following directions, and acceptance of physical contact, Mark's family takes him into the community on a regular basis to participate in family activities. Table A.1 summarizes Mark's changes.

TABLE A.1   Mark's Summarized Changes

Skill Area	Before Inclusion	After Inclusion
Physical contact with peers and adults	Avoided contact; resisted physical assistance	Initiates physical contact in socially acceptable manner; initiates hand touching for assistance; accepts physical assistance from known adult or peer
Involvement with peers in play and class activities	Played alone; looked at books and objects stereotypically	Independently interacts with peers; actively participates in classroom activities
Latency	Continued in same activity; did not respond to directions	Responds to directions; attends to class activities as they occur
Communication	Avoided eye contact with adults and peers; could verbally communicate in one-word utterances but usually used gestures or pointing; did not respond to questions; repeated last phrase	Makes eye contact with adults and peers; uses short phrases, along with gestures and pointing, when initiating requests; responds to questions with short phrases; sings
Attention	Attended to classroom activities at times, especially coloring and music; did not attend to directions	Performs classroom jobs with peer partners; follows directions most of the time; attends to tasks for up to ten minutes
Community involvement	Seldom taken into community	Participates in family activities in community on regular basis
Self-care	Occasionally wet self	Rarely has accident; follows schedule

Including Jason in First Grade

Student Description Prior to Inclusion in First Grade

His home school district temporarily placed Jason, a six year old with severe mental retardation, speech delays, and physical delays, in a home school kindergarten with no services from special education and no individualized education program (IEP). During this temporary placement the school district formally was recommending his placement in a self-contained class in a self-contained building approximately thirty miles from his home, while Jason's parents challenged this recommendation through due process procedures. The parents were attempting to procure inclusive educational services.

At the end of this kindergarten experience, Jason was placed again in kindergarten with minimal special education support. After two years of kindergarten, Jason displayed disruptive behaviors (e.g., throwing tantrums; refusing to complete tasks, touching others inappropriately by hugging or kissing someone's hand). He appeared to have a very short attention span, as demonstrated by staying on task for only short periods of time, though he constantly watched his peers. He communicated by using a few one-word utterances and a few signs. At times Jason would use gestures and vocalizations, progressing toward screams. Jason appeared to be more comfortable interacting with adults than with peers, choosing to interact with them even when peers were present. Jason's disability included degeneration of muscles as he aged. At this time he walked with a wide gait, climbed stairs one foot at a time while holding the railing for support, and had tantrums if strongly encouraged to participate in a new physical activity. Throughout the day Jason visibly grew fatigued and frequently fell asleep during activities in the afternoon. He had difficulty holding a writing implement, using scissors, and completing other fine motor tasks because of weak hand muscles.

After the two years of kindergarten, Jason's school district and parents reached a settlement through the due process procedures. They decided that the next academic year Jason would be included in first grade with assistance from a part-time aide, along with special education and related services support. The education team completed the curriculum content identification process and yielded the following results.

Prioritized Results from Inventories

Family Inventory

1. Improve verbal language
2. Limit touching to appropriate situations
3. Initiate conversations with peers
4. Increase interactions with others (i.e., adults, siblings, peers)
5. Improve daily living skills
6. Increase responsibilities at home

Community Inventory

1. Participate in recreational activities (i.e., bowling, karate)
2. Increase participation in church activities (i.e., religion class, social events)
3. Increase independence in dangerous situations in the community (e.g., street crossing)

Peer Inventory

1. Increase interactions with peers
2. Increase communication through words and signs

General Education Setting Inventory

1. Participate in extracurricular activities (i.e., library club, band)
2. Order and purchase own lunch
3. Increase participation in music, art, gym, and library

General Education Curriculum Inventory

1. Increase responsibilities at school (e.g., caring for personal belongings and school materials)
2. Speak in complete sentences
3. Participate in all first grade reading activities
4. Participate in all first grade writing activities
5. Participate in all first grade math activities

Goals Derived from Inventories

Goal 1   Jason will increase his ability to interact with peers and adults in a manner that is age appropriate during school and community experiences.

Goal 2   Jason will increase his expressive language skills *from* using one-word utterances *to* using complete sentences across the day.

Goal 3   Jason will participate as fully as possible in all first grade reading activities including, science and social studies, focusing on the use of letters, words, and sentences across the day.

Goal 4   Jason will participate as fully as possible in all first grade writing activities, focusing on letter, word, and number reproduction, and volunteering personal experiences for the purpose of classroom creative writing.

Goal 5   Jason will participate as fully as possible in all first grade math activities, focusing on use of numbers, time, money, measuring, and shapes.

Summary of Progress on Goals During First Year of Inclusion

Goal 1   Increase interaction skills
          Jason is more comfortable with his peers, relying more on them than on adults for clarification of directions through modeling. He follows peers' examples well. He seldom touches people in an inappropriate manner. Tantrums no longer occur, possibly due to his modeling peers' behaviors.

Goal 2   Increase expressive language skills
          In the first grade classroom Jason has increased the number of words he uses per utterance and periodically speaks in a complete sentence. With his speech therapist, however, Jason talks in multiple, full sentences without prompting. Generalization to other adults and peers is necessary. Tantrums no longer occur, possibly due to his increased communication skills.

Goal 3   Participation in reading activities
          Jason recognizes the letters of the alphabet. He has acquired a word bank from first grade curriculum and personal experiences. Tantrums no longer occur, possibly due to the relevance and importance of the curriculum content to Jason.

Goal 4   Participation in writing activities
         Jason prints his name. He is improving his number and letter repro-
         duction skills through classroom activities. The education team is
         considering giving him use of an electric typewriter or computer to
         supplement his hand-written responses to tasks. When encouraged,
         Jason asks questions and shares experiences for creative writing exer-
         cises.

Goal 5   Participation in math activities
         Jason purchases his own lunch and snacks. He is working on telling
         time and recognizes certain times of the day (e.g., lunch time is 12:00
         P.M.). Jason is expanding his number recognition skills by working on
         recognizing larger numbers.

Student Description After Inclusion in First Grade

After his inclusion in first grade with special education and related services support, Jason participates in all classroom activities, including motor activities and
physical education, and dramatically has increased the amount of time he is on
task during instruction. Jason follows directions and communicates his needs to
adults and peers in the classroom by using three-to-four word sentences. With his
speech therapist, however, Jason spontaneously uses multiple sentences to answer
questions, indicating that the education team needs to address his generalization
of sentence use from the speech therapist to peers and other adults. Jason also initiates interactions with both peers and adults. His classmates have been reinforcing this as friendships have begun to develop.

In the area of motor skills, Jason's desire to complete tasks as his peers has
proven to be a large motivator for him to persevere in tasks, even when he is becoming fatigued. He stays awake longer during the day and for complete days as
the year has progressed. He completes more fine motor tasks with less need for
physical support. He participates in all physical education and motor activities
without prompting, by watching his peers and modeling their behaviors. He walks
with a narrower gait and climbs stairs with alternating feet. Table A.2 summarizes
Jason's changes.

Including Alice in Fifth Grade

Student Description Prior to Inclusion in Fifth Grade

Alice, an eleven year old with spastic quadriplegic cerebral palsy, developmental
delays, and probable moderate mental retardation, had attended a self-contained
private agency during preschool and early elementary years. During this time she
displayed many disruptive behaviors (e.g., refusing to work, biting, screaming,
noncompliant behaviors). At this time her educational program focused on daily
living skills and physical management needs.

Alice then attended her home school, where the district placed her in a self-
contained class, with part time integration in third grade activities. Her objectives

TABLE A.2   Jason's Summarized Changes

Skill Area	Before Inclusion	After Inclusion
Behavior	Had tantrums; refused to participate in new motor activities; inappropriately touched others; refused to do tasks	Tantrums no longer occur; participates in all activities; seldom touches inappropriately; completes tasks as requested
Attention	Did not stay on task	Completes tasks as requested
Communication	Used one-word utterances; used few signs	Uses more words per utterance, periodically uses sentences; uses multiple sentences with speech therapist
Socialization	More comfortable with adults	Relies more on peers than adults for clarification of directions; follows peers' examples
Reading	No reading skills	Recognizes letters of the alphabet; uses word bank from first grade curriculum and personal experiences
Writing	No writing skills	Prints his name; improving on number and letter reproduction; asks questions and shares experiences for creative writing
Math	No math skills	Purchases lunch & snacks; recognizes times of day
Motor	Refused to participate in new motor activities	Participates in all motor activities in classroom and physical education by modeling from peers; walks with narrower gait; climbs stairs with alternating feet; sits upright for longer periods; stays awake most days; uses writing implements and scissors independently

at this time included: (1) identifying numerals 1 to 30, counting up to four objects, and identifying values of coins, (2) identifying functional sight words and matching printed letters to samples, (3) producing the "sign" of seven functional words upon request, pointing to pictures and words on a communication board, and labeling her emotions, (4) remaining on task with cues and cooperating throughout the day, (5) moving her electric wheelchair from classroom center to center, (6) completing ten functional tasks daily (e.g., hand washing, coat removal), and (7) playing board games. The following year she was included in a fourth grade class. During this year her educational program focused on improving social skills, acquiring appropriate behaviors to replace inappropriate behaviors, and increasing communication skills throughout general education settings.

Her education team decided that Alice would be included during fifth grade with an aide available to assist with her self-care needs. She would receive speech therapy, occupational therapy, and physical therapy on a direct and indirect basis. Upon transitioning to fifth grade, the education team completed the curriculum content identification process and yielded the following results.

Prioritized Results from Inventories

Family Inventory

1. Increase responsibilities at home
2. Increase independence in daily living activities
3. Increase communication skills
4. Increase self-control when upset or angry
5. Request assistance when necessary

Community Inventory

1. Increase use of community resources
2. Increase number of choices made while in the community
3. Increase independence when purchasing items

Peer Inventory

1. Participate in after school activities with peers
2. Increase socialization with peers outside of school

General Education Settings Inventory

1. Complete activities with appropriate social interactions
2. Comply with teacher requests
3. Transition more efficiently between classes

General Education Curriculum Inventory

1. Increase responsibilities at school
2. Improve listening comprehension skills
3. Increase sight word vocabulary
4. Improve math computation skills
5. Increase independence on personal computer
6. Improve communication skills (i.e., articulation, signs, gestures)

Goals Derived from Inventories

Goal 1   Alice will increase reading skills related to fifth grade curriculum across all subjects.

Goal 2   Alice will increase her active participation in, and the number of, community activities in which she participates *from* two activities (i.e., going to a restaurant and shopping) *to* four activities (i.e., use the bank and library) within one school year.

Goal 3   Alice will increase her use of the computer *from* needing assistance to boot it up *to* booting it up and using it independently within one school year.

Goal 4   Alice will increase number recognition *from* numerals 0 to 9 *to* numerals 0 to 20 and use a calculator to add and subtract one-digit numbers within one school year.

Goal 5   Alice will increase her self-control *from* inappropriately expressing
             anger or frustration (e.g., refusing to comply, biting, screaming) *to* ex-
             pressing her feelings in a more age appropriate and socially accept-
             able manner.

Summary of Progress on Goals

Goal 1   Increase reading skills in the fifth grade curriculum
             The education team selected words that were most meaningful to Alice
             either functionally across her environments or for participation in fifth
             grade activities for reading, spelling, and social studies. On an average,
             Alice has increased her sight word vocabulary by three words per
             week.
Goal 2   Increase number of community activities
             Alice continues to work toward independence at restaurants and in
             stores and is beginning to complete basic banking tasks and steps for
             use of the library. Her physical disabilities require personal assistance
             from a peer or an aide, but her decision making and indication of next
             steps has increased dramatically.
Goal 3   Increase computer skills
             Alice either independently boots her personal computer or seeks assis-
             tance from her peers when she is physically unable to perform some
             part of the task.
Goal 4   Increase number recognition and computation skills
             Alice consistently recognizes the numerals 0 to 9 but does not consis-
             tently recognize numerals 10 to 20. She uses a calculator or her person-
             al computer to add and subtract one-digit numbers with assistance for
             positioning the equipment and materials.
Goal 5   Increase self-control
             Alice uses her Touchtalker, vocalizations, gestures, and signs to express
             her feelings, rather than screaming, biting, and refusing to comply. Oc-
             casional outbursts still occur but have diminished significantly in
             length and frequency.

Student Description After Inclusion in Fifth Grade

Alice interacts well with peers and enjoys being part of a group. She expresses herself by using alternative means of communication, including gestures, signs, vocalizations, and a Touchtalker. Alice's noncompliant behaviors have diminished
significantly, and when noncompliance is exhibited, one of two situations is occurring; Alice either does not want to complete an activity, and a simple redirection returns her attention to the task at hand, or Alice is attempting to communicate
something and is getting frustrated. In this second situation, Alice will answer yes-
or-no questions about why she is being noncompliant. Through this process it has
become clear that noncompliance occurs when she is asked to do something (1) that

TABLE A.3   Alice's Summarized Changes

Skills Area	Before Inclusion	After Inclusion
Behavior	Refused to work; bit; screamed; was noncompliant	Compliant unless frustrated and unable to communicate; completes tasks; no biting or screaming
Communication	Had computer, but no independent use; expressed anger and frustration through inappropriate behaviors	Boots and uses computer independently, seeking peer assistance when physically unable; uses Touchtalker, vocalizations, gestures, and signs to express all feelings; few instances of inappropriate behavior
Socialization	Smiled in situations and with people she liked	Interacts well with peers; enjoys being part of a group
Reading	A few functional sight words	Learned three new sight words per week
Math	Recognized numerals 0 to 9; no counting of objects	Inconsistently recognizes numerals 10 to 20; uses calculator or computer to add and subtract one-digit numbers
Community	Accessed restaurants and stores with minimal active participation	Increased decision making and indication of next steps across four community settings

she has already completed, (2) at a time when she is supposed to do something else, or (3) when she does not have the materials or information to complete the task. In each of these situations it is clear that the instructor is in error, and Alice is trying to communicate that this is the case and why. Table A.3 summarizes Alice's changes.

Including Tony in Fifth Grade

Student Description Prior to Inclusion in Fifth Grade

Tony, a ten-year-old with spastic quadriplegic cerebral palsy, scoliosis, and profound mental retardation, had received no educational services until he was eight years old due to family issues and medical concerns. He cried about 90 percent of the day, wore a body jacket, received a great deal of physical and occupational therapy, had very little volitional movement in only one arm, was not toilet trained, and was fed through a gastrointestinal tube. When initially receiving educational services, Tony's school district had placed him in a self-contained class with periodic opportunities for him to participate in third grade activities. His IEP goals had consisted of (1) reducing crying, (2) responding correctly to yes-or-no questions, and (3) beginning oral motor control for sucking and chewing.

Tony entered a fourth grade inclusion class, in spite of his lack of progress on IEP goals, almost constant crying, and numerous physical and medical needs. His educational program now focused on decreasing crying, increasing communication skills through visual responses to yes-or-no questions or object identification, improving tolerance of community-based instruction, and addressing health issues. Upon transitioning to fifth grade, Tony's education team implemented the curriculum identification process. It yielded the following results.

Prioritized Results from Inventories

Family Inventory

1. Increase communication skills
2. Increase use of adaptive switches
3. Partially participate in daily living activities
4. Express need to use the bathroom
5. Improve lip and mouth closure for eating and drinking

Community Inventory

1. Partially participate in community activities
2. Increase amount of time spent in the community

Peer Inventory

1. Collect and trade sports cards with peers
2. Increase interactions with peers through an Introtalker

General Education Settings Inventory

1. Participate as fully as possible in gym, art, music, and library
2. Partially participate in cooking activities with a peer during home and careers class
3. Take daily medication without resistance

General Education Curriculum Inventory

1. Recognize numbers 0 to 9
2. Indicate need for attention and make choices through eye gazing at options
3. Decrease crying and increase listening skills
4. Attend to filmstrips and movies
5. Answer concrete yes-or-no questions

Goals Derived from Inventories

Goal 1   Tony will participate as fully as possible in all fifth grade activities, including all academic areas and specials.

Goal 2   Tony will increase expressive communication skills from using zero symbols on his Introtalker to using four symbols, by the end of the school year.

Goal 3   Tony will increase the amount of time he tolerates community-based instruction without crying from an average of fifteen minutes to an average of sixty minutes, by the end of the school year.

Goal 4   Tony will operate electronic equipment (i.e., pencil sharpener; blender; tape player; computer) with an adaptive switch, from using it once a day to using it three times a day.

Summary of Progress on Goals

Goal 1   Increase participation in fifth grade activities
Tony is actively engaged in fifth grade activities, without crying, for 70 percent of the day. In addition to decreased crying and apparent listening to class activities, Tony's classroom "jobs" include passing out papers to classmates. He accomplishes this with a sticky band attached to his wrist, which he lowers to a stack of papers on his wheelchair tray. As he raises his arm, one paper stays attached to the band for a classmate to grasp. He then lowers his arm for the next paper. Tony's participation in fifth grade activities also consists of him responding to yes-or-no questions on concrete content.

Goal 2   Increase expressive communication skills with the Introtalker
Tony shows a great interest in communicating with both peers and adults through his Introtalker. Encouragement from his peers reinforces this. Tony consistently uses four symbols on his Introtalker to indicate his needs across the day through an eye gaze, and he indicates his desire to use the Introtalker by ringing a classroom bell positioned at midline. The education team found that Tony's crying was frequently accompanied either by his wetting or soiling himself, or by his body jacket fitting uncomfortably, leaving red marks on his trunk. Of particular interest is his use of symbols to identify his need to go to the bathroom and his desire to have his body jacket checked. By responding to his use of these two symbols Tony's crying has decreased to occurring for only 30 percent of the school day.

Goal 3   Increase time spent in community-based instruction
Tony gradually increased the time he spends in community-based instruction without crying. Because of the education team's inability to predict when he needs to go to the bathroom or when his body jacket will begin to be uncomfortable, however, he still cries periodically in the community excessively, necessitating an early return to school.

Goal 4   Increase use of adaptive switches
Tony uses adaptive switches during home and careers class, computer class, and within his fifth grade classroom. His classroom "jobs" include running the electric pencil sharpener at specified times of the day for classmates. Tony's family has also expressed interest in using switches at home.

TABLE A.4   Tony's Summarized Changes

Skill Area	Before Inclusion	After Inclusion
Behavior	Cried 90% of the day	Actively involved in fifth grade activities without crying 70% of the day; cries 30% of the day when Introtalker or correct symbol not available
Volitional movement	Limited movement of one arm; no use of switches	Uses vertical movement to pass out papers; uses movement to midline to ring bell for attention; runs electric pencil sharpener for classmates
Communication	Cried 90% of the day; no other communication (e.g., yes-or-no responses; eye gaze; Introtalker)	Responds to yes-or-no concrete questions on class activities; uses four symbols on Introtalker; uses bell to indicate desire to use Introtalker
Socialization	Cried 90% of day; no other consistent responses to others or situations	Interested in communicating with peers; frequently requests to be with peers
Self-care	Fed through gastrointestinal tube; not toilet trained	On toileting schedule; chewing and sucking instruction terminated due to frequent pneumonia; fed through gastrointestinal tube
Community	Cried after fifteen minutes	Cries less frequently, after longer periods

Student Description After Inclusion in Fifth Grade

Tony is able to follow one-step directions, operate adaptive switches with one hand when they are positioned either at midline or under the hand at his arm's length, and use an Introtalker to indicate four of his needs. He continues to increase the amount of time he spends with peers, frequently requesting to be with his friends. Tony's crying has decreased to situations when his Introtalker is not available to him or when an appropriate symbol is not available on the Introtalker.

Tony is strongly motivated to participate in activities with his peers. They provide him support, encouragement, and reinforcement for his efforts. During fifth grade the team observed Tony (1) visually attending to his fifth grade teacher passing out papers, (2) moving his arm to midline to ring the classroom bell for attention, and (3) moving his arm up and down, indicating to his support person that he wanted to do his classroom "job," which the teacher was doing. While not appearing to be important, it must be remembered that upon entering fourth grade, Tony was considered to be profoundly retarded, have little volitional movement, and no manner of communicating beyond crying. The intellectual processes Tony required to recognize that somebody (i.e., the fifth grade teacher) was completing an activity that was "his" (i.e., passing out papers), realizing that he needed to get somebody's attention (i.e., through the use of the bell) to create the opportunity for him to do his own "job" (i.e., getting them to realize what was happening by moving his arm as if he were doing the "job"), were beyond expectations that education team members had for Tony. In addition, the fact that Tony chose to demonstrate these abilities at this time indicated the degree to which he is motivated to participate in class activities. Table A.4 summarizes Tony's changes.

Including Dave in Ninth Grade

Student Description Prior to Inclusion in Ninth Grade

Dave, a seventeen year old identified with moderate autistic behaviors, previously received educational services in self-contained classes in a segregated building. Dave responded to verbal cues from adults and peers and engaged in both appropriate and inappropriate interactions with classmates in the self-contained classroom. Interactions between Dave and nondisabled peers, however, were frequently more inappropriate, unnatural, and repetitive, presumably because of his limited exposure to them and the characteristics of his disability. Interactions were characterized by echolalic responses or initiating discussions on irrelevant and inappropriate topics. Academically, Dave was strongest in mathematics. He solved math problems independently, using a calculator to check his answers. Dave was reading at a sixth grade comprehension level and was learning the aspects of compositional writing (e.g., paragraph formation, spelling, punctuation, capitalization). Vocationally, Dave had limited prevocational experience and no vocational experiences on actual jobs.

Dave's education team decided to change his services and place him in general education classes in his home high school. While receiving services in the self-contained settings, however, Dave had become accustomed to a highly structured school environment with consistent routines and guidelines. These and other factors were taken into consideration by his education team, and they believed that Dave's best chances for success were at the ninth grade level.

Prioritized Results from Inventories

Family Inventory

1. Express his feelings and emotions more clearly
2. Initiate hygiene routine at home when getting ready for school, before meals, etc.
3. Participate in after-school activities
4. Explore vocational opportunities
5. Stay with his family when in the community and keep to the schedule when given time on his own

Community Inventory

1. Go to and use the library
2. Go to fast-food restaurants with friends, order, and pay for a meal

3. Go to a book store and buy a book
4. Go to a video store and rent a preferred video

Peer Inventory

1. Participate in school-based extracurricular activities (e.g., sports, clubs)
2. Go to a mall to shop and socialize with peers
3. Cope with his feelings about sexuality
4. Get a part-time job after school

General Education Settings Inventory

1. Take notes in class
2. Move between classes within four minutes

General Education Curriculum Inventory

1. Display problem solving behaviors
2. Increase reading comprehension during high school course work
3. Write complete sentences and paragraphs
4. Improve math computation and application skills

Goals Derived From Inventories

Goal 1	Dave will increase social interaction skills with peers *from* relying on verbal cues during conversation *to* engaging in reciprocal conversations during social situations at school and extracurricular activities.
Goal 2	Dave will increase his independence during activities in and out of school *from* relying on adult assistance *to* engaging in activities either independently or by requesting assistance from peers.
Goal 3	Dave will increase his reading and writing skills *from* present level *to* grade-appropriate level across all academic courses.
Goal 4	Dave will increase expression of his emotions *from* not discussing his feelings *to* discussing them with adults in structured situations.

Summary of Progress on Goals During First Year of Inclusion

Goal 1	Social interaction skills
	Dave initiates conversations with peers and adults at appropriate times throughout the school day. He is a member of the track team and an active member in a school club. During interactions, however, his conversation often is repetitive and lacks spontaneity and flexibility. While he periodically continues to be echolalic, this behavior has decreased dramatically, especially with peers. In the structured settings of general education classes, Dave's language skills usually are adequate. He continues, however, to have great difficulty in unstructured situations.

Goal 2   Increase independence

On the track team, Dave participates in both practice and competitions with support only from his peers. To increase his independence in academic tasks, Dave independently uses a personal computer to take notes during classes.

Goal 3   Increase reading and writing skills

Dave demonstrates easily comprehension of short reading passages of ninth grade course material (e.g., sentences, paragraphs). His comprehension difficulties continue to be apparent, however, when reading longer passages (e.g., short stories, novels). Dave participates in all written classroom assignments, focusing on both reading and writing content appropriate for each topic. He writes answers to questions involving facts found in his textbooks. Creative writing, however, is still a challenge for him.

Goal 4   Increase expression of emotions

Teachers, family, and friends address this goal with Dave, explaining and practicing appropriate social behavior with him. He has demonstrated tremendous growth in identifying other's feelings, following the social amenities for high school students, and using body language. When faced with new situations, however, Dave continues to need assistance and feedback.

Student Description After Two Years of Inclusion

At nineteen years of age Dave has been included in general education classes for two years and is completing the tenth grade. His classes include U.S. Government, English, Introduction to Occupations, Physical Education, and Business Math, during which Dave independently uses a lap-top computer to take notes. Dave's education team identifies the general education content per class that would be most useful for him in his current and future life and focuses instruction on that content. Because of this, he is responsible for less content than his peers. His instruction focuses mainly on reading, writing, increasing independent work, and interacting appropriately with adults and peers across all settings, both in school and in the community. In spite of this, however, he has learned much more of the academic content than the education team expected.

In addition to taking class notes with a computer, Dave has used his computer skills during his summer job experiences. He has held part-time jobs filing, entering information into a computer, and shelving library books. The education team expects that his employment training will continue across different types of jobs, leading to an after-school job.

Socially, Dave continues to be a member of the track team, and his team mates report that he is well-liked by both male and female members of the team. His social interaction skills have improved dramatically, with Dave initiating interactions at appropriate times with both adults and peers. His communication skills during those interactions are much more understandable to strangers and more extensive in content. Table A.5 summarizes Dave's changes.

TABLE A.5   Dave's Summarized Changes

Skill Area	Before Inclusion	After Inclusion
Behavior	Used echolalic responses constantly; relied on adults for assistance; refused to discuss emotions, especially when angry or frustrated	Periodically is echolalic; participates in school activities with support only from peers; uses personal computer for class notes; identifies others' feelings; follows high school social amenities; uses body language appropriately
Social interactions	Interactions were frequently inappropriate, unnatural, stifled; echolalic responses to overtures from others; initiated interactions on irrelevant and inappropriate topics; needed verbal cues to respond appropriately	Initiates interactions at appropriate times; actively participates in school clubs and teams; interactions often lack spontaneity and flexibility and are repetitive
Math	Solved problems independently; used calculator to check answers	
Reading and Writing	Comprehended sixth grade material; learning compositional writing	Comprehends ninth grade material in sentences and paragraphs (not books); does assignments where answers are in texts; has difficulty with creative writing
Community	No independent use of the community	Independently attends school functions held on evenings or weekends
Vocational training	Limited prevocational experiences; no vocational experience	Part-time summer jobs

Note: After five years of being included in general education classes, Dave has progressed dramatically. He gradually became responsible for more of the general education content so that now he is responsible for *all* of it. He is receiving his high school diploma because he has met *all* of the academic requirements for graduation. His language and interactions with others are much more appropriate, although he still is noticeably different from his peers. Dave has shown some ability with computers and recently completed an introductory course on microcomputers at a local community college.

PORTRAIT OF MAUREEN BEFORE AND AFTER INCLUSION

DIANE LEA RYNDAK

Maureen Prior to Inclusion

When the education team first considered inclusion for Maureen, she was fifteen years old and labelled as having moderate mental retardation and speech delays. She had received special education and related services for the last ten years from seven different teachers in self-contained classes, each class located in a different school district within one hour of her home school. Maureen's most recent self-contained classroom was comprised of twelve students, a special education teacher, a full-time classroom aide, and a part-time aide available to Maureen for academic reinforcement. She also received one-to-one speech and occupational therapy on a pull-out basis.

Overall Performance Levels

The progress report the education team wrote at the end of the previous year in a self-contained class stated that Maureen had low social maturity but displayed appropriate social interactions with nondisabled peers. Her speech and language records indicated that Maureen had a receptive vocabulary of six years ten months but an oral vocabulary of only three years five months. Maureen's speech delay resulted in numerous difficulties with conversational skills, both with adults and nondisabled peers. Few people (e.g., family members, peers from neighborhood) could understand Maureen's verbalizations, though her vocabulary was extensive enough for her to participate in lengthy conversations. In addition, Maureen demonstrated what appeared to be a difficulty with word retrieval. When faced with situations where she anticipated being misunderstood, Maureen responded with contrived phrases that quickly extricated her from further interactions. Her speech services consisted of one-to-one speech therapy for thirty minutes, five times a week. During these sessions Maureen received therapy for articulation, vocabulary expansion, and role playing interactions during games.

Academically, Maureen's records indicated that she performed at a third grade level in math. While Maureen's reading test scores indicated a comprehension performance of second grade fourth month, she behaved in a manner that was inconsistent with that score and that educational personnel could not explain. For example, at night Maureen frequently was under the covers of her bed with a flashlight and an adolescent love story. Though these novels did not include pictures and were not from a high interest–low vocabulary series, Maureen answered global questions about these stories. She refused, however, to read any section of these novels or other reading materials either silently in front of an adult or aloud to any person. To extricate herself from adults' requests for her to read or situations which required reading, Maureen consistently resorted to a repertoire of coping behaviors. This especially occurred when Maureen was in an one-to-one instructional setting, a testing situation, or any situation in which she expected that she would perform poorly. In addition, when Maureen became aware that she did not understand a concept required in a desired activity, she would refuse any assistance and use her coping strategies to bluff her way through the situation. When pressed to (1) read or complete an academic task (e.g., use math functionally), (2) perform a task or activity in which she expected that she would do poorly, or (3) accept assistance to complete a desired activity, Maureen usually "tantrummed" by yelling, walking away angrily, or sitting down and refusing to acknowledge anyone. Interpreting them as noncompliance and behavior management problems, Maureen's education team addressed these behaviors by developing behavior management programs and goals for responding appropriately to authority figures.

In relation to physical development, Maureen exhibited generalized hypotonia, poor balance, and a variety of visual motor, motor planning, and visual perception problems. In addition Maureen fatigued easily, so that during activities that required strength or endurance from either fine or gross motor muscles (e.g., writing; physical education activities; walking quickly or for a long distance) she would perform much better at the beginning of the activity than at the end. Physical fatigue also was a factor during afternoons. Maureen frequently arrived home after school exhausted and unable to participate in family activities without a rest.

Pre-Inclusion Program and Performance

Behaviors and Social Interactions
Though the objectives on her individualized education program (IEP) included adding appropriate comments to conversations with adults and peers (see Figure B.1), Maureen's education program provided limited opportunities for her to develop the skills necessary to hold a conversation with nondisabled peers. For instance, while she and her classmates ate in the school cafeteria at the same time as

1. Improve proper behavior
2. List ways of contributing to her family and community
3. Verbally express her feelings
4. Add appropriate comments to conversations with adults and peers
5. Improve her understanding of her location in space and other spatial relations
6. Improve the organization of work on her paper
7. Read, spell, and use in sentences new vocabulary from a phonics book and basal reader
8. Improve phonics and comprehension skills to the second grade fifth month level
9. Write complete sentences
10. Improve leisure skills by reading materials (e.g., newspapers, magazines) during free time in the self-contained classroom
11. Read and write dollar amounts
12. Solve three- and four-digit addition and subtraction problems from a workbook or teacher-made worksheets
13. Demonstrate knowledge of body parts
14. Improve work skills by alphabetizing ten words within fifteen minutes

FIGURE B.1   Maureen's IEP Objectives Before Inclusion

nondisabled peers, the self-contained class was assigned to a separate table. In addition, there were no strategies for facilitating either interactions or conversations between the students from the self-contained class and their nondisabled peers. This resulted in Maureen and her classmates eating lunch in isolation from nondisabled peers and with limited conversations even among themselves. Maureen's main opportunities to interact with nondisabled peers came daily when she left her self-contained class to attend either sixth grade girls' chorus or sixth grade physical education class (see Figure B.2).

Maureen demonstrated differentiated behaviors between situations which did and did not include nondisabled peers, as between her self-contained special education room and the sixth grade music and physical education classes. When in the self-contained room, Maureen (1) refused to complete her work, (2) yelled across the room at classmates and adults, (3) kicked other students, especially boys, when seated together, (4) refused to follow directions, and (5) avoided eye contact with nondisabled peers as they passed in the hallway. As soon as Maureen crossed the threshold into the hallway on her way to sixth grade music or physical education, however, she became quiet and observant while moving to her assigned room. During those classes, Maureen attended to the teacher and quietly followed directions to the best of her ability.

For instance, before chorus began, Maureen obtained her folder of music (which she could not read), moved to her assigned seat, opened her folder, and alternated between surreptitiously observing her nondisabled peers and pretending to read the music. Once class started Maureen followed the teacher's directions by participating in the warm-up exercises, opening her materials to the named sheet of music (by modeling her neighbor's behaviors), and singing with the group when she knew the words of the song. When she did not know the words, Mau-

FIGURE B.2   **Maureen's Schedule Before Inclusion**

Time Period	Monday	Tuesday	Wednesday	Thursday	Friday
9:05–9:50	M-T-TH-F: Language in self-contained room W: One-to-one occupational therapy				
9:50–10:35	Reading in self-contained room				
10:35–11:20	Odd days: sixth grade girl's chorus Even days: sixth grade physical education				
11:20–12:00	Math in self-contained room				
12:00–12:35	Lunch in cafeteria				
12:35–1:20	Home and careers with self-contained classmates				
1:20–2:05	M: One-to-one occupational therapy T-W-TH-F Odd days: Seat work in self-contained room T-W-TH-F Even days: Functional skills in self-contained room				
2:05–2:30	Science and social studies in self-contained room				
2:30–3:00	Seat work in self-contained room				
3:00–3:30	One-to-one speech therapy				

reen "faked it" by moving her mouth while not producing any sound. To assist her in learning the songs, the music teacher made an audio tape of every song she presented to the class, both with and without full accompaniment. Maureen independently used these tapes at home to memorize the songs.

At no time outside of special education settings did Maureen demonstrate inappropriate social behaviors, refuse to follow directions or complete her work, or resort to her coping behaviors. In spite of these differentiated behaviors and Maureen's demonstrated ability to act appropriately when with nondisabled peers, her IEP included an objective to improve proper behavior (see Figure B.1).

Reading and Math

For her math and reading instruction, Maureen received either teacher-made worksheets or copies of pages from elementary workbooks. Because the education team based Maureen's educational program on her learning developmental skills in these areas, she was not allowed to use a calculator or other adaptive devices when doing her work (see Figures B.3 through B.6). When faced with tasks or activities in her daily life which required academic skills she did not have, Maureen found numerous ways of either getting out of doing the work, or getting somebody else to do it for her.

Therapeutic Services

Maureen received one-to-one occupational therapy services for thirty minutes, two times a week, on a pull-out basis. When observed, Maureen's therapy consist-

FIGURE B.3 Sample of Maureen's Math Work on Time after Ten Years of Special Education and Before Inclusion

ed of her (1) walking forward, backward, and sideways on a line made with masking tape on the floor of a small equipment room off the school stage, and (2) walking toward a poster with the parts of a business letter labelled in their proper place and attaching a card with the label of each part in the proper place. The occupational therapist explained that these activities were selected "to help

Name

FIGURE B.4   Sample of Maureen's Math Work on Addition after Ten Years of Special Education and Before Inclusion

Maureen develop better balance... a better sense of spatial relationships...and better organization skills."

Program Structure
Upon observing Maureen's education program throughout the school day, it became clear that both her IEP objectives and the delivery of educational and related services to meet those objectives were both disjointed and fragmented. Staff members never met as a team except for the annual review of Maureen's IEP, and there was no communication system to replace periodic team meetings. This resulted in each staff member providing services related to one or more IEP objective in isolation from the other objectives. Education team members did not solicit from the parents or other support network members information about relevant instructional content. In fact, when the education team developed the last IEP, the parents requested therapy support to assist Maureen in acquiring the skills necessary to complete two activities with which she had great difficulty: (1) walking on icy

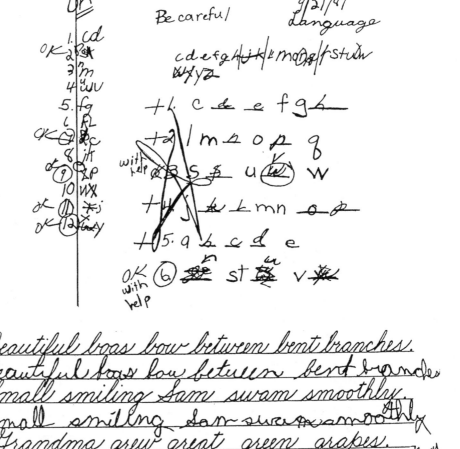

FIGURE B.5　**Sample of Maureen's Writing Work after Ten Years of Special Education and Before Inclusion**

pavements without falling, and (2) riding a two-wheel bicycle as a potential means of future community mobility. The remainder of the education team translated these requests into the need to acquire balance skills, and the requests resulted in the occupational therapy services described in the Therapeutic Services section. In addition to these concerns, the parents frequently questioned the lack of age-appropriate materials and activities in the self-contained class. These types of experiences resulted in a serious lack of communication both among education staff member and between the education staff members and the family.

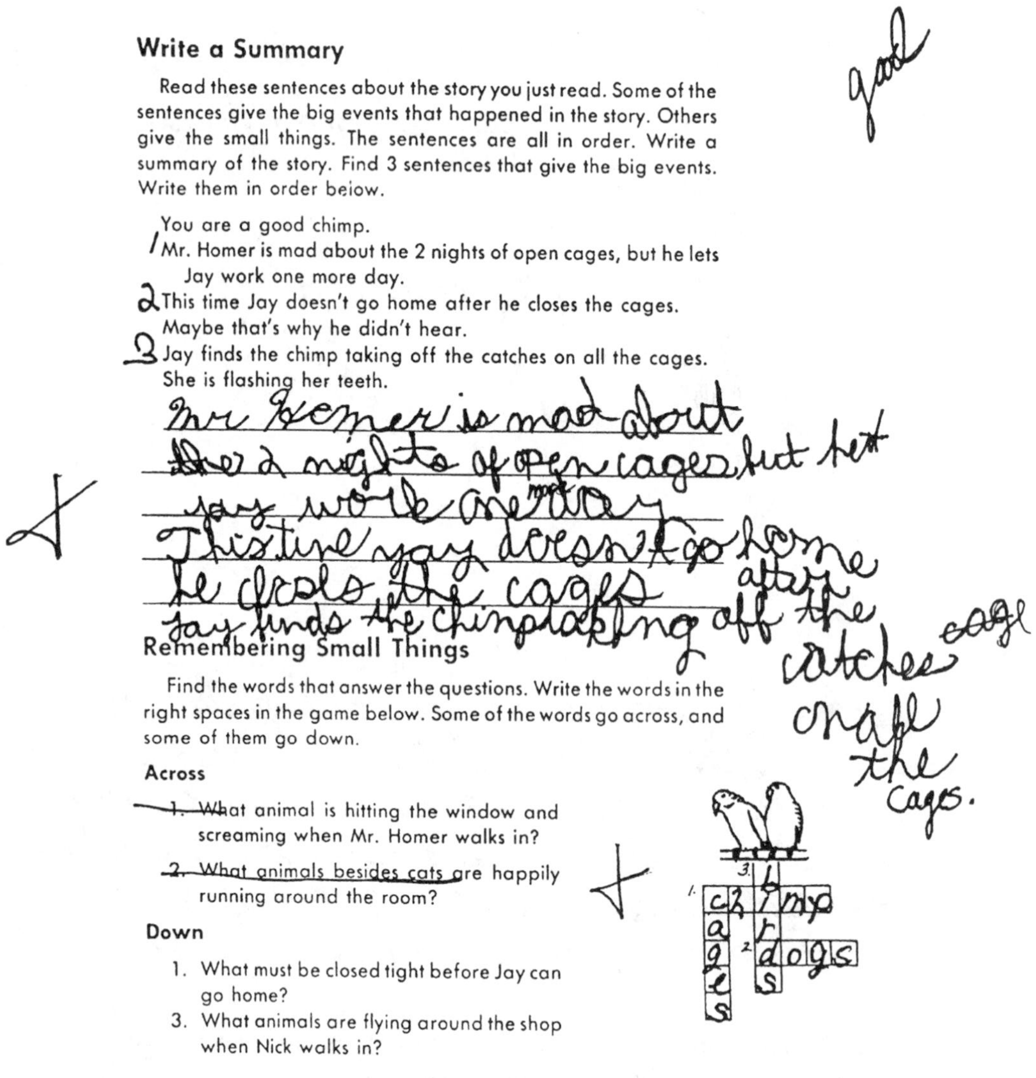

Write a Summary

Read these sentences about the story you just read. Some of the sentences give the big events that happened in the story. Others give the small things. The sentences are all in order. Write a summary of the story. Find 3 sentences that give the big events. Write them in order below.

You are a good chimp.

1 Mr. Homer is mad about the 2 nights of open cages, but he lets Jay work one more day.

2 This time Jay doesn't go home after he closes the cages.

Maybe that's why he didn't hear.

3 Jay finds the chimp taking off the catches on all the cages. She is flashing her teeth.

[handwritten] Mr Homer is mad about the 2 nights of open cages, but let Jay work one day. This time Jay doesn't go home he closes the cages. Jay finds the chimp taking off the catches of the cage. after the catches on all the cags.

[handwritten margin note] good

Remembering Small Things

Find the words that answer the questions. Write the words in the right spaces in the game below. Some of the words go across, and some of them go down.

Across

1. What animal is hitting the window and screaming when Mr. Homer walks in?
2. What animals besides cats are happily running around the room?

Down

1. What must be closed tight before Jay can go home?
2. What animals are flying around the shop when Nick walks in?

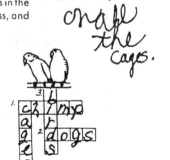

FIGURE B.6   Sample of Maureen's Reading Work after Ten Years of Special Education and Before Inclusion

Maureen Immediately After Inclusion

Reluctantly, Maureen's home school district "included" her on a trial basis in seventh grade classes (see Figure B.7) for the last month of the school year and modified her IEP objectives to reflect Maureen's use of skills in situations that naturally occurred for seventh graders (see Figure B.8). While the district did not provide special education support for the seventh grade teachers whose classes Maureen

FIGURE B.7   **Maureen's Schedule While Included in Seventh-Grade Classes in the Last Month of School Year**

Time Period	Monday	Tuesday	Wednesday	Thursday	Friday
8:55–9:05	Seventh grade homeroom				
9:05–9:50	Seventh grade library				
9:50–10:35	Computer lab				
10:35–11:20	Odds days: seventh grade physical education Even days: seventh grade girls chorus				
11:20–12:05	Resource room: language development				
12:05–12:35	Lunch				
12:35–1:20	Technology				
1:20–2:05	M: occupational therapy in natural situations with nondisabled peers T–TH: seventh grade science W–F: resource room science				
2:05–2:50	Seventh grade math				
2:50–3:00	Study hall				
3:00–3:30	Speech therapy in natural situations with nondisabled peers				

attended or for her participation during class activities, Maureen did receive pull-out services from a resource room teacher one period per day for support with language development. In addition, there was a great deal of confusion and discussion about how Maureen would receive speech and occupational therapy services without the therapists isolating her from nondisabled peers in a separate room. For this reason, Maureen received few, if any, therapy services during this month, even though services were part of her schedule (see Figure B.7). Despite the lack of well-structured special education and related services support, Maureen flourished during this month and the next full year of inclusion, demonstrating more progress than anticipated across a number of areas.

Behaviors and Social Interactions

Maureen never exhibited inappropriate behaviors (i.e., yelling, refusing to work, kicking classmates) in general education settings. When speaking she focused on articulating so that her classmates and teachers could understand her. When in classes, Maureen attended to the instruction presented, and acquired a great deal of the general education curriculum content. She completed both classwork and homework, some of which her education team had adapted to challenge her while allowing mostly independent performance, and some of which did not require adaptation (see Figures B.9 through 12). Maureen earned the nickname "Mayor" of her middle school because of her friendly and enthusiastic social interactions with schoolmates and adults throughout the school. Despite this honorary title, during her first year of inclusion Maureen consistently stated that her nondisabled peers

1. Verbally communicate in social, vocational, academic, and stressful situations
2. Verbally request assistance of adults and peers when a stressful situation occurs in which support is needed
3. Improve use of articulation skills throughout the day so adults and peers understand
4. Display age-appropriate behaviors by interacting with nondisabled peers in seventh grade classes
5. Develop coping mechanisms in life situations where balance is uncertain
6. Ride a two-wheel bicycle
7. Apply life skills to academics
8. Complete activities independently by using a systematic approach
9. Apply reading skills to adapted seventh grade social studies, geography, and science curriculum
10. Improve current reading skills through recreational reading, use of the computer, and life situations
11. Improve writing skills through use of the computer
12. Apply math skills to life activities

FIGURE B.8   Maureen's IEP Objectives While Included in Seventh-Grade Classes in the Last Month of School Year

did not like her. After receiving detention as a disciplinary measure that was consistent with school policy for all students, Maureen quickly learned the school rules about being on time, using hallway passes, and accessing restrooms at appropriate times—all rules she previously never had had a reason to know because of the logistics of her self-contained classes. Maureen spent her lunch break talking and eating with nondisabled classmates, though her lunches consisted mainly of french fries! After observing Maureen in a local grocery store, a woman from the community asked Maureen's mother what she "had done to Maureen"—that she looked "entirely different." Upon considering these comments, Maureen's mother realized that her daughter's physical appearance had changed. She now walked with her head up, body erect, and with a spring in her step, instead of using the "special education shuffle" she had used for a number of years. Nondisabled classmates congratulated her for "graduating from that [special education] room."

Academic Performance

When observed in her seventh grade classes, two interesting facts were found in relation to Maureen's time-in-instruction and time-on-task during instruction. First, when comparing Maureen's time-in-instruction and time-on-task during instruction between the self-contained and general education settings, it was found that Maureen was both in-instruction and on-task during instruction significantly more in general education settings. When comparing Maureen's time-in-instruction and time-on-task during instruction with her nondisabled peers in general education settings, it was found that Maureen was in-instruction, and on-task during that instruction, the same amount of time as her classmates. In fact, Maureen's performance on these variables was differentiated across seventh grade teachers in the same manner as her nondisabled classmates' performance. That is, when her classmates had a high rate of time-in-instruction and time-on-task during instruction

NAME: _____ PERIOD: *18-20*

HUMAN ANATOMY AND PHYSIOLOGY NOTES File: HSN.1

THE HUMAN SYSTEMS

<u>THE SKELETAL SYSTEM</u>

This system has 3 major functions:

A. ~~pro~~ *provides support*

B. *protects vital organs*

C. *supplies red blood cells*

Three major types of bones exist:

Long   round

flat

Irregular

<u>PARTS OF A BONE</u> (L-S): FEMUR (UPPER LEG BONE) *spongy marrow*

periosteum   marrow   calcified layer

FIGURE B.9 Sample of Maureen's Science Work Immediately after Inclusion

throughout a class period with one teacher, so did Maureen; when they had a low rate with another teacher, so did Maureen.

Maureen after Five Years of Inclusion

At the age of twenty, Maureen "graduated" from high school with classmates she had since the last month of seventh grade. She and her family made plans for her

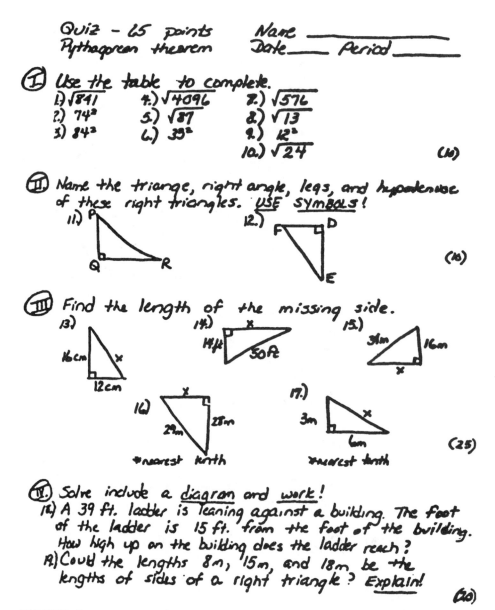

FIGURE B.10   An Eighth-Grade Math Test on Pythagorean Theorem

to be included in a college program and live in a dormitory. During the years she received special education and related services in inclusive settings, Maureen had grown in many ways. Some of her growth occurred in areas that were targeted by her education teams, which finally included her family. Some, however, occurred in areas that the entire education team never considered for Maureen due to her disabilities, her lack of prerequisite skills, or the perceived lack of importance of the skills for Maureen's life.

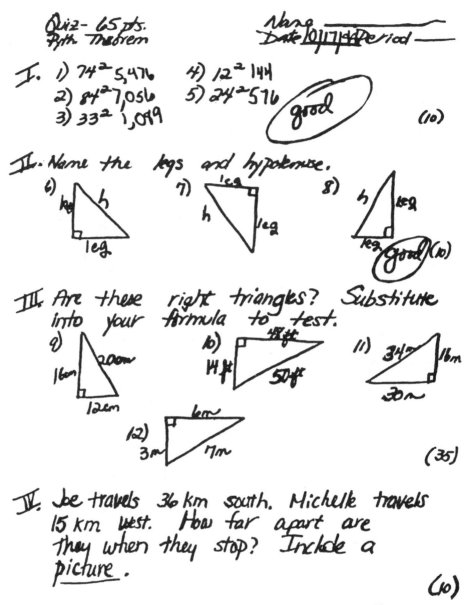

FIGURE B.11   Maureen's Adapted Math Test on Pythagorean Theorem
Shortly after Inclusion

Behaviors and Social Interactions

In relation to the coping behaviors Maureen had used to extricate herself from difficult situations in inclusive settings, Maureen developed good problem solving skills and more appropriate coping behaviors. She still, however, encountered sit-

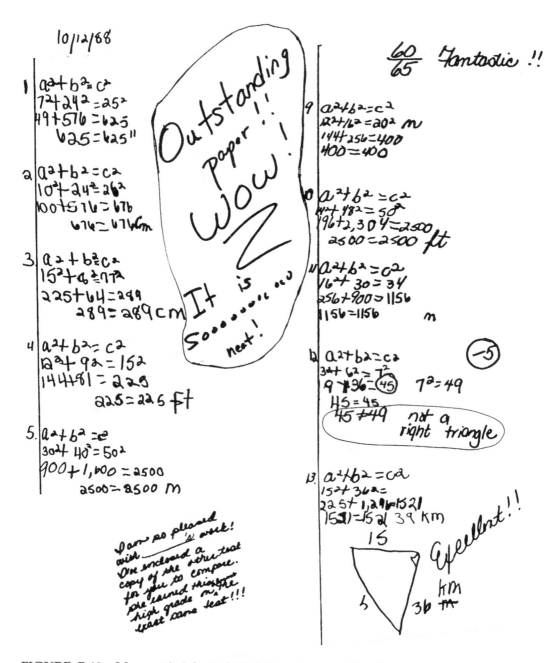

FIGURE B.12   Maureen's Adapted Math Test Answers Shortly after Inclusion

uations for which she did not have all the necessary skills to cope appropriately. In these situations, Maureen still periodically refused assistance, though she usually accepted assistance from familiar adults who understood her resistance to help and applied strategies that accommodated for this resistance. Maureen did best when assistance was paired with praise and when people explained how she could do things by herself, rather than relying on other people. When faced with the realization that she did not understand a concept, Maureen had begun to request assistance. For instance, when discussing the score from one of the girls' soccer team games, Maureen was able to recite the final score but, when asked, could not explain what the score meant (i.e., which score correlated with which team and, therefore, which team won). Upon realizing she did not understand, Maureen asked her mother to explain how to interpret the scores. This was a major change in Maureen's acceptance of her lack of understanding, as well as her willingness to admit that lack to another individual and request assistance. It resulted in much less frequent use of her contrived phrases and coping behaviors to extricate herself from difficult situations.

Socially, Maureen had been involved in numerous extracurricular activities during her high school years. Initially she had become involved with the girls' soccer and field hockey teams as a team manager. In this capacity she had attended every practice and game, assisting the coach and team members in a variety of tasks. She had participated in school musicals and been involved in school sponsored clubs (e.g., Volunteers Interested in People, Distributive Education Clubs of America). Because of her involvement in school activities, Maureen left home at 7:15 A.M. and did not return from school before 6:00 P.M. When participating in night games she did not return home until 8:30–9:00 P.M. Despite this more extensive schedule, Maureen quickly adjusted to the physical demands and did not exhibit fatigue beyond that of other high school students.

In her interaction with nondisabled peers, Maureen's initial growth had been in the areas of articulation and vocabulary. As she became more intelligible to classmates and adults, Maureen developed behaviors that demonstrated a heightened awareness of her nondisabled peers and their reactions to her, although she still had difficulty interacting maturely with boys. For instance, Maureen participated in disability awareness sessions in each of her high school classes. During these sessions she helped explain her disability, the things with which she had difficulty, and the most effective manner in which to respond to her when she "fell apart" (e.g., when she was angry or frustrated and unable to cope) (see Figure B.13). Through these continued discussions and observing classmates' responses to her, Maureen became aware of her reactions to difficult situations and learned to identify when she was "falling apart". Once she had the ability to identify these situations, Maureen began to tell people when she was "falling apart" and request that they "give her a minute." In addition, as she began to cope with these situations more effectively the frequency with which she actually "fell apart" decreased dramatically, and she began to use humor to defuse her own anger.

Maureen also recognized two important facts about herself. First, she learned that she could learn; that she was a capable individual who just needed instruction and repetition provided in specific manners in order to learn more efficiently. Maureen also recognized a tendency she displayed to focus so intently on something that she was unable to respond to changes by restructuring her thoughts and expectations. This inflexibility, or hyperfocusing, kept her from participating in many activities and presented situations in which she "fell apart." With information about this inflexibility, Maureen was able to modify her own behavior and learn to "go with the flow" of life.

Maureen also learned inappropriate behaviors from her nondisabled classmates, as well as the societal consequences that result from those behaviors. For instance, when Maureen realized that a lot of her classmates smoked cigarettes between classes in the restrooms, even though it was not permitted, she joined them. The embarrassment of being caught by a teacher and the ensuing detention that forced her to miss one of her team's field hockey games, resulted in no recurrence of this behavior.

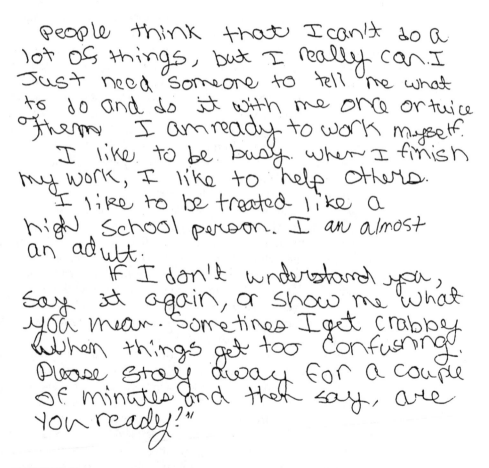

People think that I can't do a lot of things, but I really can. I just need someone to tell me what to do and do it with me one or twice them I am ready to work myself.
I like to be busy. when I finish my work, I like to help others.
I like to be treated like a high school person. I am almost an adult.
If I don't understand you, say it again, or show me what you mean. Sometimes I get crabby when things get too confusing. Please stay away for a couple of minutes and then say, are you ready?"

**FIGURE B.13   Maureen's Disability Awareness Statement after
Five Years of Inclusion**

Reading, Math, and Other Academic Performance

During the five years in which Maureen received special education and related services in general education settings, she developed a number of decoding skills that assisted her in reading new material. In addition, she learned numerous functional vocabulary words and developed a "word bank" from which she could retrieve words for a first draft of written work (see Figure B.14). With this draft Maureen worked with a peer or adult who would facilitate the development of her thoughts into complete sentences and assist Maureen in writing them either on the computer or by hand. The combination of these strategies allowed Maureen to develop written material and read it at will. For instance, using these strategies Maureen wrote and read testimony for the Education Committee of the State Assembly related to her State's implementation of the least restrictive environment component of the Individuals with Disabilities Education Act (see Figure B.15). In addition, Maureen used these strategies to participate in high school class activities. When her English class was studying Shakespearean plays, Maureen participated by reading study versions of the plays that summarized the stories, practiced reading aloud specific sections of the play to facilitate her participation in class readings, watched videotapes of the plays, and used the library to prepare six posters about the author and his plays. She also took adapted tests (see Figure B.16).

In relation to math, Maureen learned systematic approaches to problem solving and applying math formulas to real life situations. Specifically, Maureen learned to apply formulas to work-related issues (e.g., wages, depositing paychecks) and budgeting the use of her funds for life activities (see Figure B.17).

Therapeutic Services

During her high school experiences, the education team determined that Maureen's speech impairment partially was due to an inability to hear and reproduce all the syllables in some words. Speech therapy then expanded from articulation and vocabulary training to focusing on syllables and practicing words that were particularly problematic. For instance, Maureen could not differentiate the sylla-

---

October Tuesday 20,92

I help manager field hocey and keep score, take out equpent keep time,

The Coach is Mrs. Baker.
we won the championship last year is very good.The teams is sue jones and Jeanie Boss, sue Black. the use slicks cleats shin pads the hurt the self.

FIGURE B.14   Sample of Maureen's Independent Writing after Five Years of Inclusion

I was in special class for ten years. I was very Angery. I used to put my head down on the Desk and look out the Door and see the kids. I want to be with Them.

Now I have a locker And take government, Journalissm, marketing, economics and Health. The kids I used to look at are my friends now.

I learn Better in the regular class. I watch my friends and Do what they Do. Sometimes my friends help me and teach my Stuff. Sometimes I help them. My special Educations teacher, my speech teacher and my o.t. help me, too. I am very good in school. I also have a new Job. I have a lot of friends there. I get paid. I pay taxes.

if someone said That I could Go back to the special class I would say "no" I will never Go back?

Please change the laws to help kids like me be in Regular classes with Their friends.

February 12, 1993

FIGURE B.15 Maureen's Testimony on Least Restrictive Environment to the Education Committee of the State Assembly

bles in the word *iron*, but she could pronounce the word correctly by thinking about articulating and blending the words *I* and *earn*. While practicing her testimony for the State Assembly Education Committee (see Figure B.15), Maureen had similar problems with the word *economics*. She could say it correctly however, if she first thought of the word *echo* and then added *nomics*. During her actual testimony Maureen read her statement smoothly up to the word *economics*. She then paused

Name _____   Date 10/22/97

Choose the best meaning for the following terms:

✓ 1. plot
        (a) the list of characters
        b) events that make up the story
        c) the place where the story happens

✓ 2. moral
        a) lesson
        b) events that happened in the past
        (c) world as it is

+ 3. flashback
        a) world as it is
        (b) showing events that happened in the past
        c) time and place where the story happens

+ 4. idealism
        a) world as it is
        (b) world as the author would like it to be
        c) the main idea of the story

✓ 5. climax
        (a) unusual events, characters, or situations
        b) highest point of interest or emotion
        c) the lesson

+ 6. setting
        (a) time and place where the story takes place
        b) lesson to be learned
        c) list of characters

+ 7. theme
        a) stage set
        b) main idea
        (c) way the author sees the world

+ 8. realism
        (a) the way the world is
        b) the lesson of the story
        c) the props the director uses

+ 9. fantasy
        a) the way the world is
        (b) unusual events, situations, or characters: not real.
        c) realism

+ 10. antagonist
        a) the main character
        b) the hero
        (c) the character who is against the main character.

(70)

Use the word setting in a sentence:

+ The Setting is where the story takes place.

FIGURE B.16   Sample of Maureen's Adapted Tests after Five Years of Inclusion

"Review" (40) (36) Name _____
good work!

Find your total wages for a week: Hours x Wage = Total Wage

(a) You work 10 hours   at $4.65 an hour. $46.50 ✓

(b) You work 15 hours   at $4.65 an hour. $69.75 ✓

(c) You work 20 hours   at $4.65 an hour $93.00 ✓

How much money do you have to spend?

Ex: Total Wages $80.00
  − Taxes   − 22.00
                        58.00
  − Bus Tickets   −11.00
                      $47.00

(a) Total Wages $71.25   (b) Total Wages $95.00
  − Taxes $17.80   − Taxes   23.75
                       53.45 (.2)   (7) $71.25
  − Bus Tickets   11.00   − Bus Tickets $11.00
                      $42.45   60.25

✱Bonus Points: Which is less expensive?

        Riding the Bus   Taking a taxi.
                                  $60.25

MAUREEN   0104
                                           10-2/220
                         Sept. 21, 1992

PAY TO THE
ORDER OF Lynne | $61.44

sixty-one and 44/100 ~~~~~~~~~ DOLLARS

FOR Sony wm   M

⑈:0 2 2000 20⑈: 7 288 273 10⑈ 0104

© HARLAND 1991

FIGURE B.17   Sample of Maureen's Math Work after Five Years of Inclusion and said *echo nomics,* paused again and smiled at her mother. She then continued reading the remainder of her testimony smoothly.

Through her occupational therapy Maureen accomplished several tasks with which she previously had had a great deal of difficulty, such as opening the lock on her locker and walking up and down the stairs between high school classes with the other 900 students in her school. Maureen also was able to accomplish class-related tasks with the assistance and training provided through occupational therapy. For instance, because Maureen demonstrated difficulty with visual perception skills, organization skills, and coordination, the development of six large posters on Shakespeare for English class required the integration of occupational therapy into her work. Visual perception skills, organization skills, and coordination were critical when visually locating appropriate material for the posters and preparing materials through photocopying, cutting, placing materials in a coordinated manner, and gluing materials in place. In addition, Maureen developed some materials on the computer, which required the incorporation of occupational therapy into keyboarding skills. Finally, Maureen's occupational therapy became part of the components of the jobs for which she received instruction during part of her last two years of high school and over those summers.

AUTHOR INDEX

SUBJECT INDEX

Domain, 25, 156
Domestic skills, 157

E.H.A. (PL 142), 271
Ecological analysis, 115
Ecological domains, 156
Ecological inventory, 25
Education Team, 78
Educational Reform, 13
Electives, 196
Emergent literacy, 183
Environment, 26
Environmental control, 260
Excess behavior, 228
Explicit language, 184
Expressive communication, 179
Extended evaluation, 304
Extinction, 131

Fair Labor Standards Act (FLSA), 302
Family inventory, 37
First aid, 279
Friendship, 141
Friendship facilitation, 120
Full inclusion, 7
Functional, 182
Functional analysis, 135, 231
Functional assessment, 231
Functional reading, 182
Functional skills, 5
Functional writing, 182

Gastronomy, 280
General education activity analysis, 113
Generalization, 20, 134
Generic instructional plan, 112
Guardianship, 309

High technologies, 260
HIV positive, 244

I.D.E.A. (1990), 271
Implicit language, 184
Inclusion, 228
Individualized family service plan (IFSP), 294
Individualized transition plan (ITP), 291
Individualized written rehabilitation plan (IWRP), 304
Infant and toddler services, 294
Institutional writing, 185
Integration, 10, 12
Interagency agreement, 297
Interdisciplinary team, 83
Intervention, 230

Inventory of general education curriculum, 49
Inventory of general education settings, 48

Job analysis, 163
Job Training Partnership Act (JTPA), 307

Language arts, 185
Learning, 134
Learning rate, 35
Least restrictive environment, 244
Library/information use, 199
Light technologies, 260
Literacy, 183
Long-term advocacy, 309
LRE, 9

Mainstreaming, 10
Maintenancy, 126
MAPS, 68
Mathematics, 189
Medical services, 270
Medically fragile, 271
Medicare, 312
Modeling, 134, 147
Motor skills, 186
Multidisciplinary team, 82
Muscular dystrophy, 246
Music education, 198

Nasogastric tube, 280
Natural support, 145
Natural support network, 62
Negative reinforcement, 130
Negotiation, 51
Next future environment, 157
Non-electronic and electronic aids, 260
Nonsymbolic communication, 179
Normalization, 6

On-the-Job Training (OJT), 306
Ongoing services, 298
Operant Behavior, 128
Oral and written language, 179
Orthotic and prosthetic devices, 260
Ostomy, 282
Other activities, 196

Peer inventory, 42
Peer partners, 120
Peer tutoring, 149
Performance periods, 237
Personal management, 222
Physical and health challenges, 245
Physical education, 186